THE INDIAN CORPS IN FRANCE

[*W. & D. Downey.*

His Majesty The King-Emperor.

Frontispiece.]

The Indian Corps in France

LT.-COLONEL J.W.B. MEREWETHER, C.I.E.
AND
THE RT. HON. SIR FREDERICK SMITH, BART

With an Introduction by
THE RT. HON. EARL CURZON OF KEDLESTON

MANOHAR
2022

First published 1917
Reprinted 2022

ISBN 978-93-91928-81-0

Published by
Ajay Kumar Jain *for*
Manohar Publishers & Distributors
4753/23 Ansari Road, Daryaganj
New Delhi 110 002

Printed at
Replika Press Pvt. Ltd.

THE INDIAN CORPS IN FRANCE

BY LT-COLONEL J. W. B. MEREWETHER, C.I.E.,
INDIAN ARMY

AND THE RT. HON. SIR FREDERICK SMITH, BART.,
HONORARY FELLOW OF WADHAM COLLEGE, OXFORD,
TREASURER OF GRAY'S INN

WITH AN INTRODUCTION BY
THE RT. HON. EARL CURZON OF KEDLESTON

WITH PORTRAITS, ILLUSTRATIONS AND MAPS

PUBLISHED UNDER THE AUTHORITY OF HIS MAJESTY'S SECRETARY OF STATE FOR INDIA IN COUNCIL

INDIAN EDITION
OBTAINABLE FROM THE AGENTS FOR THE SALE OF INDIAN OFFICIAL PUBLICATIONS

LONDON
JOHN MURRAY, ALBEMARLE STREET, W.

PRICE SIX RUPEES

TO

HIS MAJESTY THE KING-EMPEROR

THIS NARRATIVE OF THE VALOUR OF

HIS TROOPS IS BY PERMISSION

DEDICATED.

INTRODUCTION

I AM not at all clear why an Introduction should be needed to this important and thrilling narrative of the deeds of the Indian Corps in France in the early days of the Great War, in addition to the excellent Preface which has already been contributed by the Authors. Still less is it clear why a remote spectator should have been urged to undertake the task. It can only be because a former Viceroy must have enjoyed many opportunities during his term of office in India of making the acquaintance and realizing the superb qualities of the Indian Army, that he should be invited, or would consent—as I have willingly done—to join in this tribute to their latest achievement.

I have seen it frequently stated, even by high authority, in the course of the present War, that the Indian Army is raised, trained, and equipped for service in India alone or upon its frontiers, and that the call to external warfare was therefore both novel and disconcerting. Such a claim would not only be indignantly repudiated by the Indian Army itself, but it finds no foundation in history. During the past half-century, the foreign campaigns in which that Army has been employed, greatly to its credit and glory, have extended from Egypt and even Ashanti on the West to China on the East, and have embraced most of the intervening countries. Even before this War began it was the pride of the Indian Army that its British units saved Natal in the Boer War of 1899–1900, that it rescued the Legations at Peking in 1900, and that on its banners were inscribed the names of hard-fought engagements in almost every part of the African and Asiatic Continents.

The Indian Army, in fact, has always possessed, and has been proud of possessing, a triple function: the preservation of internal peace in India itself; the defence of the Indian frontiers; and preparedness to embark at a moment's notice for Imperial service in other parts of the globe. In this third aspect India has for long been one of the most important units in the scheme of British Imperial defence, providing the British Government with a striking force always ready, of admirable efficiency, and assured valour.

None the less there was a vast and vital difference between the field of war for which the Indian Expeditionary Force left the shores of India in August 1914, and any previous campaign in which its predecessors had been engaged. These had for the most part been conflicts in which the Indian Forces had had to encounter an enemy of minor importance and at no high level of military organization. Only once, nearly 40 years earlier, when Lord Beaconsfield had brought 7000 Indian troops to Malta, as an evidence of Imperial unity and purpose, had an Indian Military Contingent been seen to the West of the Suez Canal. Now, however, General Willcocks' Army Corps was to be pitted against the most powerful military organization on the globe, against a European enemy who had brought to the highest pitch of sinister perfection both the science and the practice of war, and who was about to plunge not Europe alone, but the entire civilized world, into such a welter of continuous devilry and horror as the mind of man had never imagined and history had never known. The landing of the two Indian Divisions, numbering 24,000 men, on the quays of Marseilles in September and October 1914, was a great event, not merely in the annals of the Indian Army, but in the history of mankind.

This book describes the manner in which that force, and the drafts and reinforcements by which it was followed, comported themselves in the fearful struggle of 1914–15. That the Indian Expeditionary Force arrived in the nick of time, that it helped to save the cause both of the Allies and of civilization, after the sanguinary tumult of the opening weeks of the War, has been openly acknowledged by the highest in the land, from the Sovereign downwards. I recall that it was emphatically stated to me by Lord French himself. The nature and value of that service can never be forgotten.

Neither should we forget the conditions under which these Indian soldiers served. They came to a country where the climate, the language, the people, the customs, were entirely different from any of which they had knowledge. They were presently faced with the sharp severity of a Northern winter. They, who had never suffered heavy shell fire, who had no experience of high explosive, who had never seen warfare in the air, who were totally ignorant of modern trench fighting, were exposed to all the latest and most scientific developments of the art of destruction. They were confronted with the most powerful and pitiless military machine that the world has ever seen. They were consoled by none of the amenities or alleviations, or even the associations, of home. They were not fighting for their own country or people. They were not even engaged in a quarrel of their own making. They were plunged in surroundings which must have been intensely depressing to the spirit of man. Almost from the start they suffered shattering losses.

In the face of these trials and difficulties, the cheerfulness, the loyalty, the good discipline, the intrepid courage of these denizens of another clime, cannot be too highly praised. If disappointment, and even failure, sometimes attended their efforts, their accomplishment was nevertheless solid and striking. The writer was at Neuve Chapelle, just after that historic combat. No record in it excelled that of the Indian troops. This volume contains the tale of other deeds not less heroic and daring. When the first V.C. was pinned on to the breast of an Indian soldier, not only was the promise given by the King-Emperor at the Imperial Durbar of 1911 redeemed, but the valour of Hindostan received at last the full recognition of its supreme merit.

This volume deals chiefly with the stormy incidents of war. But any one who visited the Western front during the period which it covers, and saw the Indian regiments either in the trenches or in reserve, will also carry away with him many a picture of the good fellowship prevailing between British and Indian soldiers, of the deep and characteristic devotion of the latter to their British officers, and of the happy relations between the men in *pagris* and the inhabitants of the country. The letters of the Indian soldiers to their folk at home would stand comparison with any that the official post-bag has conveyed to England from our own heroes at the front, in their uncomplaining loyalty, their high enthusiasm, their philosophic endurance, and their tolerant acceptance of the privations and sufferings of war.

That this record should have been compiled seems entirely right and just. That it will stand forth as one of the most radiant chapters in the glorious history of the Indian Army is certain. That it will act as a stimulus to the martial spirit and loyalty of India for generations to come, cannot be doubted. Nor will it be less a source of congratulation to its readers, that the Indian Army will, in more ways than one, receive a well-earned recognition of its great achievement.

CURZON OF KEDLESTON.

October 1917.

PREFACE TO THE SECOND EDITION

THE first edition of this book appeared in the month of December 1917. It was reprinted in March 1918, and again in April 1918. The third impression was immediately sold out and the book has now been out of print for many months. In the meantime it has been translated into several dialects in India.

It was not thought desirable to print a second edition until a sufficient period had elapsed to give an opportunity to every critic in Great Britain, India, or Mesopotamia to make observations upon the facts stated in the first edition. It is a source of great satisfaction to the authors that, although they have received hundreds of letters from officers and men who have served with the Corps, the accuracy of their story as told in the first edition has in no point of real importance been substantially impeached. On many small points suggestions have been offered and accepted. The present edition therefore contains a large number of unimportant alterations and modifications: but in its integrity the story remains as it was told in the first edition, and the authors are satisfied that later research can add very little to the account as it is presented in the following pages.

The second edition had been fully prepared for

the press before the Armistice was signed or indeed thought of. It was not therefore possible in this edition to examine the whole history of the Corps, and of its Commanding Officer, with complete freedom from those Military restrictions which, as long as the War lasted, were prohibitive. The authors hope to make such additions to their work as this task may render proper in a later edition, if one should be called for.

But they may point out even now that Lord Kitchener in appointing Sir Frederick Smith to serve on the staff of the Indian Corps had in his mind the extreme importance first of preserving a permanent historical record of the services of the Indian troops, secondly of supplying a contemporary record in India of the fortunes of the Corps *with the object of stimulating recruiting in India.* Lord Harding, who was at that time Viceroy of India, continuously and most wisely urged the importance of supplying the peoples of India with something else to read about the War besides the long and melancholy lists of casualties. General Sir James Willcocks, the enlightened Commander of the Corps, who knew India well and Indian soldiers even better, consistently held the same view. But those who in France were responsible for the censorship of news from the seat of War on the Western Front, took a different view. It is not for us to criticize them. But we record the fact that they refused to allow a single battalion to be mentioned by name for fear of giving information to the enemy of the *Ordre de bataille,* at a moment when every single Battalion in the Corps had lost prisoners to the enemy. They also refused to allow mention in a despatch, which had been passed by General Willcocks himself, of the names of two most gallant officers who had given their lives in one of the most desperate battles of those bloody days. We may further note that restrictions of the above class have since been either completely withdrawn or largely modified.

In the last three years India has been allowed to know in reasonable detail what Indian troops have suffered and what they have achieved on the field of battle. The result has been (exactly as Lord Kitchener foresaw) that recruiting has undergone an immense development in India. The authors feel that if the martial population in India had been adequately and closely informed of the sufferings and the glory of their troops in France and of the needs of the Empire, three-quarters of a million men could have been recruited in 1914 and 1915. No student of our campaigns in the East will fail to realize the difference which such a recruitment would have made in the duration of the War.

We have at least been able to carry out Lord Kitchener's first wish, expressed to Sir Frederick Smith in 1914, that there should be preserved a history, which we venture to believe will endure, of the extraordinary valour and tenacity of the Corps which perished in Flanders. We hope that a history, not less detailed, will one day be written of every Corps which in this long struggle has preserved and added to the imperishable records of British valour.

PREFACE

THIS book is an attempt to describe the fortunes of the Indian Army Corps in Flanders. Sir Frederick Smith was asked by Lord Kitchener to undertake duties in relation to the records of the Corps, and he served upon the Staff from the month of October 1914, until he became a member of the Coalition Government in the late spring of 1915. The War Office then appointed Lt-Colonel Merewether to take his place. Both these officers in the course of their duties had access to the Corps and Divisional Diaries, and to regimental and other records, and both were honoured, as far as was proper, with the confidence of the General Officer commanding the Corps, Sir James Willcocks. But the account which follows of the fortunes of the Corps does not, of course, pretend to anticipate the official War Office history. It is published at the desire and under the authority of the India Office; but the authors, and no one else, must be answerable both for allegations of fact and for expressions of opinion.

Far the greater part of the labour involved in the preparation of the book has fallen upon Colonel Merewether, who has been retained in England by the India Office in order that he might devote himself to the work. It was, however, his earnest desire that his predecessor should assist him in dealing with the period before he joined the Corps, and the

History has therefore been produced as the result of joint authorship, for which both writers are responsible.

The present struggle has been waged upon so immense a scale: so vast have been the numbers engaged, so infinitely varied the theatres, and so sedulously preserved the "fog of war," that it seems certain no single writer will ever produce a complete history of it, and probable that no combination of writers will present an adequate account in our lifetime. But the piety and industry of individual students may shed a tiny ray of light upon the small segment of ground where their comrades lived and fought and died. And in this way some deeds of shining heroism may be rescued from the frosty grasp of the military censors. It may even be that the confluence of many individual efforts will afford the only prospect of that ultimate History of the Great War which will at once affright and inspire our grandsons, and reduce every other military history to the remoteness of Cæsar's "Commentaries."

Many immortal deeds have been wrought in this war without record and without recognition. Of these many had a flame and quality of valour far transcending achievements which have lived for centuries in the pages of historians, or have been made musical in the verses of great poets.

All the Armies of all the Allies have suffered by the suppression of contemporary narrative.

Perhaps we shall never have a complete story of the Guards Brigade before it became a Division; of the Territorial Army hardening into veterans in a sea of blood; or of that Scottish Army—the largest under one standard since Bannockburn—

which fought and perished in the unhappy but glorious struggle of Loos.

Many units of all kinds have failed to receive contemporary justice, but perhaps none more conspicuously than those of the Indian Army Corps. Ludicrous expectations were formed of the part they were to play. The most exaggerated statements were rife as to their numbers. Legendary accounts of their performances in the field filled the press before they had left their place of concentration at Orleans. And at the end when, broken and bruised with fighting, they were carried (what was left of them) bleeding from Flanders, there were many who in perfect good faith said that the Indians had been failures. It would be truer to say that the Indian and British Regiments which together composed the Indian Army Corps in their turn saved the Empire.

No one who saw it will ever forget the landing from the great transports which began to swing into the harbour of Marseilles in the autumn of 1914, or the laughing, sunburnt, careless faces of the young British officers who leaned over the bulwarks and called aloud to learn whether they were coming too late. In six months nearly all were dead. The arrival of the Indian Corps was an event to him who could presage the future, as fraught with tragedy and pathos and "the purple thread of doom" as the landing of that earlier force which marched to Mons with the same gaiety, the same valour, and the same bloody predestination.

We have claimed in an earlier passage that the Indian Corps saved the Empire. The proposition to those who know the facts is almost self-evident. The original Expeditionary Force, with the supplementary Divisions, had gone through the Retreat, the Marne, the Aisne, and the bloody hand-to-hand fighting which at every step marked the race to the sea.

At the time when the Indians landed, the resistant power of the British Army, cruelly outnumbered, and exhausted by constant fighting against superior artillery and a more numerous equipment of machine guns, was almost overcome. And except the Indian Army there were no other trained regular soldiers in the Empire available at that moment for service.

The Territorial Army—the finest material in the world—had not completed its training, and was not used and could not be used, in its own unitary organization for many months. The Kitchener Armies were still a shadowy embryo in the womb of improvization.

The Empire was saved by an alternation of shifts and expedients, each of which just succeeded because of the deathless valour and devotion of the human beings who were associated with each endeavour.

It was saved first by the Expeditionary Force, secondly by the Indian Corps, thirdly by the Territorial Divisions, and fourthly by the Overseas and Kitchener Armies. And there is enough glory and enough sacrifice for all.

Of the Indian Corps it may be said that as much was asked of them as has been asked of any troops at any period or in any theatre of this war. They stemmed that first German onslaught through the late autumn of 1914, which ended in the bitter fighting at Givenchy. They played a glorious part in the battle of Neuve Chapelle. The second battle of Ypres, the struggle for the Aubers ridge, and the desperate assaults of Loos—all claimed a toll of blood from this devoted Corps. They were asked to do much, and they tried to do everything they were asked.

In the pages which follow, small attempt has been made at rhetoric. It seemed to the authors, as they examined laconic diaries and soldierly notebooks, that the story was too noble, and in many ways too terrible, to require or indeed to justify the use of rhetoric. If the account of the fighting seems in places cold and uninspired, those who are responsible can only plead in extenuation that the story itself is one of almost monotonous heroism among surroundings which hardly ever vary, and they hope that the simplicity and sameness of the narrative will not have impaired its power to interest.

They are bold enough to believe that they have in the main overcome the extreme difficulty of disentangling the narrative. Unless they are too sanguine, the account which follows of the principal actions in which the Corps was engaged will in its main features be found accurate, and they do not believe that it will be discredited, or very much modified, by later research. No pains at any rate have been spared in the examination of the available material, or in interviewing surviving officers upon incidents in which they bore a part.

The authors will be repaid for their labours if they make it easier for the Empire to do justice to the Force of which they were humble members, and whose stubborn valour they witnessed with a determination to preserve some memorial, however inadequate, of its quality.

CONTENTS

LIST OF ILLUSTRATIONS AND MAPS

THE
INDIAN CORPS IN FRANCE

CHAPTER I

ARRIVAL OF THE CORPS IN FRANCE

The German conception of India—A tottering Empire—The truth—A German or a British India—The Indian National Congress—Disillusionment—Outbreak of war—Mobilization of Indian Expeditionary Force A—Embarkation—Voyage—Arrival at Suez—Cairo—Re-embarkation at Alexandria—Sirhind Brigade and Indian Mountain Artillery retained in Egypt—Arrival at Marseilles—Disembarkation—Warm reception by the French—Appointment of Lt-General Sir James Willcocks, K.C.B., K.C.M.G., K.C.S.I., D.S.O.—Entrainment for Orleans—Enthusiasm en route—Halt at Orleans—Entrainment for the Front.

German policy had long and deeply calculated upon the effect of an European War upon our Indian Empire. The conclusions which the Germans reached were largely based upon their own Colonial methods and upon the materials for forming a decision which were furnished by those methods. They saw an immense Oriental Empire, peopled by a teeming population, and controlled thousands of miles away by the Government of these Islands. Having no conception of the essential principle upon which the relationship of governor and governed is determined in the Anglo-Saxon tradition, it seemed to them axiomatic that the governed population should be awaiting an opportunity to revolt against its governors. German literature was very fertile for many years before this conflict in speculations upon the stability and cohesion of the British Empire when submitted to the strain of war.

Their conclusions were very clear. The German nation, of all the nations in the world, had mastered the essential secrets of Kultur, organization and discipline. No nation which had not mastered those secrets—such was their view—could survive the maëlstrom of a great world war. In particular the British Empire was doomed to disappear ; it depended upon principles which, when analyzed, were everywhere found to be the antithesis of every Prussian principle. It was undefined, it was undisciplined, it was sloppy, and it was sentimental.

We find traces of these conclusions in all the writers who represent German thought during the ten years which preceded the war. German observers brooded attentively over every resolution of the Indian National Congress. They watched over the movements of the North-West Frontier with at least as much care as the Indian Staff, and they expected India under the Anglo-Saxon Government to behave as they knew India would have behaved under Prussian Government. General Bernhardi told us with perfect frankness of the hopes which his countrymen entertained of Indian disaffection. Herr Karl Peters has quite recently informed the world that the two principal disappointments which Germany has experienced in the war have been in relation to South Africa and India.

The explanation of errors which may ultimately prove to be very costly is not difficult. The Prussian mentality is well acquainted with its own Colonial system ; it has no understanding whatever of ours ; and so it happened that when the challenge was given in August, 1914, to the British Empire and all it stood for, perhaps the most serious Prussian error was made in relation to our great Empire in the East.

It is difficult even now to state with precision what were the ambitions which the megalomania of Germany had formed. We know that their rallying cry was the march to the East. We know that the conquest of Egypt must at certain periods of this World War have seemed to them not an impossible dream. And given a conquered Egypt and a disaffected India, Germany might well have realized and even exceeded the dreams of Napoleon.

The outbreak of war, unexpected anywhere in the British Dominions, and of all places in the British Dominions most unexpected in India, afforded a swift and chilling disillusionment to the hopes of the German General Staff. Perhaps the leading spirits of that Staff had made an error, surprising in any thoughtful man, but most surprising among Prussians. They had taken their opinions, not from the soldiers of India, but from the agitators of India. In fact, from the first moment that it became clear that a powerful European antagonist was challenging the greatness of England and the position of that Empire of which England is the centre, there followed a hardening and consolidation of feeling in India, which on the whole must be pronounced more remarkable than that which was exhibited in any part of the Empire. Intelligent Indians are under no delusion as to the power of India to stand alone. The alternative therefore presented itself sharply as between a British Empire and a Teuton India, and in this division lobby there was no minority. The telegram sent from the Viceroy on the 8th September, 1914, will live for ever in the annals of India, and will be regarded by later ages as the greatest tribute ever offered by a constituent state to a great Empire. The rulers of the Native States in India, the Viceroy telegraphed, numbering nearly 700 in all, had with one accord rallied to the defence of the Empire, and offered their personal services and the resources of their States for the war. The rest of the Viceroy's telegram may be set out in full. It contributes a shining page to the history of the British Empire :—

"From among the many Princes and Nobles who have volunteered for active service, the Viceroy has selected the Chiefs of Jodhpur, Bikanir, Kishangarh, Ratlam, Sachin, Patiala, Sir Pratap Singh, Regent of Jodhpur, the Heir-Apparent of Bhopal and a brother of the Maharaja of Cooch Behar, together with other cadets of noble families. The veteran, Sir Pratap Singh, would not be denied his right to serve the King-Emperor in spite of his 70 years, and his nephew, the Maharaja, who is but 16 years old, goes with him.

"All these have, with the Commander-in-Chief's approval, already joined the Expeditionary Forces. The Maharaja of Gwalior and the Chiefs of Jaora and Dholpur, together with the Heir-Apparent of Palanpur, were, to their great regret, prevented from leaving their States. Twenty-seven of the larger States in India maintain Imperial Service Troops, and the services of every Corps were immediately placed at the disposal of the Government of India on the outbreak of War. The Viceroy has accepted from 12 States contingents of Cavalry, Infantry, Sappers and Transport, besides a Camel Corps from Bikanir, and most of them have already embarked. As particular instances of the generosity and eager loyalty of the Chiefs the following may be quoted: Various Darbars have combined together to provide a Hospital Ship to be called 'The Loyalty' for the use of the Expeditionary Forces. The Maharaja of Mysore has placed Rs. 50 lakhs at the disposal of the Government of India for expenditure in connection with the Expeditionary Force.

"The Chief of Gwalior, in addition to sharing in the expenses of the Hospital Ship, the idea of which originated with himself and the Begum of Bhopal, has offered to place large sums of money at the disposal of the Government of India and to provide thousands of horses as remounts. From Loharu in the Punjab and Las Bela and Kelat in Baluchistan come offers of camels with drivers, to be supplied and maintained by the Chiefs and Sardars. Several Chiefs have offered to raise additional troops for military service should they be required, and donations to the Indian Relief Fund have poured in from all States. The Maharaja of Rewa has offered his troops, his treasury, and even his private jewellery for the service of the King-Emperor. In addition to contributions to the Indian Fund some Chiefs, namely, those of Kashmir, Bundi, Orchha and Gwalior and Indore have also given large sums to the Prince of Wales' Fund.

"The Maharaja of Kashmir, not content with subscribing himself to the Indian Fund, presided at a meeting of 20,000 people recently held at Srinagar, and delivered a stirring speech, in response to which large subscriptions were collected.

"Maharaja Holkar offers, free of charge, all

horses in his State Army which may be suitable for Government purposes. Horses have also been offered by the Nizam's Government, by Jamnagar and other Bombay States. Every Chief in the Bombay Presidency has placed the resources of his State at the disposal of Government, and all have made contributions to the Relief Fund.

"Loyal messages and offers have also been received from the Mehtar of Chitral and tribes of the Khyber Agency as well as the Khyber Rifles.

"Letters have also been received from the most remote States in India, all marked by deep sincerity of desire to render some assistance, however humble, to the British Government in its hour of need.

"Last, but not least, from beyond the borders of India have been received generous offers of assistance from the Nepal Durbar; the military resources of the State have been placed at the disposal of the British Government, and the Prime Minister has offered a sum of Rs. 3 lakhs to the Viceroy for the purchase of machine guns or field equipment for British Gurkha Regiments proceeding over-seas, in addition to large donations from his private purse to the Prince of Wales' Fund and the Imperial Relief Fund.

"To the 4th Gurkha Rifles, of which the Prime Minister is honorary Colonel, the Prime Minister has offered Rs. 30,000 for the purchase of machine guns in the event of their going on service. The Dalai Lama of Tibet has offered 1000 Tibetan troops for service under the British Government. His Holiness also states that Lamas innumerable throughout the length and breadth of Tibet are offering prayers for the success of the British Army, and for the happiness of souls of all victims of the war.

"The same spirit has prevailed throughout British India. Hundreds of telegrams and letters have been received by the Viceroy, expressing loyalty and desire to serve the Government either in the Field or by co-operation in India. Many hundreds have also been received by local administrations. They come from Communities and Associations, Religious, Political and Social, of all Classes and Creeds, also from individuals offering their resources or asking for opportunity to prove their loyalty by personal service. The following may be mentioned as typical examples:—

"The All-India Moslem League, the Bengal Presidency Moslem League, the Moslem Association of Rangoon, the Trustees of the Aligarh College, the Behar Provincial Moslem League, the Central National Mohammedan Association of Calcutta, the Khoja Community and other followers of Aga Khan, the Punjab Moslem League, Mohammedans of Eastern Bengal, the Citizens of Calcutta, Madras, Rangoon and many other Cities, Behar Landholders' Association, Madras Provincial Congress, Taluqdars of Oudh, Punjab Chiefs' Association, United Provinces Provincial Congress, Hindus of the Punjab Chief Khalsa, Diwan representing orthodox Sikhs, Bohra Community of Bombay, Parsee Community of Bombay.

"The Delhi Medical Association offer the Field Hospital that was sent to Turkey during the Balkan War; Bengali students offer enthusiastic services for an Ambulance Corps, and there were many other offers of medical aid; Zemindars of Madras have offered 500 horses, and among other practical steps to assist Government may be noted the holding of meetings to allay panic, keep down prices and maintain public confidence and credit. Generous contributions have poured in from all quarters to the Imperial Indian Relief Fund."

This memorable message, sent after personal communication with many of the rulers of India, rang through the Empire and established the attitude of the natural leaders of Indian thought. But it may, perhaps, be asked, what was the attitude of the ordinary Indian officer and the ordinary private soldier ? Did the men who mobilized from all parts of India to join the Colours appreciate any of the issues of this world-wide struggle ? Had the Gurkhas who sharpened their kukris as the train neared Calcutta, under the impression that they were about to engage the enemy, any conception of the quarrel in which they were to fight and die ? The answer is quite simple, and nothing is to be gained by evading the criticism contained in the question. The Indian soldiers knew nothing about the merits of the quarrel and cared less about them. They fought because they were told by officers whom they trusted that the interests of the King-Emperor and of his Empire were being menaced by enemies ; they cared nothing who those enemies were, and they asked only the opportunity of proving their soldierly valour upon the bodies of those enemies.

No greater tribute has ever been paid to the character and quality of British rule in India than the passionate eagerness of Indian soldiers to fight against any enemy who assailed the system of which they formed so small a part.

In India the first week of August, 1914, was full of vague and alarming rumours. It was not until the 8th that any definite military orders arrived. On that day the Lahore (3rd Indian War) Division under Lt-General H. B. B. Watkis, C.B., and the Meerut (7th Indian War) Division under Lt-General C. A. Anderson, C.B., received orders to mobilize. The news was greeted with the wildest enthusiasm by all ranks. The Indian Army had been excluded on grounds of policy from any share in the South African War. Until this moment the disappointment had never been forgotten.

The long years of patient training, varied only by the constant frontier expeditions in which the forces of the King-Emperor have had so many opportunities of putting to the test the lessons learned in peace, were at last to bear fruit. The night was past; to them, too, the day, DER TAG, had arrived.

The curtain of a world-wide theatre of war was rising, but the secret of the ultimate destination of the Indian Expeditionary Force was well kept. The East is the forcing-bed of rumour and lived up to her reputation in those great days of speculation. For once rumour has not exceeded fact. From Neuve Chapelle to far Kiao Chao, from the forests and uplands of East Africa to the graves of Gallipoli, from the sands and swamps of Mesopotamia to the scorching deserts of the Aden Hinterland, the earth has shaken with the tread of the Sikh, the Gurkha, the Pathan, the Rajput, the Jat, the Garhwali; and the enemy, who affected to disbelieve their fidelity to their King-Emperor, has learned to know their truth and soldierly valour.

Their destination was unknown, but the troops

never concealed their hope that they would be called on to face the foe in Europe, shoulder to shoulder with the British comrades-in-arms whom they knew so well alike in peace and in war.

And here let it at once be placed on record that from first to last, in sunshine, in storm, in billet or in trench, the superb British regiments which formed part of the Indian Expeditionary Force to France have never failed to justify the supreme confidence placed in them by their country and by their Indian fellow-soldiers. Their gallantry was beyond all praise; their cheerfulness under terrible conditions presented an example of incalculable value to their Indian comrades. The deeds of the Manchesters, the Black Watch, the Leicesters, the Connaughts, the Highland Light Infantry, the Seaforths, are being retailed now throughout the length and breadth of India. Common memories of suffering and heroism have set a final seal upon the brotherhood between the British and Indian soldier.

It is convenient to give in this place a complete statement of the fighting units of which the Lahore and Meerut Divisions were originally composed.

Lahore Division.

Commander: Lt-General H. B. B. Watkis, C.B.

Ferozepore Brigade.

Commander: Brigadier-General R. M. Egerton, C.B.

1st Battalion Connaught Rangers.
129th Duke of Connaught's Own Baluchis.
57th Wilde's Rifles (Frontier Force).
9th Bhopal Infantry.

Jullundur Brigade.

Commander: Major-General P. M. Carnegy, C.B.
1st Battalion Manchester Regiment.
15th Ludhiana Sikhs.
47th Sikhs.
59th Scinde Rifles (Frontier Force).

Sirhind Brigade.

Commander: Major-General J. M. S. Brunker.
1st Battalion Highland Light Infantry.
1st Battalion 1st King George's Own Gurkha Rifles.
1st Battalion 4th Gurkha Rifles.
125th Napier's Rifles.

Divisional Troops.

15th Lancers (Cureton's Multanis).
Head Quarters Divisional Engineers.
No. 20 Company Sappers and Miners.
No. 21 Company Sappers and Miners.
Signal Company.
34th Sikh Pioneers.

Artillery Units.

Head Quarters Divisional Artillery.
5th Brigade R.F.A. and Ammunition Column.
11th Brigade R.F.A. and Ammunition Column.
18th Brigade R.F.A. and Ammunition Column.
109th Heavy Battery.

MEERUT DIVISION.

Commander: Lt-General C. A. Anderson, C.B.

Dehra Dun Brigade.

Commander: Brigadier-General C. E. Johnson.
1st Battalion Seaforth Highlanders.
1st Battalion 9th Gurkha Rifles.

2nd Battalion 2nd King Edward's Own Gurkha Rifles.

6th Jat Light Infantry.

Garhwal Brigade.

Commander: Major-General H. D'U. Keary, C.B., D.S.O.

2nd Battalion Leicestershire Regiment.

2nd Battalion 3rd Queen Alexandra's Own Gurkha Rifles.

1st Battalion 39th Garhwal Rifles.

2nd Battalion 39th Garhwal Rifles.

Bareilly Brigade.

Commander: Major-General F. Macbean, C.V.O., C.B.

2nd Battalion Black Watch.

41st Dogras.

58th Vaughan's Rifles (Frontier Force).

2nd Battalion 8th Gurkha Rifles.

Divisional Troops.

4th Cavalry.

No. 3 Company Sappers and Miners.

No. 4 Company Sappers and Miners.

Signal Company.

107th Pioneers.

Head Quarters Divisional Engineers.

Artillery Units.

Head Quarters Divisional Artillery.

4th Brigade R.F.A. and Ammunition Column.

9th Brigade R.F.A. and Ammunition Column.

13th Brigade R.F.A. and Ammunition Column.

110th Heavy Battery.

The mobilization was carried out without a hitch, and the Lahore Division embarked at Karachi on the 24th August; the Meerut Division, less some units which embarked at Bombay, sailed from Karachi on the 21st September, having completed its mobilization on the 26th August.

When the machinery works so perfectly, the embarkation of a Division is merely that of any unit multiplied many times. The ordinary routine was followed in each case. The heavy kit and machine guns were sent in advance, with generally a working party of fifty men to load them on the ship. Next followed the machine-gun mules, individuals into whose philosophy no idea of discipline or system ever entered, and the officers' chargers. Last of all came the battalion, and the power of discipline is well illustrated by the fact—to take a concrete instance—that the 2/39th Garhwalis arrived at the dock at 11.15 a.m., and were all on board the transport with their kit by noon.

The convoys were escorted by ships of the Royal Navy, the Royal Indian Marine, and at a later stage by ships of the French Navy.

The voyage was uneventful, and the weather perfect. Every opportunity was taken to exercise men and animals. Much enthusiasm was caused by the receipt of a wireless message announcing the naval victory off Heligoland, and by Lord Kitchener's statement in the House of Lords that two Indian Divisions were on their way to France. This was the first authentic news received by the troops of their real destination.

Between the 9th and 13th September, the Lahore Division arrived at Suez, whence the

Ferozepore and Jullundur Brigades entrained for Cairo. On the 16th September a Divisional route march through the city took place. The impression made by the fine appearance and equipment of the troops was very marked, and the knowledge that so many Musalman soldiers were on the way to fight for the Empire had at the moment great political value.

The Division re-embarked at Alexandria on the 19th September, leaving behind it the Sirhind Brigade and the 3rd Mountain Artillery Brigade, and arrived at Marseilles on the 26th September.

The Sirhind Brigade, on arrival in Egypt, was ordered to assist in guarding the Canal, 4 companies of the Highland Light Infantry moving to Port Saïd and 4 companies to Suez, the remainder of the Brigade occupying Ismailia, where they camped in a grove on the shore of the lake. Eventually the Brigade was ordered to stand fast, pending relief by Territorials from England, and it finally reached Marseilles on the 30th November, in time to take part in some of the heaviest fighting of the year, but a few days too late to qualify for the 1914 Star.

The work of preparing for the arrival of the Indian Expeditionary Force at Marseilles was, as can be easily imagined, extremely arduous.

On the 15th August, the advanced party, consisting of about thirty officers under the command of Lt-Colonel T. Fraser, R.E., left Bombay for an unknown destination, eventually landing in Egypt, where the necessary arrangements for the disembarkation of the Indian Corps were made. Orders were then received to re-embark at Alexandria, and the journey came to an end at Marseilles. Here

[*Daily Mirror.*

THE CAMP AT MARSEILLES.

eighteen officers of the Royal Indian Marine were attached to the party.

From this time onwards the work was never-ending. The duties of the Staff in surroundings so novel can perhaps be imagined. The wharves had to be prepared in order to provide proper forming-up places for the troops on arrival; arrangements were necessary to water men and animals; sheds were needed for the reception of vast quantities of stores; berths required allocation for ships to unload. Camping-grounds were got ready; arrangements were made for the issue of new arms and ammunition; and last, but not least, the most accurate time-tables had to be prepared to ensure the punctual railing of the troops to the concentration area.

Throughout their task the Staff received the most cordial and tactful co-operation from the French authorities.

Marseilles presented a very lively appearance to the eyes of our officers, whose previous acquaintance with the city was made in times of peace. Now there were no acrobats or lace-sellers on the quays, no itinerant musicians with their eternal "Funiculi, Funicula." Everything was given over to war: almost daily French transports arrived filled to the brim with Algerian troops, Zouaves, Chasseurs d'Afrique and Senegalese; and it was very interesting to our Staff to compare these French Colonial troops with our Indian forces.

The first convoy arrived on the morning of the 26th September with the Lahore Division and part of the Indian Cavalry Corps. Two of the earliest ships to be berthed were the British India Company's *Mongara* and *Castilia*, having on board elements so diverse as a battery of Royal Horse Artillery, a Signal Company, a Field Ambulance, part of a Mule Corps, and account details.

These were soon disembarked, but the landing of Supply and Transport stores went on all night, and the two vessels were away again by 9 a.m. next morning, their places being immediately taken by two ships laden with the 15th Lancers.

As illustrating the accuracy and completeness of the arrangements, it may be recalled that this cavalry regiment, with its horses and all paraphernalia, was on its march to camp within four hours from the time of the berthing of the ship. And so day after day the work went on.

The scene on the quays was bizarre and incongruous. Working parties of the Indian troops in their sombre but business-like khaki were mixed with assistants in the shape of French seamen, French labourers, stevedores, and our own Army Service Corps men. Nobody understood any one else's language ; parties of Indians could be seen gesticulating and illustrating their wants by vigorous pantomime to sympathetic but puzzled Frenchmen. However, all was good humour and an intense desire to help, so matters soon arranged themselves.

On marching away from the docks to their camping-ground the troops met with a remarkable reception. Our warm-hearted Allies, men, women, and children, vied with each other in showing honour and kindness to the men who had traversed so many weary miles by land and sea to play their part in the World War at its most critical period.

The bearing and condition of the troops were splendid, and the local newspapers gave generous

[*Langfier, Ltd.*

GENERAL SIR JAMES WILLCOCKS, G.C.M.G., K.C.B., K.C.S.I., D.S.O.

17.]

expression to the popular feelings. The equipment was especially the subject of much praise, and the inhabitants of Marseilles are competent judges in such matters, for they have seen many thousands of their own Colonial troops pass through.

Apart from its geographical position, no more suitable port than Marseilles could have been chosen for the disembarkation of so many thousands of Indian troops, for by its constant association with every form of Eastern trade, the city was able to provide many articles of supply which would otherwise have had to be brought from India. For example, a suitable quality of "atta" (flour) was at once procurable at rates little higher than those obtaining in India.

On the 30th September, Lt-General Sir James Willcocks arrived with his Staff by the s.s. *Malwa.* His appointment as Corps Commander of the Indian troops in France had been announced on the 27th September, and was received with the greatest enthusiasm by all ranks. Nor was his great reputation undeserved. His name stood high in the Army as that of a very stout, skilful, and efficient soldier, who had carved out a career for himself without the aid of patronage, and in complete indifference to social and political influences. Born in 1857, he joined the Leinster Regiment in 1878. He served in the Afghan campaign 1879–80, and in the Waziri expedition of 1881, for which he was mentioned in despatches. He was promoted to the rank of captain in 1884, and took part in the Soudan campaign of 1885. The years 1886 to 1889 saw him engaged in the Burma expedition, from which he brought away a medal with two clasps and a D.S.O. He fought in the Chin Lushai expedition of 1889–90, and in the Manipur expedition of 1891. In 1893 he gained his majority, and in 1897 served with the Tochi Field Force and obtained the brevet of Lieutenant-Colonel. In 1898 he served as second in command of the West African Frontier Force, receiving, when the expedition ended, the special thanks of H.M. Government. From 1899 to 1900 he commanded the West African Frontier Force, and in the latter year the Ashanti Field Force, with which he relieved Kumasi. On this occasion he was granted the freedom of the City of London, was presented with a sword of honour by the corporation, and was mentioned in the King's Speech at the opening of his first Parliament. In 1902 he joined the Field Force in South Africa, adding a medal and a clasp to his soldierly record. Finally, in 1908, he commanded with distinction the Zakka Khel and Mohmand expeditions.

Such was the remarkable record of the General who led the Army of India to their great adventure in Flanders. No man in the British Army wore more decorations on his breast for active service than James Willcocks, and none bore his honours more modestly and more gallantly. He was now to be tested in surroundings which were novel even to his vast military experience. He was to be placed in situations more difficult, it may be boldly claimed, than any other Corps Commander had to face. His task demanded a subtle and intuitive insight into the mentality of the East: much sympathy, much allowance, and yet on occasion an unpitying severity. He had at once to hold, with two small, untried

Indian Divisions, a line which had tested the endurance of the two Divisions of English veterans under General Smith-Dorrien whom he relieved, and through all his difficulties, which were far graver than even at this time it is permissible to explain, he never faltered in his courage and never lost the devotion of the troops whom he understood so well. One of the writers will never forget his conversation, after the battle of Neuve Chapelle, with an Indian officer of a shattered but heroic battalion. "There are very few of you left, Subadar Sahib," said the General with deep emotion. "There are twice as many as there were until the General Sahib visited us," replied the officer, bleeding as he spoke from two severe wounds.

General Willcocks has preserved a complete documentary record of the whole period during which he commanded the Indian Corps. His advice as to the demands which it was possible to make upon the troops for which he was responsible was not always accepted by superior authority; perhaps imperious necessity sometimes prescribed a different course. But he was seldom wrong in his estimate, and a close study of his confidential papers establishes more and more clearly his sagacity, his prescience and his courage.

The Lahore Division remained at Marseilles till the 30th September, the interval being utilized chiefly in re-arming with new rifles and ammunition, and in providing the troops with warm clothing.

On the 30th September the Division entrained for Orleans, where it arrived on the 3rd October. Throughout the journey the greatest hospitality and kindness were shown to the troops by the generous-hearted French people. Enormous crowds gathered at all the stations where the trains stopped; fruit, flowers, coffee and biscuits were lavished on the men, and each station was a surging mass of humanity, waving flags and cheering "les Hindus," as the people called our men.

The Division camped at the Champs de Cercettes, about six miles from Orleans, where it remained till the 18th October. This period was utilized in completing transport, etc., in which many difficulties were experienced. As General Service wagons were not available, their place was taken by tradesmen's vans very similar to those used by English railways for luggage; these were drawn by two horses and, if carefully packed, could carry about 2000 lbs.

On the 18th October, a very wet day, the Division entrained, still without the Sirhind Brigade, and at Arques and Blendercques, where they arrived on the 20th October, the men had their first experience of billets, and the campaign could be said to have begun.

CHAPTER II

THE FIRST BATTLE OF YPRES

First battle of Ypres—Arrival of Lahore Division at the front—Ferozepore Brigade attached to British Cavalry Corps—General situation—Attack on German position—Fighting spirit of the troops—Enemy's attack on Messines front—Gallantry of Captain Forbes' Company 57th Rifles—129th Baluchis heavily attacked—Attack on Messines by nine German battalions—Heavy losses of British officers—Sepoy Khudadad Khan's Victoria Cross.

On the 21st October, the Lahore Division, without the Sirhind Brigade, marched to the area round Wallon Cappel and Lynde.

Orders were then received for the 1st Battalion Connaught Rangers, under Lt-Colonel H. S. Ravenshaw, to move by motor-bus viâ St Sylvestre and Bailleul to Wulverghem, which they reached in the early morning of the 22nd October, coming under the orders of General Allenby, Commanding the Cavalry Corps, by whom they were attached to the 1st Cavalry Division under General De Lisle.

The 57th Rifles, under Lt-Colonel F. W. Gray, D.S.O., on the return of the motors, moved up to Wulverghem, about seven miles south-west of Ypres, and were attached to the 2nd Cavalry Division under General Gough. Half of the battalion was then placed at the disposal of General Bingham, Commanding the 4th Cavalry Brigade, and half with General Chetwode's 5th Cavalry Brigade, both Brigades being in the vicinity of Wytschaete.

This arrangement continued till the 26th October, the 57th remaining in the trenches. On the same date the remainder of the Ferozepore Brigade marched to Bailleul and billeted.

Thence the 129th Baluchis, under Lt-Colonel W. M. Southey, proceeded by bus to St Eloi, where they were also attached to the 2nd Cavalry Division and placed at the disposal of General Vaughan, Commanding the 3rd Cavalry Brigade. The honour of being the first British battalion of the Indian Corps to enter the trenches therefore belongs to the 1st Battalion Connaught Rangers, the first Indian battalion being the 57th Rifles, closely followed by the 129th Baluchis.

The position at this moment was briefly as follows in the immediate front occupied by the Cavalry Corps to which the units of the Ferozepore Brigade were attached.

The key to Ypres in the south lay in the ridge which commences in the west with the Mont des Cats and runs eastward for some eleven miles to Wytschaete, between the Poperinghe—Ypres road on the north side and the river Lys on the south. Rising as it does in places to a height of several hundred feet, with a maximum breadth of two miles, the occupation of this position by the enemy would have entailed the evacuation by the British of Ypres, Vlamertinghe and Poperinghe. It was imperative, therefore, at all costs to prevent the Germans from gaining a footing on the ridge.

The Cavalry Corps, the strength of which was barely 4,500 sabres, was holding the space between Zandvoorde and Wytschaete with its right resting on the north-east corner of Ploegstert wood, which will always be known to the British soldier as "Plug Street." This wood was a sparsely treed patch, nearly two miles long by three-quarters of a mile broad. The ground was mostly bog, while the slightest rain rendered the road almost impassable. Here the Cavalry Corps joined hands with the 3rd Corps, which held the front from the eastern extremity of the wood through Le Gheir, crossing the river Lys about a quarter of a mile south of Frelinghien.

On the 22nd October the 1st Cavalry Division took over the section of the defence from the river Douve to a point east of Messines, linking up with the 4th Division on the right, and the 2nd Cavalry Division on the left, which carried the line on northwards for $3\frac{1}{2}$ miles, its right on Messines in touch with the 1st Cavalry Division, and its left at the canal bridge east of Hollebeke in touch with the 3rd Cavalry Division.

The fighting for some time past had been of a hammer and tongs order, with alternate gains and losses on both sides. The 21st October may be taken as the turning-point, as on that day the Germans commenced an offensive along the whole line from La Bassée in the south to Menin in the north, the British, except on the extreme left, being pinned down to the defensive.

The position was critical, for the Allies were outnumbered and outgunned. There was no prospect for several days of our receiving any substantial reinforcements, while it was known that the enemy was bringing up large bodies of troops from the east. Sir John French had no illusions on the subject. In his despatch of the 14th November, he remarked,—

"I fully realized the difficult task which lay before us and the onerous rôle which the British Army was called upon to fulfil. That success has been attained, and all the enemy's desperate attempts to break through our line frustrated, is due to the marvellous fighting power and the indomitable courage and tenacity of officers, non-commissioned officers and men. No more arduous task has ever been assigned to British soldiers; and in all their splendid history there is no instance of their having answered so magnificently to the desperate calls which of necessity were made upon them."

On the 23rd October, two companies of the Connaughts relieved the Essex Regiment in front of Messines, the remaining two companies taking over cavalry trenches at the same place on the 24th. The battalion Head Quarters occupied a convent in Messines, which was shelled on the 26th, but without casualties. This notice to quit was accepted in the spirit in which it was meant, and it was fortunate that the move was made without delay, for the convent was shortly afterwards very heavily bombarded, the church being burnt down. Orders were then received to hand over the trenches to the cavalry.

The relief was commenced in daylight, and was carried out with considerable difficulty, as the Germans had the range to a nicety, their shrapnel and rifle fire causing several casualties. The 57th Rifles occupied trenches near Oost Taverne with the Afridi Company, the Dogra Company being between Wytschaete and Messines. Their first casualties took place that night during a small German attack which was repulsed.

The temper of the men was strikingly illustrated during this affair. Sepoy Usman Khan (55th Rifles attached) was hit by rifle fire but refused to leave; he was again hit, and again declined to give way. Finally, a large piece of flesh was blown away from both legs by a shell splinter, and he was carried back. For his grand example he was awarded the Indian Distinguished Service Medal.

On the 26th October, orders were issued for an attack on the enemy's lines. The general idea was that the 1st Cavalry Division should hold Messines. The Connaughts and 57th, pivoting on Messines, were to attack towards the line Gapaard—west of Wambeek, while the 2nd Cavalry Division attacked the line from west of Wambeek—Houthem, the operations being supported by the 1st Cavalry Division at Messines, and by fire from our trenches.

The 2nd Cavalry Division was directed to commence the attack at 3 p.m. The 129th Baluchis, under the orders of General Vaughan, were to co-operate with the attacks on the right and left towards the line west of Wambeek—Houthem. The 4th and 5th Cavalry Brigades were held in close reserve.

The ground over which the attack was to be made was of a difficult nature, consisting of a series of low hills, the slopes of which fell towards the Gaapard—Oost Taverne line. There was little or no cover, while in the vicinity of Oost Taverne there was a small wood which served to mask the movements of the enemy.

The morning of the 26th October broke grey and misty. Rain had fallen throughout the night, and the trenches were deep in mud and water.

The trenches of those far-off days were very different from the elaborate field fortifications of the present time. As often as not they were merely ordinary ditches, improved to the best of our ability, as time, means and opportunity might allow. The line of defence was not continuous. Gaps existed everywhere, through which snipers crept at night and shot our men from the rear. It was no uncommon occurrence for a company to find in the early morning that a section of trench on their right or left had been evacuated by our men during the night, and had been occupied by the enemy. The first notice of the change of tenants was frequently given in the shape of a shower of bombs or an enfilade rifle or machine-gun fire.

Such attempts at drainage as could be made were of the most primitive description. In the lower-lying ground, the water-level was so high that trenches could not be sunk to a depth sufficient to give adequate cover. A few hours' rain sufficed to fill them knee-deep with mud and water.

The communication trenches, where they existed, were very imperfect, and there were many instances of wounded men being drowned in them when attempting to find their way back from the firing line. It would be impossible to imagine conditions more terrible for Eastern troops. No language can describe their sufferings, carried swiftly from a fierce tropical sun to the wet and winter of Flanders.

The attack commenced at 3 p.m., and by 5 p.m. had progressed without much opposition to a distance ranging from 200 to 1000 yards at different points. The Connaughts on the right unfortunately lost direction while feeling for the 57th in the growing darkness.

The detachment advanced with C company under Captain R. L. Payne leading, and B company under Captain R. G. Eyre in support, the two companies being under the command of Major S. J. Murray.

C company unfortunately lost direction while feeling for the 57th Rifles on their left in the growing darkness, but they pushed on towards the German trenches, three lines of which they rushed, capturing an officer and one man of the 9th Dragoons and a man of the 1st Bavarian Jaegers, and killing a number of the enemy.

Further progress was stopped by a strongly held farm house, which was too hard a nut for a handful of about one hundred men to essay to crack, so the Connaughts held on to a trench at the edge of the orchard in the hope of the arrival of reinforcements, but in addition to a fierce fire from the enemy, bullets from our men in rear began to fall in the trench.

Major Murray was faced with the necessity for a rapid decision as to whether he should hold on with the probability of being attacked in force, and the almost absolute certainty of being shelled by our own guns at daylight, or whether he should make certain of his prisoners and information by retiring while yet the way was open.

The situation left no room for doubt, and Major Murray withdrew, still under fire from friend and foe, until he reached our cavalry support line with a loss of 1 man killed, 15 wounded, and 1 missing. The prisoners were then handed over to the 2nd Cavalry Division.

The Connaught Rangers gave a foretaste in this affair of the dash which they showed throughout, and distinguished themselves by being the first battalion of the corps to capture a German trench or prisoner.

The 57th Rifles had begun the day with bad luck. The enemy shelled Wytschaete heavily. Lt-Colonel Gray, the Commanding Officer, who had just returned from the trenches with the adjutant, Captain W. S. Trail, was severely wounded in the right shoulder by shrapnel. The absence, even temporary, of an officer of his experience was a heavy blow to the regiment at the very outset of the campaign. The 57th got on by degrees, but darkness fell before they reached their objective, and the order to retire was then received from Head Quarters. Their casualties were slight, being, in addition to Lt-Colonel Gray, only 11 rank and file wounded.

The 129th Baluchis, operating with the 3rd Cavalry Brigade, made slow progress, owing to the difficulties of the ground and the necessity of keeping touch with the other units. The attack came under fairly heavy shell, machine-gun and rifle fire. Early in the advance, Captain Hampe-Vincent, while gallantly leading his men, fell mortally wounded, the first officer of the Indian Corps to lose his life in the war in Europe.

Lance-Naik Nek Amal at once went out alone and attended to him in the open under heavy fire. As he was unable to bring him in single-handed, he returned to his company, and with the aid of Sepoy Saiday Khan he succeeded in carrying the officer back.

The Indian Order of Merit was conferred on

both of these brave men, who thus early set an example of devotion which was later followed by so many others.

Darkness had begun to fall when No. 2 Company at last succeeded in pushing to a point within 200 yards of the German trenches. The men were very keen to carry the assault through, but as the attack had not progressed in other sections, and the darkness was now rendering movement very uncertain, orders were given to retire to their original line.

The orders were fortunate, for the position, protected as it was by at least four skilfully placed machine guns, would probably have proved too strong to offer any chance of success to so small an assaulting force. The 129th lost in the action Captain Hampe-Vincent and 9 other ranks killed, 48 wounded and 4 missing. This concluded the day's operations.

Nothing of any value was effected, and had not this been the first action in which Indian troops were engaged, it would not have received so much notice. It served, however, to test the fighting spirit of the men under novel and trying conditions, and it is satisfactory to note that the behaviour of the troops was throughout admirable, their disappointment at being ordered to retire before coming to conclusions with the enemy being very marked.

On the 27th October the Connaughts were with the 1st Cavalry Division, the 129th Baluchis with the 3rd Cavalry Brigade; of the 57th Rifles half a battalion was with the 4th and half a battalion with the 5th Cavalry Brigades, Head Quarters being at Wytschaete. On the 28th, two companies of the 57th were transferred to the 1st Cavalry Division at

Messines to relieve the Connaughts, who, with the Brigade Head Quarters, left to join the Division further south. The 9th Bhopal Infantry had, since the commencement of operations, been with Brigade Head Quarters. They left on the 26th October to rejoin the Division.

The 27th, 28th and 29th October were not marked by any very resolute attack on the part of the enemy, but a fairly heavy bombardment was kept up, to which our guns, inferior in strength as they were, replied to the best of their ability. Messines was continually shelled by night as well as by day, while the enemy made frequent half-hearted attacks.

During the night of the 29th–30th October reports were constantly received from the outposts that considerable movements of the enemy were in progress along our front. Owing to the easterly wind which brought up heavy mist, aeroplane reconnaissance could reveal nothing, but the early morning of the 30th brought a plain explanation of the movements.

At 6 a.m. the Germans opened a very heavy fire with howitzers and field guns against the left of the 2nd Cavalry Division, the sounds heard during the night having evidently been due to the bringing into position of these guns. At the same time the position on the Zandvoorde ridge, held by the 3rd Cavalry Division under General Byng, was bombarded with great violence. Messines suffered very severely. Shells fell fast in every part of the town, but luckily all the inhabitants had been evacuated, and casualties were confined to the troops.

The 7th Cavalry Brigade was most severely tested. Their trenches were hammered with heavy shells and were practically obliterated, many men being buried under the ruins. At the same time the attack was pressed home by overwhelming masses of infantry.

The 2nd Cavalry Division fought hard to hold its position. A squadron of the 1st Life Guards under Lord Hugh Grosvenor, and another of the 2nd Life Guards under Captain Vandeleur were surrounded in their trenches by the Germans. Scorning surrender, they fought to the last, and were absolutely wiped out in hand-to-hand fighting against hopeless odds.

The Division was compelled to fall back to the ridge of Klein Zillebeke, about a mile to the north and slightly to the east of the now famous Hill 60. Here, with the aid of two regiments from the Cavalry Corps, it managed to hold its position until relieved at nightfall.

In the meantime, the 2nd Cavalry Brigade, with which were the 129th Baluchis and 2 companies of the 57th Rifles, was passing through a critical period. The hostile artillery fire became heavier and heavier. It was soon evident that some forty guns were in action instead of the six which had been firing for the past few days.

At noon it was ascertained that the enemy was massing all along the front, but especially opposite the salient held by the 5th Lancers, whose strength at that point was only ninety rifles. At 12.30 p.m. two battalions attacked the 5th, who held on until the enemy was almost upon them, and only retired after losing over thirty of their small number.

The Division, in fact the Corps, had become so weak numerically that the defensive line consisted, not of a continuous line, or even of a broken line, of trenches, but merely of a thin scrawl of more or less detached posts. As a result, the enemy, having once gained a footing in a section of the line, was able to enfilade each post in succession. The position was untenable, and a general retirement was imperative.

This movement, always one of great danger and difficulty in the face of an enemy superior in numbers and in guns, was as a whole carried out deliberately and in good order during the afternoon, the enemy's infantry pressing hard.

A troop of the 20th Hussars, which did not commence its retirement until the enemy was within three hundred yards, lost very heavily. Captain L. Forbes was in command of No. 3 Company (Punjabi Mahomedans) of the 57th at this point, near Oost Taverne. For some unknown reason, but probably because all communication had been cut by the enemy's shell fire, the order to retire did not reach Captain Forbes in time to permit of the movement being made deliberately. Not having received any order to retire, he saw no reason to do so, and held on to the last. When eventually the order did arrive, it was too late. The enemy's infantry were upon them, and both flanks of the company were enveloped in a murderous machine-gun fire.

During the retirement, the half company under the command of Lieutenant Clarke was threshed out by machine guns, and practically none escaped. The remains of the company, now reduced to some sixty men of its original one hundred and forty, retired to Wytschaete, where it took up a previously prepared position about a quarter of a mile north-east of the village.

On the right of the line the bombardment had not been quite so heavy, and Major Willans was able to withdraw his company of Sikhs and the machine guns to a position slightly east of the Wytschaete—Messines road. During the night the Germans continued to bombard the trenches as also the village of Wytschaete, which was now a mass of ruins.

In the meantime, the 129th Baluchis under Lt-Colonel Southey had been undergoing a searching test. No. 1 Company under Captain Adair and No. 2 under Major Humphreys relieved C Section of the line and the reserve, while No. 3 under Major Hannyngton and No. 4 under Major Potter were relieved by the cavalry, and ordered to billets early in the morning of the 30th. No. 4 Company was successfully withdrawn under fairly heavy fire. No. 3 Company's progress rearwards was arrested by very heavy shelling, and it had to take refuge behind a farm slightly in rear of the trenches.

At about 6.30 a.m. the enemy opened a very heavy artillery fire on the whole of our position, Major Humphreys being mortally wounded in the reserve trenches; a number of other casualties also took place at this time.

Shortly after noon, all available men of the battalion were ordered to reinforce the firing line, which was being hard pressed by artillery fire as well as by infantry with machine guns. The Germans had chosen the moment for attack very skilfully. The fact that reliefs of this part of the line were taking place was doubtless known to them through their elaborate system of espionage, and greatly added to the confusion. In some cases orders did not arrive at all, in others they were incorrectly delivered or were misunderstood.

Three platoons of No. 3 Company had taken refuge behind the farm before mentioned, one platoon only having managed to get back. Colonel Southey took No. 4 Company and the one platoon of No. 3 back towards the firing line, but found the whole line, British and Indian, retiring. He then sent his men to hold a wood on the right flank and rallied those who were retreating, ordering them to hold positions covering the right and centre of the château. In the meantime, Lieutenant Lewis, who had replaced Major Humphreys, when that officer was mortally wounded early in the day, returned from the front line, and with Subadar Adam Khan held the position against heavy odds until ordered to retire, which he did very deliberately, holding the enemy in check with his fire.

About 4 p.m. orders were received from the General Officer Commanding 3rd Cavalry Brigade to withdraw to the trenches north of the château. After a brief interval to allow our guns to clear, this movement was successfully carried out.

The day had been a very trying one, and our losses were correspondingly heavy. Between the hours of 3 and 4 a.m. on the 31st October a fierce onslaught was made on Messines by nine German battalions, a very heavy bombardment having been kept up throughout the night. The enemy advanced at the jog-trot which later became so familiar, accompanying the movement with the usual raucous guttural sounds. They poured over the trenches of the 57th in wave after wave.

Major Barwell, who was in the 57th support

trenches, hearing a prolonged burst of fire from No. 4 Company, at once rushed forward to get to the front line, but before he had gone many yards was shot dead; several men were killed or wounded in gallant attempts to bring him in.

Captain Gordon, in command of No. 2 Company, seeing that No. 4 was being very heavily attacked, called on his company to counter-attack. As he rose to lead them, he too was shot, and died almost at once.

Lieutenant Molony, company officer of No. 2, heard the Germans charging on his right and suddenly saw three distinct masses of the enemy at a distance of about seventy-five yards. They had apparently just taken the trench on his right. Lieutenant Molony had no thought of retreat, and opened rapid fire, which soon put an end to the German cheering, and the enemy began digging himself in. Our trench was to some extent protected by a thick hedge and trees, which made it difficult for the enemy to see exactly where they were shooting. The duel went on for almost two hours, when suddenly a sweeping enfilade fire was opened from the right on the devoted little party, by this time very gravely reduced in numbers. Lieutenant Molony got his men out of the trench, and they lay down in the open about 20 yards behind, in prolongation of a cavalry trench, keeping up rapid fire as long as the ammunition lasted. At this moment Lieutenant Molony was badly hit in the arm, but before he became unconscious he ordered Jemadar Ram Singh to hold on, only retiring should the cavalry do so. The wounded officer eventually managed to crawl back to a trench in rear, whence he was taken to an aid post established in a cellar.

Jemadar Ram Singh was about the only survivor of this party, the remainder being wiped out by the frightful fire which the enemy brought to bear on them as they were lying in the open.

Jemadar Kapur Singh also fought it out until all but one wounded man had been put out of action, and then, rather than surrender, shot himself with his last cartridge.

Even this war can present few more devoted pictures than the death of these noble-hearted Dogras and the heroic Indian officer who chose rather to follow his men than to surrender.

The 57th in this part of the field were now left without a single British officer.

Subadar Arsla Khan, the senior Indian officer remaining, seeing that No. 4 Company was being overwhelmed, made a counter-attack with the bayonet in a gallant but vain attempt to succour it. He was, however, quite outnumbered, and was pushed back to the support trench by sheer weight, losing heavily in the process. Recognizing the hopelessness of the position, he succeeded, with the greatest coolness, in retiring the remnant of his men to Messines. His gallantry was recognized by the award of the Order of British India, 2nd Class, with the title of Bahadur.

While this was going on, a determined attack had been made on No. 3 Company north of Wytschaete, under Captain Forbes, who held on until the enemy's numbers again told, and enabled them to force their way through, Captain Forbes being badly wounded in the shoulder.

Havildar Gagna was holding a portion of this trench with a few men. When the Germans burst upon him, sanguinary hand-to-hand fighting took place in which most of the 57th were put out of action. The Havildar fought it out and killed five Germans before his bayonet broke. With a sword which he picked up, he continued the unequal combat until, after receiving six wounds, he collapsed. Happily, when the trench was retaken, he was found still alive and was afterwards rewarded with the 2nd Class, Indian Order of Merit.

A counter-attack was at once organized and delivered with the bayonet by a squadron of the 5th Dragoon Guards and a company of the 57th. After ferocious hand-to-hand fighting, the 57th were reinstated in a portion of their trench.

During the night the enemy continued to press his advantage on the left of the line, and in the morning of the 1st November, when Major Swifte and Captain Trail went up to the front line, they believed that the hundred men with them were all that remained of the 57th. To their delight, they found Major Willans with about another hundred men, mostly Sikhs, with whom he had held out during the night against all attacks, although the Germans were well past him on both flanks.

With Major Willans was Lieutenant Fowler, in charge of the regimental machine guns, which he fought with great gallantry throughout the action. While crossing a road under heavy fire in search of information, he was wounded in several places by a high explosive shell which burst quite close to him. For his gallant conduct he was awarded the Military Cross.

Captain Trail, the adjutant of the 57th, had been

conspicuous for his disregard of danger, and had rendered the most valuable assistance to the Commanding Officer. For his services he received the Military Cross.

The 57th nobly sustained the reputation which they had earned in other fields. Sikhs, Dogras, and Afridis vied with each other in heroism, inspirited by the bravery of their British officers.

We must now return to the 129th Baluchis, whom we left holding a wood and covering the right and centre of a château.

Early in the morning of the 31st October, the enemy was observed to be moving infantry up to Oost Taverne and the wood slightly to the west, but our artillery prevented them from pressing very seriously. The second Division was reinforced at noon by three French battalions with twelve guns, which arrived at St Eloi, whence they moved forward towards Oost Taverne and Hollebeke and to a great extent cleared the front of the 3rd Brigade, which had hitherto been closely pinned down to its trenches. The Brigade was thus enabled to assemble by nightfall, but before this could be effected, it was necessary to turn a body of the enemy out of a farm in which they had been allowed to gain a footing, under the impression that they were French. This operation is described by Major-General Gough, Commanding the 2nd Cavalry Division, as having been very well carried out by Lt-Colonel Southey and some of the 129th.

In the early morning of the 31st three companies of this regiment were sent up to support the 18th Hussars, and at dark took over four of their trenches. Shortly afterwards, a heavy fire was opened on their right, which steadily increased. News was then received that Captain Maclean had been wounded.

About midnight, Colonel Southey received a message from the General Officer Commanding the 3rd Cavalry Brigade that a farm which was held by Major Potter with part of No. 4 Company had been taken by the enemy. It appeared that a small body of Germans had advanced on the farm with the utmost assurance, so much so that No. 4 Company, not well versed in the difference in appearance between French and Germans—this at first was a constant and very serious difficulty for our Indian troops—believed that they were French. Fire was consequently not opened until they were practically in the farm, which was only held by a few of our men. After a brief struggle, Major Potter withdrew the men to a trench about fifty yards to the rear of the farm, having accounted for some fifteen of the enemy.

Colonel Southey then came up, and at about 3 a.m. on the 1st November, he attacked the left of the farm, while Major Potter attacked on the right. The 129th were thoroughly in their element in this kind of fighting, and chased the enemy from room to room of the building, killing ten and wounding three. Those who had not bolted then surrendered, to the number of fourteen. As one of the 129th remarked, " It was a very good game."

Shortly after this, the 129th were ordered to hand over their trenches to the French cavalry and to rejoin the Ferozepore Brigade. On their way south, they were inspected by Major-General H. P. Gough, Commanding 2nd Cavalry Division, who thanked the battalion for its assistance, and added that he would send in a very favourable report on its behaviour.

The 57th Rifles and 129th Baluchis, both under Lt-Colonel Southey, rejoined Head Quarters a few days later.

Thus ended their part in the famous First Battle of Ypres, the first serious engagement in which Indian troops fought in the war. Both regiments possessed previous experience of fighting in parts beyond the confines of the Indian Empire, for the 57th saw service in China in 1900, while the 129th bear on their Colours "Tel-el-Kebir" and "Egypt, 1882." During this long-drawn-out and fiercely contested battle, they fully sustained their own reputations and the honour of the Indian Army.

The casualties, as was to be expected from the nature of the fighting, were heavy. The 57th lost Major E. E. Barwell and Captain R. S. Gordon killed, Captain L. Forbes, Lieutenants E. K. Fowler and C. W. Molony wounded, while Lieutenant H. S. Clarke was missing. Indian officers: one killed, one wounded, two missing. Other ranks: 192 killed or wounded and 98 missing, of whom the majority were killed.

The losses of the 129th Baluchis were Major G. G. P. Humphreys, Captains W. F. Adair and P. C. Hampe-Vincent killed, while Captains F. A. Maclean and R. F. Dill, with Lieutenant H. V. Lewis were wounded. Of the Indian officers, three were killed and two wounded. Other ranks: 164 killed or wounded and 64 missing, of whom again the majority were probably killed.

The respect and affection felt by the Indian

[*Daily Mirror.*

SEPOY KHUDADAD KHAN, V.C., 129TH BALUCHIS.

41.]

soldier for his British officers is well known. No officers of any army in the world at any period of the world's history have ever fought with more valour and devotion than the British officers of the Indian Army Corps. Those who fought and fell in these first engagements were typical of a very noble and heroic class.

Major Humphreys is spoken of as having on every occasion commanded his company with the greatest coolness and judgment.

Captain Adair had shown himself to be a most gallant leader. When mortally wounded and lying under heavy fire, Havildar Zauf Khan and two men, with that devotion to their officers which has so often been shown, attempted to get Captain Adair away. He refused to be an encumbrance to them, saying that he was mortally wounded.

Captain Dill was in command of the machine guns. When one gun was put out of action, he ordered the men to retire. He then continued to fight the other gun until he was severely wounded in the head by a shell. His gallantry was recognized by the award of the D.S.O.

His men remained in action until they were rushed by the enemy in overpowering numbers, and all died fighting to the last, except Sepoy Khudadad Khan, who, although grievously wounded and left by the enemy for dead, managed to crawl away and escaped with his life. For his very conspicuous bravery he was awarded the Victoria Cross, being the first Indian soldier to receive this great honour.

The names of these gallant machine gunners deserve special record. They were—Havildar Ghulam Mahomed, Sepoys Lal Sher, Said Ahmed,

Kassib and Lafar Khan. They were honoured in death, for the Havildar received the Indian Order of Merit, while the sepoys were awarded the Indian Distinguished Service Medal.

Major-General Allenby, Commanding the Cavalry Corps, reported to the Indian Corps Commander in terms of great praise of the behaviour of the 57th and 129th while under his command.

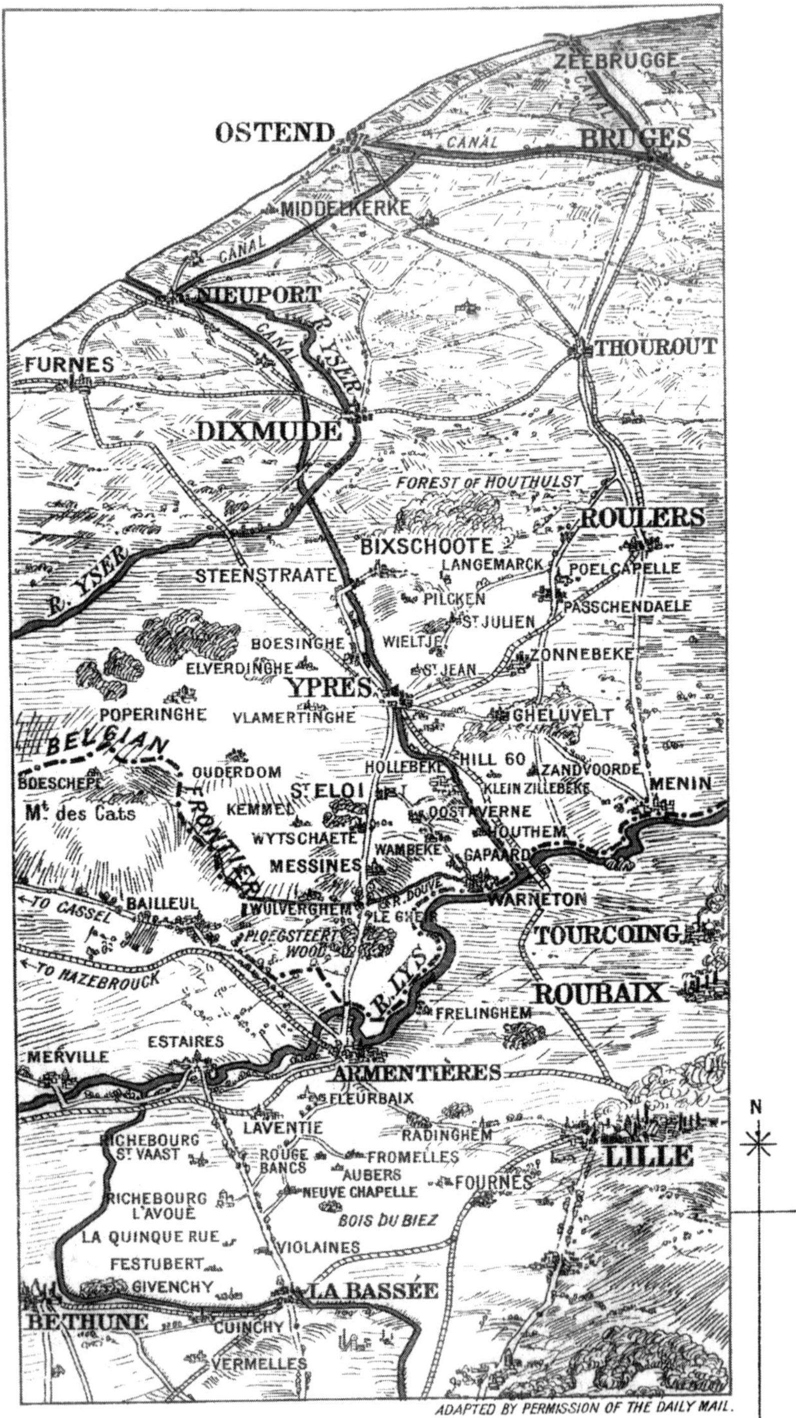

General map of the country from the Sea to the La Bassée Canal.

CHAPTER III

RELIEF OF THE FRENCH CAVALRY UNDER GENERAL CONNEAU BY THE JULLUNDUR BRIGADE

Position of the 2nd Corps under General Smith-Dorrien—British attempt to strike towards Lille—Heavy German offensive—Jullundur Brigade in trenches—Sir John French's appreciation—Trouble with spies—Last reserves brought up—Casualties.

WHILE this battle was taking place in the north, stirring events were happening further south.

It is necessary to describe briefly the position of the 2nd Corps under General Sir Horace Smith-Dorrien, with which the Indian Corps was destined to be intimately connected.

As already stated, the line from east of Messines and Armentières to a front west of Radhinghem was held by General Allenby's Cavalry Corps and General Pulteney's 3rd Corps, with General Conneau's French Cavalry on its right. The Germans, opposed by our 2nd Corps, were attacking from the direction of Lille towards La Bassée and Béthune.

On the 19th October, the 2nd Corps held a line from Givenchy, near the La Bassée Canal, forming a salient eastwards to the north of the La Bassée—Lille road to Herlies, thence to Aubers on the famous ridge which has cost us so many brave lives, both British and Indian; thence north-east to a point near Radinghem, where it connected with General Conneau's Cavalry.

The 5th Division held the right of the line, the

3rd Division the left. La Bassée was held by the Crown Prince of Bavaria, as also was the La Bassée—Lille Canal and the country immediately to the south and east.

Our first endeavour was to strike through Fournes at the La Bassée—Lille line, and thus to cut off La Bassée. The Germans, however, anticipated this move, and after the 20th October General Smith-Dorrien found that he could not at the best hope to do more than to hold his ground and keep the enemy off Béthune.

On the morning of the 22nd October, the enemy made his first attack on a large scale. The 5th Division on the right was pushed out of Violaines between Givenchy and Lorgies, the further progress of the German advance being only checked by a vigorous counter-attack by the 3rd Worcesters and 2nd Manchesters. It was evident from the strength of the attack that the 3rd Division on our left would be unable to hold its ground. On the night of the 22nd October, therefore, the line was withdrawn to a position running east of Givenchy, in front of Neuve Chapelle to a salient near Aubers and so on to Fauquissart, south-east of Laventie. At this time the 2nd Corps consisted of two Divisions, the 3rd and 5th, together with one Brigade, amounting to about 32,000 men in all, amongst which were some French units.

On the 24th October, the whole line was vigorously attacked, but, mainly by the help of our artillery, the assault was beaten off before it reached our trenches. In the evening the 3rd Division was sorely tried, but the position was saved by the 1st Wiltshires and 1st West Kents.

By this time the Corps, which had been fighting for ten days, was beginning to feel the strain. Luckily, the Lahore Division under Lt-General Watkis had just arrived, without, however, the Ferozepore Brigade, which was with the Cavalry Corps near Messines, and the Sirhind Brigade, still in Egypt.

The remaining Jullundur Brigade was at once utilized on the left of the Corps, taking over the ground held by General Conneau's Cavalry, which was moved northwards. The 15th Sikhs, 34th Sikh Pioneers and 59th Rifles were pushed up to support the French Cavalry, with orders to counter-attack if the French were driven out that day. If not, they were to relieve the Cavalry at nightfall. This relief was advisable for two reasons—because the French were filling a gap between two of our Brigades, and because they had been in the trenches for ten very strenuous days.

From this date until the 1st November the three battalions were fated to undergo a harassing experience. Space does not permit of a very detailed account, but a brief description will give some idea of the conditions under which our troops had to fight in those far-off days, when they were outnumbered and outgunned, and were without the bombs, grenades and other munitions which are now provided as naturally and as regularly as their daily food.

The 15th Sikhs on the right were in touch with the Gordon Highlanders, who were the left battalion of the 8th British Infantry Brigade; the 59th Rifles carried on the line to the left, where one company of the 34th Pioneers under Captain Bailey took over an advanced post from the French and linked up the 59th with the 19th British Brigade.

This detachment was attacked within an hour of its relieving the French, and during the night Captain Bailey was wounded severely and Lieutenant Browne slightly. The defence was very ably carried on by Subadars Sher Singh and Natha Singh till the evening of the 26th, when Major Gib took over command. Subadar Sher Singh received the Indian Distinguished Service Medal for his gallant leadership.

This relief was the first experience by Indian troops of the difficulties of moving at night across unknown country, cut up by wire entanglements and deep ditches full of water and mud. The men were, moreover, under fire for a great part of the time, and had much difficulty in finding the French trenches.

On arrival, it was seen that the front was far too long for the number of men available. The 59th, for instance, had to occupy a front of 1500 yards. There was no help for it, as there were no more men to be had. The relief was successfully carried out between 6 p.m. and midnight.

At about 8 p.m. the Gordons on the right were heavily attacked, and their line was broken. The first intimation of this occurrence received by our men was the sound of Germans shouting in rear of the right of the 15th Sikhs, and it was evident that an unknown number of the enemy had got through. In the inky darkness it was impossible to find out exactly what had happened, but after a time everything became quiet, and it seemed that the Germans had not followed up their advantage. As a matter of fact, the 4th Middlesex, gallantly led by Lt-Colonel

Hull, had at once counter-attacked, and, hurling back the enemy at the point of the bayonet, had restored the position.

During the night there were intermittent attacks, which, although they were not pressed home, caused a number of casualties. The difficulty of the position was increased by the fact that telephonic communication with Brigade Head Quarters could not be established, owing partly to the wires being cut by shells, and partly to the operations of spies, of whom there were at this period many behind our lines.

On the 25th we were repeatedly attacked. Captain Scott of the 59th was shot through the head and killed. Lt-Colonel Gordon and Lieutenant Henderson of the 15th were wounded, and the command of the regiment devolved on Major Carden.

The enemy's artillery fire became heavier and heavier, and it seemed that he was meditating an attack on the section held by the 59th. Two companies of the 34th were brought up, with orders to counter-attack if the 59th were driven back. About this time the German snipers became very active and caused many casualties, occupying every point of vantage with very great resolution.

Throughout the day the 15th Sikhs were subjected to very heavy shell fire, and after dark our centre and right were hard pressed, but held their own till 3 a.m., when the attack ceased. The remainder of the 34th reinforced the firing line, leaving absolutely no Brigade reserve, but at 7 p.m. half of the 47th Sikhs arrived, a very welcome addition, as the situation was rapidly becoming critical.

The night was a trying one, very wet and cold,

and the men, who had now been fighting without sufficient food and with little or no sleep for two days, were soaked to the skin.

The question of rations was an anxious one. The only way in which they could be brought up was by collecting them at some central spot, about 400 yards behind the line, and then waiting for a lull in the firing. If there was no lull, there were no rations.

The position of the Regimental Staffs was no enviable one, for they had several times been shelled out of the houses in which they had established themselves. This was undoubtedly due to the activity of spies, for everywhere along the British front it had been remarked that, however often Head Quarters might be changed, the enemy's guns were soon able to re-locate them.

The 26th passed fairly quietly, but the Germans were reported to be massing in front of our centre. On the 27th at 7 a.m. the 59th were heavily attacked, and No. 3 Company under Captain Martin was losing men fast. In attempting to reinforce him, Captain Murray was severely wounded. A vigorous fire fight followed, and after an hour's hard tussle the enemy was beaten back to his trenches all along the line, Captain Vaughan-Sawyer, the interpreter of the 34th, falling a victim to a sniper during the attack.

The rest of the day passed more quietly than usual, except for the activities of the snipers, who prevented rations from being brought up till after dusk. During the day the men were greatly encouraged by a message from Sir John French, warmly commending the manner in which the Jullundur

Brigade had maintained its position during the day's fighting.

The 15th Sikhs had been so worried by snipers that a house-to-house search was carried out in the village. Several of the haunts of these gentry were discovered by the presence of empty German cartridge cases. In the end a number of men were sent off to Head Quarters under escort, and for a time there was comparative peace. There is no doubt that at that period the spying and general observation arrangements of the enemy were much superior to ours, for it was noted that whenever a few officers were collected together, that part of the trench was at once subjected to heavy fire.

The 28th was marked by two determined attacks, which, with the aid of our artillery and machine guns, were both repulsed with considerable loss. Curiously enough, the Germans did not support their night attacks by artillery fire, although our guns were largely instrumental in beating them back. The 29th passed quietly, but by this time the front, always far too extended for the men available, was very thinly held, as the casualties had been heavy and continuous.

The position was most grave. On the 27th, the 15th Lancers had been sent up as reinforcements. They represented absolutely the last available reserves. In the event of a really strong attack, nothing remained but for our men to die where they stood. Happily, the attack did not come, and by the 1st November the defenders were relieved by the two remaining regiments of the Brigade, one of which, the 47th Sikhs, had meantime been heavily engaged in the attack on Neuve Chapelle, and was in consequence only able to take over the front of three companies.

The casualties during the period 24th October to 1st November were severe.

The 15th Sikhs lost 3 British and 3 Indian officers wounded; other ranks, 11 killed, 240 wounded, and 12 missing. These casualties were largely due to shrapnel, and occurred chiefly on the 26th and 27th, before the regiment was properly entrenched.

The 59th Rifles had 1 British officer killed, 1 British and 2 Indian officers wounded, 13 other ranks killed and 189 wounded.

The 34th Pioneers lost 1 British officer killed, 2 British and 3 Indian officers wounded, 15 other ranks killed and 89 wounded.

The 47th Sikhs had 2 British officers and 118 other ranks wounded.

CHAPTER IV

ATTACK BY INDIANS ON NEUVE CHAPELLE

Situation round Neuve Chapelle—British evacuate village—Counter-attack by Indian troops—Gallantry of 47th Sikhs and Sappers and Miners—Heroism of British officers—Lieutenant Nosworthy, R.E.—Counter-attack unsuccessful—Heavy casualties—Honours awarded—Daring reconnaissance by Lieutenant Brunskill, 47th Sikhs—Legendary achievements of Indian troops.

It is now necessary to move slightly southwards towards the village of Neuve Chapelle.

On the 26th October, the enemy managed to gain a footing, after a violent struggle, on the north-east side of the village, having advanced under cover of the Bois du Biez, which lies slightly to the east.

During the 27th desperate hand-to-hand fighting took place for the possession of the village. In spite of vigorous counter-attacks, the Germans still clung to their hold for the greater part of the day, but towards dark we gradually retook most of the ground held by the enemy. At this juncture heavy German reinforcements were brought up, and our troops, fighting with the greatest valour, were forced back by sheer weight of numbers, the entire village being taken from us.

The troops engaged in this fighting were mostly of the 7th and 9th British Brigades. Amongst them the West Kents especially distinguished themselves, holding on to their isolated trenches from beginning to end until relieved, eventually coming out of action with only two officers, both 2nd Lieutenants, who were rewarded with the D.S.O.

This success on the part of the Germans drove a salient into our line which it was imperative to rectify without delay. At 5 p.m. on the 27th, a message was received to the effect that the Commanding Officer and the Adjutant of the West Kents had been killed, and that the Germans were coming on very fast through the south of Neuve Chapelle. This was followed quickly by a report from the Wiltshires and South Lancashires that they were nearly surrounded, and had been forced to retire, but were engaging the enemy on the west side of the village, in order to check them, before retiring further after dark.

This news pointed to the probability of a gap being created between the 3rd and 5th Divisions, which would seriously affect the whole position of the 2nd Corps. The 9th Bhopals, under Lt-Colonel Dobbie, were at once ordered to counter-attack in the direction of Pont Logy, with the object of taking in flank the enemy who was reported to be advancing west of Neuve Chapelle.

The Bhopals moved off across enclosed country cut up by bogs and barbed wire, which in the darkness caused some confusion; but eventually the whole battalion reached the neighbourhood of the West Kent trenches and established touch. Confused fighting took place in the hamlet south of Neuve Chapelle, during which No. 1 Company, under Captain Jones and Lieutenant Wade, put about thirty Germans out of action.

The position at this juncture was very critical,

as the enemy had almost succeeded in enveloping the West Kents and were actually firing into them from the rear. At this most opportune moment the Bhopals arrived on the right flank of the Germans, who were forced to retire with some loss.

During the chaotic fighting, Lieutenant Mullaly of the Bhopals was unfortunately captured, and Lt-Colonel Anderson was mortally wounded while the battalion was entrenching under heavy fire.

By now, the 20th Company Sappers and Miners, under Captain Paris, R.E., and the 21st Company under Captain Richardson, R.E., had come up, while the 47th Sikhs under Major Davidson had moved up into line on the left of the Bhopals. Darkness stopped further advance, and it was found that a considerable gap existed between the 47th and the Bhopals. Brigadier-General McCracken considered it necessary to utilize the Sappers and Miners to fill this gap, as they were the only troops immediately available, although it was, of course, not intended that such highly and specially trained men should be used for the ordinary fighting duties of infantry.

Frequent attacks were made during the night by the enemy, but were repulsed, and the trenches on the north-east side were swept by machine-gun fire, while a German searchlight was playing on the left of the position from the outskirts of Neuve Chapelle. At 10.30 a.m. on the 28th, our artillery commenced a bombardment which continued for half an hour.

A portion of the Bhopals remaining with the West Kents, the 47th Sikhs advanced on the village with the 20th and 21st Companies Sappers and Miners, and covered the 700 yards of open ground, alternately firing and rushing. Casualties were numerous, but the excellence of our fire control saved us a much heavier loss.

When our men were about 100 yards from the outskirts of the village, the Germans in the front trenches began to bolt, pursued by the gallant Sikhs and Sappers with the bayonet, a few being killed and some captured. The Indians then tore on into the village, Sikhs and Sappers mixed together, and worked in parties up the streets, under a furious fire from the roofs of buildings.

By degrees the houses were cleared after desperate hand-to-hand fighting, in which a man of the 47th is reported to have captured three Germans out of eight, having previously killed the other five. From another house the 47th recovered a wounded British soldier (a relic of the previous hard fighting) and two wounded Germans. The latter were searched, and one of them lifted up his voice and wept bitterly, evidently thinking that our men were feeling for a soft place in which to insert a bayonet. He refused to be comforted until a stalwart Sikh patted him kindly on the back and said, "Be not afraid!"

On reaching the cross-roads in the centre of the village, the troops came under a frightful machine-gun fire. Captain McCleverty, always in advance, cheering on his men just as he had cheered on the regimental hockey team, dashed across the roads, the rest following close on his heels, but he was shot dead at a corner house by a German concealed only a few yards away. Major Davidson and others tried to stalk the man with revolvers, but he was not to be drawn.

A Punjabi Mahomedan of the Sappers calmly put the others aside, telling them to leave it to him. He knelt down in the road, and quietly waiting until the German put his head out for another shot, killed him on the spot. He continued to wait, amidst the machine-gun bullets drifting like rain, for a chance at a second man whom he believed to be there, but if the sniper existed, he was too wary to show himself. In the turmoil, the name of this hero could unfortunately not be ascertained, or he would have been recommended for a very high honour.

Our losses were rapidly becoming serious from the rifle fire of the enemy in the houses, and of several machine guns posted outside the village which swept the main street. Lieutenant Hayes-Sadler of the 20th Company Sappers and Miners determined at all costs to put a stop to the ravages of the machine guns, and headed a splendid charge against the nearest, but without avail. His men were mown down and he fell shot through the head.

The blood of our men was up, and nothing could stop them ; after a prolonged and ferocious struggle, the whole of the main street was captured. The Germans held on like a vice, and each house formed a small fortress which had to be stormed before further advance could be made.

Captain Paris of the 20th Company was wounded several times, but refused to leave, and was eventually taken prisoner.

The 21st Company was also doing its part manfully, but its losses were terrible. Captain Richardson charged with impetuous valour ahead of his men, and was actually killed on the far side of the village after the main street had been captured. His two subalterns, Lieutenants Rohde and Almond, fit followers of a dauntless leader, fell just as victory appeared to be within their grasp. Lieutenant Fitzmaurice was badly wounded, but kept going as long as he could stand, and then managed to crawl back to safety.

The fighting went on, counter-attack following counter-attack, the Germans using the bodies of their own dead as cover. Major Davidson was collecting his men for a final charge, when the enemy came on in overpowering numbers from the north and east, and at the same moment the machine-gun fire redoubled its fury down the main street.

Without immediate reinforcements, the position of the 47th was now quite untenable, as their losses had been very heavy. Reinforcements there were none, and Major Davidson was compelled to give up all he had won at such fearful cost, and retire. The line of retreat lay over about 500 yards of open ground exposed to a tornado of shell and machine-gun fire, and the bodies of our men soon lay thick on the ground, but eventually the remains of the half battalion got back to comparative safety, only 68 out of 289 actually collecting on the La Bassée road.

The troops were suffering terribly from want of water and were absolutely dead beat, but the enemy was counter-attacking all along the front, and every man was required. Major Davidson was ordered to collect at Rouge Croix as many of the battalion as were left, with a view to holding the cross-roads, which were almost certain to be attacked. He asked his men whether they could do it, exhausted as they were, and to his delight found that they clearly resented such a question. Off they marched again towards Rouge Croix, but were met by orders to go into billets.

Such was the spirit of the Indian Corps, and it is on record that during the retreat from the village, under a fire described as hellish, the men were laughing and joking with each other, and Captain Brown, afterwards killed at Neuve Chapelle, stood up at the halts to fire, his example being followed by many of the men.

Major Davidson had throughout this confused and ding-dong fighting shown the highest qualities of bravery and leadership, and was awarded a brevet Lt-Colonelcy in recognition of his services.

The 47th Sikhs were raised in 1901 and have no battle honours on their Colours. Throughout its service in France, this magnificent regiment never failed to answer all calls; its reputation would be secure, and its right to fight shoulder to shoulder with our best troops would be established, if based only on the record of Neuve Chapelle; but this action was only one of many in which the 47th distinguished themselves.

In the meantime, the Bhopals had made some progress, and a portion of them under Major Jamieson even reached the original trenches of the Wiltshires, while another party arrived at the same line of trenches further to the east, after forcing their way through a part of the village. Here, however, they found themselves confronted by very superior forces of the enemy, and without support. The remnants of these small detachments eventually made their way back through Neuve Chapelle, losing heavily as they went by the fire from the houses.

Lieutenants Nosworthy and Rait-Kerr of the 20th Company Sappers and Miners now found themselves in the centre of the village, with only about twenty men left, as the casualties had been very heavy, and in the absolute chaos which reigned the company had become split up.

Speedy reinforcement was necessary, so Lieutenant Rait-Kerr volunteered to go back over the bullet-swept open to try and bring up more men, but he was hit before he had gone two hundred yards. Sapper Dalip Singh ran to his officer's assistance and helped him under cover. He then stood over him and kept off several parties of Germans by his fire. On one occasion—a feat almost incredible, though well established—he was attacked by as many as twenty of the enemy, but beat them off, and got Lieutenant Rait-Kerr away. This officer's indomitable spirit is shown by the fact that when Lieutenant Nosworthy eventually retired, he found him just recovering from the shock of his wound, but preparing to try and crawl back to the fight. For his signal act of bravery and devotion Sapper Dalip Singh received the 2nd Class of the Indian Order of Merit.

Prominent among the few men still left with Lieutenant Nosworthy, was Subadar Gunpat Mahadeo, who throughout fully merited by his bravery the reward of the 2nd Class of the Order of British India which he received.

Subadar Malla Singh, too, fought with supreme disregard of danger, and when retreat was inevitable, he conducted his small party with the greatest skill and coolness. For his gallantry throughout the action he received the Military Cross.

Lieutenant Nosworthy is known in an army of very brave men for his genuine and irrepressible love of fighting ; in the most awkward and dangerous positions he is always the same, gay, self-possessed, and resourceful. He was wounded on this as on other occasions, but nothing seemed to damp his spirits. His last achievement was to be shot through the heart at the battle of Ypres in April, 1915, and to recover, destined to take part, with nerves unaffected, in other conflicts. You could, until all was lost, as easily have moved the three Musqueteers from their famous breakfast as you could have moved this man from Neuve Chapelle.

With the scanty remnant of his company, he proceeded to build a barricade in the cross-road off the main street, and thus checked the enfilade machine-gun fire. He then ensconced himself in a couple of houses and held his position while waiting for the reinforcements which were never to arrive. Two other messengers were sent off, but neither got through.

At about 3.30 p.m. a weary battle-worn party of Indians with one British officer was seen approaching by the road which the Sappers were holding. These proved to be Major Jamieson and a small body of Bhopals who, having penetrated to the Wiltshires' trenches, had been forced to retire in the face of numbers. On their arrival Lieutenant Nosworthy, still full of fight, led a charge against one of the numerous machine guns, but it failed, and it was evident that the only possibility of avoiding death or capture lay in immediate retirement.

Of the company of Sappers only thirteen men retired with Lieutenant Nosworthy. Many of the others had died gallantly, while some, cut off from their officer, had retired with Subadar Malla Singh. The 21st Company had vied with the 20th in bravery, Subadars Ganga Charan Dixit, who was wounded, and Ismail Khan being prominent amongst brave men for their gallantry. They received the Indian Distinguished Service Medal.

The attack was magnificently carried out, and was within an ace of success. As usual in those days, our hands were tied by the lack of men; and by degrees we were learning the lesson that to take a position was one thing, to hold it another, involving the employment of a sufficient depth of troops. It seems probable that, had reinforcements been available, the 47th and Sappers would have held the village which they took with such superb élan and at such a heavy cost.

The stubbornness and bravery with which our men fought can be gauged by the losses. The 47th lost Captain McCleverty, one Indian officer and 16 men killed, and Major Browne, three Indian officers and 156 men wounded, out of a total of 289.

The 9th Bhopals lost Lt-Colonel Anderson and one Indian officer killed, Captain Jones and Lieutenant Wade wounded and missing, Captain Irvine wounded (since died of wounds in Mesopotamia), Lieutenant Mullaly a prisoner, the casualties amongst other ranks being 262.

For his gallantry Captain G. D. Martin received the Military Cross, while Subadar Major Bhure Singh and Havildar Amar Singh were awarded the Indian Distinguished Service Medal.

[*C. Vandyck, Ltd.*

FIELD-MARSHAL VISCOUNT FRENCH OF YPRES, K.P., G.C.B., O.M., G.C.V.O., K.C.M.G.

61.]

Not a single one of the British officers of the Sappers and Miners came out scathless.

In the 20th Company, Lieutenant Hayes-Sadler was killed, Captain Paris wounded and missing; Lieutenants Nosworthy and Rait-Kerr were wounded, while the losses in other ranks amounted to 54 out of 150 who went into action.

The casualties of the 21st Company were Captain Richardson, Lieutenants Rohde and Almond killed, and Lieutenant Fitzmaurice wounded, the losses in other ranks amounting to 57.

The magnificent conduct of the troops was recognized by Field-Marshal Sir John French, who, in his despatch, dated 20th November, 1914, remarked as follows:—

"On the 28th October especially the 47th Sikhs and the 20th and 21st Companies of the Sappers and Miners distinguished themselves by their gallant conduct in the attack on Neuve Chapelle, losing heavily in officers and men."

General Sir Horace Smith-Dorrien also sent his warmest congratulations on the splendid conduct of the troops.

The history of the Indian Army contains few nobler pages than that of the 28th October, 1914.

On the 3rd November volunteers were called for to undertake the dangerous work of reconnoitring the ground in front of our lines, and securing as much information as possible about the German trenches. The 47th Sikhs were then holding a section of the line near Picantin, and from amongst the many competitors for the work, Lieutenant Brunskill was selected, and he decided to take with him only one man, Scout Havildar Munshi Singh.

The weather conditions were perfect for such work, for, although there was a heavy ground mist, the bright moon penetrated it and made it possible to see fairly clearly up to a distance of about thirty yards, and to sketch and make notes as well as in broad daylight.

Lieutenant Brunskill and Havildar Munshi Singh crawled out, and stealthily advanced for about five hundred yards, making a rough field sketch as they went along. Suddenly they sighted what appeared to be a German trench about thirty yards ahead; they lay absolutely still for some time, listening and hardly daring to breathe. The ground was full of shell holes, and it hardly seemed possible that they could have approached so near without being heard by the enemy, who, at any moment, might open rapid fire on them, the result of which at thirty yards' range can easily be imagined.

To make doubly sure, Lieutenant Brunskill decided to creep back, make a détour to a flank and approach the trench at a fresh spot. The manœuvre succeeded admirably; the pair of adventurers crawled right up to the parapet with their hearts, stout as they were, in their mouths. Not a sound was to be heard. Was the enemy asleep or was he only waiting for them to show themselves over the parapet before disposing of them with the bayonet? It was impossible to say, so the audacious couple slowly crept over and looked in. As they had suspected, it was the German front line trench, and, by the mercy of Heaven, unoccupied. A thorough inspection of the trench was made. It proved to be a wide ditch, with dug-outs for two men at every ten yards, and snipers' posts for men lying down.

After collecting a helmet, some letters and empty cartridge cases, Lieutenant Brunskill decided to return at once with his information. When he had accomplished about half of the return journey, both British and Germans opened fire, apparently at nothing, but luckily the bullets went high.

During this expedition the gallant Munshi Singh had, owing to excitement and the exertion of prolonged crawling over broken ground, developed such unusually stertorous breathing as to cause Lieutenant Brunskill to fear that he might be heard before he was seen. On his next two hazards, therefore, he took in his place Sepoy Tawand Singh.

On both these occasions he calmly crawled through the first line of German trench and to within thirty yards of the second line, which was about a hundred yards in rear of the first. He was thus enabled to make a fairly accurate map of the ground between our trenches and the enemy's second line on a front of about 250 yards.

On his last approach to the German second line, which was evidently strongly held, as the sound of talking was very audible, Lieutenant Brunskill received unpleasant proof that the enemy was wide awake, for an advanced post opened fire at thirty yards' range, and the fire was soon taken up by every one in the neighbourhood. The ground was hissing with bullets, and was lit up by numerous flares. By some miracle, neither the officer nor his companion was hit, and both succeeded in making their escape, only to be greeted, when nearing our own wire, by rapid fire from their friends, who took them for Germans. However, no harm was done, and Lieutenant Brunskill was able to make a most valuable report. In addition to the sketch of the ground, he had, by careful listening, been able to locate the route by which supplies were brought up to the German line, and our guns were thereafter enabled to pay the road the attention which it merited.

A few days later he was severely wounded while making, in broad daylight, a sketch of the front of our line. The gallantry and skill shown by him during his very dangerous reconnaissance well deserved the Military Cross which was bestowed on him.

Remarkable features of this reconnaissance were the facts that the German front-line trench was unoccupied night after night, and that no German patrols were out. This state of affairs can only be ascribed to the extraordinary legends which at that time were current in both German and English newspapers concerning the uncanny properties of the Indian troops. Pathans with glittering eyes, knives, and teeth were (so it was said) crawling up to German trenches, and extracting the occupants from their lairs; Gurkhas with long grey beards were being landed from transports along the Belgian coast, and were making a practice of blowing up German munition depôts miles in rear of the enemy's lines. When our scouts were caught in an awkward place they were never nonplussed, for in the twinkling of an eye (so a German paper gravely announced) they threw the end of a rope in the air, and climbing up it, disappeared, one by one, from view. It is not surprising that the enemy was alarmed, or that the British public expected miracles where only good honest fighting qualities were forthcoming.

The casualties of the Corps up to and including the 3rd November, 1914, amounted to:—

	Killed.	Wounded.	Missing.
British officers . .	18	28	8
Indian officers . .	6	22	5
Other ranks, British .	25	63	6
,, ,, Indian .	133	1342	333
Total .	182	1455	352

CHAPTER V

THE CORPS TAKES OVER THE LINE HELD BY THE 3RD AND 5TH BRITISH DIVISIONS, 2ND CORPS

Arrival of the Meerut Division and Secundrabad Cavalry Brigade—Indian Corps now complete, except Sirhind Brigade still in Egypt—Corps takes over portion of line held by 2nd Corps—Description of existing conditions—2nd Battalion 8th Gurkha Rifles bombed and shelled out of their trenches—Very heavy casualties—Counter-attack partially successful—Casualties of 58th Rifles in counter-attack.

THE Meerut Division, under the command of Lt-General C. A. Anderson, C.B., the greater portion of which left Karachi on the 21st September, and was joined by the remainder of the Division at sea on the 23rd September, arrived at Marseilles, after a fine and uneventful voyage, on the 11th October.

Amongst the first arrivals were Their Highnesses Maharaja Sir Pratap Singh, the Maharaja of Jodhpur, and the Maharaja of Bikanir, who came to place their swords at the service of the King-Emperor.

The Division remained there till the 19th October, when it entrained for Orleans, where it was completely concentrated on the 22nd October.

The scenes at Marseilles and on the journey by rail were very similar to those enacted during the progress of the Lahore Division. Nothing was too good for the troops, and the inhabitants of each town on the route flocked to the railway stations to welcome our men, who were almost overwhelmed by their kindness.

[*Official.*

MARÉCHAL JOFFRE, FIELD-MARSHAL SIR DOUGLAS HAIG, AND HON. LT-GEN. H. H. MAHARAJA SIR PRATAP SINGH

The Division arrived at the front on the 29th October, followed a few days later by the Secundrabad Cavalry Brigade * and the Jodhpur Lancers under Brigadier-General F. Wadeson.

The Indian Army Corps was now complete in France, with the exception of the Sirhind Brigade still in Egypt, and the moment had arrived for it to play its part in the general scheme.

Orders were at once issued for the Corps to take over the portion of the line held by the 3rd and 5th British Divisions, the Corps being strengthened by 10½ units of British infantry and artillery, pending the arrival of the Sirhind Brigade and the return of a portion of the Lahore Division from operations with the Cavalry Corps further north.

The line to be occupied extended from just north of Givenchy in the south, past the front of Richebourg l'Avoué, making a re-entrant round the rear of Neuve Chapelle, on past Chapigny to Fauquissart, and then eastward to Rouges Bancs just north of Fromelles. The order of Brigades from south to north was as follows :—

Bareilly, Garhwal, Dehra Dun, then the four British battalions temporarily attached from the 2nd Corps, and finally the Jullundur Brigade of the Lahore Division.

The relief of the 2nd Corps was successfully carried out during the night of the 29th October. A heavy downpour of rain made the whole country into a vast quagmire. Communication trenches in those days were practically non-existent. The troops had to reach the front line as best they could, crawling

* Consisting of N Battery, R.H.A. (the Eagle Troop), the 7th Dragoon Guards, 20th Deccan Horse, and 34th Poona Horse.

up any ditches which led in the required direction, crouching behind banks and sheltering behind trees. By the time they arrived in the fire trenches they were soaked through and through, and caked with mud from head to foot. In spite of these drawbacks, there were few casualties, and the men were in high spirits at attaining the goal which they had sought from so far across the sea. The 2/3rd Gurkhas had to evacuate their Head Quarters during the night, as they were heavily shelled by way of a welcome to the front.

As has been seen earlier, our offensive towards Lille had been brought to an abrupt conclusion, and for some days the Germans had been attacking heavily along the whole line from La Bassée to Messines, keeping us in our turn pinned down to the defensive. The term "defensive" is, however, a little misleading when referring to the state of affairs which exists when two bodies of troops are entrenched within a few yards of each other, and both are straining every nerve and muscle to do the greatest possible damage to the opponent.

The line held by the Indian Corps from the time of its arrival at the front to that of its final departure for other theatres of war may be fairly described as one of the least attractive sections, either from the picturesque point of view or from that of comfort. On taking a hasty survey from our trenches, the eye was met by a vast expanse of low-lying cultivable land, cut up by innumerable roads and lanes, and dotted with small villages and isolated farms. During a great part of the year, as far as the eye could reach there stretched a dismal sea of mud, almost the only break consisting of suspicious-looking pools of water, which proved, on further investigation, to be flooded shell holes, with which the ground was thickly pitted. The only prominent objects, to some extent relieving the eternal monotony of the scene, were a few copses or woods, amongst which was the Bois du Biez, so long a stronghold of the enemy, and in the distance the Aubers ridge, so near and yet so far.

The fields were interspersed with orchards and the roads fringed with trees. In consequence, extended observation was impossible except by means of aeroplanes, of which, at that period, we possessed relatively very few. The short distance below the surface at which water was found rendered the digging of deep trenches impossible in places, while even a moderate fall of rain reduced the inhabitants of the trenches to a state of discomfort quite indescribable.

The chief industry of the natives of this forlorn district is the cultivation of beetroot for sugar. The beets are stacked in a kind of silo, the aroma from which has often seriously perturbed men who could endure the proximity of a dead German without flinching. In winter the beet fields became morasses, over which any rapid movement was almost impossible. The outlook in summer, when No Man's Land was carpeted with poppies and daisies and the mud of winter had given place to straggling self-sown crops, was not unpleasing, but on a typical winter's day, with a steady cold downpour converting the fire trenches into fetid waterlogged ditches, and the communication trenches into bottomless muddy streams, the drear and chilly discomfort of the whole scene was enough to appal the stoutest heart.

The feelings of Orientals coming from fierce sunshine to surroundings like these cannot be described and can hardly be imagined. Those who saw them in the trenches in these months will never think without emotion of the shining courage and the superb devotion which they never ceased to display.

At the outset, the Allies laboured under a heavy handicap. The Germans, with the foresight and thoroughness which have throughout marked their conduct of the war, had provided themselves with every description of apparatus necessary for such close-quarter siege warfare as this. They possessed bombs, trench mortars, rifle grenades, searchlights and "sausage" observation balloons, and, looking still further ahead, they were, as we found to our cost, even then preparing their devilish gas and flame throwers.

We had none of these things, and for quite a considerable period our only bombs were those manufactured locally from empty jam tins. Under such conditions, and considering the thinness of our line, it is marvellous that it was kept intact during all those weary months. The Germans were to learn that the fine-drawn khaki cord was whipcord: it strained; it bent; but it never broke.

The enemy was not long in greeting the Corps, for shortly after midnight of the 29th–30th October, he attacked the 2/8th Gurkhas in a half-hearted manner, and three times during the night delivered a burst of fire on our trenches, each burst being preceded by shelling and an exhibition of fireworks. The Gurkhas were in a most unenviable position. They had only just arrived in their trenches, which were already half full of mud and water, while the pitiless rain showed no signs of ceasing. But far more serious than the weather was the fact that the trenches had been adapted for taller men, and the little Gurkhas were unable to fire over the parapet. Steps were at once taken to remedy this defect, but the constant shelling and rifle fire gave the men little chance of effecting any material improvement.

The position held by the Gurkhas was in the triangle formed by the Quinque Rue and the road from Festubert, the line being extended southwards towards Givenchy by the Devons. The trench was merely a ditch which had been adapted, the original brick culverts still existing in some places. By daylight on the 30th the telephone wires had all been cut by shell fire, and shortly afterwards the Germans made a determined attack which was beaten off.

The shelling went on all day, and culminated in a concentration of heavy guns and howitzers upon the Gurkha trenches. This continued without the slightest pause for about four hours. The enemy had got the exact range of the trench occupied by Major Wake. Shell after shell dropped right in the trench, burying many men and blowing others to atoms. Still the Gurkhas held on and drove back several attacks between 8 a.m. and noon. At this moment the supply of ammunition began to run low, but Lt-Colonel Morris was able to get a message through to General Macbean, to say that he was all right, except as regarded ammunition.

Affairs, however, had not yet reached the climax. At 1 p.m. the enemy in great force attacked the trench held by Captains Hayes-Sadler and Wright, who succeeded in keeping them at bay for over an hour. To add to Colonel Morris's anxieties, a message came from Major Wake that he was very hard pressed and in urgent need of reinforcement, followed by an appeal from the Devons on the right, who were also being heavily attacked, had used up all their supports, and were badly in need of assistance.

The position was extremely critical. In many places the parapet and trench had been obliterated; numbers of the defenders were buried beneath the debris, and the ammunition was nearly exhausted. Colonel Morris, gallant officer as he so often proved himself to be before he met his death at the battle of Loos in September, 1915, was determined to hold on at all costs. He sent an urgent appeal to General Macbean for assistance, at the same time telling Major Wake and the Devons that they must at all hazards hold out till dark. Shortly afterwards, Major Barlow, himself already thrice wounded but still carrying on in the way the British officer does, sent Captain Davidson over to help Major Wake, closely followed by Captain Stack, who was immediately wounded in the neck, but managed, mortally hurt as he was, to stagger back to ask for more men. Captain Davidson was also wounded, and was last seen firing at the oncoming enemy with his revolver, as he lay on the ground.

Major Barlow sent fifteen men, and himself moved up to the right, whence he succeeded in driving the Germans back; but it was too late. The enemy had managed to work round the right trench, in which there were now only ten survivors, and Colonel Morris had himself to move hastily to the left to avoid being captured.

At the same time Major Barlow, being unable to leave the front line and having no combatant officer left, despatched Captain MacWatters, I.M.S., to report the situation, and to get the guns turned on to a red farmhouse situated about 300 yards to the right front of our line. This house had been occupied by the Germans, who, from the upper and lower stories, kept up an infernal fire which commanded and enfiladed the right of our trenches. As the latter were completely blocked by the debris of the parapet and by dead and wounded, any reinforcements moving up from the left were compelled to get out in the open, when they at once became targets for a storm of bullets. It was in this manner that Major Barlow had been twice hit, the bullets entering his right shoulder within a couple of inches of each other and inflicting terrible wounds.

Owing entirely to reinforcements being held up by the fire from the farm, the Germans were eventually enabled to break through the right and take the remainder of the defenders in the rear. Otherwise the surviving officers felt convinced that the trenches would have been held, however vigorously they might have been shelled.

Captain MacWatters had a difficult and dangerous task to perform, for he had to get out of the trench, cross the open under heavy fire, and, crawling through a hedge, to reach a farmhouse in which Head Quarters had been established. By the time he had overcome the dangers, it was too late. The fire from the farm had done its deadly work. Major Wake, Captains Hayes-Sadler, Hartwell, and Wright had fallen victims, and the regiment was the poorer by the loss of four splendid British officers and many good men.

The 2/8th Gurkhas were fortunate in embarking on this war in possession of a particularly fine body of officers, and it was by the cruellest of bad luck that the regiment at the very outset suffered the loss of no less than nine of their small number.

Major Barlow was now in a most perilous position, for his men had to fire both to front and rear to keep the enemy off, while he himself was too weak to stand. However, game to the end, he ordered a few men to try and hold some adjacent farm buildings, and then he fainted from loss of blood, just as another attack was commencing. He fell, luckily, into a ditch, where he remained unobserved by the Germans, until, recovering consciousness, he managed to crawl back, being shot at several times on the way. By this time there were no unwounded officers on the right, and it was impossible to hold on any longer. The trenches were blotted out; many of the brave defenders were buried; the enemy was all round, and still coming on in overwhelming numbers.

Colonel Morris, still undefeated, although badly wounded in the leg, tried to bring up reinforcements, but, unable to keep up, lost his way and was challenged by Germans. To escape, he threw himself into a ditch, and knew no more till he found himself being put into a stretcher by his own men.

Major Cassels, who had been holding his own most gallantly on the right centre, was pushed out by sheer weight of metal and numbers, and narrowly escaped being captured. A part of the battalion succeeded in reoccupying a section of their support trenches, and remained in them, reinforced by half of the Bedfords and the whole of the West Ridings, except those who reinforced the Devons on the right.

So ended a terrible night and day, an experience which, as an eye-witness testified, would have shaken the moral of any troops, however seasoned. Much more trying was it, then, to the Gurkhas, newly arrived, fresh to the work, handicapped by imperfect and unsuitable trenches, by the failure of ammunition, and, above all, by the heavy losses suffered by their British officers, on whom the Indian soldier, be he Sikh or Gurkha, Pathan or Dogra, is dependent (and most generously owns it) for leading and control.

The casualties of the 2nd Battalion 8th Gurkha Rifles on this occasion were :—

Killed: Major Wake, M.V.O., Captains E. R. Hayes-Sadler, Hartwell, Wright and Stack ; 2 Gurkha officers ; other ranks, 37.

Wounded: Lt-Colonel Morris, Major Barlow and Lieutenant MacLean ; 1 Gurkha officer ; other ranks, 61.

Missing: Captain Davidson, 2 Gurkha officers, and 109 other ranks, of whom many were doubtless buried by shell fire.

A counter-attack was at once organized, consisting of the following troops :—

Half Battalion West Ridings and Bedfords respectively, with the 58th Rifles and half of the 107th Pioneers in support, Lt-Colonel Griffith of the Bedfords being in command.

The enemy was still keeping up a heavy fire, but the attack pushed steadily through it, with slight casualties, to within reach of that portion of the Gurkha support trenches which was in the hands of the Germans. At this point it was necessary to make a close reconnaissance of the enemy's trench—a dangerous task which was undertaken by Captain W. Black, Adjutant of the 58th Rifles, who succeeded in getting close to the trench, but was then killed.

Meanwhile the 58th were ordered to move up through the firing line, with a view to retaking the trenches. At 2.30 a.m. the position was rushed, the Gurkha support line was captured, and two farmhouses, which had been occupied by the enemy, were also taken. The casualties of the 58th were slight during the assault, as the enemy fled without offering much opposition.

The position was at once consolidated against the expected counter-attack, but the Germans contented themselves with a heavy shell and rifle fire, which speedily increased our casualties. Just as day was breaking, the commanding officer, Lt-Colonel Venour, was killed, as was shortly afterwards Lieutenant Craig of the 57th Rifles, who was attached to the 58th.

During the whole of the 31st, and until the 58th were relieved at midnight, the trenches were deluged with rifle and shell fire, varied by mortar bombs and hand-grenades, which destroyed the parapet in many places and caused a number of casualties.

These trenches were striking examples of what trenches should not be. They were badly sited, varied in breadth from 12 feet to 25 feet, and were entirely without traverses. The result was that the enemy's shells and bombs frequently fell into the trench, and the full force of the explosion was felt, owing to the absence of traverses.

In spite of all, the 58th held their ground until relieved. Their casualties were 3 British officers and 5 other ranks killed, 4 Indian officers and 79 other ranks wounded.

Havildar Karam Singh gained the 2nd Class, Indian Order of Merit by his fine display of endurance and pluck in continuing to command his men, although dangerously wounded, until he was removed at night.

The net result of the counter-attack was that while the Gurkha support trenches and two farm-houses were retaken by us, three of the advanced trenches still remained in the hands of the Germans.

CHAPTER VI

ATTACK ON 2ND BATTALION 2ND GURKHAS

Heavy attack on trenches held by 2nd Battalion 2nd Gurkhas—Forced to evacuate trenches—Gallantry of officers and men—Reinforced by Connaught Rangers—Brilliant leadership of Lt-Colonel C. Norie, D.S.O.—Casualties of 2nd Gurkhas—Honours awarded—Losses of 34th Poona Horse—Connaughts rush German trench—Four officers killed—Gurkha trenches recaptured by two battalions of the 8th British Brigade—Rifle and hand grenades first issued—German attack on 1st Battalion Seaforth Highlanders repulsed with loss—Raid on German trenches by 2nd Battalion 39th Garhwal Rifles under Major Taylor—Raid by 2nd Battalion Royal Highlanders (Black Watch).

THE Germans were not long in following up this temporary success, for on the 2nd November they turned their attention to the trenches held by the 2nd Battalion 2nd Gurkhas. These trenches were situated slightly north-north-west of Neuve Chapelle, and formed an acute salient in our general line. The salient was caused by the evacuation of Neuve Chapelle by our troops some days before, when the village was occupied by the enemy. The trenches were in a very isolated position, being cut off from the rear by a small copse and orchard, and when, as often happened, the telephones were cut, communication was very difficult.

The 2nd Gurkhas had only moved into this position during the night of the 29th–30th October, and were consequently very imperfectly acquainted with their surroundings. It was subsequently ascertained that the enemy was in occupation of what were either old trenches or deep irrigation ditches at a distance of some fifty yards from the Gurkha trenches, towards which they were sapping from the east.

The trenches in this part of the line were of the very worst. Since the evacuation of Neuve Chapelle, there had not been time to effect any material improvements, and they were really little more than boggy ditches, affording very imperfect cover from frontal fire, and in many cases open to enfilade. Unfortunately, the enemy was at least as aware of the weakness of this part of our line as we were, and he hastened to take advantage of it.

Early in the morning of the 2nd November, the Germans opened the attack with a murderous fire of high explosives, partly from heavy guns and partly from one or more trench mortars in Neuve Chapelle. At about 8 a.m. they concentrated on No. 1 Double Company trench. The explosions were followed by spouts of mud mixed with every kind of object usually found in a trench; the mangled remains of Gurkhas hurtled into the air, and the trench was almost obliterated. The men held on as long as they could, but there is a limit to human endurance, and the survivors were forced into No. 2 Company's trench on the left, while some took refuge in a drain about fifty yards in rear. One man alone remained, keeping up a rapid fire on the enemy, until at last compelled to retire, when the trench was occupied by the Germans. This was Naik Padamdhjog Gurung, whose unflinching determination was rewarded with the 2nd Class, Indian Order of Merit.

The Germans next turned their guns on to

No. 2 Company, and speedily rendered their trench untenable. Explosion followed explosion in quick succession. The mortars had the range to an inch, and a large proportion of the shells fell either on the parapet or in the trench. Men were either buried or blown sky high. One shell blew four men into the air with the debris of the parapet, rifles and a machine gun, and killed Lieutenant Lucas of No. 1 Company while rallying his men. At the same time Major Becher was killed while trying to get his men back to the cover of an old trench.

Feeling that, at all costs, something must be done, Lieutenant Innes, the officer in charge of the machine gun which had been blown up, collected as many men as he could of No. 2 Double Company, and with Lieutenant Walcott headed a most gallant counter-attack against the German infantry, who were swarming into the trenches. With them went also a party of ten or twelve men under Naik Rampershad Thapa, who had held desperately on to a corner of the trench. By sheer dint of reckless bravery, this little force drove back the enemy in ferocious tooth-and-nail fighting, but both the British officers were killed, as well as Subadars Tekbahadur Gurung and Gopal Sing Rawat. The survivors, forced back step by step, had to retreat again to their drain, Subadar Chet Sing being killed on the way. For his bravery, Naik Rampershad Thapa received the Indian Distinguished Service Medal.

Next, Major Ross, with Subadar-Major Man Sing Bohra, collected a few men, and went straight at the Germans, who had now occupied the trenches of Nos. 1 and 2 Companies. Once more a terrible hand-to-hand struggle took place, which ended with the death of the heroic Major Ross, the Subadar-Major, and most of the men.

The survivors, now only some eight or ten in number, managed to gain the trenches of No. 3 Double Company, where Lieutenant Reid was in command, Captain Barton having been killed early in the action. Lieutenant Reid sent off to the Connaught Rangers on his left for reinforcements, and rallied No. 3 Double Company, telling them that help was coming. He then, under an appalling fire, went back and guided the reinforcement of the Connaughts to the trench, where he and the sergeant in charge of the Connaught detachment were both shot dead.

There now only remained behind Subadars Dalbahadur Rana, Fateh Sing Newar and Jemadar Suba Sing Gurung, with some men of No. 4 Company. These, with the party of Connaughts, held on with the grimmest determination until, borne down by numbers, they were forced to retreat to a communication trench.

Not even here were their troubles ended, for a machine gun was turned on to them, and the trench was soon blocked with dead and wounded to such an extent that those who were still on the side nearest the enemy could not pass, and had to turn round and face it out. To add to their appalling trials, our reserves, thinking that the trench was occupied by Germans, commenced a counter-attack on it.

The party in the communication trench were thus now being fired on from the rear by our own men, and by the enemy from the orchard and from the front. They held on, facing outwards, and kept the enemy at a distance. A company of the Connaughts now reinforced them, but in moving up, had to cross an open space in a hedge running parallel to the front. The enemy evidently had this opening marked down, for a machine gun was turned on and a number of the Connaughts fell, including Lieutenant Abbott.

After dark, by order of the officer in command of the Connaught detachment, Subadar Fateh Sing retired the remnant of his men, and fell in with the reserves about a quarter of a mile in rear. This officer had behaved with the greatest gallantry and coolness throughout, and thoroughly merited the Order of British India, 2nd Class, which was bestowed on him.

A certain number of men who did not hear the order to retire remained all night with the Connaughts, and eventually retired with them.

So far, we have only followed the fortunes of the companies in the front line trenches, but the reserves under the commanding officer, Lt-Colonel C. Norie, D.S.O., had meantime played their part nobly. With Colonel Norie were Captain McCleverty, Lieutenant and Adjutant Corse-Scott, and Major Norie, brother of Colonel Norie, who was attached as interpreter.

When the attack commenced, Colonel Norie at once advanced to the right of the forward trenches, and succeeded in locating the German trench mortar which was playing such havoc with our men. He opened fire on it, and it was soon silenced and removed. He then took his men to the left of the 1/9th Gurkhas, whence he kept up a heavy fire on the enemy until his ammunition ran short, and he had to retire to his original position to refill.

Here he met three dismounted squadrons of the 34th Poona Horse, whose commandant, Lt-Colonel Swanston, had just been killed in a brave attempt to reinforce the Gurkhas across the open. Thence he moved forward towards the left trenches. These, however, had in the meantime been occupied by the enemy in force. In spite of many casualties, Colonel Norie kept them engaged until 2 p.m., when the terrible machine-gun fire forced him to retire, under a deluge of high explosives, to the reserve trenches. In the evening he was reinforced by a company of the Royal Scots Fusiliers and a composite Indian battalion, while the 9th Gurkhas were strengthened by a double company of the 6th Jats and three squadrons of the 7th Dragoon Guards. With these, Colonel Norie made a final effort to recapture the lost trenches.

The Jats were pushed forward on the left, and the remnant of the 2nd Gurkhas continued their line to the left. Colonel Norie himself took up a company of the Scots Fusiliers with a view to reoccupying the right section of the Gurkha trenches and picking up survivors. This party advanced under a devastating fire and found the enemy in possession. Led by Colonel Norie, they made a most gallant attempt to rush the trench, and actually got to within twenty yards, but were met with a furious machine-gun and rifle fire, which inflicted such losses that the little party had to retreat. Of the six officers, one belonging to the Royal Scots Fusiliers was killed; Major Norie and Captain McCleverty were wounded, the former very severely, while, by a strange chance, the remaining three escaped untouched.

Although this attack failed in its objective, it produced valuable results. It made the enemy nervous about his position, and caused him to retire to his own trenches.

The losses of the 2nd Gurkhas were:—7 British officers killed, 1 wounded; 4 Gurkha officers killed 3 wounded. Other ranks, 31 killed and 101 wounded or missing; of the latter, the majority were buried in the ruins of the trenches.

Although the battalion was forced to evacuate its line, or the remains of its line, the bravery displayed by all ranks fully sustained the great reputation of the regiment. The heroism of the British officer has seldom been more brilliantly demonstrated than on this occasion. Not a single officer in the front trenches returned alive, several being killed while leading forlorn hopes against overwhelming numbers of the enemy.

Lt-Colonel Norie, whose excellent leadership (as remarked by Sir John French in his despatch dated 20th November, 1914) saved the situation, was granted the brevet of Colonel.

Major F. H. Norie, who behaved with the greatest gallantry throughout, and who was severely wounded, received the D.S.O.

A number of non-commissioned officers and men gained the Indian Distinguished Service Medal.

Sowar Madhu of the Poona Horse received the Indian Order of Merit, 2nd Class, for his gallantry in carrying Rissaldar Rathore Hamir Singh, who was wounded, under heavy fire to a first-aid post, whence he returned to the firing line.

The Poona Horse had the great misfortune to lose their Commandant, Lt-Colonel Swanston; the interpreter, 2nd Lieutenant Sturdee, was wounded, and there were 36 casualties in other ranks.

The Connaughts lost Lieutenant Abbott and five men killed, Lieutenant Hewitt and 32 men wounded.

The Irishmen were not at the end of their troubles with these trenches, for on the 4th November it was decided to try and rush a trench which ran out on the right of the Connaughts' front line, and to fill it in.

The scheme does not appear to have been well planned. The enemy's main trench was only at a distance of two hundred yards, and it was certain that his full fire would fall on the digging party, while the fire from the Connaughts' main trench would be, to a great extent, masked, for fear of hitting our own diggers.

At midnight, the signal was given by the Royal Scots Fusiliers opening rapid fire. A Company of the Connaughts, less two platoons, commanded by Captain Hack, with Lieutenants Tulloch and George, rushed forward under heavy fire and captured the trench. Captain Payne at once sent on the digging party, who doubled over and started filling in the trench. The enemy's fire steadily increased, while A Company's decreased, and it was afterwards ascertained that numbers of the bolts of our rifles had jammed. The result was that, when the filling in was half completed, the digging party had to go forward to keep up the fire. Eventually, nearly all the bolts jammed and the rifles were useless.

Captain Payne ascertained that no further filling

in was possible and that all the officers had been killed, and ordered a retirement.

Captain Hack was shot early in the attack.

Lieutenant George, the Adjutant, was hit before he reached the enemy's trench, and fell. Lance-Corporal Kelly at once went over the parapet of the Connaught trench and picked him up. The next instant Lieutenant George was shot dead in his arms. Corporal Kelly's act was one of great bravery, as the enemy's fire was very heavy at the time. He well merited the Distinguished Conduct Medal which he received.

Lieutenant Tulloch was also wounded early in the fight, but carried on till he was killed.

The retirement was carried out, the enemy's fire growing fiercer every moment.

As A Company was practically without rifles, Captain Payne asked for reinforcements, and two platoons of the Middlesex were sent up. The result was that the trench became overcrowded. A number of the Connaughts got out in rear of the trench to clear it, and tried to cross to a farmhouse known as the "moated grange." In doing so, they came under what an officer describes as a "hellish fire," and Lieutenant Ovens and a number of men were killed. Towards dawn, Lieutenant Badham collected the remnant of the company and took them back to the support trenches.

Of the small number engaged in this unfortunate enterprise, four officers were killed, and there were 36 other casualties. Captain Payne, who commanded this operation, had distinguished himself during the fighting round Messines, and again when the 2nd Gurkhas were driven out of their trenches on the 2nd November. He was awarded the D.S.O., his cool valour on this occasion having undoubtedly saved a number of needless casualties.

There is not as much humour in a battle as some writers would have us believe; all is not cheering and hilarity, although sometimes a subject for mirth offers itself. On this occasion, a man who was supposed to be badly injured was being carried off on a stretcher. Both the bearers were hit by shrapnel and dropped the sufferer. The wounded hero at once jumped to his feet and ran like a hare to the nearest cover, leaving his bearers to look after themselves, and pursued by the cheers of his comrades.

For some days after this action little of special note occurred. The enemy kept up a constant fire on our trenches and the roads in rear, varied by occasional light attacks, which were easily repulsed.

On the 5th November, battalions of the Royal Scots Fusiliers and of the Middlesex Regiment, part of a British Brigade attached to the Indian Corps, retook the trenches which were evacuated by the 2nd Gurkhas on the 2nd November. The trenches were filled in and the battalions returned to their own line.

The 6th November marked a new epoch in the equipment of our troops, for on that date rifle and hand grenades were first issued, and met with warm appreciation, for the lack of them had been very severely felt.

On the 7th November, the enemy made a determined attack on the 1st Seaforths, using, during the preliminary bombardment, a trench mortar with a range of 600 yards. One of its shells made a hole 15 feet wide by 8 feet deep, and buried Colour-Sergeant Baker and several men. About three hundred Germans attacked the right of the battalion, and two of them actually got into our trench, where they were killed. The attack was ultimately repulsed with considerable loss to the enemy.

The Seaforths lost Captain Wilson and 17 men killed, 2nd Lieutenant Macandrew and 63 men wounded. At the same time, Captain B. O. Duff, son of the Commander-in-Chief in India, and several men of the 2nd Gurkhas were killed while supporting the Seaforths in their trenches. On the 8th November, patrols found some 40 dead Germans in front of the Seaforths.

On the night of the 9th–10th November, an enterprise was undertaken by parties of the 1st and 2nd Battalions 39th Garhwal Rifles, which deserves a brief description, as typical of the raids which our men were frequently called upon to carry out. The party consisted of 100 rifles all told, under the command of Major Taylor of the 2/39th. The German trench was within 50 yards of the right of the 2/39th, and as there was great danger of the enemy sapping up to our trenches or mining, it was considered necessary to make an attempt to fill it in.

When the time for the attack arrived, the men were lined up in an irrigation ditch in front of our position, a portion of them having picks and shovels to fill in the trench when captured. The party got safely across without being detected, and lay under the German parapet where they could hear the enemy talking. Major Taylor then gave the signal by firing his revolver at a German. The men cheered and climbed over the parapet. The enemy only stayed to fire a few rounds and then bolted. The Garhwalis entered and searched the trench, taking six prisoners, who made no resistance. The work of filling in was then begun and was found to present great difficulties. The trench was seen to be about 8 feet deep, strongly revetted and shrapnel-proof. It was soon evident that it was impossible in the time available to fill it in; further, that even if filled in, it could easily be re-dug.

The enemy, meantime, was keeping up a heavy fire on the party, to which they replied with spirit. Finding that the work could not be completed, and foreseeing a heavy counter-attack, Major Taylor and his party retired, taking with them their prisoners.

This little affair was extremely well carried out, and only four casualties occurred. For their good service on this occasion, Havildars Ranjir Sing Pandir and Diwan Sing Padhujar received the Indian Distinguished Service Medal, and Major Taylor was mentioned in despatches.

It was found, however, that the cheering of the men on charging was a mistake, as it gave warning to the enemy in his main trench.

Although in this case the principal object of the raid could not be accomplished, there is no doubt that such enterprises had a very heartening effect on our men, while tending to make the enemy nervous, and to keep him from getting any rest. Frequently, too, the information given by prisoners proved to be of great value.

During the early morning of the 9th November, one of a party of scouts of the 2/39th was mortally wounded. Although fully exposed to view and fire of the enemy, Rifleman Ganesh Sing Sajwan stopped, picked the wounded man up, and carried him back to our trenches, an act for which he received the Indian Order of Merit, 2nd Class.

Before dawn on the same day, a similar raid on a smaller scale was carried out by the 2nd Black Watch, with the object of capturing or destroying a machine gun which was tormenting our men. Captain Forrester with twenty men rushed the German trench, and had a hand-to-hand scrimmage with the enemy, of whom they killed ten. The gun, however, had been removed, and the party were lucky to get back to their own trench with only Captain Forrester and one sergeant wounded.

The casualties amongst British officers of Indian units were observed to be very much out of proportion to those amongst other ranks. This was no doubt due to the fact that the enemy's snipers had special orders to pay particular attention to the British officers, also, of course, to the risks which the officers had necessarily to take in leading their men, who, under such strange conditions, were more than ever dependent on them. In order to reduce the risk as much as possible, British officers were now ordered to be dressed and equipped like the men, a measure which was found to be attended by a certain amount of success.

FIELD-MARSHAL EARL ROBERTS INSPECTING THE INDIAN CORPS, 12TH NOV. 1914.

CHAPTER VII

VISIT AND DEATH OF FIELD-MARSHAL EARL ROBERTS

Lord Roberts arrives—His gratitude to the Army in India—He inspects the Corps—His last public speech—His warning to the Empire before the War—His death.

AMID these scenes of strife and bloodshed, an incident must now be recorded which produced a deep and a very moving impression upon all ranks of the Corps.

On the 12th November, Lord Roberts, in the course of a visit to the front, arrived at the Corps Head Quarters in order to observe under war conditions those Indians, whom perhaps of all troops in the world he loved the best, and who in their turn looked upon him with a degree of reverence and affection which few British generals have been able to evoke.

Sixty-two years had passed since this wonderful old man, still trim, erect and soldierly, had set sail as a cadet from Southampton to Calcutta. Forty-one years of his career had been passed in India. He had himself written in the closing words of his book :—

"To the discipline, bravery, and devotion to duty of the Army in India, in peace and war, I felt that I owed whatever success it was my good fortune to achieve."

As a proof of this feeling, he chose as the supporters of his coat-of-arms the figures of a Highlander and a Gurkha.

Lord Roberts took part in more than thirty engagements; he was mentioned more than thirty times in despatches, and in 1902 received the thanks of both Houses of Parliament for his incomparable services to the Empire.

In India the profession of a soldier is often hereditary, and it is certain that among those he visited in 1914 were men whose grandfathers had remained loyal in the Mutiny, and whose fathers had stormed, under his direction, the last entrenched position before Kandahar. To the Indian troops Lord Roberts stood as the link of sympathy between the exalted General and the humble soldier, as the Captain who carried with him everywhere the shining talisman of success; and above all as one who recalled, amid the mud and blood of Flanders, the radiant sunshine, the spacious range, the dear dusty atmosphere and aroma of the country which he loved almost as much as they did.

On the bitterest and coldest day of all the cold and bitter autumn of 1914, the Corps Staff assembled outside the château at Hinges, where a few weeks earlier General Willcocks had taken over the line from General Smith-Dorrien. Soon afterwards the motor from St Omer was heard in the grounds, and in a moment the Field-Marshal was recognizing old friends and being introduced to officers hitherto unknown.

One of the writers may perhaps be forgiven for recalling that, as he shivered himself in the half-hour which the proceedings occupied, the presage crossed his mind that long exposure to the cruel east wind must carry great peril to one so old.

The next visit was to Divisional Head Quarters at Locon, where, besides the Staff, a few selected units had been assembled for inspection. The Field-Marshal walked up and down the lines and then made a brief address—the last of his life—to the assembled units. It was not possible to take notes at the time, but the present writer, on learning of Lord Roberts' death, immediately put in writing his recollection of the simple words he spoke. They were substantially as follows :—

"*I am greatly moved to find myself again with the troops by whose side I have fought in so many campaigns. Many persons feared that the strange surroundings in which it is now your duty to fight would be too hard and too severe for the Indian troops. I never shared that fear. I have fought with them too often in every kind of climate, and against every kind of enemy, not to be sure that there are no conditions so hard that they will not do their duty as soldiers. How well you are doing it I have heard from your Commanding Officer, General Sir James Willcocks, and the account he has given me has filled me with emotion. You are suffering much, but you are fighting in loyalty to your Empire and King. You are fighting far from your homes. Yet that for which you fight is as important to those whom you have left at home as it is important to those who live in the shattered villages around us. For if public law and liberty be destroyed in Europe they cannot long survive in India. You will then fight on as long as may be necessary. And it may be long. Do not think that the enemy is already defeated. He is strong: he is still very strong: and his organization is very great. But the Empire and the Allies of the Empire are strong too, and they will become stronger. And they are even now only beginning to organize for war, for they greatly desired peace. Let every man then do his utmost until the enemy is defeated. In this way you will do your duty to the Empire to which you belong, and the glory of your deed will live for ever in India.*"

The prescience of the great soldier has been justified by time. At the moment when he was warning his hearers that the struggle would be a long one, and that the enemy was still wholly undefeated, Staff Officers of the highest distinction were boldly claiming that the Germans had shot their bolt, that the lines opposite to us were weakly held, and that the war would be over in a few months. Both Lord Kitchener and Lord Roberts took the long view and the right view. The victory of the Marne destroyed the sense of perspective in the minds of some of the most distinguished generals in France, so that it became a common criticism of Lord Kitchener, when issue was first joined at the Aisne, that he was wrong to prepare great armies for the future when the war would be over, and that he ought to send out at once to France every man fit to bear arms and every trained officer. Fortunately for the Allied cause, Lord Kitchener pursued his own line, and his sagacity and tenacity of purpose placed at the disposal of his critics the superb armies which shattered at the Somme the illusion of German invincibility.

If another digression be permitted, it may be pointed out that not once in France, nor so far as it is known in England, did Lord Roberts, when war was once declared, dwell upon his own neglected warnings to his countrymen. Those who are recording in this chapter his last effort on behalf of his country cannot resist recalling the solemn warning which he uttered to the Empire at Manchester two years before the war:—

"I am doing, I trust, no wrong to the memory of Cobden and Bright when I point out that in the very month that they were cherishing illusions of perpetual peace, the mightiest and most disciplined force that this earth has ever contained was silently being drilled from the Rhine to the Elbe and the Oder, and from the North Sea to the Bavarian Frontier, until that army disclosed itself in its unmatched capacity for destruction and war. And amid these dreams of peace, for what was that army being trained? Königgratz, Metz, St Privat, and Sedan are the answer . . . At the present day in the year 1912, as in 1866 and in 1870, war will take place the instant the German forces by land and sea are, by their superiority at every point, as certain of victory as anything in human calculation can be made certain. Germany strikes when Germany's hour has struck. This was the policy relentlessly pursued by Bismarck and Moltke in 1866 and 1870: it has been her policy decade by decade since that date. It is her policy to-day . . . We stand still; Germany always advances, and the direction of her advance is now most manifest. It is towards one consummation—a complete supremacy by land and sea . . ."

These warnings passed as unheeded as the prophecies of Cassandra, and indeed an Under-Secretary apologized to the German nation for the speech from which we have quoted an extract. No word of reproach, so far as we know, ever crossed the lips of this far-seeing and modest soldier.

His visit to the Indian Corps has been described. Three days later, within the sound of the great guns, *felix opportunitate mortis,* he was dead. His last warning was uttered: his last battle fought: and with a rare gleam of chivalry a German writer dismissed him well:—

"And so the old warrior has passed to Valhalla. God rest his soul."

CHAPTER VIII

EPISODES OF TRENCH WARFARE

Raid by 2nd Battalion 3rd Gurkha Rifles and 2nd Battalion 39th Garhwal Rifles—Enemy prepared—Gallantry of Lt-Colonel Brakspear and others—Casualties—Honours—Enemy sapping up to our line—Raid by 6th Jat Light Infantry and Sappers and Miners—Curious behaviour of German prisoner—Casualties—Honours—Invention of our first trench mortars—First used by Lieutenant Robson, R.E.—Frostbite—Comparison of casualties from sickness in British and Indian units—Causes of disparity—Visit of H.R.H. the Prince of Wales—Capture of German aeroplane and two officers—Bitter weather—Patrol work hindered by snow—Inactivity of enemy's artillery—Enemy either saving ammunition for a big offensive or moving guns—Likelihood of attack on Indian Corps front—Value of example of British soldier—His never-failing cheerfulness—Comradeship of British and Indians—Dependence of Indian soldiers on their British officers.

On the 13th November, an attack was launched on a German trench, fifty yards from the junction of the trenches of the 1/39th and 2/39th Garhwalis. The assaulting party consisted of six platoons of the 2/3rd Gurkhas with 50 rifles of the 2/39th Garhwalis under Major Taylor, the whole under the command of Lt-Colonel W. R. Brakspear, 2/3rd Gurkhas. With the detachment, as a working party, were two sections of No. 4 Company Sappers and Miners and two platoons 2/3rd Gurkhas, who were to follow the party and fill in the trench. The assault was to be prepared by artillery fire, from 9 to 9.15 p.m., on the main German support trenches, and the withdrawal of the party was to be covered by artillery from midnight to 12.20 a.m.

The operation orders directed that the assault should be made in silence, but shortly after the advance commenced, cheering was started on the right. It was impossible to ascertain by whose fault this occurred, as all who could have given information were either killed or missing. It is doubtful, however, whether the cheering had any bad effect, as the enemy was evidently prepared for the attack, and was firing heavily before it commenced. Moreover, it was found later that, since Major Taylor's raid on the 9th November, the enemy had provided against further surprise by throwing back the line on the left and prolonging the flank to meet the support trench. A search-light and machine guns had also been installed.

On hearing the cheer, the men charged and ran into a withering fire, with the result that all the British and Gurkha officers in the centre and on the left were shot down, with the exception of one Subadar, and that part of the attack was held up.

Meanwhile Lieutenant McSwiney with some of C Company had got into the left of the German trench, where they engaged in a hammer and tongs fight, killing about thirty of the enemy and capturing four. Lt-Colonel Brakspear had already been knocked out by a fall into a deep shell hole, but managed to reach this party, and led them along the main trench until they were pulled up by Germans posted behind a traverse.

Lieutenant McSwiney, without a moment's hesitation, jumped on to the near slope of the trench to get at the enemy over the traverse, but was at once shot down. Captain Alexander was at this moment lying just outside the parapet with a shattered ankle, but still cheering on his men.

The position of this part of the attack was now critical. Only a small portion of the left of the trench was in our hands; our main attack was still held up, and of Lieutenant McSwiney's small party of about twenty, two British officers and at least five men had been put out of action.

Colonel Brakspear, although still in a very shaky condition from his fall, decided to leave Subadar Dalkesar Gurung to hold the trench, and himself to take the risk of returning to bring up men to finish the Germans. He managed to get back in safety through the bullet-swept zone, Subadar Dalkesar meantime holding bravely on to his position, in spite of rapidly increasing odds.

The advance of the supports was for some time prevented by the enemy's use of their searchlight, which they turned on to our main trench, keeping up, with its aid, a heavy fire on any one who showed himself.

To carry on the assault, Colonel Brakspear and Major Drummond, the latter of whom had only joined from England a few hours before, exposing themselves to almost certain death, climbed over the parapet and lay down in full view of the enemy, calling on their men to join them. Major Drummond was at once shot dead, a gallant ending to a gallant officer.

The searchlight being occasionally turned off, the advance began again, and was proceeding favourably, when a number of high explosive shells fell among the party, leaving only four men with

Colonel Brakspear, who appeared to bear a charmed life. Quite undaunted, he returned to his trench to organize another party.

By this time it was 12.30 a.m. and past the hour fixed for the retirement of the attack, a fact which was emphasized by the falling round the assaulted trench of numerous shells from our own guns which, as pre-arranged, were covering the retirement of the party. Lieutenant McSwiney, seeing that there was nothing to gain and everything to lose by staying, ordered Subadar Dalkesar Gurung to retire, and sent a party to bring in Captain Alexander. The men got back with few casualties *en route* to our trenches.

There, however, news was received that Captain Alexander, refusing to be an encumbrance to his men in their precarious retirement, had ordered them to leave him and help the other wounded men. Lieutenant McSwiney, badly wounded as he was, at once took Subadar Dalkesar Gurung and six men out as a search party, and went back to the spot near the German trench where he had last heard Captain Alexander's voice, but failed to find him, and only just succeeded in getting back to our trench when he collapsed from loss of blood.

The devotion of these two officers, the one to his men, the other to his brother officer, is one of many instances which explain the intense admiration, love and respect felt by the Indian soldier for his British leaders. It is pleasing to record that Captain Alexander survived, being now a prisoner of war, while Lieutenant McSwiney, for his great gallantry, was rewarded with the Military Cross.

The affair was marked by many instances of

bravery, but the losses were heavy in proportion to the small number engaged. The Gurkhas lost Major E. G. Drummond killed, Captain Alexander wounded and missing, and Lieutenant McSwiney wounded, while Captain Bennett was missing. Amongst the Gurkha ranks there were 57 casualties.

The small detachment of the 2/39th Garhwalis lost Major Taylor and Captain Robertson-Glasgow missing, and had 38 casualties in the ranks.

Subadar Dalkesar Gurung had throughout displayed great gallantry, coolness and leadership, and headed his company right down the German trench with the bayonet. He also went back with Lieutenant McSwiney to rescue Captain Alexander. For his services he was mentioned in despatches, and later, having again distinguished himself at Neuve Chapelle, where he was wounded, was awarded the Cross of the Russian Order of St George, 4th Class.

Naik Rupdhan Pun, who had been to the fore throughout, received the Russian Medal of St George, 2nd Class for this action combined with his services at Neuve Chapelle.

For his conspicuous gallantry, Rifleman Ganpati Thapa received the Indian Distinguished Service Medal.

Three men of the 1/9th Gurkhas displayed great bravery in bringing in wounded under heavy fire. Of these, Lance Naik Jhaman Sing Khattri received the Indian Order of Merit, 2nd Class, while Rifleman Gajbir Bisht and Ran Bahadur Sahi were awarded the Indian Distingished Service Medal.

About this time it became evident that the enemy was systematically sapping up to our trenches along the whole front. This proceeding was open to one of two explanations. Either it was with a view to bringing on a general engagement as soon as parallels had been established near enough for the enemy to issue on a sufficiently broad front to offer a prospect of success, or it may have been to guard against an attack by us. Whatever the object, it was daily becoming more evident that the situation could not last much longer, as one side or the other would shortly be compelled to take the offensive and drive the other back.

The Indian Corps had one Division in reserve, and it therefore seemed probable that it would fall to the lot of the Corps to initiate the offensive, and thus anticipate that of the enemy. During the night of the 15th–16th November, the Ferozepore and Jullundur Brigades were relieved by the 8th British Division, which thus took over the northern portion of our line and reduced the front held by the Corps to about 3½ miles, extending from just north of Givenchy to the junction of the ill-famed Rue du Bois with the main La Bassée—Estaires road.

During the night a dashing little raid was carried out by a party of 125 men of the 6th Jat Light Infantry, under Major P. H. Dundas, with Lieutenant Liptrott, and half of No. 3 Company Sappers and Miners under Captain Kelly, R.E., with Lieutenant Wheeler, R.E. Two German saps had been pushed up to within a very uncomfortable distance of the trenches held by the 107th Pioneers, and it became necessary to clear the enemy out and fill in the saps.

In this, as in most of these rushes, the element of surprise was very essential. It was therefore decided by Colonel Roche, commanding the 6th Jats, in consultation with Major Dundas, that no preliminary bombardment was advisable. As soon, however, as our men had got in, the heavy guns were to open on the enemy's reserve trenches and, later on, the field guns would join in. Major Dundas was ordered to hold the trench between the enemy's saps sufficiently long to admit of the 107th rebuilding a section of their parapet which had been blown down, and of the Sappers and Miners filling in the saps.

At 8.55 p.m. the attack was launched, with orders not to fire until the objective was reached. As the men cleared the wire entanglement in our front, some casualties were caused by fire from the sap on each flank, but they pressed on, passing a deep drain, and further on a fire trench, which had been abandoned by us and afterwards used by the enemy.

On reaching the right sap, Major Dundas at once set to work to clear the enemy out with the bayonet, in order to cover the Sappers who were working just behind. The space was very cramped, and there was only room for one man to advance at a time; the bullets were falling fast and thick, and men were dropping. There was nothing for it but to draw back to the mouth of the sap, where we were better protected, our reply to the heavy fire drawing forth many curses and yells.

In the hand-to-hand fighting some loss was inflicted on the enemy, and one prisoner was captured, whose behaviour was a striking illustration of the terror then inspired by the Indians, due doubtless to the stories of their barbarity with which the Germans had been regaled. This man, on being taken, absolutely refused to be left alone with the Indians. He clung to Major Dundas's hand and declined to leave him, being eventually killed at his side by a shot from his own trenches.

The left sap was entered without much difficulty by Lieutenants Liptrott and Wheeler, who found the enemy in full retreat, but did not pursue them, as it was vitally necessary to fill in the sap as quickly as possible. The Sappers accomplished this for a distance of about thirty yards, working with their usual devotion under fire, and sustaining several casualties.

Meanwhile Captain Kelly's party in the right sap were having a hand-to-hand tussle, during which they bayoneted several of the enemy and destroyed as much as they could of the work.

The whole party retired shortly before 10 p.m., but unfortunately came under heavy fire from the abandoned trench which they had passed during the advance, into which some Germans had apparently managed to steal. The result was that the casualties were as heavy here as during the advance, amongst others one Indian officer being killed and a second wounded, the German prisoner being shot at this point, still constant to the side of Major Dundas.

This little exploit earned the warm praise of the General Officer Commanding the Meerut Division. Major Dundas had shown good leadership throughout, and was awarded the D.S.O., while Lieutenant Liptrott, who was unfortunately killed a few days later, was mentioned in despatches. Captain Kelly, R.E., received the Military Cross, Lieutenant Wheeler being mentioned.

Jemadar Abdul Aziz and Colour-Havildar

Chagatta, 1st Sappers and Miners, were awarded the Indian Distinguished Service Medal, the latter being already in possession of the Indian Order of Merit. Among the 6th Jats, a fine regiment which performed excellent service throughout its career in France, Havildar Badlu and Sepoy Risal received the Indian Distinguished Service Medal. The Havildar led the attack in the right sap until he was seriously wounded, and Risal continually exposed himself to fire while holding off the enemy on our right.

Jemadar Incha Ram received the Military Cross for his bravery in continuing to command his men when badly wounded, and Havildar Jai Lal was awarded the Indian Order of Merit for his gallantry in the close fighting.

The casualties of the Jats were 29, of whom three were Indian officers, the Sappers and Miners losing three killed and one wounded.

The next few days passed fairly quietly, in the sense that nothing occurred beyond the usual shelling, sniping, and bombing. The weather was very cold and frosty, rendering the roads slippery and difficult for horse transport.

It is interesting to note that on the 19th November our first trench mortars were fired. These ingenious contrivances were the invention of Major Paterson, R.F.A., and were constructed by No. 3 Company Sappers and Miners. At first only two were made, of which one was of wood and the other of cast iron.

The details of this early attempt at the construction of a weapon which has since developed into a most formidable instrument of warfare, are too technical to recount here. It is sufficient to mention that the shell, weighing 3 lbs. 12 oz., was made out of an 18-pounder shell case with three inches cut off the end. This was filled with melinite or flaked cotton. The success of the operation depended on the fuse lighting from the flash of the powder charge at the moment the shell left the mouth of the gun. The charge consisted of three ounces of powder tied up in a piece of sacking.

The mortars were brought into action against the enemy's saps by Lieutenant Robson, R.E., who was not long in getting to work, as he had only joined the day before. One or two direct hits were obtained in twenty rounds, which was encouraging for a first attempt.

It was found necessary to omit the sacking envelope of the charge, as it was blown from the mouth of the mortar and left a trail of smoke or flame which enabled the gun to be located. Still, everything has a beginning, and the use of even these primitive weapons cheered up our men who had suffered severely from the enemy's mortars without the power of replying in kind.

There was, however, another side to the question. The usual procedure of the trench mortar specialist was to fire as many rounds as possible, and then to pack up and remove his infernal machine with the utmost expedition to another part of the trench, to avoid the wrath to come.

At first, our officers and men watched the proceedings with the greatest sympathy and interest, but when, as soon happened, they awoke to the fact that the firing of our mortars was the signal for a bombardment of that part of the trench by the enemy, sympathy gave place to intense dislike, and after a time, as one gallant officer testifies, it was only a very astute bomb-gunner who could obtain a free hand.

The British soldier never fails to see the humorous side of even the blackest day, and at one point in a trench which had suffered severely through the zeal of those whom its occupants knew as the mortar maniacs, a notice was put up which read, "No hawkers, organs or trench mortars permitted."

About this time there was a great increase in the number of cases of frostbite, the 41st Dogras especially suffering severely. As far as possible arrangements were made to supply braziers and charcoal in the trenches, where the conditions were most bitter.

The fighting strength of the two Divisions of the Corps was then 3500 British rifles, 9500 Indian, added to which was the Secundrabad Cavalry Brigade of four regiments, mustering 1700 sabres.

The proportion of sickness in British and Indian ranks of the Corps respectively is of interest. It would naturally be imagined that the Indian troops, accustomed for the most part to the warmth and dryness of the plains of India, would have suffered more severely than their British comrades from the extremely trying conditions under which they now existed. The contrary proved to be the case, for while the casualties in the British ranks due to sickness amounted to some 400 out of a total of 3500 men, those in the Indian units totalled only 449 out of 11,200.

This disparity can be ascribed to two main causes. The British troops suffered from the effects of a long sojourn in the enervating climate of India, which, as is so often the case, brought out the fever frequently only latent in Europeans who have lived in the East. Colour is lent to this theory by the fact that the chief sufferers amongst the Indian regiments were the 2/3rd Gurkhas, who had been delayed for three weeks at Kotawara in the fever-laden atmosphere of the Terai, and in tropical rain, during their march from the hills in India prior to embarkation. This regiment felt the effects of the malaria thus induced during the whole period of their stay in France.

On the other hand, the evil effects of the unaccustomed climate of Northern France in winter were successfully combated, in the case of the Indians, by the unceasing care and solicitude with which they were watched over by their regimental and medical officers. Other factors in their well-being were the excellence of the food supply, the sanitary measures adopted by the medical officers, and the quantities of extra comforts which were showered on the men by the forethought and kindness of those at home, largely through the instrumentality of the Indian Soldiers' Fund.

On the 21st November, H.R.H. the Prince of Wales visited the Corps and spent some time in assuring himself of the welfare of the men to whom this visit, so shortly to be followed by that of the King-Emperor, was a source of unfeigned pleasure.

On the same date the enemy commenced a series of attacks with heavy trench mortars, directed chiefly against the 6th Jats in the left centre of the Bareilly Brigade, which occupied the section of the line nearest to Givenchy. These monster bombs caused a large number of casualties, and gave the men no rest, for the trenches were broken up, repaired and broken up again, repaired and re-occupied; and so it went on until the troops were worn out with constant strain and want of sleep.

A novel excitement was caused by the descent, owing to engine trouble, of a German biplane, the two aviators, both officers, being captured.

At first it was very difficult to stop the Indians from firing with the utmost impartiality at every aeroplane, Allied or hostile, which hove in sight. They found it difficult to believe that such uncanny monsters could have any but malevolent intentions. By degrees, however, the novelty wore off, until the appearance of an aeroplane hardly excited remark.

The cold was now intense, heavy snow having fallen. Patrol work was rendered almost impossible, as the snow made every movement clearly visible. The hardness of the ground, however, brought its compensations, for our primitive hand-grenades, which had often proved ineffective, now exploded with cheerful frequency on striking the ground.

On the morning of the 22nd November, the Bareilly Brigade was again heavily bombed, as many as sixty projectiles falling in the trenches of the 58th Rifles; and the 6th Jats once more suffered severely. The news that Hales' rifle grenades were on their way from England was therefore very encouraging.

The proximity of the enemy's line hampered us very greatly, for not only did it enable the Germans to throw bombs into our trenches, but it prevented the artillery from shelling the enemy, on account of the risk to our men. The only remedy lay in frequent attacks on the hostile sapheads, but the effect of these raids was purely temporary, as there was seldom time to allow of the saps being effectually filled in.

It was noticed at this juncture that the enemy's guns were markedly inactive. This admitted of one of two possible explanations: either he was saving up ammunition with a view to a big effort, or he was removing his heavy guns to another area. The former appeared to be the most probable hypothesis, as the natural point for attack, the link most likely to be the weakest in the chain, was at the point of junction of the Allied forces, in this case about opposite Festubert and Givenchy. It seemed probable, therefore, that an attack on a large scale was impending, and that the Indian Corps might have to bear the brunt of it.

The enemy doubtless believed that the mixture of British and Indian troops in our line would prove to be a source of weakness. In this, as in so many similar surmises, he was to find his mistake. Throughout the period during which our British and Indian troops were so intimately associated, the strongest feeling of comradeship prevailed. On the part of the Indian soldiers there existed the greatest admiration for the tenacity, the cool courage, the unfailing cheerfulness under the heaviest trials of their British friends. It must never be forgotten that the Indians were fighting under the strangest and most unfavourable conditions imaginable. Transported many thousand miles from their own sunny land, dumped to face a cruel winter in a country of which the inhabitants, language, and customs were entirely unknown to them, it is to their everlasting credit that they came so nobly through the ordeal. Faced by the most treacherous and bloodthirsty foe that the world has ever seen, whose many years of preparation gave him innumerable advantages over our hasty improvisations, they preserved a degree of composure and attained to a standard of courage which has not been surpassed even in this war.

It was here that the example of the British soldier proved to be of such supreme value. There was no question of the inherent courage of the Indian soldier. It had been proved in many a hard-fought field. The only doubt was whether he would rise superior to the appallingly depressing nature of his surroundings. For him, be it remembered, there was no short leave home to instil fresh heart and spirits. To visit England was merely the exchange of one unknown country for another, and such visits could only be the result of wounds or sickness. The British soldier, on the other hand, fighting as he was in a country and climate not very unlike his own, amongst people whose manners and customs were not altogether dissimilar to his, was not exposed to quite the same depth of depression. Always cheerful himself, his cheerfulness was infectious to all around him, and the Indians at once came under the spell.

Instances of the best form of comradeship are numberless. Often, when it was impossible to bring up rations to the trenches, have the British shared the remains of their supplies with their Indian friends.

There are many instances, too, some of which

will be found in these pages, of British soldiers risking their lives to save Indians, and *vice versâ*. Camaraderie was there in its highest sense, and without it the Corps could not have existed.

The one calamity of all those which he was called on to face, which could in any degree shake the moral of the Indian soldier, was the loss of his beloved British officers. Accustomed from the very commencement of his military life to look to them at every turn for example and guidance, treated by them with the utmost justice tempered by kindness, regarding them almost as a child regards a much-loved father, the Indian would have been less than human had he not felt that the world was slipping away from him when he saw, amid such strange and terrible surroundings, the leaders who constituted the one link between his native land and this foreign country killed one after the other, leaving him to the guidance of the Indian officers who, gallant in the extreme as they have so often proved themselves to be, were as much strangers to the land and conditions as himself.

The heroism of the British officer in this war is beyond the power of the pen to describe, nor would he encourage or welcome a literary advertisement of his valour. The scope of this history only permits of the description of a small number of instances of conspicuous self-sacrifice and bravery on the part of British officers, but the abiding proof of their loyalty to their tradition, to their duty, and to their men, is to be found in the graves in Flanders, which are the only record of so much devotion and so much glory.

CHAPTER IX

THE ACTION OF FESTUBERT

Conditions obtaining at time of battle of Festubert—Indian Corps heavily handicapped, but line never broken—Description of sapping operations—Relief of Meerut Division by Lahore—Heavy attack by enemy before relief completed—Gallant defence by Connaught Company—34th Sikh Pioneers, 9th Bhopal Infantry and 58th Rifles forced out of their trenches—Lt-Colonel Southey saves position on left flank—Captain Bull, 58th Rifles—Corps Commander orders trenches to be retaken at all costs before dawn—Counter-attack in the afternoon—Major Cassels and 2/8th Gurkhas—Held up by bombs—1/39th Garhwalis attack under Lt-Colonel Swiney—Plan suggested by Lieutenant Robson, R.E.—Bombing party of 57th Rifles led with great bravery by Lieutenant Robson with Captain Acworth—58th Rifles retake their trenches—Gallantry of four privates of the 2nd Black Watch—Success of the 1/39th Garhwalis—Naik Darwan Sing Negi earns the Victoria Cross.

Before proceeding to an account of the action of Festubert, it seems advisable to give a brief sketch of the conditions which obtained at the moment.

For a month past, the Indian Corps, numbering only some 14,000 rifles and 1700 sabres, with the usual proportion of artillery, had been holding the line previously occupied by the 2nd Corps strengthened by an extra Brigade, its total numbers amounting roughly to 32,000 men.

It can thus be easily seen that the position was extremely hazardous, in view of the pitiful weakness of our line and the proximity of a daring and pertinacious enemy, whose numbers greatly exceeded ours, while his resources in guns, trench mortars and grenades were vastly superior to anything which we could oppose to them. The Corps had therefore been pinned down to a defensive attitude, varied only by the necessity for occasional local attacks when the enemy's sapping operations brought him into such dangerous proximity as to threaten to render our trenches untenable.

In spite of all the disadvantages under which it laboured, the Corps had so far won through without relinquishing any material portion of its original line. Wherever the Germans had succeeded in making a breach, the position had always been restored. From the enemy's continuous and determined efforts to bring his line up as close as possible to ours, it was obviously his intention to make, at some not distant date, a determined attempt to break our front.

The term "sap" has occurred very frequently in this history, and its precise meaning may not be clearly understood by the non-military reader. As sapping operations have played, and continue to play, a very important part in the general scheme, a short and non-technical explanation may be helpful.

The distance between the opposing trenches varied at different points in the line from between 500 to 50 yards, or even less, being governed chiefly by the configuration of the ground. Everywhere the space between the trenches, known as "No Man's Land," could be swept by machine-gun and rifle fire. Where the trenches were divided by a sufficient interval, artillery fire of an appalling density could be brought to bear. It was obvious, therefore, that in order to give an attack the best chance of success, it was necessary, as far as possible, to curtail the distance to be traversed in the open before reaching the hostile trenches. The closer to our trenches, as before remarked, the less had the enemy to fear from our artillery. Moreover, the existence of approaches below surface-level rendered reinforcement of the front line a safer operation.

The method pursued to accomplish these ends was briefly as follows.

Saps, or winding trenches, were commenced as a rule from points in the enemy's line some 300 to 400 yards from our trenches. After progressing perhaps 100 yards, the various saps would be connected by a new fire trench, parallel to the original trench from which the saps proceeded. As the distance became less, the difficulties of course increased, and it was necessary to establish a fire to cover the diggers. This was managed by making short lines of trench, with loopholes at the bends or angles of the saps from which men could keep up fire.

At last, by repeated advances, the front trench was established at a distance of perhaps fifty yards from our line. From this a further sap was frequently (in the days when we were scantily provided with bombs and grenades) pushed up to within a few feet of our parapet. The advantages resulting to the enemy are, of course, obvious. His men could be massed within a very short distance of their objective. Our artillery could do them no harm without certain damage to our own men. The successive lines in rear could be occupied quietly by supports which could come up at the required moment under cover of the zig-zag approaches.

Finally, when all was ready, the attack was made with bombs and grenades. If this succeeded, the sections opposite the sapheads were rendered untenable, and the defence was split up. The bombs and grenades supplied the place of the enemy's artillery which could not shell our trenches without injuring his own men.

The attack commenced on the 23rd November, and was preceded by extensive operations of the foregoing character which were greatly assisted by the nature of the ground. The saps had been brought up to within a few yards of our line, with the result that, by incessant bombing, the position of the 34th Pioneers on the left of the right section of the defence was rendered untenable, and they were forced to evacuate their trenches.

The enemy had, from one point of view, chosen his time well. The relief of the Meerut Division by Lahore was fixed for the nights of the 22nd–23rd and 23rd–24th November. On the morning of the 23rd, half of the left section, east of Richebourg l'Avoué, and the left and centre sub-sections of the right section east of Festubert had been relieved. The right section of our line was thus composed of units of both Divisions.

From left to right, the troops were in the following order :—

129th Baluchis	57th Rifles	1 Company 1st Connaughts	34th Pioneers	9th Bhopals

These all belonged to the Lahore Division, but to their right were two units of the Meerut Division, the 58th Rifles and a half-battalion Black Watch.

The enemy doubtless counted on this state of affairs as a likely cause of confusion.

On the other hand, the units of the Meerut Division, which had just been relieved, were still in proximity to our line, and were thus readily available as reinforcements. These were the other half of the Black Watch, the 41st Dogras, 2/8th Gurkhas and 107th Pioneers, while the 6th Jats were in reserve near Festubert. Major-General Macbean of the Bareilly Brigade was still in command of this section of the line.

During the night of the 23rd November, the enemy pushed up his sap to within five yards of the trenches of the 34th, and as dawn broke, he commenced a storm of hand grenades from his nearest sapheads, with especial violence at the junction of the 34th and the company of Connaughts on their left, where a maxim of the 34th was in position.

Subadar Natha Singh was near the machine gun, round which bombs fell fast, killing a number of men. He at once took charge and held his position against the enemy, who had broken in, until he was eventually forced to retire. This officer had previously distinguished himself on several occasions, and now received the Indian Order of Merit, 2nd Class.

Havildar Nikka Singh, when all the men of the machine-gun team had been killed or wounded, carried the gun by himself under a withering fire back to the support trenches, for which act of bravery he also received the 2nd Class, Indian Order of Merit.

Captain Mackain was in command of the company

next to Subadar Natha Singh. Although already wounded in the head, he rushed through a storm of bombs to a traverse, over which he shot several of the enemy with his revolver, but was then killed by a bullet through the head; a splendid end to a very brave young officer, whose many good qualities had endeared him to all ranks in the regiment. Sepoys Ishar Singh, Sachittar Singh, and Kanhaya Singh at once carried him through the bursting bombs to a shelter. Of these three devoted soldiers, Ishar Singh was selected to receive the Indian Distinguished Service Medal.

Lt-Colonel G. H. Kelly then rallied a party of his men and headed a most gallant charge which, however, was foredoomed to failure, and the intrepid leader fell mortally wounded.

Captain Mackain, whose splendid example was reflected in the spirit of the men under his command, was mentioned in despatches.

Lance-Naik Tota Singh stuck to Captain Mackain to the very last and was killed by his side, after giving every proof of his fidelity and valour, for which he was posthumously awarded the Indian Order of Merit.

Sepoy Katha Singh, Captain Mackain's orderly, was severely injured by the same bomb which inflicted the first wound on his officer, but he refused to leave until ordered back to the aid post. He received the Indian Distinguished Service Medal.

Colour-Havildar Chanba Singh, Havildar Narayan Singh, and Sepoy Teja Singh (the latter already wounded) held on to their position. When the enemy entered the trench, they blocked up the traverse and fired through loopholes in it until, after Narayan Singh had been wounded, they were ordered to retire.

Narayan Singh was again, and this time mortally, wounded while being carried to the aid post; his bravery was recognized by the award of the Indian Distinguished Service Medal.

Subadar Sant Singh rallied his half company and held them in position when the enemy broke in. He behaved with great courage in our subsequent counter-attack, in which he was wounded. He received the Military Cross.

Naik Bir Singh held on to the traverse nearest to the enemy, and kept up rapid fire until he was shot through the face. He was awarded the Indian Distinguished Service Medal.

During this attack, the building in which the regimental aid post was established came under heavy shell fire, the house being repeatedly struck. Sub-Assistant-Surgeon Harnam Singh and Havildar Pala Singh, who was the hospital havildar, removed all the wounded, the stretcher-bearers being away near the firing line, and carried them into safety along the road, which was being shelled. These two men showed absolute disregard of danger, and were awarded the Indian Order of Merit, 2nd Class.

The 34th were overpowered by numbers and by bombs, and their left was pushed out into the Connaught trench, while the Germans continued to clear out each traverse with grenades as they advanced. A brave attempt was then made by Captain Crookshank with one company to retake the trench, but just as they were advancing, a machine gun enfiladed them, and they were forced to fall back.

This left the right of the Connaughts, under Captain Callaghan, in the air, and the enemy with a machine gun and bombs were forcing their way through the communication trench. The Connaughts fought them traverse by traverse, but owing to the want of bombs they suffered considerable loss and could do little injury to the enemy. Step by step they retreated, until, to avoid being taken both in flank and rear, they had to seek cover in the trench on the right of the 57th Rifles, where they built a rough barricade and defied all the efforts of the enemy to move them.

A counter-attack was immediately organized and carried out by the 34th with portions of the 6th Jats and 9th Bhopals, but they were at once held up by machine guns. Subadar Natha Singh again distinguished himself by getting into the enemy's trench on the left with only twenty-six men. The Commanding Officer reported that his conduct during the whole of these operations was an exceptional example of the highest courage and coolness. He well merited the Indian Order of Merit bestowed on him, to be followed later by the Order of British India, 2nd Class. At 9.30 a.m., some of the 58th Rifles on the left of the right section of the defence were forced out of their trench, and affairs began to look critical. At 12.30 p.m., Brigadier-General Egerton of the Ferozepore Brigade was sent up to take command of the centre.

The position here was saved by the coolness and grasp of Lt-Colonel Southey of the 129th Baluchis, who sent 1½ companies to entrench themselves on the road from Festubert to Ligny-le-Petit and to hold the neighbouring houses. This refusal by Colonel Southey of his right flank, and the determination with which the position was held by his detachment, prevented the enemy from extending his success to the left.

Before evacuating their trenches, the 58th had gone through a trying time. Lieutenant Reilly had been killed in a gallant and successful attempt to carry bombs and ammunition up to the firing line. Havildar Hawinda immediately took out a party under very heavy fire and brought his body in, having already rescued a mortally wounded havildar. For these brave acts he was promoted to Jemadar and received the Indian Distinguished Service Medal. Later in the war, having frequently shown marked courage, he was awarded the Military Cross.

Captain Baldwin found a ditch which enfiladed the enemy's approach, in which he held on with great determination, but he was killed later in our counter-attack and was mentioned in despatches for his bravery. The command of the company was then taken by Havildar Indar Singh, who held the position against heavy assaults until relieved next morning, for which he also was promoted to Jemadar and later received the Military Cross.

Captain Willis, D.S.O., was wounded in the head by a bomb at noon, but continued to command his men, and was finally ordered out of action after taking part in the counter-attack in the afternoon. He was mentioned in despatches.

Captain Lind's company was heavily bombed and was enfiladed by a machine gun, with the result that it lost nearly 75 per cent. of its strength, including its gallant commander.

Captain Bull had been sent up to relieve the wounded Captain Willis, who, however, declined to budge. Captain Bull then got into a ditch with a few men of the 58th and Black Watch, and there they held out with grim determination, although they were heavily bombed from a distance of fifteen yards. The enemy was dominated at this point; the bombing stopped and the position was secured.

There is little doubt that Colonel Southey's action on the left, and Captain Bull's on the right, saved the situation, for had they been less determined in holding their ground at all costs, the whole of this section of our line must have been lost.

The position at 1.30 p.m. was by no means satisfactory: on the extreme right the Black Watch, under Major Harvey, had succeeded in keeping their line intact, but the whole line of the 58th had been evacuated, except the small portion where Captain Bull and his devoted little party of Black Watch and 58th still held out. The entire front of the 34th Pioneers and 9th Bhopals was in the hands of the enemy, as was that of the company of the Connaughts, who were, however, still holding out behind their barricade. On the left, the 57th Rifles and 129th Baluchis, under Colonel Southey, had not budged.

At this juncture uncompromising orders were received from Sir James Willcocks that the original line must be restored before dawn and held at all costs.

General Egerton had come to the conclusion that a preliminary artillery preparation was necessary to the success of a counter-attack, and arrangements were made for all our available guns to shell the trenches taken by the enemy, prior to the assault at 4.30 p.m. On the right, three companies of the 2/8th Gurkhas, under Major Cassels, were ordered to retake the trenches lost by the Bhopals. At the same time, the detachment of 34th Pioneers and 6th Jats in support under Colonel Roche were to move forward, and carrying with them the troops under Major Dundas, which were immediately in front of them, to reoccupy the original 34th Pioneer trenches, in co-operation with 3 companies 2/8th Gurkhas and supported by the Connaughts.

The support trenches vacated by Colonel Roche were to be occupied by the 107th Pioneers. At the same time the 58th were to recapture their own trenches.

The artillery opened fire at the appointed time and got the range at once, a large number of dead and wounded being found when the attack was pushed home, while the trenches themselves were much battered. At 4.30 p.m. the infantry attack was launched and at first made good progress on the right. By 8.30 p.m. Major Cassels was able to report that the 2/8th Gurkhas had reoccupied the right trenches, that the 58th Rifles had also got into their old position, while the Bhopals had captured part of the original line, taking some prisoners, including an officer.

The movements of our men were greatly hampered by the snow-covered ground, which showed them up distinctly and made them an easy mark, with the result that the casualties, in face of heavy rifle and machine-gun fire, were severe, especially in the case of officers.

Much of the success of the 2/8th Gurkhas was

due to the determined and skilful leading of Captain Buckland, who headed a party of his regiment which bombed and bayoneted the enemy out of traverse after traverse until the whole of the right trenches had been retaken.

The business of clearing a position at night is a most eerie one under the best of circumstances, but in this case it was rendered doubly difficult because the 2/8th had been split into two parts, three companies being on the right under Major Cassels and three on the left. The result was that as both parties were working inwards towards each other, neither knew whether they would meet friend or foe round the next traverse.

The difficulty was solved by the use of the Gurkha language. As Captain Buckland at the head of his party crept up to a traverse, bombs and bayonets ready for whatever might be round the corner, one of his men whispered "Koho?" ("Who?"). If there was an answering grunt of "Mon" ("Me"), all was well; if not, the party at once rushed round the corner, hurling bombs and stabbing with the bayonet anyone they met. In this way Captain Buckland cleared a long stretch of trench in the inky darkness, being wounded in the process, and for his gallantry in this as well as other actions received the D.S.O.

Havildar Hari Parshad Thapa, 2/8th Gurkhas, greatly distinguished himself by heading a party which, advancing in single file, rushed traverse after traverse and killed a number of Germans. The Havildar, who was severely wounded during the fight, was awarded the 2nd Class, Indian Order of Merit, for his gallant conduct.

Lieutenant Macpherson having been severely wounded, Major Cassels was the only British officer left in that section, but on being joined by some of the 6th Jats, he went on gradually working towards the left of the line.

The Jats, fighting with their usual dash, had suffered severely. Captain Dudley was killed by a sniper at about ten yards' distance, when standing by the side of Colonel Roche. Major Dundas and Captain Moore were severely wounded. Lieutenant Cockburn, since killed in Mesopotamia, showed great gallantry in leading his men to the assault, and afterwards in heading bombing parties of Gurkhas, with whom he drove the Germans from traverse to traverse, and captured a number of prisoners. For his bravery he received the Military Cross.

The 6th Jats lost between 150 and 200 men, and by this time were reduced to a total of 300. At one point, when very heavy machine-gun fire caused a temporary hesitation, Lance-Naik Maru and Sepoy Bhagmal earned the Indian Distinguished Service Medal by rushing on and carrying the company forward. Jemadar Lakhi Ram and Havildar Harpul received the same award for similar action at another critical moment.

Major Cassels, who had by this time been wounded, continued to work towards the left with his own Gurkhas and a collection of men of other units, until he was held up by bombs, to which he had no means of reply. The 107th were then ordered to hold on to the line and to try to get into touch with the 58th on their right. In the meantime the 58th were busy further to the right. Major Davidson-Houston, their Commanding Officer, himself led the assault at 4.30 p.m., and the original trenches were re-occupied with little opposition, but Lieutenant Gaisford was killed just as he jumped into the trench.

The small casualty list was greatly due to the close and accurate support of our artillery.

Sergeant-Major Kennedy and fifty men of the Black Watch were with the 58th, and were among the first to reach the trench.

An incident occurred here which showed once again the spirit of comradeship pervading all ranks, British and Indian. Just as the 58th were about to make the final rush into the trench, there was a slight momentary hesitation. Four men of the Black Watch, Privates Venters, Boyd, McIntosh, and Stewart, dashed in front of the Dogra Company and headed the charge by the side of Major Davidson-Houston, thus helping him to take the company on; and the trench was carried at once. Major Houston then put the four men into a sap which had been cut right into our old line, where they held out against heavy bombing until relieved. He testified that their sangfroid and cheeriness made a most marked impression on the men of the 58th. For their gallant bearing on this occasion they received the Distinguished Conduct Medal.

The losses of the 58th during the action were:—Killed: Captain Baldwin, Lieutenants Gaisford and Reilly, Jemadar Wazir Singh and 42 other ranks. Wounded: Captains Lind and Willis, Subadar Gujar Singh and 61 other ranks, while 11 men were missing.

Major Davidson-Houston and Captain Bull received the D.S.O. in recognition of their determined leadership.

Leaving the 58th firmly re-established in their old trenches, we must follow the fortunes of the 1/39th Garhwalis under Lt-Colonel Swiney, who was ordered shortly after 9 p.m. to retake the left of the centre section.

In General Egerton's words, the battalion was "to move to the left flank of the centre section, to effect a lodgment at its extremity, and to work along the line towards the right."

A series of unavoidable delays occurred, and the attack did not commence till about 3.45 a.m. on the 24th. Apparently some misunderstanding existed as to whether a frontal attack was intended. Colonel Swiney was under the impression that the orders admitted of no doubt on this point, whereas General Egerton, in forwarding Colonel Swiney's report on the action, remarked that his orders were not understood in the first instance, as he never ordered a frontal attack.

Lt-Colonel Southey, commanding the left section of the line, reported that Lieutenant Robson, R.E., suggested to him that the German tactics should be adopted, viz., to bomb the enemy out from a flank and to follow up with the bayonet. This suggestion was conveyed to General Egerton, who ordered Colonel Swiney to attack at once, using his own discretion as to the method to be adopted, and the plan put forward by Lieutenant Robson was followed.

A detailed account of one of the most gallant episodes of the war will perhaps not be out of place.

On the night of the 22nd–23rd November the 57th Rifles took over the right flank of the left section of the Brigade line. The right rested on a road through which a very shallow and bad communication trench had been cut for a distance of about 40 yards, connecting the 57th with the left of the centre section, whose line was about ten yards in front of the 57th trench.

When, early on the 23rd, the enemy bombed the defenders out of the centre section, Captain Acworth, 55th Rifles, attached 57th, was erecting a barricade on his right, but had to hasten his efforts on our men rushing in with the news that the enemy were close behind them. Luckily, however, the Germans advanced no further than the left of the centre section, for we had no bombs at that point and would certainly have been unable to hold our ground.

About midday Lieutenant Robson arrived with some of his sappers, and with his usual marvellous energy and coolness began to organize the flank. He demolished the barricade hastily completed by Captain Acworth and rebuilt it more substantially. More important than all, he brought with him a supply of bombs. None of those on the spot had ever handled these weapons before, but as an officer records, Robson soon taught them all that was necessary, and they threw a few bombs into the houses in front of the communication trench and dislodged some snipers who had been very objectionable.

At about 2 p.m. Robson went down the communication trench alone to reconnoitre, and found that the Germans were hard at work improving the position. This, in itself, was a feat of great daring, for the trench was only about three feet deep, and so winding that it was impossible to see more than five yards ahead, and at any turning the intruder might be confronted by a German with his finger on the trigger.

Not satisfied with this exploit, he again went down the trench alone, and threw six bombs into the German working party with gratifying effect. His reply to remonstrances was that any one with him would only have been in the way. An eye-witness remarks that this was one of the most gallant individual acts of which he had ever heard.

Shortly afterwards Robson returned to Head Quarters to bring up more bombs, the supply of which ran out at dark. Had the Germans then attacked, the position would have been most critical. At 10 p.m. he returned with an ample supply, which, with his usual energy, he had prepared in the interval; the flank was thus rendered fairly secure.

At 3 a.m. on the 24th he again came up and explained that a counter-attack was to be made by the 1/39th Garhwalis from the 57th trench. He proposed to lead the assault with a small party of bombers of the 57th, and, in inviting Captain Acworth to accompany him on his perilous task, he said, half laughingly and half apologetically, "I wouldn't ask you to come, but we want two anarchists on this show."

Captain Acworth accepted with delight, and the assault was carried out as planned by Robson.

When all was ready, the barricade was partially pulled down and the party slipped over the top, three Afridis leading with fixed bayonets, followed by the two officers with bombs and a few more Afridis carrying a further supply.

They crept stealthily up the shallow communication trench until they were within an easy throw of the enemy, and then the two officers pitched bombs well into the first traverse, and advancing still further, got several into the nearest bay.

The surprise was complete, and a number of the Germans were killed and wounded, while the rest put up their hands.

The bombing party hastily flattened themselves against the side of the trench, and Robson shouted to the Garhwalis to charge. The leading men jumped over the officers and went down the trench, as an eye-witness relates, like tigers.

Just as they started, the enemy opened a hot fire from his trench. To prevent the Germans from breaking in on the flank of the assault, the two officers at once rushed up and bombed the point from which the firing came until it ceased altogether.

They then, exhausted as they were with their unceasing efforts of the night and the previous afternoon, tried to get to the head of the attack, but the trench was so crowded and the Garhwalis had got on so rapidly that they had to give up the attempt, and with only a few bombs left, they returned to the 57th trench, Captain Acworth being slightly wounded on the way.

Lt-Colonel Southey brought to notice the splendid behaviour of the two officers who, he said, throughout the afternoon exposed themselves while bombing the enemy, and volunteered for the same work at night, preceding the 1/39th, and bombing out the men who were in the trenches.

Major Wardell and his men pushed on, bayoneting all who resisted.

Naik Darwan Sing Negi, V.C., 1st Bn 39th Garhwal Rifles.

Captain Lumb, not to be outdone, jumped with a section and a half into the trench ahead of Major Wardell and proceeded to rush the traverses, bayoneting many of the enemy and taking some prisoners. In this work Rifleman Kalamu Bisht showed great courage, and earned the 2nd Class, Indian Order of Merit.

Affairs then began to look a little awkward, as Major Wardell's party had been much weakened by casualties during this operation, and could do no more than hold the portion of trench already taken. A gap was thus fast arising between him and Captain Lumb. Luckily, at this moment, Lieutenant Welchman brought up the remainder of Captain Lumb's men, and together they pushed on along the trench.

Foremost among many heroes was Naik Darwan Sing Negi who, from the beginning to the end, was either the first, or among the first, to force his way round each successive traverse, facing a hail of bombs and grenades. Although twice wounded in the head and once in the arm, he refused to give in, and continued fighting without even reporting that he was wounded. When the struggle was over and the company fell in, his company commander saw that he was streaming with blood from head to foot. For his most conspicuous valour Naik Darwan Sing was awarded the Victoria Cross, being the second Indian soldier to receive this honour.

He was ably seconded by Lance-Naik Sankaru Gusain and Rifleman Ghantu Rawat, who from start to finish were in the first rush at each traverse, and continually climbed into such exposed positions as the top of parapets or traverses in order to get a better chance at the enemy.

Rifleman Dhan Sing Negi, although wounded in the face, also fought throughout the action with complete disregard of danger.

Havildar Alam Sing Negi led three successive bayonet charges of his company.

Each of these brave men received the Indian Order of Merit.

The remainder of the trench having being taken, the 39th joined hands with the 107th just as dawn was breaking. While this was taking place, Captain Lane brought up reinforcements of the 1/39th, but while occupying the left of the recaptured trench, he came under a heavy enfilade fire which knocked over a number of his men. Equal to the occasion, as the British officer generally is, he improvised a barricade out of the debris lying round, although exposed all the time to the enemy's fire, and held it until relieved, for which he received the Military Cross, a reward which also fell to Subadar Dhan Sing Negi for the cool determination shown by him throughout the fight.

An outstanding figure of this action was undoubtedly Lieutenant R. G. G. Robson, R.E., who not only suggested the plan of bombing the Germans from the flank, but carried it out himself with the greatest gallantry, gallantly backed by Captain Acworth who received the Military Cross, while Lieutenant Robson was mentioned in despatches. Sad to relate, his valiant and most promising career was cut short, as he was killed exactly one month later while carrying out an almost equally dangerous enterprise.

On the 23rd December, our trenches near Port Arthur, already deep in water, became flooded to such a degree and so rapidly as to threaten to become untenable. Although our men did everything possible with the primitive appliances then available, the water still gained on them. The Officer Commanding on the spot came to the conclusion that the enemy was deliberately pumping water out of his trenches, which were here quite close, into ours.

As usual in moments of doubt and difficulty, a Sapper officer was summoned and arrived in the person of Lieutenant Robson, who agreed with the Commanding Officer's opinion, and characteristically at once took the danger on himself. Borrowing a shovel, he crawled out towards the German trench with the intention of listening for the sounds of pumping and endeavouring to find the channel through which the water flowed towards our trenches.

The enemy was keeping up a heavy rifle and machine-gun fire, and a little later a non-commissioned officer in our trench, observing a shovel sticking up in the air, and being aware that Lieutenant Robson had not returned, crept out to reconnoitre. Lying near the German trench, he found the gallant officer dead, killed apparently by machine-gun fire. Such was the end of one whom Lieutenant-General Sir Charles Anderson described as having "at all times and in all ways shown himself to be as brave and capable an officer as ever wore the King's uniform." Had he lived, it is permissible to suppose that he would have been granted a high reward for his valour.

Of the eight men of the 57th, four received the

2nd Class, Indian Order of Merit, and four the Indian Distinguished Service Medal.

For his determined leadership, Captain Lumb of the Garhwalis received the Military Cross, and Subadar Jagat Sing Rawat the Order of British India, 2nd Class. Seven men received the Indian Order of Merit, 2nd Class, and five men the Indian Distinguished Service Medal.

Lt-Colonel Swiney's valuable services were recognized by the grant of a brevet Colonelcy. It was greatly owing to this officer's careful preparation and foresight, and to the skilful manner in which the attack was carried out, that the losses of the regiment were small in comparison to the results.

The casualties were:—Major Wardell wounded and missing; Captain Orton severely wounded; 1 Garhwali officer and 17 men killed; 2 Garhwali officers and 33 men wounded.

The 1/39th Garhwalis, having only been raised in 1887, had little chance until this war of showing their mettle, but they have most valiantly proved their right to take place beside the best regiments in the army. It is noteworthy that the Victoria Cross has been won by men of both the 1/39th and 2/39th Garhwalis.

In this action the battalion captured two machine-guns, one trench mortar, a large number of rifles, and a quantity of trench equipment. Inside the trench 32 Germans lay dead, and many bodies were scattered outside.

The losses of the 2/8th Gurkhas were:—Major Elliott and Lieutenant Macpherson, both attached from the 7th Gurkhas, killed; Major Cassels, 2/8th Gurkhas, and Lieutenant Peploe, 2/6th Gurkhas, wounded; Lieutenant Maxwell, missing; 1 Gurkha officer killed, 2 missing, the casualties in the ranks being 71.

Shortly after the 1/39th were sent up to attack on the left, General Egerton decided to make a further attempt on the right flank, where the 107th Pioneers had previously been held up by bombs.

Accordingly, two companies of the 2nd Leicesters under Major Gordon, and two companies of the 107th Pioneers got into position at about 4 a.m. on the 24th, by moving up a communication trench to within about seventy yards of the Germans. B Company of the Leicesters was on the right of one company of the 107th in the front line. On the advance commencing, some confusion was caused by the left company crowding in on the right. Captain Grant of the Leicesters led his men through heavy machine-gun and rifle fire into the enemy's trench, where he and Lieutenant Seton-Browne were almost immediately killed. Sergeant Foister gained the Distinguished Conduct Medal by a gallant attempt to rescue the last-named officer.

After a short rough-and-tumble fight, the enemy bolted, as was generally the case even then when they came to grips with our men, and a number of them were killed in their flight.

With this party of the Leicesters a few men of the 107th had entered the trench, but the remainder of the company had suffered severely and were unable to advance. On learning the situation, General Egerton ordered a retirement, which was effected at about 6 a.m., the last wounded being removed by 7 a.m. In the meantime, as before mentioned, the 1/39th Garhwalis joined hands with the 107th.

In this brief but sharp fight the Leicesters lost two officers and 3 men killed, 14 wounded and 12 missing. Major Gordon received the D.S.O. for his gallant leading; Captain Grant and Lieutenant Seton-Browne were mentioned in despatches; and Privates Chatten, Chamberlain, and Taylor were awarded the Distinguished Conduct Medal.

The 107th lost Major Bruce and 17 other ranks killed; Captains McLaughlin, Davis, Turnbull, and Mangin, Lieutenant Wallis, one Indian officer and 39 men wounded.

The services of Subadar-Major Labh Singh, Subadar Hashmat Dad Khan and Havildar Bhagat Singh were recognized by the award of the Indian Distinguished Service Medal.

Little has hitherto been said of the work done by the 2nd Black Watch under Major Harvey. This magnificent regiment had, however, been true to its traditions and had not given one inch of ground, although at one time the enemy was firing into their rear. The regiment as a whole was not called on to attack during the fight, but a party of 50 men, under Company Sergeant-Major Kennedy, as before mentioned, materially assisted the 58th Rifles in regaining their trenches, for which Sergeant-Major Kennedy, Sergeant Drummond and Private Swan received the Distinguished Conduct Medal, while a few of the men were with Captain Bull in his gallant defence of a portion of the 58th trench.

Major Wauchope of the Black Watch, as always when fighting was forward, was in the thick of it, and assisted the final attack by leading a charge of about twenty men under Lieutenant McMicking against the nearest German saphead. He then found that a gap of about 300 yards existed between the left of the 58th Rifles and the right of the 2/8th Gurkhas. Calmly occupying this gap were the four men of the Black Watch who had been posted there by Major Davidson-Houston. Quite undaunted by the showers of bombs and bullets to which they were being treated by the Germans, they were keeping up a steady and very effective fire. They only retired when Major Wauchope ordered them to do so, taking with them one of their number who had been severely wounded.

Throughout this action, our artillery, under Lt-Colonel Duffus, continued to render most active support to the infantry ; evidence of the accuracy of their fire was everywhere forthcoming when the trenches were retaken. The parapets were much battered and the German losses were fairly heavy, as in one place 100 corpses were found.

This, the most important battle in which the Indian Corps as a whole had hitherto been engaged, ended with our reoccupation of all the trenches seized by the enemy. The chief lesson learnt from the action was the vital necessity for more guns, more high explosives, more machine guns, more bombs and grenades.

However stubbornly our men might fight, it was trying them very severely to expect them to hold out, without the means of replying, against an enemy numerically greatly superior and provided in superabundance with the weapons which we lacked. How well the Corps did its duty under such unequal conditions was recognized in a message received from Sir John French, in which he congratulated the troops on the counter-attack, and remarked that the units engaged had done splendidly.

On the 23rd November, a detachment of the 34th Poona Horse, under the command of Captain Grimshaw, took over a portion of the trenches of the Ferozepore Brigade.

On arrival, at 4 a.m., it was found that the enemy had driven a sap right up to the parapet, in which a breach of some 8 feet in breadth was made.

As soon as it was daylight, Captain Grimshaw inspected the breach, which had been guarded by a party under Lieutenant F. A. De Pass, and called for a volunteer to reconnoitre along the sap towards the enemy. Sowar Abdulla Khan at once came forward and proceeded to crawl out.

On his return, he reported that the Germans had erected a sand-bag traverse at a distance of about ten yards from our trench at the first bend in the sap. The traverse was loopholed and a sentry was on guard, a fact which Abdulla Khan ascertained by being fired at and missed.

At 8 a.m., the enemy began to throw bombs into our trench from their side of the traverse. This went on all day and caused several casualties.

Early in the morning of the 24th, Lieutenant De Pass determined at all costs to put an end to this state of affairs, and, accompanied by Sowars Fateh Khan and Firman Shah, he entered the sap and crawled along it until he reached the enemy's traverse. With the utmost coolness, he proceeded to place a charge of guncotton in the loophole and fired it; the traverse was completely demolished, and the bend of the sap was rounded off to such an extent as to expose some thirty yards to our fire. When the explosion occurred the enemy threw a bomb at our little party, but by good luck

[Rugby Memorials.

LIEUT F. A. DE PASS, V.C., 34TH POONA HORSE.

it exploded behind Lieutenant De Pass and did no damage, the trio returning to our trench in safety.

All bombing was put a stop to during the remainder of the 24th, and there was only one casualty, compared with six on the previous day and nine on the 25th, by which time, under cover of darkness, the Germans had managed to replace their traverse.

On the 24th, Lieutenant De Pass visited the neighbouring trench which was occupied by the 7th Dragoon Guards. On his way he observed a sepoy of the 58th Rifles lying wounded outside our trench. Accompanied by Private C. Cook of the 7th, he at once went out in broad daylight and brought the man in, although he was exposed to the enemy's fire for a distance of about 200 yards. He then once more volunteered to enter the enemy's sap and attempt to blow up the traverse, but as this meant almost certain death, permission was refused.

On the 26th, the enemy's bombing increased in violence, and De Pass went to the saphead to superintend the repair of our parapet which had again been seriously damaged. Observing a sniper at work behind the traverse, he tried to shoot him, but was himself shot through the head and killed.

Many brave deeds have been performed during this war, but there are few instances of gallantry more conspicuous than that displayed by this heroic young soldier. He was the very perfect type of the British officer. He united to singular personal beauty a charm of manner and a degree of valour which made him the idol of his men. He was honoured in death by the Victoria Cross. No one in the war earned it better.

Sowars Abdulla Khan, Fateh Khan, and Firman Shah received the Indian Distinguished Service Medal, while Private Cook was awarded the Distinguished Conduct Medal.

By the 24th November the Lahore Division had completed its relief of the Meerut Division, and Lt-General Watkis took over command of the line.

On the 26th, the two first anti-aircraft guns joined the Corps. About this time the weather was warmer, but the sky very cloudy, rendering air reconnaissance impossible.

On the night of the 27th–28th November, a party of twenty men of the Manchesters, under 2nd Lieutenant Connell, with Lieutenant Buller, R.E., rushed two German saps about 40 yards from our trench. The enemy were completely taken by surprise, and were still working when our men got in. A hand-to-hand fight took place, in which about ten of the enemy were killed. After the saps had been searched and one partly filled in, the party retired. In doing so, they were caught by machine-gun fire, Lieutenant Connell and 2 men being killed; 6 men were wounded, and 2 were missing. Lieutenant Buller got back safely, but at once went out again to bring in a wounded man, and was himself wounded. For his gallantry he received the Military Cross, while Lieutenant Connell was mentioned in despatches.

The remainder of the month passed in a manner which is known as "quietly." The usual bombing went on wherever the trenches were close enough to each other, while at intervals the artillery on each side woke into spasmodic activity.

On the 30th November the enemy pushed a saphead right into the trench in front of Le Plantin. Sergeant Coldwell and four men of the Connaughts rushed into the gap, drove the Germans out and built a "block." For his courageous conduct Sergeant Coldwell received the Distinguished Conduct Medal.

This non-commissioned officer is described by an officer of the regiment as "the bravest of the brave." He subsequently distinguished himself at the second battle of Ypres, when all his company officers were hit, and he received the 4th Class of the Russian Cross of St George. Unfortunately, he was killed on the 14th October, 1915, when reconstructing in front of our line a listening post which had been blown in by an 8-inch shell.

The 57th Rifles and 129th Baluchis suffered a great loss on the 23rd November by the death of their Medical Officers, Captain Indrajit Singh and Major Atal.

The combined dressing stations had been established at about 1500 yards behind the fire trench. In the afternoon the enemy put several large shells into the house, which was entirely demolished. Working parties made desperate efforts to clear away the ruins and get out those who had been buried; but apparently a spy was concealed somewhere near, for as soon as the men approached the ruins, heavy shell fire was opened on them, and the place was speedily in a blaze, which exploded quantities of ammunition. Major Atal's body was eventually recovered, but Captain Singh's remains were not found till a day later. Both these officers had greatly distinguished themselves by their gallantry in attending wounded under fire, and their loss was deeply felt by their regiments. In a gazette published after his death, Captain Indrajit Singh was awarded the Military Cross.

CHAPTER X

VISIT OF HIS MAJESTY THE KING-EMPEROR

Visit of His Majesty to the Indian Corps—Delight of the troops—Casualties to date—Arrival of the Sirhind Brigade from Egypt—Catapults for grenades and searchlights improvised by Sappers—Good work of Sappers appreciated by Sir John French—Weather prevents aerial reconnaissance—Conditions in trenches very bad—Jullundur Brigade relieve the French at Givenchy—Comparison of British and French trenches.

On the 1st December, 1914, the Corps had the honour of receiving the King-Emperor. The event was a most memorable one, for this was the first occasion on which a British Sovereign had appeared in the field with his troops since George II headed his forces at the battle of Dettingen.

The secret of the Royal visit had been well kept, and was only known to the troops at a late hour on the previous night, when officers and men detailed from the various units were warned to be in readiness to parade next morning for inspection by His Majesty. The troops were drawn up, lining both sides of the road, when the King-Emperor arrived, accompanied by the Corps Commander, Lt-General Sir James Willcocks. H.R.H. the Prince of Wales was also present.

After the Staff had been presented, His Majesty walked down the lines to inspect the men. The morning was dull and the recent heavy rains had converted the roads into a perfect quagmire. Just before the King arrived, a German aeroplane appeared, making straight for the place of parade. Our guns at once opened fire on it, and after one or two ineffectual attempts to approach, it was driven off to the north and was seen no more.

His Majesty paused at frequent intervals to converse with the officers and men, and made most searching inquiries after their welfare. He was particularly struck with the appearance of the men of the 2nd Leicesters, who had come straight out of the trenches and were caked with mud from head to foot.

The troops were delighted at the sight of their King. To many of the Indians it recalled the last occasion on which they had seen His Majesty, which was during the visit to India in 1911. Every man to whom the King spoke was a hero in the billets at night, and the Royal words were retailed and pondered over for long afterwards. The Oriental is particularly susceptible to the personal influence of his Sovereign, and His Majesty's graciousness and keen solicitude for the well-being of his soldiers were intensely appreciated by them.

After the departure of the King, General Willcocks translated His Majesty's message to the troops, in which he told them that he was extremely pleased with all that he had seen and heard, that they were always in his thoughts and those of the Queen, and that he intended to visit them again. The visit was charming in its simplicity, and the strong impression left by it of His Majesty's personal anxiety for the welfare of his troops greatly heartened the men for the hard task which lay before them.

Up to and including the 1st December, 1914, the casualties of the Corps were:—

	Killed.	Wounded.	Missing.
British officers . .	61	100	26
Indian officers . .	27	58	10
Others, British . .	151	609	90
Others, Indian . .	546	3148	1041
Total .	785	3915	1167

On the 3rd–4th December, the Lahore Division was reinforced by the Meerut Division, and each was allotted half of the defensive line, one Brigade being kept as Corps reserve.

On the 7th December, the Sirhind Brigade, under Major-General Brunker, arrived from Egypt, the Lahore Division being thus completed.

About this time the Sappers and Miners were very busy improvising catapults for bomb throwing. With their usual skill and ingenuity, they evolved a weapon which could throw with fair accuracy a light grenade to a maximum distance of 300 yards, the range varying according to the number of strands of elastic used. At the same time, the Sappers contrived a form of searchlight for use in the trenches. Motor headlights fitted with electric bulbs were employed, the power being supplied from certain available sources.

Both of these temporary contrivances were found to be of the greatest value in subsequent operations. In these directions, as in so many others, the Scientific Corps has rendered most important aid to the men in the trenches, and, as it always does, has fought both with valour and with brains. In his despatch, dated 20th November, 1914, Sir John French records the following appreciation of its work :—" The Corps of Indian Sappers and Miners have long enjoyed a high reputation for skill and resource. Without going into detail, I can confidently assert that throughout their work in this campaign they have fully justified that reputation."

The weather during this period was extremely trying; heavy cold rain falling almost daily made life in the trenches well-nigh unbearable. There were many cloudy days accompanied by thick mists, which rendered aerial reconnaissance impossible.

During the 11th–12th December, the Jullundur Brigade under General Carnegy relieved the French in their trenches at Givenchy and at Cuinchy across the La Bassée Canal, embracing the Béthune—La Bassée road.

It was observed that the French fire trenches were, as a rule, not so deep as the British. This was partly because their men are generally shorter than ours, and that they use few loopholes, firing mostly over the parapet. The French communication and support trenches were considered to be superior, which was probably due to the fact that they employed more men per yard of front, and were thus able to do more work. In Givenchy itself the French had practically double as many men as we had.

CHAPTER XI

THE BATTLE OF GIVENCHY: THE MEERUT DIVISION

An attack decided on—Raid by 129th Baluchis on German trenches—Saps taken, but evacuated—Casualties—Position of the Indian Corps—Orders for attack—Assault by 2nd Leicesters and 3rd Gurkhas—Enemy's trench taken—German attack on the "Orchard"—2nd Gurkhas bombed out—Take up line in rear—Leicesters withdrawn from captured trench—Casualties.

TOWARDS the middle of December, the moment appeared to General Head Quarters to be favourable for an attack by the Indian Corps, amongst other units.

A succession of orders was issued. On the 14th December, the Indian Corps was directed to carry out "other local operations with a view to containing the enemy now in their front," and thus to assist General Smith-Dorrien, who was then attacking near Messines.

On the 16th December, therefore, the Ferozepore Brigade under Brigadier-General Egerton delivered an attack, in which the 129th Baluchis behaved with great gallantry. The Brigade consisted of the 1st Connaughts, 57th Rifles, and 129th Baluchis, the 142nd French Territorial Battalion being attached for the time being.

The general idea was to attack two German saps opposite the trenches of the 15th Sikhs, which lay slightly to the west of Givenchy, and, after carrying the saps, to seize as much of the enemy's main trench as possible. At 5.20 a.m. the 129th moved off, followed by the 57th, and took up position ready to assault at 8.30 a.m. The Connaughts remained in support with the French battalion in reserve. On the signal being given, Major Potter dashed with his company of the 129th across the twenty-five yards of open ground which separated our trench from the enemy's left saphead, while a second company attacked the right sap, about fifty yards distant.

The assault was carried out with great élan in the face of heavy fire, and was pushed home up both saps to within a few yards of the enemy's main trench. In a few moments nothing was to be seen from our trench except some fifteen of our men, who were lying dead or wounded round the saphead. A few of the less severely wounded tried to dive into the sap or run back towards our trench, but the fire was so heavy that none got through. In face of the storm of bullets, it was impossible to reinforce until a communication trench could be cut to join our trench with the sapheads.

At this moment it appeared that the right attack had failed. Under the circumstances, it seemed useless for Major Potter to attempt to go on; but the difficulty was to communicate with him. Eventually, it was solved by tying a message to a light weight and throwing it into the sap. An hour later it turned out that, so far from the right attack having failed, two platoons had taken the sap and had almost reached the main trench.

To bring up supports under such heavy and concentrated fire was out of the question, and it was evident that the communication trench could not be made before dark.

Matters grew worse and worse, and the men were gradually being bombed back into the sapheads. Major Potter was holding his own with his usual bravery, but Lieutenant Browning and the Indian officers of the party in the right sap were all wounded. The men had to give way until the remnant was collected in the saphead, where, in spite of all the efforts of the enemy, it held on till dark.

Under the orders of Lt-Colonel Hill, working parties of the 15th Sikhs, ten in each party, had followed up the 129th, and had at once commenced to dig back from the saphead to the Sikh trench. It was necessary to keep Colonel Hill informed of events, and Havildar Mastan Singh of the 15th Sikhs made two perilous journeys under a torrent of lead between the sap and our trench. He tried to get across a third time, but was shot dead.

Lieutenant Barstow, Adjutant of the 15th, happening to look through a loophole when there was a sudden burst of firing, spotted a German peering over a small parapet which commanded the sap, and firing into it. He seized the nearest rifle and shot ten Germans in quick succession. This stopped the firing into the sap, but the enemy now began throwing bombs into it. The sap was by this time crowded, but by the greatest good luck the fuzes of the bombs were too long, and our men were often able to pick them up and throw them back.

In the meantime, parties of the 34th Pioneers and of the 21st Company Sappers and Miners under Captain Battye, R.E., were hard at work digging the communication trenches towards the sapheads, of which the left trench was finished by evening. The right communication trench was a more difficult matter, as it was longer, and, being open to a cross-fire from both flanks, a parapet had to be thrown up on each side, which made progress very slow.

By dusk, only some 12 yards remained to be dug, but the party in the saphead was *in extremis*, having fought all day without a British officer, and having been heavily bombed without the means to reply. They were unable to hold out any longer, and tried to get back across the open after dark; but every one of them was either killed or wounded in the attempt. The enemy then reoccupied the sap and fired down the shallow communication trench, rendering further work impossible. A barricade was hastily built, and operations ceased for the time being as regards the right sap.

Major Potter held on with dogged pluck in the left sap until the communication trench got through to him at about 6 p.m., when he managed to withdraw his men to the Sikh trench. The 129th behaved throughout this very trying affair with the greatest gallantry, but their losses were heavy. Captain Ussher, Subadar Adam Khan, and 53 men were killed; Captain C. A. G. Money, Lieutenant C. Browning, Jemadars Nawab Khan and Imamdar, and 67 men were wounded.

The splendid leading of Major Potter was brought to notice by his Commanding Officer in the following words:—"The leading platoon in the initial stage of the attack hesitated at the lip of the saphead. Major Potter, seeing this, dashed forward and carried them right on. During the whole day, when heavily bombed and pushed, he kept perfectly cool and never allowed himself to get flustered. He was in a very nasty position—cut off for twelve hours—knew I could get no help to him, and by his bearing so kept up the spirits of his men that the sap was held and fortified, and made good."

It is sad to have to record that this heroic officer was reported as missing during the operations of the 20th December, and it is now certain that he was killed.

When Lieutenant Browning was wounded, Jemadar Mir Badshah took command in the right sap, and it was said that, had it not been for his splendid behaviour, the whole party would have been lost.

Sepoy Sahib Jan also showed great courage. On one occasion, at a critical moment, he charged three Germans single-handed, and drove them back.

The Indian Order of Merit was conferred on both of these brave soldiers.

On the 17th December, the Corps was directed, in conjunction with the 2nd, 3rd, and 4th Corps, "to attack all along the front on the 18th December." This was followed by a further order which was received after 10 p.m. on the 17th. To assist the French in their operations near Arras, the 3rd, 4th, and Indian Corps "will demonstrate and seize any favourable opportunity which may offer to capture any enemy trenches in their front." These last two orders were conflicting, and the first was also vague.

A demonstration is a totally different matter to an attack all along the line; the one is incompatible with the other. But even after this rapid succession of orders, a modification was issued, according to which the Indian Corps was "to demonstrate along the whole front, and to seize every favourable opportunity which may offer to capture any of the enemy's trenches."

This final order was received at 5.30 p.m. on the 18th December, and is open to the criticism that it was somewhat indefinite, in the absence of any indication that Sir James Willcocks considered the moment to be favourable for an attack.

Sir John French, in his despatch of the 2nd February, 1915, remarks :—

"In his desire to act with energy up to his instructions to demonstrate and occupy the enemy, the General Officer Commanding the Indian Corps decided to take advantage of what appeared to him a favourable opportunity to launch attacks against the advanced trenches in his front on the 18th and 19th December."

Unless some explanation were offered, the inference might be drawn from this passage that Sir James Willcocks' judgment was at fault in considering the opportunity to be favourable.

To remove this impression, it is perhaps sufficient to mention, that so far from considering the opportunity to be favourable for an attack by the Indian Corps, General Willcocks had a short time previously reported that, owing to the strain of the preceding seven weeks of incessant trench warfare, practically without any relief, the Corps was urgently in need of rest, and he had requested that it might be relieved. With this view Sir John French fully agreed, but owing to the exigencies of the moment, in place of rest the Corps was directed to extend its already thinly held line and to take in the village of Givenchy, that hotbed of trouble.

From this it is evident that Sir James Willcocks did not consider the moment to be favourable for an attack by the Indian Corps, which, as he had reported, was not in a condition to take the offensive.

However, it was of course necessary to obey, and the operations of which the story is now to be given were the result.

That Sir John French approved of the work performed on the 18th is shown by the orders received at 7 p.m. on the 19th December :—

"The operations undertaken yesterday were attended in several cases with marked success. Although the ground gained has not in all cases been maintained, the balance of advantage rests with us and promises well for further progress.

"The 2nd, 3rd, 4th, and Indian Corps should continue until further orders to prosecute similar enterprises under Corps arrangements, taking every possible measure to consolidate and extend all successes achieved."

Moreover, at midday on the 18th December, an order was received from Sir John French to this effect—"The efforts of the 3rd, 4th, and Indian Corps should be concentrated only on such objectives as are reasonably favourable."

It was subsequent to this order that Sir John French, by his approval of Sir James Willcocks' action, stamped it as reasonable.

At this juncture the Indian Corps was disposed as follows :—

The Meerut Division, under Lt-General C. A. Anderson, held the left half of the defensive line, the Garhwal Brigade occupying the section from the cross-roads south of Neuve Chapelle to the cross-roads on the Rue du Bois.

Thence the Dehra Dun Brigade continued through the "Orchard," north-east of the cross-roads at La Quinque Rue, to the cross-roads half a mile south, near which point, on the extreme right of the Brigade, was the "Picquet House," held by the 1st Seaforths.

Hence the Lahore Division, under Lt-General H. B. Watkis, continued the line with the newly arrived Sirhind Brigade, running, with an indentation on the west, more or less parallel to the Festubert road, to near the north-east exit of the village of Givenchy.

The left of the Ferozepore Brigade lay just east of the eastern extremity of Givenchy, and continued south to the La Bassée Canal. Further south, across the Canal and slightly to the front of Givenchy, were the 1st Connaughts. The point of junction between the Lahore Division and the French was on the Béthune—La Bassée road.

On the left, it was intended that the Meerut Division should take by surprise the portion of the German line opposite the left of the Dehra Dun Brigade, *i.e.* near the "Orchard," during the night of the 18th–19th, and consolidate the captured position. This attack was to be carried out by one and a half battalions of the Garhwal Brigade, which joined with the left of the Dehra Dun Brigade, and was to be supported by artillery fire, by activity in other parts of the Divisional line, and further, by an attack in the neighbourhood of the "Orchard" by the Dehra Dun Brigade, in the event of the effort of the Garhwal Brigade being successful.

On the right, the Lahore Division was to attack

the enemy's trenches opposite the point of junction of the Sirhind and Ferozepore Brigades, on a front of 300 yards. This attack was to be undertaken by one battalion from each Brigade, supported by Sappers and Pioneers to consolidate the ground gained.

The assault was to be preceded by a short but heavy artillery preparation, the 47th Sikhs from the Corps reserve being attached to the Lahore Division, with a view to following up any success which might result.

To simplify the account of the operations, it is as well to divide the action into three phases.

1. Operations under the orders of Sir James Willcocks.

2. The enemy's counter-attack.

3. Operations of the 1st Division, 1st Corps, under Sir Douglas Haig.

The orders were clear enough as regards the first phase, but the action which followed as a result of the German counter-attack was both obscure and complicated.

The night of the 18th–19th December was stormy, with a high cold wind, and rain which chilled the men to the bone, so the order to move silently out in front of our trenches was a welcome break in the dreariness of waiting under such conditions.

At 3.15 a.m. on the 19th December, the 2nd Leicesters, under Lt-Colonel Blackader, crept out with scarcely a sound until they had cleared the front of our trenches, and at 3.30 a.m. advanced with two companies in the front line and two in support, each accompanied by a bombing party. The left company under Captain Romilly had barely moved twenty yards when a machine gun opened on them from the right, but they pressed on, men beginning to fall, until a few yards further on they were stopped by a hedge with a ditch in front of it protected by barbed wire. This held them up for a few minutes, but they eventually got through, only to find themselves harassed by a second machine gun.

With the dash which has distinguished this splendid regiment throughout the campaign, they rushed the trench with the machine guns playing on them. The guns were captured, but the enemy had fled while our men were climbing over the parapet. Captain Romilly came to the conclusion that there must be another trench close in rear, and got his company out for a second advance. Machine guns immediately opened on him from both flanks. He at once charged, but arrived in the ditch from which the left gun had been firing only to find it gone.

As the men were reforming to attack the other gun, our own shells began to burst over them. Thinking he had got too far on, Captain Romilly retired to the first trench, where he found the supporting company. As dawn was breaking, the trench was consolidated, and Captain Romilly held on where he was.

The company of the Leicesters on the right lost direction and missed the first German trench, but rushed on under heavy machine-gun and rifle fire and took about one hundred yards of the next trench. With the bombing party in front, they advanced along the position, and found themselves nearing one of the main trenches whence heavy fire was opened, which quickly put seven of the eight bombers out of action.

At the same time the company was so heavily enfiladed that it became necessary to erect a barricade, which was effected under a galling fire and incessant bombing.

In the meantime, two double companies of the 2/3rd Gurkhas, under Major Young, with Major W. L. Dundas, had been working in support of the Leicesters. The party under Major Dundas followed up the rear company of the Leicesters until a gap occurred on the right, which the Gurkhas, rushing across the open ground, quickly filled up. Having joined hands with the party of Leicesters which had become detached, Major Dundas tried to extend along the trench to his left, to link up with the rest of the Leicesters, but found that this section was still held by the Germans, whom he at once attacked, and drove them with some loss out of the nearest portion. He then tried to get along the German communication trench, but found that it had not been completed. Not to be denied, he tried again to advance along the main trench, but was at once met by enfilade fire, at a range of about ninety yards, which caused heavy casualties, Major Dundas himself being slightly wounded. He quickly improved a traverse into a barricade with sandbags, and thus to a certain extent kept off the enfilading fire. The bombing party was sent for to clear the enemy out, but was found to have gone on with another detachment.

As soon as it was light enough Colonel Blackader set the company of the 107th Pioneers to work to convert the communication into a fire trench. The captured trench on the right was found to be commanded and enfiladed by the enemy's main trench. Being narrow and without traverses, it was very difficult to work in it.

Shortly afterwards, the enemy began to bomb this trench, and, pushing up a machine gun, blew the barricade down. Our small party was steadily pushed back until it only held some thirty yards of the trench. At this point Captain Bamberger, R.E., was killed while directing with the utmost coolness the building of a new barricade. Two machine guns now began to enfilade the communication trench, and the parapet had to be rebuilt again and again. As fast as it was put up, the stream of bullets brought it down.

It now became evident to Major Dundas that he could not push on further to his left, and at that moment the platoons of the Leicesters who were with him received orders to rejoin their company. This so weakened his small party that he was forced to retire, taking with him his casualties, which amounted to 26 out of the 55 men engaged.

The Leicesters, although heavily bombed and suffering under enfilade fire, clung throughout the day to the three hundred yards of trench which they had captured.

The enemy, having failed to turn our men out by fair means, attempted one of the many ruses peculiar to the children of "Kultur." A party of Germans advanced up a communication trench with their hands up in token of surrender. As they got nearer, we discovered that behind them were machine guns ready to fire on any of our men who might show themselves. This enterprising party met with a suitable reception.

At about 10 a.m. aviators and artillery observers

reported that the enemy was massing in considerable strength to the south of the "Orchard" and east of La Quinque Rue, evidently with the intention of making a formidable counter-attack. The 41st Dogras were at once ordered up from the Divisional reserve to support the line near the captured position.

It soon became clear that unless pressure was brought to bear upon the enemy, the Leicesters would be unable to hold out in the trench which they had taken so gallantly. An attack by the Dehra Dun Brigade was accordingly ordered to take place from the front held by the 6th Jats and 2/2nd Gurkhas. The enemy, however, anticipated this move, and from shortly after noon the "Orchard" was deluged with heavy trench-mortar bombs.

The first intimation of the enemy's intentions was received when two monstrous bombs dropped, and the shattered bodies of several Gurkhas were hurled high into the air amidst the debris of the parapet. These were closely followed by about twenty more bombs. A number of men were killed and wounded, and the eastern face of the position was completely obliterated, the south face also being badly knocked about. The Gurkhas were very severely handled, and, in view of the evident strength of the German counter-attack, it became necessary to retire to a new line slightly in rear.

This unfortunately rendered it imperative to abandon the proposed attack and to withdraw the Leicesters from their exposed position. The retirement was successfully carried out after dark without a single casualty, but the evacuation of the "Orchard" caused a dent in the front of the Dehra

Dun Brigade which could not be filled up during the current operations.

The enemy, unaware that the trench had been evacuated by the Leicesters, wasted much good ammunition on it in a bombardment which lasted throughout the next day.

The right of the 6th Jats, who were on the left of the Gurkhas, was now completely in the air, but Captain Ross at once set to work, and under a heavy fire succeeded in consolidating a new right flank, and effectually barred the German advance, if any such movement was really intended at the time, which seems doubtful. The arrival of the 1/9th Gurkhas, under Lt-Colonel G. Widdicombe, shortly afterwards rendered the position reasonably secure.

So ended the first phase of the attack by the Meerut Division, a marked feature of which was the gallantry of the detachment of the 2nd Leicesters, a quality of which this splendid regiment has throughout shown itself to be possessed in the highest degree. The 2/3rd Gurkhas also distinguished themselves by the tenacity with which they held on to the captured trench.

The Corps Commander showed his appreciation by the following message to the Division :—

"I congratulate you on the good work done last night, which shows what can be done by enterprise and care. Please send my hearty congratulations to Major-General Keary, the Leicesters, and the 2/3rd Gurkhas, for their gallant behaviour."

The casualties were comparatively small, owing to the skill with which the operation was planned and carried out.

Killed: Captain Bamberger, R.E.

2nd Leicesters:—Wounded: Major Knatchbull, D.S.O., Lieutenant J. E. Harris, and 44 men. Missing: Lieutenant H. A. Tooley and 6 men.

2/3rd Gurkhas:—Wounded: Major Dundas and 16 men. Missing: 10 men.

CHAPTER XII

THE BATTLE OF GIVENCHY: THE LAHORE DIVISION

Attack by Highland Light Infantry and 4th Gurkhas—Simultaneous attack by 59th Rifles—Enemy's trench taken—Captain Cramer-Roberts, 4th Gurkhas—Gallantry of Sappers and Miners and 34th Pioneers—Retirement of Highland Light Infantry and Gurkhas—Difficulties of 59th Rifles over unknown ground at night—Trench taken and held—Net result of attack—Casualties—Minor attack by 1st Gurkhas—German attack on 20th December—Highland Light Infantry and 4th Gurkhas—Rifles jamming as usual—Our trenches evacuated—Casualties.

We must now turn to the operations of the Lahore Division, under Lt-General Watkis.

The objective was the main line of German trenches in front and to the north-east of Givenchy. The left section of the attack was entrusted to two companies each of the 1st Battalion Highland Light Infantry and 1st Battalion 4th Gurkha Rifles, both belonging to the Sirhind Brigade lately arrived from Egypt. The whole operation was under the command of Lt-Colonel R. W. H. Ronaldson, Highland Light Infantry.

The right section of the attack was to be delivered by the 59th Scinde Rifles of the Jullundur Brigade, specially lent for the purpose, simultaneously with the left.

The left section was divided into four lines—the first under Major B. U. Nicolay, 1/4th Gurkhas, with whom was Lieutenant Anderson, Highland Light Infantry; the second under Captain Pringle,

Highland Light Infantry. Major Brodhurst, of the Gurkhas, who was seriously ill, but with characteristic courage had begged to be allowed to join in, accompanied Captain Pringle, and was of great service. The third line was commanded by Captain Cramer-Roberts, 1/4th Gurkhas, with Lieutenant Kerr, Highland Light Infantry; the fourth being under Captain G. M. Knight, Highland Light Infantry.

Captain Inglis, Adjutant of the 1/4th Gurkhas, was detailed to guide the attacking force to its correct position during the night, a difficult duty which he performed admirably. He then volunteered to accompany the assault, in the course of which he was unfortunately killed.

At 5.30 a.m., the 18th Brigade Royal Field Artillery and one section 57th Howitzer Battery opened a rapid and most accurate fire for the brief space of four minutes, during which time, in pouring rain and inky darkness, the first line went over the parapet. As soon as the bombardment ceased, they rushed over the open, a distance of about 180 yards, followed shortly afterwards by the second line. The advance was at first completely successful, and the casualties in the rush were small, but later events tended to show that the enemy had been put thoroughly on the alert by the earlier attack of the Meerut Division and the subsequent bombardment.

Owing to the German system of holding the front trenches lightly, the enemy's losses here were small. About 80 prisoners were taken, and some dead and wounded were found in the trench; others were discovered in the open, evidently caught by our shrapnel.

Any further advance was stopped by heavy fighting on the right of the 59th, who were hampered by the difficulties inseparable from night operations over totally unknown ground.

Major Nicolay at once set about consolidating the position. As the light improved, it was found to consist of about 200 yards of trench, in which was included a sap running out from the centre towards the British line. The trench was narrow and had very few traverses.

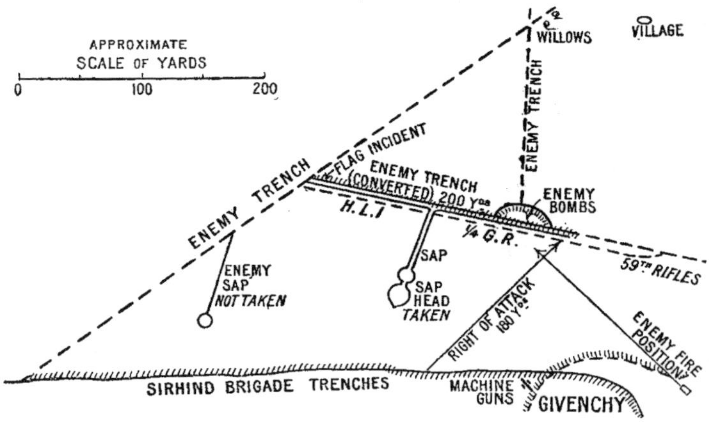

By this time the third line, under Captain Cramer-Roberts, had arrived on the scene. Shortly afterwards Lieutenant Kerr and most of his platoon were killed by machine-gun fire. The trench was already crammed with the 1st and 2nd lines, and there was no room for the 3rd line, which had to lie down in the mud in rear of the trench, where they were not only useless, but exposed to fire which soon caused a number of casualties. They were therefore sent back, but Captain Cramer-Roberts remained with Major Nicolay.

In the meantime our Sappers and Miners were hard at work, under Captain Hunt, 34th Pioneers, at the dangerous task of trying to connect the saphead by a shallow communication trench with our original line; but the enemy's fire swept them away, and all were killed. Needless to remark, with their usual bravery, the Sappers renewed the attempt again and again.

The German fire now increased and took us from both flanks and front, and when daylight broke fully, Colonel Ronaldson was in great uncertainty as to the real situation, since it was found impossible to connect the German sap with our line of entrenchment. His only information from the front line consisted of a report, brought back at great risk by Major Brodhurst, to the effect that the trench was over-crowded. About 9 a.m. Major Nicolay received a message which led him to believe that his men were suffering from the fire of our own main trenches. Communication had not been established, and the fire was so heavy that it seemed impossible to get a message through.

At about 10 a.m. Captain Inglis was killed. An eye-witness gives a stirring picture of this gallant officer, who met his death through his keenness in volunteering to accompany the attack. Captain Inglis had seized hold of a German rifle and bayonet, and was firing away in the full joy of battle, when he fell, shot through the head. At first it was feared that he had been shot by accident from the rear, but this idea was afterwards disproved.

Captain Cramer-Roberts set to work to explore the sap running in the direction of our main trench, and found that the Germans were working in towards it. Our men were being driven in by bombing from both flanks and the sap was becoming overcrowded.

The truth of the position, as later discovered, was that on the right of the trench taken by us, and running at right angles towards our main trench, there was a bank. From behind this the Germans were throwing bombs from a position which had been overlooked in the darkness of the advance, and were taking our men in rear with rifle fire. It was from this direction that Captain Inglis was shot, and there is no doubt that the bullet came from a German rifle. Captain Inglis is described by Major Nicolay as a very gallant officer, whose assistance and example had been invaluable.

At this moment the enemy tried another discreditable trick. A party of Germans carrying a dirty-looking flag appeared in front of the Highland Light Infantry section on the left, from which firing had practically ceased, partly owing to the number of casualties and partly because the majority of the rifles had become clogged with mud. Rapid fire was opened from the other sections of the trench, which was the signal for the enemy to put on Balaclava caps evidently taken from our dead; by this means apparently they hoped to deceive us into believing that they were British. Fire was continued, and some of the enemy were knocked over. The remainder disappeared after capturing the few men of the Highland Light Infantry who were still alive in that section.

It was now evident that something must be done to re-establish communication with the main trench. To attempt to cross the bullet-stricken, shell-tormented interval was to court death, but Captain Cramer-Roberts, knowing the vital necessity, determined, whatever the risk, to make the attempt. No advantage was to be gained by waiting for a lull, for there were no lulls.

Nearly two hundred yards of open ground which was swept by hissing bullets and churned up by heavy bombs had to be crossed. Captain Cramer-Roberts started, alternately running and crawling, followed by the Subadar-Major of the 59th Rifles. All went well for a short time, both officers seeming to possess charmed lives, but when nearly halfway across, the Indian officer, of whose presence Captain Roberts was unaware, was badly hit and could go no further. Captain Roberts, however, got on unharmed until, just as he was nearing our parapet and a few feet more would have put him in safety, he was severely wounded in three places by machine-gun fire, and was hauled into the trench, more dead than alive, by the Highland Light Infantry. Before he collapsed he was able to give Colonel Ronaldson news of what was taking place in front. For his great devotion and gallantry Captain Cramer-Roberts received the D.S.O.

Meanwhile the men of the 20th Company Sappers and Miners under Major Gardiner, R.E., and the 34th Pioneers were continuing their efforts to connect our trench with the saphead, but little progress could be made, owing to the proximity of the enemy's fire trench and the want of sand-bags.

The position in the front line was rapidly becoming hopeless. As the day wore on, Major Nicolay discovered that the enemy had a fire position in his right rear, on high ground in front of Givenchy village, from which his line was enfiladed. By the early afternoon he had only about eighty effectives left, and had been driven by rifle fire and bombs out of the trench into the sap.

By a lucky chance at this moment, having long since exhausted his own supply, he found three German bombs. He explained their use to his bombing party, who immediately threw them with great effect, and the enemy's bombing ceased abruptly. Had it not been for this lucky find, we could not have held out much longer.

As dusk came on, finding that there were no signs of the completion of the connecting trench, and as many of the wounded men were in great need of treatment, Major Nicolay was forced to decide on evacuating the position which he had held so long and so gallantly, before the enemy, under cover of darkness, could make a determined effort to capture his party. The retirement was carried out with the utmost steadiness between 4.30 and 5 p.m., the unwounded helping the wounded across the open.

Thus ended an anxious day, during which all ranks had done their duty nobly. They failed, but they failed splendidly.

The casualties were heavy. The Highland Light Infantry lost Lieutenant Kerr killed, Captain Pringle and Lieutenant Anderson missing. In the 1/4th Gurkhas Captain Inglis was killed, Captain Cramer-Roberts severely wounded. Owing to the continuous fighting during this period, it was impossible to ascertain the casualties of each day amongst the rank and file.

In the meantime the 59th Rifles had been going through a very trying experience.

The original intention was that the left of the Ferozepore Brigade should co-operate with the right of Sirhind, the 129th Baluchis being detailed for this purpose, as the position to be assaulted lay in front of their trench and they knew the ground well, having attacked over it so recently as the 16th December. The 129th had, however, on that occasion lost heavily and were not in a condition to take part in any immediate attack.

The 59th Rifles of the Jullundur Brigade were therefore placed at the disposal of Ferozepore. The Battalion suffered under the very serious handicap of having had no opportunity of reconnoitring the ground, and they had to take up their position for attack in the dark.

The 59th moved up into the trenches of the 129th Baluchis, and as soon as our four minutes' bombardment ceased, No. 1 Company under Captain J. D. Scale, and No. 4 under Captain B. E. Anderson, climbed out and advanced. One platoon of No. 1 Company, under Jemadar Mangal Singh of the 52nd Sikhs, was ordered to take the German sap on the right, which they accomplished with a rush. They continued to hold this sap against every effort of the enemy, for 18 hours, until the Sappers and Miners, coming to the rescue as usual, managed to dig through, and thus enabled a party of the 129th Baluchis to relieve them.

Meanwhile Jemadar Mangal Singh's party, in spite of heavy losses, had killed a number of Germans and captured a wounded officer. For his gallantry the Jemadar received the Indian Distinguished Service Medal.

The confusion in the pitch darkness was indescribable. One company, on getting out of our trench, was unable to find the sap which was their objective. Even the real direction of the German trenches was uncertain. As an officer tersely put it, " they advanced towards the German fire," which led them to a trench in which they found British soldiers, Gurkhas and Germans hopelessly mixed up.

The confusion was rendered even worse by the fact that the German regiments in front of the 59th had very similar numbers, and when officers of the 59th tried to collect their men, the enemy frequently answered.

Captain Anderson's party got up to a trench, and in order to avoid a possible fight with our own men, he asked the occupants who they were. They replied, " Highland Light Infantry and Gurkhas," and promptly opened fire. Captain Anderson then saw by their bayonets that they were Germans, so he and his men went at them, on which they at once ran, and Captain Anderson occupied the trench. A support of another regiment now came up, and with the greatest difficulty they were persuaded not to attack our men with the bayonet, thinking them to be the enemy.

Germans were continually being pulled out of dug-outs and made prisoners, which only added to the confusion. An officer relates that almost every other officer who met him put a revolver to his head and threatened to blow his German brains out.

Meanwhile Lieutenant W. Bruce with a platoon had lost direction, but eventually got into the trench further to the left. As he drew near, the enemy put up their hands and called out that they would surrender. As soon, however, as our men put their heads over the parapet they were shot. Lieutenant Bruce jumped into the trench and was immediately killed. Captain Anderson was carrying a rifle and was hit by a bullet on the revolver in his belt, at close range. He was completely knocked out, but soon returned to the fight. Lieutenant Atkinson was killed actually lying on the German parapet and firing with the utmost coolness into the trench.

Havildar Dost Mahomed took command after Lieutenant Bruce's death, chased the enemy out and held on all day, a large number of dead Germans being eventually found in front of his position.

Here, too, as was the case everywhere on this occasion, the rifles jammed and our fire waned.

Finally, the enemy brought up a trench mortar, and after a number of his men had been killed, Dost Mahomed ordered the survivors to retire. This they absolutely refused to do, for their Sahib, Lieutenant Bruce, they said, had ordered them to hold out to the end.

Faithful to their dead British officer, the proudest tribute any man could wish, they fought on until all but Dost Mahomed and a wounded man had been killed. The two survivors then crawled out and eventually got back, guided by the bursting of German shells, to our trench, where, in the darkness, they were promptly fired on, but on their shouting that they were "men from India," they were let in.

For his bravery and devotion Havildar Dost Mahomed received the Indian Order of Merit.

A portion of the two companies in support in our main trench now pushed up into the left sap, under Captains Lee and Gilchrist, with whom went Lieutenant Kisch, R.E., always to be found where the fight was thickest. The two former were shortly afterwards hit through the head, and Captain Anderson met Lieutenant Scobie in the midst of the turmoil, making attempts to get the two officers away under a heavy fire from three sides, while Havildar Abdul Wahab with a few men was pluckily holding the head of the trench close up to the Germans. This non-commissioned officer distinguished himself throughout the action, and was awarded the Indian Order of Merit, 2nd Class, receiving later the Russian Medal of St George, 2nd Class.

Cool as ever, Lieutenant Kisch was sketching the plan of a barricade which he proposed to erect. Captain Lee was dead; Captain Gilchrist was brought back by Lieutenant Scobie behind our barricade, but died very shortly afterwards. It could be seen that the Germans were in strong force, for their heads were silhouetted against the dawn at about two feet interval along the parapet, over which they were keeping up rapid fire. Most of our rifles had by this time jammed with the mud, and were being passed back and others passed up in their place. Lieutenant Scobie's example was invaluable at such a time, and he well earned the Military Cross which he received.

There were many instances of individual gallantry. Numbers of wounded men were brought in under a murderous fire, but the turmoil and darkness prevented the rescuers from being identified.

By this time the shallow communication trench was blocked with dead and wounded, and with the dawn it became evident that, as no bombs were available, the only thing left to do was to make a "block" in the communication trench and hold the small portion of the front trench which we had captured. This "block" was made as quickly as possible, under heavy fire, by Lieutenant Kisch, and a short description will serve to show the kind of work which our Sappers were continually called on to carry out under most dangerous circumstances.

The first step was to make a temporary block at the most forward point held by us. This consisted of sandbags or anything which would afford some shelter to those working on the real block further back. Behind this advanced block the zigzags of the trench were straightened out for a distance of at least 25 yards—40 yards, if possible—so as to give immunity against hand-bombing. The object of straightening the trench was to give our men a clear field of fire from behind the main block. At the near end of the straight portion, a substantial barricade of sandbags was made, in which was fitted a steel loophole taken from a German trench. The straight portion of the trench was then cleared of dead and wounded, and a double sentry posted behind the loopholed main barricade. The term and system "double block" were, it is believed, invented by Captain B. C. Battye, R.E., and have since been generally adopted.

The rest of the day was spent in consolidating the captured trench and getting ready for the probable counter-stroke. In the evening, the enemy made an attack for the purposes of reconnaissance, which was repulsed, and after dark the 59th were relieved.

So ended the assault delivered by the 59th. It was carried out most gallantly, but the Germans were in great strength, their wire was intact, and last, but not least, they had unlimited bombs, of which we possessed but few, and those of a very inferior type improvised in the field.

The net result was that one platoon succeeded in holding about 90 yards of the enemy's sap on the left, while another platoon on the right, with some of the 129th Baluchis, kept its grip on a sap in front of that battalion. With these exceptions, the night of the 19th December fell with all the ground lost which at bloody price we had gained during the day. The Brigades were holding their original line, except for the indentation at the "Orchard," where the 2nd Gurkhas, having been driven back, were occupying a retrenched line, previously prepared.

The losses of the 59th in this very gallant attack were heavy. Captains Lee and Gilchrist, Lieutenants Atkinson and Bruce, with 22 men, were killed; and Captain J. D. Scale and 85 other ranks wounded.

In co-operation with this attack, an assault on a German saphead on the left of the Sirhind Brigade by two platoons of the 1st Battalion 1st Gurkhas, under Captain Burke and Lieutenant Rundall, was timed for 5.30 a.m. Owing partly to the terrible condition of the trenches, an unfortunate delay occurred, and the attack was delivered in broad daylight, starting at 10 a.m.

Although under such circumstances the attempt was foredoomed to failure, the two officers led the assault with the greatest determination and dash. They were met by a deluge of machine-gun and rifle fire, but it was not until both British officers were killed that the attacking party recoiled, only a

[*Daily Mirror*.

INDIAN TROOPS IN THE TRENCHES: WINTER, 1914.

175.]

small remnant regaining our trenches. In addition to Captain Burke and Lieutenant Rundall, 24 men were killed or wounded, representing over 50 per cent. of the number engaged.

The night of the 19th–20th December passed without any marked incident, but with the first streak of dawn the enemy opened a heavy fire from artillery and trench mortars upon the whole front of the Indian Corps. This was followed up by infantry attacks in especial force against Givenchy and the line between Givenchy and La Quinque Rue.

The elements were warring on the side of the enemy, for torrential rain during the night had made the trenches almost untenable. In many places the fire-step had been washed away, and the men were consequently unable to stand high enough to fire over the parapet. The trenches were knee- and in some places even waist-deep in mud and icy water, which clogged a large number of rifles and rendered them useless.

At about 9 a.m. a series of ear-splitting explosions took place along the whole front of the Sirhind Brigade round the village of Givenchy, and it was evident that the enemy had succeeded in mining under the parapet from the numerous sap-heads along our front.

In the right sub-section were one company Highland Light Infantry and two double companies of the 1/4th Gurkhas. Of these, one double company of the Gurkhas and half a company of the Highland Light Infantry were either blown to bits or buried under the ruins of the trench. There were few survivors, but these included Lieutenant Barry, Highland Light Infantry, with Colour-Sergeant

Brisbane and a small party on the extreme right, who held out until overwhelmed and captured. Lieutenant Cowan and Captain Money, 1/1st Gurkhas, with a few men on the extreme left, missed the full force of the explosion, and continued to bomb the enemy until, when Captain Money had been killed, Lieutenant Cowan had to retreat into the Gurkha trench.

Private Black, Highland Light Infantry, stuck to his post and went on serving his trench mortar until the ammunition was exhausted, and when the retirement took place he refused to leave a wounded comrade until he had taken him to a place of safety. He received the Distinguished Conduct Medal for his bravery.

Immediately after the explosions, the enemy advanced in dense masses, but met with a stubborn resistance by the remaining double company of the 4th Gurkhas, who inflicted considerable loss. The rifles were jamming as usual, and in spite of all our men could do, the Germans gained a footing in the trench at several points, where ferocious hand-to-hand fighting took place, and the enemy had an opportunity of appreciating to the full the skill with which the Gurkhas can use their beloved kukris in a circumscribed space.

Our men were outnumbered and outbombed from the start. Our bombs, however gallantly and skilfully handled, were limited in number, and were no match for the scientifically devised German missiles. The greatest difficulty was experienced in getting them to light, and many failed to explode.

About this time Captain Rundall of the Gurkhas

was killed while leading a bombing party, after shooting two Germans with his revolver. The Gurkhas lost heavily, but left their mark deep in the enemy.

No amount of gallantry could prevail against such odds. The position was enfiladed, and the few remaining rifles were rapidly being put out of action by the mud. To remain meant annihilation, without serving any useful purpose.

A retirement was ordered at 1 p.m., under Major Travers, who succeeded in getting the remains of No. 4 Double Company through Givenchy village, which was then being heavily shelled. The movement was most gallantly covered by the Gurkha machine guns, under Captain Wylie, and those manned by a party of the 125th Napier's Rifles; but in the midst of their devoted work another terrible explosion took place, and of this noble little band not a man returned.

The extent to which luck determines the incidents of war is illustrated by the fact that Captain Phayre, who was in charge of the Gurkha machine guns, was relieved by Captain Wylie only a few minutes before the mine was exploded. It was afterwards ascertained that by some freak of fortune Captain Wylie escaped death and was taken prisoner. Of E Company, under Captain Yates, not a trace has ever been found.

In the firing line of the left sub-section were one company Highland Light Infantry, under Major Murray, with two machine guns, and two double companies 1/1st Gurkhas with two machine guns, under Major Bliss, C.I.E. As in the case of the right section, frightful explosions took place, destroying several lengths of trench with their defenders. At the same time, it was reported, an aeroplane attacked the line.

The enemy advanced in swarms up their saps and across the open. It seemed that the majority of the Germans were armed with bombs. A large number were killed by rifle and machine-gun fire, but they still came on in waves and forced their way over the parapet, where their superiority in bombs at once told heavily in their favour. After a short but sanguinary fight the remains of the trenches passed into the hands of the enemy.

Of the Highland Light Infantry, Lieutenant Guthrie-Smith was blown up near the Picquet House; Major Murray and Captain Cameron with their men held on to the very last, and are all believed to have been killed. Lieutenant Pitts-Tucker made a desperate attempt to take reinforcements up to Captain Cameron, but he and all his party were mown down by machine-gun fire. Seeing their officer fall, Lance-Corporal Barr and Private Carmichael rushed out and managed to bring Lieutenant Pitts-Tucker back some way under a terrible fire, but he was killed by another bullet as they were carrying him. For their gallant conduct they received the Distinguished Conduct Medal.

Meantime Lieutenant Stewart, Highland Light Infantry, who was in the support trench with 80 men and two machine guns, barricaded himself in, and held out against all attacks, although he was practically isolated. A small reinforcement of 30 men succeeded in reaching him just before dark, and with this assistance Lieutenant Stewart fought on, with splendid pluck and tenacity, till relieved by the South Wales Borderers on the evening of the 21st December. His gallant conduct very materially helped to stay the further advance of the enemy, and gave us time to bring up fresh troops.

This achievement was the more noteworthy because the men of the Highland Light Infantry who were with him had been for over 72 hours in the trenches without a moment's rest. When relieved, they were utterly worn out, but still remained to bury Lieutenant Pitts-Tucker and many of our dead, and they brought away with them their two machine guns.

After sending the 30 men to Lieutenant Stewart, only 60 remained to hold the left of the reserve trenches in rear of him. Nevertheless, the position was retained by Colonel Ronaldson until the 3rd Brigade reached him on the afternoon of the 21st December. This was only rendered possible by the action of our artillery, which maintained an unceasing fire by night and day on the enemy's trenches, and thereby deceived them as to our strength in rear, and kept them from advancing.

Meanwhile the Gurkhas, under Major Bliss and Captain Kennedy, were putting up a very stubborn fight against heavy odds; and the enemy only succeeded in getting a footing at one spot, being driven back everywhere else. Captain Kennedy organized and led bombing parties, which prevented the enemy from emerging from his saps.

Major Bliss then headed a desperate bayonet charge and drove the Germans back some distance along their sap, but he lost his life in this gallant effort.

Captain Tarrant, Highland Light Infantry, now took command, and tried to establish communication with the Gurkha Head Quarters, but the telephone wires had been cut by shell fire, and all attempts to repair them failed.

It was then found that the Germans had managed to get into both flanks of the trench, and had bombed us out of two traverses near the centre, killing or wounding the whole of our bombing party in doing so, and destroying one of our machine guns. The other gun was still working, although its water jacket had been ripped open. It was therefore only a question of how many rounds it could fire before becoming overheated.

The position was now hopeless, and retirement was unavoidable. This movement was carried out in good order to the support trenches, where, however, there was no rest, for the enemy had bombed our men out of the left of the trench, and we had run out of bombs. A further retirement was therefore made to Festubert, under cover of a small rearguard, armed with the few serviceable rifles remaining.

This operation was carried out very steadily. The conduct of the troops was throughout admirable in the face of overpowering numbers and every conceivable disadvantage.

The trenches, owing to the thick and holding mud, became veritable death-traps. Only the slowest movement was possible; men had their boots, and even their clothes, pulled off by the mud. Most of the rifles jammed, and bombs gave out.

As soon as the retirement was fairly under way, our artillery opened a heavy fire on the trenches taken by the enemy, which prevented him from making any further advance, and in some places even forced him back.

The casualties on the 19th and 20th were very serious, as may be gathered from those of the 1/4th Gurkhas, who lost 302 of all ranks, including 7 British and 10 Gurkha officers. On the 20th December alone, the 1/1st Gurkhas lost 2 British officers killed and had over 200 casualties amongst the other ranks, including the Subadar-Major and three other Gurkha officers.

From the 19th to the 22nd, the 1st Highland Light Infantry had 2 officers and 55 men killed, 63 men wounded, and 8 officers and 276 men missing. Of the 8 officers returned as missing, all have since been ascertained to have been killed, as were also the great majority of the men.

Shortly afterwards, Sir John French inspected the battalion, and warmly congratulated it on having upheld the famous traditions of the regiment.

Colonel Ronaldson, who had shown marked qualities of leadership in a very difficult position, was awarded the C.B., while Lieutenant Stewart received the D.S.O. in appreciation of his gallant conduct.

CHAPTER XIII

GERMAN COUNTER-ATTACK

German attack on Givenchy—Sirhind Brigade lose trenches—Givenchy taken by the enemy—Counter-attack by 1st Manchesters—Counter-attack forced back—Heavy casualties—Arrival of 1st Brigade, 1st Division—Operations of the Secundrabad Cavalry Brigade under Brigadier-General Macbean—First attack unsuccessful—Second attack takes trenches, but forced to retire—Casualties—Causes of failure.

We must now turn to the rest of the Lahore Division front.

At 12.30 p.m. it was reported that the situation in the left section of the Sirhind Brigade was very serious, and that a counter-attack by at least a Brigade was necessary if the line was to be re-established. General Watkis was almost at the end of his resources in troops, having no reserves left except the 34th Pioneers and the 59th Rifles, which latter battalion had on the previous day suffered heavy losses. The Corps Commander therefore placed the Secundrabad Cavalry Brigade, under Brigadier-General F. W. Wadeson, and the 2/8th Gurkha Rifles at General Watkis' disposal, the whole being under the command of Major-General Macbean. To these General Watkis added the 47th Sikhs under Lt-Colonel Gunning.

Shortly after 1 p.m. on the 20th December, news was received that the left battalion of the Ferozepore Brigade, the 129th Baluchis, had fallen back, and that Givenchy was being heavily attacked. The retention of Givenchy was vitally necessary, as near this point the right of Lahore connected with the French left. General Carnegy, Commanding the Jullundur Brigade, was accordingly directed to turn his immediate attention to securing Givenchy and re-establishing the situation there. At the same time the General Officer Commanding the 10th French Army Corps placed two battalions at General Watkis' disposal. The 1st Manchesters and 4th Battalion Suffolks (Territorials), the latter of which had recently joined the Corps, were moved up to Pont Fixe on the La Bassée Canal near Cuinchy.

The main object was to get into touch with the Sirhind Brigade, and to counter-attack, as circumstances permitted, with a view to retaking our lost trenches. On arrival, General Carnegy found the position to be as follows :—

The Germans had occupied the whole of the Sirhind Brigade front, and the Brigade had fallen back to the Festubert road. The enemy had also occupied the left or northern part of the line held by the Ferozepore Brigade, while Givenchy village was itself in the hands of the Germans. East of Givenchy, the 57th Rifles with one company of the 9th Bhopals were still holding their position, while south of the La Bassée Canal the 1st Connaughts and 4th Suffolk Territorials had not moved.

The 1st Manchesters under Lt-Colonel Strickland, with one company 4th Suffolks, were ordered to attack Givenchy, and, pushing on through the village, to reoccupy the trenches vacated by the 129th Baluchis. The French Territorials on arrival were to retake the trenches formerly held by the right of the Sirhind Brigade.

The Manchesters began their attack shortly after 3 p.m., and found on reaching the village that it was held in unexpected strength by the enemy. Rough and tumble hand-to-hand fighting of the fiercest description took place, the Germans holding their position house by house, and they were not cleared out until it had become too dark to distinguish the features of the country, or to locate the position of the trenches which were the next objective. The further attack was therefore delayed until the following morning.

The desperate nature of the fighting can be gauged from the fact that only twelve prisoners were taken.

A curious incident marked the recapture of the village. Three of our Artillery observing officers had been cut off when the enemy took Givenchy, and had only escaped death or capture by hiding in a cellar. When our men entered, they emerged, none the worse for their exciting experience.

The village was held by us during the night, and another company of the Suffolks and French Territorials respectively was sent up to Colonel Strickland. Before dawn we made an attempt to locate the enemy's trenches, but were met by very heavy fire, and sustained severe losses.

At 6.30 a.m. on the 21st, Colonel Strickland launched his attack, but immediately came under fire from rifles and machine guns, which proved particularly deadly, as every movement of our men was clearly shown up by the blaze of two haystacks burning furiously behind us.

The Manchesters, however, are a regiment which takes a good deal of stopping, as the enemy to his cost has learnt on many occasions in this campaign. For over an hour they made desperate efforts to reach the German trenches, but against the torrent of bullets and shells little progress could be effected, and men were everywhere falling fast.

It was becoming evident that the attempt could not succeed, when at 11 a.m., after the village and our trenches had been vigorously shelled for 45 minutes, the enemy made a strong attack. The Manchesters held firm, and the assault was on the verge of being repulsed, when the French on the left were forced out of their position, leaving our flank in the air.

The enemy seized his advantage, and began to work round the Manchesters' left, which was compelled to retire through the village on to the road. At the same moment the Germans heavily attacked the centre and right. The situation appeared to be rapidly becoming untenable, and it was decided to retire the left supports to a position in rear, in order to cover the withdrawal of the centre and right.

The gallant Manchesters, a regiment of Ironsides, had, however, not yet shot their bolt. They held on so tenaciously that Colonel Strickland determined on a further attempt. By a splendid rush, the original trenches were reoccupied, the enemy being driven back on the left at about 2 p.m.; but this was our last expiring effort.

Soon after 3 p.m. the Germans delivered a sharp attack from the front, while large bodies appeared on the right flank and in rear. At the same moment machine guns opened on us, enfilading our line from the right.

There was now nothing for it but to retire; the casualties had been very heavy, and the men were utterly done. There were only three officers left with the companies, and in some companies there were hardly any non-commissioned officers.

The centre and right again held on with the utmost obstinacy, while the remainder, with whom were Colonel Strickland, the Adjutant, and a few non-commissioned officers, took up a position in rear, the firing line then falling back after a furious hand-to-hand fight on the road.

The retirement to Pont Fixe was conducted with the greatest steadiness, a quality for which, under all circumstances, this splendid regiment has always been known. Many wounded men were carried back under heavy shrapnel and machine-gun fire. By their wonderful staunchness the Manchesters had given time for reinforcements to be brought up, and the arrival of the Cameron Highlanders of the 1st Brigade, 1st British Division, righted the situation at this point.

The losses of the battalion were heavy. Captain Creagh, Lieutenant Norman, and 64 men were killed; Major Hitchins, Captain Rose, Lieutenant Lynch, and 123 men were wounded; while 46 men were missing. There was, however, the satisfaction of knowing that our mark had been left still more deeply on the enemy. Of this regiment it may be said once for all that none more devoted and none more valiant has passed in this war through the Valley of the Shadow of Death.

We must now hark back to the operations of

the force under Major-General Macbean, which consisted of the Secundrabad Cavalry Brigade (dismounted) under Brigadier-General Wadeson, to which were added the 47th Sikhs and the 2/8th Gurkhas.

At 2 p.m. General Macbean moved up from Marais to the 2nd line trenches to the north, in readiness to strike vigorously if opportunity offered. At 5 p.m. arrangements were made for a counter-attack by the 7th Dragoon Guards and 47th Sikhs under the command of Lt-Colonel Lemprière, D.S.O., of the 7th. These regiments came up to the right of the Sirhind Brigade and established touch with the left of Jullundur.

For various reasons, considerable delay occurred in launching the attack, and at 11.45 p.m. General Macbean was ordered to advance at once with all the troops at his disposal and to support Colonel Lemprière, if, as was expected, that officer had already started. Colonel Lemprière assaulted at 1 a.m. in two lines, the first consisting of A and D Squadrons 7th Dragoon Guards and half of the 47th Sikhs, the second line of C Squadron and the remainder of the 47th.

The attack moved steadily over the open ground, but met with heavy rifle and machine-gun fire, which caused a number of casualties. Both lines reached the support trenches about 600 yards east of Le Plantin, the 47th occupying an old communication trench on the left. The night was pitch dark, the ground in many places knee-deep in glue-like mud, and the whole country was intersected by trenches and ditches, which rendered it almost impossible to recognize the real objective. Colonel

Lemprière went forward with his Adjutant to locate the front line trench which he had to attack.

During this period the enemy was keeping up a heavy fire from the left, under which men were dropping fast. As Colonel Lemprière was returning, he was shot dead. Colonel Gunning, 47th Sikhs, then took command.

The prospects of a successful assault were hopeless. The position of the enemy's trench could only be inferred from the flash of rifles ; we were enfiladed by rifle and machine-gun fire from both flanks; while to add to the difficulties, our own guns were plastering our probable line of advance with their shells, in their endeavour to wreck the German trenches.

Captain A. C. Ross, of the 20th Deccan Horse, who had throughout distinguished himself by his gallant leading, went out under heavy fire, with Duffadars Sardar Singh and Shanka Rao of the same regiment, and at great risk managed to carry in Risaldar Amir Mahomed, who was badly wounded. For this signal act of bravery and devotion Captain Ross received the D.S.O., and the Duffadars the Indian Order of Merit, 2nd Class.

Risaldar Badan Singh, of the Poona Horse, was very prominent during the attack, in which he led his party with great dash, receiving the Indian Distinguished Service Medal.

Colonel Gunning, recognizing the futility of any further attempt, decided to retire on Festubert, which was reached at about 4 a.m., and the force awaited further orders.

General Macbean then directed a second effort to be made.

Just as the attack started, after a seven minutes bombardment, the Ambala Cavalry Brigade arrived, and orders were given for them to link up the line with the Jullundur Brigade, but in the darkness one unit lost its way, and the remainder of the Brigade was not collected until after the main attack had failed. The dawn was then approaching, and it was useless to send them in.

This second attack, under the command of Lt-Colonel Grant, 2/8th Gurkhas, started at about 5 a.m. on the 21st December, in two lines. In the first line from left to right were one squadron Poona Horse, 20th Deccan Horse, one squadron Poona Horse, half 2/8th Gurkhas, 47th Sikhs.

In the second line were one squadron Poona Horse, Jodhpur Lancers, half 2/8th Gurkhas, three squadrons 7th Dragoon Guards. The rain was coming down in torrents. In the inky darkness it was impossible to keep any sense of direction, and the front line first went off too much to the left and then too much to the right.

The Germans kept up a moderately heavy fire from the front, but the machine guns on both flanks never gave us a moment's rest. The ground was pitted with shell holes full of water, into which officers and men were continually falling, and was cut up by ditches and the remains of old trenches. Seldom has an assault been launched under more unfavourable circumstances.

On reaching the support trenches, a cheer was raised; the whole line charged the fire trench, which was occupied without much trouble, and as soon as things were sorted out, patrols were sent down the flanks to ascertain the position of the enemy. The right patrol speedily reported the trench to be held by Germans, who met them with a vigorous machine-gun fire.

During the advance, D Squadron 7th Dragoon Guards, under Captain Mansel, became detached, and, attempting to charge machine guns on the left, lost heavily. Shortly afterwards Major Edwards, 2/8th Gurkhas, reported that 500 yards of the trench on the left were unoccupied, for the simple reason that it was so full of water as to be untenable, two of his Gurkhas having already been drowned in it, and that it was enfiladed by machine guns from both flanks.

Captain Padday, 47th Sikhs, with a bombing party of his regiment, then made a gallant attempt to clear the enemy out, but the machine guns were merciless, and many of the party were killed, including their brave leader.

Day was now breaking; the position was untenable. To remain spelt certain disaster. A retirement of the whole line to Festubert was ordered, which was effected under a searching fire, the troops only reaching the village after daylight.

The casualties during this gallant but fruitless attack were as follows:—

The 7th Dragoon Guards lost their Commanding Officer, Lt-Colonel Lemprière, D.S.O., and Captain Mansel; Lieutenant Mann and 2nd Lieutenant Bryce were wounded and missing; their total casualties being 43.

In the Poona Horse, Major Loring, 37th Lancers, who was attached, was killed, adding one more to the sacrifices which this soldier-family has made in the war; Captain Grimshaw and 2 Indian officers were wounded; the total being 49.

The 20th Deccan Horse had Major Tennant, Captain Jarvis, and Lieutenant Tinley wounded; Captains McEuen and Mackenzie missing; with a total casualty list of 81.

The 2/8th Gurkhas lost one Gurkha officer killed, with 22 casualties in other ranks.

In the 47th Sikhs, Captain Padday and 7 men were killed; Major Van Someren and Captain Brown wounded; while 120 of other ranks were wounded or missing.

The Jodhpur Lancers had 11 casualties.

Amongst the causes which militated against the success of this attack, the following are noteworthy:—

1. The troops employed (except the 2/8th Gurkhas) had no knowledge of the ground.

2. The weakness of the force and the length of front of the objective, about one mile, precluded an attack in sufficient depth to push home and remain there.

3. The extreme difficulty of attacking by night over water-logged ground, cut up by channels and trenches.

4. Insufficient artillery support, due to want of ammunition.

For his services on this occasion Brigadier-General Wadeson received the C.B.

CHAPTER XIV

GERMAN COUNTER-ATTACK—*Continued*

The "Orchard"—Attack on 2nd Seaforths—Loss of trenches by 2nd Gurkhas—Gallantry of Seaforths—1st Division, 1st Corps brought up to relieve pressure—Givenchy retaken by 1st Brigade—Seaforths and 58th Rifles relieved—Heavy casualties—Indian Corps relieved—Sir Douglas Haig takes over command of the line—Successful stand of 57th Rifles—Appreciation of Indian Corps by Sir John French in despatches.

IN the meantime the neighbourhood of the "Orchard" had been the scene of heavy fighting.

On the night of the 19th, the attack contemplated by the Dehra Dun Brigade had perforce to be abandoned, and the 2/2nd Gurkhas were compelled to retire to a retrenched position slightly to the west. By this retirement the left flank of the 1st Seaforths, under Lt-Colonel Ritchie, who were on the extreme right of the Meerut Division, was much exposed.

At about 9 a.m. on the 20th, there were heavy attacks on the Seaforths and Gurkhas, and about the same time the right of the Seaforths and the left of the Sirhind Brigade were for the moment separated by the explosion of the enemy's mines.

The first portion of the Seaforths to be attacked was B Company, which was having a frugal breakfast when the onslaught began. Taken by surprise, the Company made two determined stands and killed about fifty Germans before they lost the trench.

The enemy rushed down the fire trench, hiding their advance under smoke balls, and bombing as they came. At the same time they bombed from the saphead, while snipers were picking off our men from the Festubert road.

Captain the Hon. C. St Clair, who was in command of B Company, lined the communication trench, but was at once shot dead.

Meanwhile the 2nd Gurkhas had been faring badly. At about 9 a.m. there was a terrific explosion, which shook the whole neighbourhood. The Germans had evidently exploded a mine under the parapet of the "Orchard." This was followed for a few minutes by a perfect tornado of shrapnel, high-explosive and machine-gun fire, the crescendo ending in a rush by the enemy from his trenches into our position.

Captain Bethell with No. 1 Company was in the right trench, but immediately got out of it into a trench in rear, in order to avoid being overwhelmed by numbers. Here, as usual where danger was, the Sapper was found in the person of Lieutenant Bird, R.E., with a small party. The second trench was too deep to hold, and Captain Bethell with about half of his men got out of it into a communication trench known as "the Strand." The remainder were overpowered, and the survivors captured by the enemy, who were pressing on in ever-increasing numbers.

In "the Strand" Major Boileau was met, and a small rearguard action was fought until a third trench was found, in which a final position was taken up by Majors Boileau and Watt, while Lieutenant Bird managed to get through to the Seaforth trenches to see if he could help there. The attack was stayed at this point, but a considerable portion of the trenches had been lost.

At this juncture the 58th Rifles came up in support of the Seaforths' left, and filled the gap caused by the retirement of the Gurkhas. At the same moment the 1/9th Gurkhas under Lt-Colonel Widdicombe reported their arrival as further supports, and half of them were sent up to Major Boileau, the rest remaining with the 6th Jats on the left.

The senior officer on the spot was now Lt-Colonel Roche, of the 6th Jats, who at once set to work to retrieve, as best he could, a desperate situation, and with the aid of reinforcements which streamed up during the 20th and 21st, in the shape of the Black Watch, 4th Seaforths (Territorials), 41st Dogras and 30th Lancers, he succeeded in establishing a fairly formidable hedge of steel facing the captured trenches.

For his distinguished services during this battle and on other occasions, especially at the action of Festubert, Lt-Colonel Roche was created a Companion of the Bath.

Meantime the enemy had been busy with "hair-brush" bombs, and had driven the Seaforths out of about 100 yards of trench as far as "Piccadilly," wounding Lieutenant Baker and a number of men in the process. Here, however, they were held up until a fresh supply of bombs reached the Seaforths.

At this moment about forty Germans appeared in rear. Captain Laing promptly went for them with a bombing party and succeeded after a grim struggle, in clearing them out and retaking ten traverses in the Gurkha trench, where he built a barricade and held on. In this trench alone, 22 dead Germans were counted, while our small party had 13 casualties.

In the evening the Seaforths, worthy comrades of the Manchesters and the Black Watch, were heartened by messages of congratulation from the Brigade and Divisional Commanders on the splendid behaviour of the battalion under such trying circumstances.

By 6 p.m. the 58th Rifles were supporting the Seaforths on their left, as well as in their fire and support trenches. It was again the old tale, however—shortage of bombs against an enemy abundantly supplied with them.

Nevertheless, heavily attacked as they were by fire and bombs, their trenches battered to bits, the Dehra Dun Brigade kept their front intact and maintained connection with the 6th Jats on their left. Major Wauchope, commanding half the Black Watch on the Seaforths' right, succeeded in establishing communication with that battalion during the afternoon, and before midnight with the Sirhind Brigade on his right. A continuous line thus existed throughout the Meerut Division front, although it was badly indented at the "Orchard."

The Indian Corps, which, at the end of October, had in the nick of time come to the relief of the 2nd Corps under General Smith-Dorrien, had now for two terrible months held with indomitable tenacity and never-failing courage the long line which had fallen to its share. During this period it had been constantly subjected to shell fire of a type quite novel to it. It had been assailed by a ferocious enemy by day and by night, with weapons such as bombs and hand grenades, with which our troops were not then provided. The weather conditions had been terrible enough to damp the courage of the stoutest heart. As a final test, the Corps had now for over thirty hours of most sanguinary fighting been confronted by an ever-increasing concentration of the enemy.

The men were rapidly becoming worn out, and it was evident that the situation could only be restored, and the future safe-guarded, by an immediate and substantial reinforcement. The 1st Army Corps, under Sir Douglas Haig, was in Army reserve and available for this purpose.

During the night of the 20th–21st December, the 1st Division, 1st Corps, under General Haking, arrived on the scene. The 1st Brigade, after a short rest, moved on Givenchy. The 2nd Brigade was sent to support the Dehra Dun Brigade, while the 3rd Brigade advanced on the trenches evacuated by the Sirhind Brigade.

A detailed account of the operations of the 1st British Division does not come within the scope of this history, but a brief sketch is necessary for a proper understanding of the operations as a whole.

The attack of the 1st Brigade on Givenchy, so lately the scene of the gallant exploits of the 1st Manchesters, and the assault of the 3rd Brigade on the Sirhind trenches commenced about 3 p.m. on the 21st December. The 1st Brigade succeeded in consolidating their position round Givenchy and on the left of the Ferozepore Brigade, but were unable to keep touch with the attack of the 3rd Brigade on their left. The 3rd Brigade advanced through a line held by detachments of Sirhind, Bareilly, and

Jullundur, as well as by the Secundrabad and Ambala Brigades.

By nightfall, however, the Brigade had not succeeded in reaching the Sirhind trenches, nor had it established permanent connection with the right of the Meerut Division, to which we must now return.

At about 3 a.m. on the 21st, the Germans were reported to be massing in front of the Dehra Dun Brigade. By 8 a.m. it was evident that the attack by the left Brigade of the Lahore Division had failed, and that the enemy were in considerable strength. The Seaforths were in a perilous position, and half of the 107th Pioneers were sent up to support their flank.

All other reserve troops available, *i.e.* the rest of the 107th and the 4th Cavalry, were brought up to a position in the Rue du Bois, from which they could act, in the event of the situation changing for the worse before the 2nd British Brigade could arrive. This Brigade was intended to attack about noon, on the arrival of General Westmacott, but two of its battalions were delayed en route, and the assault was not launched till about 7 p.m.

The Loyal North Lancashires were ordered to attack with their left on the "Orchard," the Northamptons prolonging to their left with the 2/60th Rifles in reserve. The 2nd Royal Sussex were detailed to relieve the Seaforths in the trenches.

By 10 p.m. the support line of the "Orchard" had been carried, and preparations were made to advance on the original fire trenches, but these had been so completely destroyed by bombs that they could not be reoccupied, a fact grimly eloquent of the gruelling to which the 2nd Gurkhas had been subjected. The support trenches were therefore held.

At 9 a.m. on the 22nd December, the enemy suddenly attacked the centre section, and the Loyal North Lancashires were bombed out, vacating several of the trenches which they had taken during the previous evening.

Lieutenant Macandrew of the Seaforths, finding his left unprotected and the Germans advancing up the trench, rallied some of the North Lancashires, and with them bombed the enemy back. He then found that, having only eleven men with him, he could not occupy such a length of trench. He dug himself in along the Brewery road facing north, and went back for reinforcements. While returning, he and eight men were killed by machine-gun fire.

The 41st Dogras and half of the 2nd Black Watch were now brought up, as also were the remainder of the Northamptons from the reserve. At 1 p.m. the line was again continuously held throughout.

By 3 p.m. the Seaforths and part of the 58th Rifles had been relieved. They had been fighting practically without a break in heavy mud and rain since the early hours of the 19th, and were utterly done. Faced by a most determined enemy in greatly superior numbers, hampered by a constant shortage of bombs and grenades, with both flanks in the air for a great part of the time, the 1st Seaforths had not only succeeded in holding out in spite of heavy casualties, but they had also retaken a portion of the trenches lost by the Gurkhas. For the Seaforths no higher praise can be accorded than that the regiment sustained and even added to a glorious reputation.

The casualties of the battalion from the 16th to the 22nd December amounted to 174, of whom 8 were officers. For their distinguished services Lt-Colonel Ritchie received the C.M.G., Captain Wicks the D.S.O., Lieutenant Macandrew was mentioned in despatches, and Captain Laing was awarded the Military Cross.

Lt-General C. Anderson, Commanding the Meerut Division, reported that in his opinion the action of the Seaforths and 58th Rifles, sustained over a period of three days and nights, under extremely difficult conditions, was worthy of the highest possible commendation, and reflected the greatest credit on officers, non-commissioned officers and men of both regiments.

The losses of the 58th Rifles were: Captain Bell, 54th Sikhs, Jemadar Mardan Ali and 24 other ranks killed, with 32 wounded.

Shortly after 1 p.m. on the 22nd December, Sir Douglas Haig took over command of the whole line which had been held by the Indian Corps.

The position was then as follows :—

South of the La Bassée Canal, the Connaught Rangers had not been attacked. Just north of the Canal, the 57th Rifles with one company 9th Bhopals, although pressed, still occupied their original trenches. The 1st British Brigade, holding Givenchy and its northern and eastern approaches, connected northwards with the Ferozepore Brigade, on whose left came the 3rd British Brigade, although touch between the two Brigades had been lost. The 3rd Brigade held a line along the east of the Festubert road, its left being in touch with the right of the Meerut Division, where a battalion of the Royal Sussex Regiment had just relieved the 1st Seaforths.

Further north the 2nd British Brigade held the line west of the "Orchard," and connected with half of the Black Watch and the 1/9th Gurkhas. From this point northwards, the 6th Jats and the whole of the Garhwal Brigade occupied the line which they had retained since the beginning.

The relief by the 1st Corps of the southern section was effected on the night of the 22nd December, but the Meerut Division remained under the orders of the 1st Corps, and was not completely withdrawn till the 27th December.

Very little has hitherto been said about the work of the 57th Rifles and one company 9th Bhopals, beyond mentioning the fact that they held their portion of the line throughout.

The share taken by them deserves more detailed mention, as it was owing to their determination and tenacious grip of their trenches that communication with the Connaughts on the south side of the La Bassée Canal, and through the Connaughts with the French on their right, was maintained, and that our line was kept intact in this section of the defence.

The 57th Rifles, under Lt-Colonel Gray, D.S.O., with one company of the 9th Bhopal Infantry, held the centre section of the Ferozepore line. In the firing line on the right was the Sikh Company of the 57th, under Major Willans, with Captain Leith-Ross attached from the 55th Rifles, and Lieutenant Taylor with 45 rifles, 9th Bhopals. In the centre was the Afridi Company, 57th, under Major Jarrett.

On the left were the Punjabi-Mahomedan Company, 57th, and 75 rifles 9th Bhopals, under Captains Jardine and Shepherd, with Lieutenant Deedes, 31st Punjabis, as machine-gun officer.

The local reserve consisted of the Dogra Company, 57th, and 75 rifles, 9th Bhopals. One machine gun was on the right and one in the centre.

On the 19th December, the parapet, owing to heavy rain and the enemy's fire, was in a very dilapidated condition. On the left a number of casualties were caused by shots through the loopholes from the German saps, only 70 yards away. Captain Mahon with 35 Dogras was brought up to reinforce this section.

At about 10 a.m. on the 20th, the enemy succeeded in occupying the trenches on the left flank of the 57th, which was thus in the air, and the Germans were able to enfilade the left company, with the result that Captain Shepherd was mortally wounded, and Captain Mahon took command of the company. The enemy, on the retirement of the 129th Baluchis on the left, worked round to some scattered houses in rear of the 57th. This forced Captain Mahon to fall back to avoid being cut off. The retirement was carried out with the utmost coolness, two or three men engaging the Germans from behind each traverse as they fell back.

Lieutenant Deedes remained at great risk, and helped to bring away Captain Shepherd's body. By his gallant conduct in this and other actions he gained the Military Cross.

In the meantime, Captain Jardine was busy making a barricade near the junction of the left and centre companies, which he held with the men of the 9th Bhopals. Captain Mahon with Subadar Arsla Khan lined an old communication trench facing north in continuation of the line of the barricade. Apparently the enemy was not sure of the strength of the position, as he only made weak attacks, which were easily beaten off, the men even climbing up on the parapet to get a better view of the enemy.

Shortly afterwards a company of the 142nd French Territorials arrived and was put in support of the left. Pressure was relieved about this time by the retaking of Givenchy by the Manchesters, as already related.

The left section of trench which the 57th had vacated remained empty, and the Germans built a barricade across it at the far end. Subadar Arsla Khan and some of his Afridis reconnoitred along this portion and brought back valuable information.

During the night, the French Territorials occupied the empty section of the trench and built a barricade at a distance of about 40 yards from that of the Germans. The French are described by an officer as having behaved with the utmost sangfroid and contempt of the enemy. They remained in this very uncomfortable position until the 57th were relieved.

On the 20th the Germans broke through the Sirhind Brigade on the left, and matters looked so bad that the Transport was taken out of billets and kept in constant readiness to move at a moment's notice. This, as it turned out, was very lucky, for the billets were shortly afterwards shelled and burnt.

During the day, a small body of Germans attempted to creep up from the eastern side, but were all shot down before they had advanced fifty yards.

At daybreak on the 21st, Subadar Arsla Khan went out with two men and reconnoitred the enemy's position. He ascertained that they were still in a section of the left trench, and succeeded in shooting several of them at their barricade.

At about 3 p.m. Givenchy was evacuated by the Manchesters, and pressure on the 57th left was greatly increased. The enemy again occupied the houses in the left rear, and were with difficulty prevented from moving further south and thus cutting off the battalion. Three separate attacks on our left were then repulsed, but matters began to look serious, as the reserve was being employed in bringing up ammunition, leaving no reinforcements in the event of a serious attack. Subadar Fateh Jang gained the Indian Distinguished Service Medal by his coolness and leadership at this critical moment.

At 4 p.m., luckily, the pressure was again relieved by the attack of the 1st British Brigade on Givenchy, and at about 8 p.m. they got into touch with the 57th left, the Scots Guards occupying a trench facing north at about 200 yards' distance.

Early on the 22nd, a body of about seventy Germans made a determined attack on the trench which had been thrown back on the left, but Subadar Arsla Khan collected all his men and charged the enemy, who fled without waiting for the assault. As they bolted, at least thirty of them, including two officers, were killed or wounded by our fire.

Subadar Arsla Khan is one of the finest specimens of the Indian officer imaginable. During the Mohmand Expedition of 1908, he was granted the 2nd

Class of the Indian Order of Merit for gallantry during a hand-to-hand fight in which he killed two of the enemy with his Mauser pistol, and turned the enemy out of an important "Sangar." In the present war he was granted the 2nd Class of the Order of British India for his good services at Messines, and at the second battle of Ypres in April, 1915, he won the Military Cross for his gallantry. The Subadar is a Malikdin Khel Afridi, and a man of considerable importance in his tribe. The 57th Rifles have every reason to be proud of him.

A company of the 59th Rifles now came up to reinforce, and were sent to the right, where Major Willans was in difficulties, as his men had been standing deep in mud and water since the 19th, and it was impossible, owing to the absence of reserves, to evacuate the sick and wounded.

On the night of the 22nd December, the 57th were relieved by the South Staffords, having been for three days and nights absolutely without rest and soaked to the skin, in consequence of which many men suffered agonies from frostbite. Their staunchness earned the hearty congratulations of the Corps Commander, and their Commanding Officer, Lt-Colonel Gray, D.S.O., whose cool courage never ceased to animate his men, was awarded the C.M.G.

This concluded the operations of the Indian Army Corps round Givenchy in 1914.

Sir John French, in his despatch dated the 2nd February, 1915, sums up his opinion of the work of the Corps during this very trying period in the following words:—

"The Indian troops have fought with the utmost

steadfastness and gallantry whenever they have been called upon."

These words, springing from the full knowledge of detailed operations which the foregoing pages have attempted to provide, are a sufficient reply to much ill-informed contemporary criticism.

CHAPTER XV

NEW FRONT TAKEN OVER AFTER A SHORT REST

Short period of rest—Changes in commands—Preparations for the future —Territorial Battalions—Trying weather—Strength of the Indian Corps—New front taken over.

AFTER two months of constant combat with the enemy and the elements, the troops were greatly in need of a rest. Death, wounds, and sickness had taken a grievous toll, and a period of at least comparative quiet was necessary to enable the Corps to recuperate its strength and to overhaul its equipment.

The extent to which the Corps had suffered in the short space of two months can be seen from the following table of casualties up to the 31st December, 1914:—

	Killed.	Wounded.	Missing.
British officers	104	148	40
Indian officers	39	96	31
Other ranks, British	349	1246	566
Other ranks, Indian	905	4370	1685
Total	1397	5860	2322

The orders which were issued towards the end of December for the troops to move into billets were therefore very welcome, but the period of rest was not to be as long as then seemed likely.

At the beginning of January, 1915, a number

of changes were made in Divisional and Brigade Commands.

Major-General H. D'U. Keary, C.B., D.S.O., succeeded Lt-General Watkis in the command of the Lahore Division, the latter being subsequently appointed a Knight Commander of the Bath.

Lt-Colonel C. G. Blackader, D.S.O., 2nd Leicesters, took over the Garhwal Brigade from Major-General Keary.

Lt-Colonel E. P. Strickland, C.M.G., D.S.O., 1st Manchesters, relieved Major-General Carnegy, who was invalided, in the Jullundur Brigade.

Colonel W. G. Walker, V.C., C.B., 1/4th Gurkhas, took over the Sirhind Brigade from Major-General Brunker, and Lt-Colonel W. M. Southey the Bareilly Brigade from Brigadier-General Macbean.

Colonel C. W. Jacob succeeded Brigadier-General Johnson in the Dehra Dun Brigade.

Although the Corps was resting in billets, it will not be supposed that it was idle. The past months of fierce fighting, of a description novel to all engaged, had revealed many flaws in our harness, many superfluities and many deficiencies in our equipment, and every use was made of the present opportunity to rectify omissions and to guard against future defects. The troops were constantly exercised in operations connected with trench warfare, such as firing trench mortars and rifle grenades, the use of bombs, and the advance on and occupation of hostile trenches.

Day after day, without a pause, the work went on, while at the same time gaps in the ranks were being closed by the reinforcements which arrived in a steady flow. Sir James Willcocks, according to his usual practice, devoted his leisure to making the acquaintance of the officers and men under his command.

During December, 1914, the 2nd Battalion Connaught Rangers, the 4th Battalion London Regiment, the 4th Battalion Suffolks, the 4th Battalion Seaforths (the last three being Territorials) had joined the Corps. The interlude gave the Commander a chance of making a thorough inspection of the Territorial units. He formed at once an opinion of their military value which later experience most fully justified.

It must be borne in mind that when in future we speak of the Indian Corps, reference is made (*a*) to the British and Indian battalions, artillery, etc., which constituted the Corps on arrival in France; and (*b*) to the Territorial and other units which joined later.

The effect of the withdrawal from the trenches and the consequent stocktaking was very striking. The constant strain and exposure of the past months had found out the weaklings, and had tended to harden those who had won through, but the lack of active exercise, so long continued, had unavoidably impaired to a serious degree the marching powers, and therefore the efficiency, of the men in the event of a prolonged advance. For weeks they had been soaking in the mud and water of the trenches, and their feet had suffered to such an extent as to render hard marching an impossibility for a large proportion of the troops.

To remedy this evil, route marching was now practised several times a week, with the result that after a short time the feet began to harden again, the number of men falling out became less and less, and by the end of its rest the Corps as a whole was once more in sound fighting condition.

At the same time the refitting of the troops proceeded apace. Trench warfare is particularly destructive of materiel, and the constant exposure to rain, snow, and mud had worn out many articles of clothing and equipment. These were now replaced, while advantage was taken of the opportunity to provide new forms of arms and equipment which past experience, gained in a cruel school, had shown to be necessary.

During the actual progress of operations it is difficult, if not impossible, to enforce modifications of existing practice, or to inculcate improved methods in such a manner as to secure the requisite degree of uniformity, and at the same time to render the changes intelligible to every grade of intellect. To this end conferences and demonstrations are necessary, and the period of rest was utilized to the full. Instruction was given to all officers of the Corps in day and night attacks, the construction of trenches, supply of ammunition in the field, and the use of bombs. The future was to show that the time available had been well employed.

On the 15th January, 1915, the Jullundur and Sirhind Brigades relieved a portion of the 2nd Division, 1st Corps, in the trenches, the last-named Brigade being in the front line with the Jullundur Brigade in reserve. The weather during January continued to be of a very trying nature. Heavy rain fell, accompanied by high, cutting winds, and in severe alternation, snowstorms were frequent. The whole country was a wilderness of mud, and offensive operations became impossible for both sides.

During this month we were very active in our mining operations, borrowing many ideas from the enemy's initiative. On one occasion a party of the 1st King George's Own Sappers and Miners were employed, under the command of Captain C. A. Bird, R.E., in making a mine gallery towards a German saphead which was about 30 yards away. A charge had been placed in position and was being tamped, when the enemy began bombarding the place with a medium trench mortar which was then new to us. A number of the men in the trench were killed or buried in debris.

Havildar Sucha Singh of the Sappers was in charge of the work in the mine shaft. He temporarily withdrew his party to assist in getting out those who had been buried. Having done this, he again went down the shaft to finish off the tamping and to complete the preparations for blowing up the mine, in spite of the fact that two trench-mortar bombs had fallen directly on the roof of the gallery, breaking two of the supporting frames, and that his party was isolated as our trench had been evacuated. Havildar Sucha Singh finished his work unperturbed and withdrew his men, afterwards receiving the Indian Distinguished Service Medal for his cool courage.

On the 24th January, the two Lahore Brigades were relieved by two Brigades of the Meerut Division. The fighting strength of the Corps on the 28th January amounted to 20,736 rifles; 880 sabres; 114 guns; 4000 artillery personnel.

Casualties up to the 1st February, 1915:-

	Killed.	Wounded.	Missing.
British officers	104	157	40
Indian officers	42	97	32
Other ranks, British	358	1293	576
Other ranks, Indian	925	4442	1687
Total	1429	5989	2335

On the 2nd February, the front already held by the Meerut Division, together with the left portion of the line occupied by the 1st Corps as far south as the Rue de Cailloux—La Quinque Rue, was taken over by the Indian Corps, the Meerut Division being in the front line with Lahore in reserve.

February passed without any special incident on the Indian Corps front. The artillery on both sides was fairly active, the enemy's guns frequently shelling Richebourg St Vaast and Rue du Bois, but the casualties caused were insignificant in number.

CHAPTER XVI

THE BATTLE OF NEUVE CHAPELLE

Success of the French in Champagne in January, 1915—German troops diverted from other fronts—Situation at commencement of March—French methods of offensive—Value of surprise—Operations round Neuve Chapelle decided on—Splendid services of the Flying Corps—Operation orders—Strength of Meerut Division—Description of ground—Preparations for attack—Special order by Sir Douglas Haig before the battle—Preparatory bombardment by 480 guns—Activity of our aviators on hostile communications—Attack by Garhwal Brigade—Gallantry of 2/39th Garhwalis—Rifleman Gobar Sing Negi gains the V.C.—Dashing attack of the 2/3rd Gurkhas—Major Tillard, D.S.O.—Rifleman Gane Gurung captures eight Germans—The 2/3rd Gurkhas the first regiment to enter Neuve Chapelle—The 1/39th Garhwalis find German wire uncut—Splendid behaviour of the battalion—Bravery of Lieutenant Cammell, R.F.A.—200 yards of trench taken, but attack isolated—All British officers killed—Colonel Swiney wounded, but continues to command—2nd Leicesters attack with their usual gallantry—Trench captured—Captain Romilly leads bombing party to assist 1/39th Garhwalis—Captain Hobart, R.E.—Private William Buckingham gains the V.C.—Attack by 1st Seaforths and 1/3rd Londons to help 1/39th Garhwalis—Splendid charge by Londons—Trench taken—Gallant conduct of Captain Taylor, I.M.S.—Heavy losses of 1/39th Garhwalis—Position on the night of 10th March.

During the months of January and February, 1915, the French under General Langle de Cary were heavily and successfully engaged in Champagne, where they carried the town of Perthes with an important hill in the neighbourhood, and towards the end of February captured a very strong position north of Beau Séjour.

The value of these operations lay, not only in

the moral and material effects of the recapture of ground from the enemy, but also in the fact that the Germans were compelled to divert large bodies of troops from the Eastern front, as well as from other portions of their line in the West, in order to stay the progress of the French. Amongst these troops were the 6th Corps from Silesia, the 8th Corps from the Crown Prince's army in the Argonne, and six battalions of Prussian Guards from the neighbourhood of Ypres. It was also believed that for the same purpose the enemy's line opposite La Bassée and Lille had been considerably depleted, and that the only immediately available reinforcements consisted of a body of troops, principally Bavarian and Saxon, which was in billets at Roubaix on relief from the trenches round Ypres.

The position at the commencement of March was as follows :—

The line from Dixmude southwards to the apex of the Ypres salient was held by French troops, interspersed amongst whom were British cavalry. To the south again was the 5th Corps commanded by General Plumer, in touch with which was the 2nd Corps. The 3rd Corps under General Pulteney occupied its old position opposite Armentières, whence the line was continued southwards from Estaires to the west of Neuve Chapelle by the 4th Corps under General Rawlinson. Thence the Indian Corps under General Willcocks held the line as far as Givenchy, where it linked up with the 1st Corps, which was in touch with General Maud'huy's 10th (French) Army across the La Bassée Canal.

The conditions created by the success of the French in Champagne were thought to be favourable to offensive operations by the British, and a decision to this effect had been arrived at by the end of February. To quote Sir John French's words in his despatch of the 5th April, 1915:—

"About the end of February many vital considerations induced me to believe that a vigorous offensive movement by the forces under my command should be planned and carried out at the earliest possible moment.

"Amongst the more important reasons which convinced me of the necessity were—

"The general aspect of the Allied situation throughout Europe, and particularly the marked success of the Russian Army in repelling the violent onslaughts of Marshal Von Hindenburg; the apparent weakening of the enemy in my front, and the necessity for assisting our Russian Allies to the utmost by holding as many hostile troops as possible in the Western theatre; the efforts to this end which were being made by the French Forces at Arras and Champagne; and perhaps the most weighty consideration of all, the need of fostering the offensive spirit in the troops under my command, after the trying and possibly enervating experiences which they had gone through of a severe winter in the trenches."

The chief lesson learned from the Champagne offensive was that, given a sufficient concentration of artillery on any section of front, and the employment of an adequate force of infantry, an attack on the section bombarded was practically certain to succeed.

The method employed by the French (to whose intuition and originality the debt of our Staff is as evident as it has been continuous) was to batter the hostile trenches and obstacles out of existence, then to lift the guns and to establish such a curtain or barrage of fire as to render the arrival of reinforcements impossible. Under cover of this fire, the infantry could advance and occupy the position with comparatively small loss. The only danger of failure lay in the possibility that the enemy, by means of aerial reconnaissance or the operations of spies, might become aware of the plan and defeat it by massing guns on the sector selected for attack.

The portion of the enemy's line chosen for the British offensive was that covering the village of Neuve Chapelle, in rear of which lay the Aubers ridge and the city of Lille. We have already seen that on the 16th October, 1914, the 2nd Corps under General Smith-Dorrien took the village, and on the 17th reached Aubers and Herlies, one battalion, the Royal Irish, even capturing Le Pilly, three and a half miles to the east of Neuve Chapelle. The Germans then developed a counter-offensive, which pushed us back until our line ran just east of Neuve Chapelle, which village was captured by the enemy on the 27th October. On the 28th it was retaken by the Indian Corps, after a most gallant action, but owing to the lack of support, we were again driven out, and from the commencement of November our line ran well to the west of the village ; and so it remained throughout the winter.

A glance at the map will show that Neuve Chapelle formed an enemy salient which it was eminently desirable to straighten out, if this object could be achieved without excessive loss. Moreover, during January and February, 1915, there had been a complete lull on this section of the line, and there was reason to hope that the Germans might here be caught off their guard. As before remarked, the one condition absolutely necessary to success was secrecy.

The task of a commander in the field has been rendered infinitely more difficult in recent years by the introduction of aerial reconnaissance. From the eye of the bird-men who hover over the scene of operations little can be concealed. Photographs are taken by them which reveal the smallest changes in the disposition of the hostile forces. Bodies of troops on the march, the movements of batteries or supply columns, the presence of any unusual amount of rolling stock at a railway station, are at once detected and reported, and inferences are drawn which may be fatal to the enterprise. In fact, if the aviators obtain free range, surprise on an important scale is impossible. The operations of the flying men can only be prevented by the opposing air squadrons or by the occurrence of fogs or of clouds lying at such a low altitude as to force scouting machines to fly within close range of the hostile anti-aircraft guns.

Such success (and it was not in perspective very considerable) as attended the operations of March, 1915, round Neuve Chapelle was rendered possible by the gallantry and zeal of our Flying Corps. To appreciate this fact, it is only necessary to consider that our attack on the 10th March, on which date the surprise of the enemy was complete, succeeded to the full. Had we then been able to push on, it is possible, though far from certain, that our more distant objectives would have been reached, but owing to unforeseen delays, the enemy obtained sufficient breathing time to enable him to overtake the advantage which the element of surprise had conferred upon us, with the result that our subsequent operations were finally checked and at last perforce abandoned.

For weeks previous to the battle, our airmen had made a deliberate and in the main a successful challenge to the German planes, with the result that they had obtained such a degree of ascendancy as rendered it impossible for their rivals to carry any constant or reliable information.

The scope of the operations was defined in an order issued on the 9th March. The attack on Neuve Chapelle was to be undertaken by the 4th and Indian Corps, the 8th Division of the former and the Meerut Division of the latter Corps supplying the assaulting troops.

The strength of the Meerut Division on the 10th March was as follows :—

British officers, 250 ; Indian officers, 148 ; British, other ranks, 4915 ; Indian, other ranks, 6369 ; total, 11,682 all ranks, exclusive of Staff, Cavalry, Artillery, and Engineers.

Composition of Brigades on the 10th March, 1915 :—

Lahore Division.

Jullundur Brigade.

Commander : Brigadier-General E. P. Strickland, C.M.G., D.S.O.

1st Manchesters.
4th Suffolks (Territorials).
47th Sikhs.
59th Rifles.

Sirhind Brigade.

Commander: Brigadier-General W. G. Walker, V.C., C.B.

1st Highland Light Infantry.
4th King's (Liverpool) Regiment (Special Reserve).
15th Sikhs.
1/1st Gurkha Rifles.
1/4th Gurkha Rifles.

Ferozepore Brigade.

Commander: Brigadier-General R. M. Egerton, C.B.

Connaught Rangers.
4th London Regiment (Territorials).
57th Rifles.
129th Baluchis.
Divisional Battalion, 9th Bhopal Infantry.

MEERUT DIVISION.

Dehra Dun Brigade.

Commander: Brigadier-General C. W. Jacob.

1st Seaforths.
4th Seaforths (Territorials).
2/2nd Gurkha Rifles.
1/9th Gurkha Rifles.

Garhwal Brigade.

Commander: Brigadier-General C. G. Blackader, D.S.O.

2nd Leicesters.
3rd London Regiment (Territorials).
1/39th Garhwal Rifles.
2/39th Garhwal Rifles.
2/3rd Gurkha Rifles.

Bareilly Brigade.

Commander: Brigadier-General W. M. Southey.
2nd Black Watch.
4th Black Watch (Territorials).
6th Jats.
41st Dogras.
58th Rifles.
Divisional Battalion, 2/8th Gurkha Rifles.

The 125th Rifles were lent to the 4th Corps for work on communications.

The immediate objective was the enemy's trenches west of Neuve Chapelle, and the occupation of a line to the east of the diamond-shaped figure formed by the main road from Estaires to La Bassée, the road by Fleurbaix to Armentières, and that which connects the two. In the northern angle of this diamond lies the village of Neuve Chapelle. The general object of the attack was to enable the 4th and Indian Corps to establish themselves on a more forward line to the east, the ultimate objective being the high ground on which are situated the villages of Aubers and Ligny-le-Grand, with the intention finally of cutting off that portion of the enemy's troops which held the line between Neuve Chapelle and La Bassée.

The artillery of the Meerut Division, reinforced by that of the Lahore Division and heavy guns, was to carry out a preliminary bombardment, commencing at 7.30 a.m. on the 10th March, and lasting for 35 minutes. The objects of this bombardment were—

(*a*) to demolish the enemy's obstacles;
(*b*) to destroy the enemy in his trenches;

(*c*) to put up a curtain of fire in rear of the hostile trenches in order to prevent the arrival of reserves ;

(*d*) to cover the southern section, which was not attacking ;

(*e*) to engage the enemy's batteries.

A short description of the ground will enable the reader to follow the course of the action with greater ease and clearness. Eastward from our front lay the village of Neuve Chapelle, in pre-war times a typical French townlet, with its centre street lined by estaminets, small shops and neat dwelling-houses, while on the outskirts were the villas of the better-to-do residents. The most prominent buildings were the white church on the left of the main street, the brewery in the south-east corner of the village, and a small château to the north-east of the church. The village was already in a half-ruined condition as the effect of the previous sanguinary fighting in October, 1914, but as compared with the state in which it was left by the bombardment and counter-bombardments of the 10th March, 1915 and following days, it might almost be described as in good repair.

Between our line and the village lay fields, intersected by deep ditches and cut up by hedges. The going was terrible, as the recent heavy rains had converted the plough into holding bog. Further to the east, at a distance of about two miles south-west of Lille, commences a ridge which, running in a horse-shoe shape, connects the villages of Illies and Aubers, both of which were occupied by the enemy. Between the two villages is a plateau, the importance of which to us lay in the fact that its capture, while depriving the enemy of the great advantages accruing from his possession of the high ground, would give us command of the approaches to the three great manufacturing centres of Lille, Roubaix, and Tourcoing.

Between Neuve Chapelle and the Aubers ridge runs the stream known as the river Des Layes, a tributary of the Lys, with a width of 6 to 10 feet, and a depth at that season of 3 to 4½ feet. The enemy had constructed a second line of defence along the eastern side of the stream, with strong bridge heads.

A large wood, consisting mainly of young trees with a thick undergrowth, called the Bois du Biez, lies to the south-east of Neuve Chapelle, while further east is the Bois de Pommereau on the ridge south of Aubers.

The preparations for the attack in that section which was committed to the Indian Corps, large-scaled as they were, were of the most minute description, and eliminated, as far as human foresight could, the element of chance. Two lines of breastworks were constructed in rear of our trenches along the Estaires—La Bassée road, from Port Arthur to the Rue des Berceaux, to afford cover to the troops when forming up for the assault. Strong communication breastworks were completed to the front line. Drains and water-courses were bridged, as many as 105 such bridges being put into position over the ditch in rear of our trenches on the La Bassée road. Numbers of step ladders were provided to enable the infantry to get over the parapets. Barricades and screens were everywhere strengthened. Bombs, rations, ammunition, spare bridges, planks, hurdles, pickets, sandbags, plain and barbed wire, were stocked at various advanced depôts.

From the 7th March onwards, all the artillery of the Lahore and Meerut Divisions and No. 1 Group G.H.Q. Heavy Artillery was brought into position and carried out registration of targets. During the first week of March several conferences took place between the Corps and Divisional Staffs, following on which instructions outlining the operations were issued, details being worked out by the Divisional and Brigade Staffs. On the 8th March, a final general conference was held, when all points were considered and settled.

The Garhwal Brigade under Brigadier-General Blackader was detailed for the assault, the Dehra Dun Brigade under Brigadier-General Jacob being in support, while the Bareilly Brigade under Brigadier-General Southey was to hold the line during the attack. The wire in front of our trenches was to be cut, and bridges were to be put in position over the ditches between our line and that of the enemy by the Bareilly Brigade, under cover of darkness, on the night of the 9th–10th March. Finally, all troops were to be in position by 4.30 a.m. on the 10th.

On the 9th March the following special order by General Sir Douglas Haig was published :—

"To the 1st Army.

"We are about to engage the enemy under very favourable conditions. Until now in the present campaign, the British Army has, by its pluck and determination, gained victories against an enemy greatly superior in men and guns.

"Reinforcements have made us stronger than the enemy in our front. Our guns are now both more numerous than the enemy's are, and are also larger than any hitherto used by any army in the field.

"Our Flying Corps has driven the enemy from the air.

"On the Eastern front, and to south of us, our Allies have made marked progress and caused enormous losses to the Germans, who are, moreover, harassed by internal troubles and shortage of supplies, so that there is little prospect at present of big reinforcements being sent against us here.

"In front of us we have only one German Corps, spread out on a front as large as that occupied by the whole of our Army (the First).

"We are now about to attack with about 48 battalions a locality in that front which is held by some three German battalions. It seems probable, also, that for the first day of the operations the Germans will not have more than four battalions available for the counter-attack.

"Quickness of movement is therefore of first importance to enable us to forestall the enemy, and thereby gain success without severe loss.

"At no time in the war has there been a more favourable moment for us, and I feel confident of success. The extent of that success must depend on the rapidity and determination with which we advance.

"Although fighting in France, let us remember that we are fighting to preserve the British Empire, and to protect our homes against the organized savagery of the German Army.

"To ensure success each one of us must play his part, and fight like men for the Honour of Old England."

The spirit and vigour of these admonitions were alike admirable. Their summary of the military situation was perhaps a little upon the optimistic side.

After dark on the 9th March, the movement of troops to their appointed positions commenced, and continued throughout the night, until by the early morning of the 10th, the Garhwal Brigade was formed for attack in Port Arthur and in trenches and breastworks along the La Bassée—Estaires road, while the Dehra Dun Brigade was assembled in position to support, the whole defensive line of the Indian Corps being occupied by the Bareilly Brigade.

The night of the 9th March was cheerless in the extreme, the cold was intense and snow fell at intervals. Later, the weather improved and a frost set in, which to some extent assisted the advance.

The morning of the 10th March broke cold and misty, low-lying clouds rendering aerial reconnaissance both difficult and dangerous. At the first streak of dawn our guns began a final registration on their objectives, and although there was nothing to differentiate the fire of that morning from the usual "morning hate," the suspicions of the enemy appear to have been aroused.

It was subsequently ascertained that German patrols had reported that our trenches were packed with men, and that requests for artillery fire were sent back from the enemy's front line, but the wiser heads in rear apparently considered it to be a false alarm, and the steps which might have had a far-reaching effect on the operations were not taken.

At 7 a.m. a German aeroplane, greatly daring, suddenly appeared over Port Arthur, flying at a height of three to four hundred feet only. The fact that our line was crammed with troops could not escape the notice of the observer, and very shortly after the machine had flown away to the north the enemy commenced a heavy bombardment of the position, which, in the crowded state of the trenches, caused a large number of casualties among the 2nd Leicesters and 1/39th Garhwalis who were assembled at that spot. At 7.30 a.m. our bombardment broke out in all its fury. The experience gained from the French operations round Perthes had been utilized to good purpose by Sir John French. The length of the front to be attacked was little more than two miles, and against this the British had massed nearly 480 guns and howitzers, while the supply of ammunition for a 35 minutes' bombardment was said to have been greater than the amount used by the French at Perthes in a week.

Many attempts have been made to describe the sound of a great bombardment, but exuberant and flowing as has been the language frequently employed, every description has failed to convey a true sense of the reality. To obtain a slight idea of what such a bombardment means to the enemy, one need go no further than to our own troops. An officer who was in the front line describes his own sensation as the shells passed overhead as one of semi-stupefaction, coupled with an intense desire to hold on to something in order to keep on his feet.

It was quite impossible to hear one's self speak, for it must be remembered that while the shells from the heaviest guns firing far in rear ascend to the height of Mont Blanc, those of the 18-pounders of the field batteries, firing with very low trajectory, pass at a height of only a few feet above the heads of the troops in the trenches, with a screech and a whirr which are peculiarly nerve-shaking, for there is always the chance that a short burst may land a shell in one's own trench instead of in that of the enemy.

If the bombardment was so disconcerting for our men, what must it have been for the Germans? The 18-pounders kept up an intense fire on the enemy's wire, the 15-inch, 9·2 and 6-inch howitzers plunged their high explosives into the entrenchments in front of the village.

The line of the German trenches could be clearly traced from a distance by the constant terrific explosions which hurled masses of earth, stones, and bricks high into the air, mingled with the shattered remains of the defenders, while over all hung a dense pall of dust and smoke, through which the flames of the bursting shells constantly stabbed a lurid path. The rapidity of fire was so great that it seemed impossible that it could proceed from single-loading guns; it sounded rather as if leviathan machine guns were at work.

So utterly was the enemy surprised and dominated, that later on, in some places, our men were able to climb out and walk about unharmed in the open. At one spot, the upper half of a German officer, with his cap still firmly fixed on his head, was blown into our trench.

While the guns were thus preparing the way for the infantry, our gallant airmen were busy on other errands. In order to prevent the enemy from bringing up reinforcements from a distance, the fastest machines were sent on a mission to destroy his communications. The railway bridge at Menin, over which reinforcements might have been sent by the Duke of Würtemburg, was attacked, as also was the junction at Courtrai, on the principal route from Belgium to this part of the front. One of our airmen dropped a bomb on Menin bridge from a height of only 120 feet, destroying a pier, while Courtrai Station, and the Don and Douai Junctions were also damaged; a troop train was hit by a bomb; a wireless installation at Lille was believed to have been destroyed; and one of the enemy's head-quarters was set on fire. In another case, as Sir John French mentions in his despatch of the 5th April, 1915, a pilot descended to about 50 feet above the point he was attacking.

The bombardment continued without a second's pause until five minutes past eight, when the guns lifted on to Neuve Chapelle itself, and put the finishing touches to the devastation commenced at the end of October, 1914.

The attack of the Garhwal Brigade was arranged as follows:—

Right attack, 1/39th Garhwal Rifles.

Right centre, 2nd Leicesters.

Left centre, 2/3rd Gurkhas.

Left attack, 2/39th Garhwal Rifles.

The 3rd London Regiment (Territorials) were in support.

In order to protect the flanks, the 1/39th Garhwalis

were to send parties, after the capture of the first objective, to clear the German trenches to the right, while the 2/39th were to act in the same way on the left, and to establish touch with the 25th Brigade, 8th Division.

The moment the guns lifted, the Brigade swarmed over the parapet, and doubling over the intervening space of from 100 to 200 yards, reached (except as regards one battalion) its first objective without a check. The effect of the accurate and intense fire of our artillery was at once evident. The German wire had in nearly every place simply ceased to exist, while the trenches were practically blotted out, burying in their ruins numbers of the defenders. Such of the enemy as were still unhurt were either in a state of stupefaction or half delirious, while everywhere lay the mangled bodies of the dead and wounded. The 2/39th Garhwalis met with some rifle and machine-gun fire from trenches further in rear, but pressed on through the first trench and took the second with a rush, capturing a machine gun and some prisoners.

Subadar Nain Sing Chinwarh, who had won the Military Cross in the earlier days of the war, here earned the 2nd Class, Order of British India, by his gallant leading of his company, which he continued to command although he had been wounded by a shell splinter.

Jemadar Sangram Sing Negi charged a machine gun in the face of a German officer who was aiming at him with his revolver, and with his company captured the officer, the gun, and its detachment. For his conspicuous bravery the Jemadar was rewarded with the Military Cross.

Still pushing on, the 2/39th took the third trench with few casualties, and then made for their first main objective, the fourth line. During their passage between the third and fourth trenches, they came under heavy fire, and lost many men from a party of the enemy on the left flank. These were engaged by the left company of the 2/39th, which had carried through the advance with equal success.

Naik Jaman Sing Bisht here distinguished himself and gained the 2nd Class, Indian Order of Merit, by leading his section up the trench and driving the occupants into the hands of the right company, a large number being captured.

During the advance, Captain Parkin, 113th Infantry, attached 2/39th, was severely wounded, when acting as Brigade bomb-gun officer, through the bursting of one of his guns.

The two assaulting companies of the 2/39th established themselves in their first objective, and the enemy, finding himself under fire from two directions, began to surrender, but, as usual, great care had to be exercised when dealing with such a treacherous foe. A party of Germans in the main trench beckoned to our men to come over and take them prisoners. A close scrutiny of the ground revealed the fact that in crossing they would come under machine-gun fire from a position which was not marked on the map. Fortunately, we were not taken in; the trench was rushed, and the machine gun captured.

Havildar Butha Sing Negi gained the Indian Order of Merit by heading his section into a trench, where he captured a number of prisoners.

During the assault on the main line, Rifleman

Gobar Sing Negi behaved with very distinguished courage. He was one of the bayonet party accompanying the bombers, and was the first man to go round each traverse in face of a most determined resistance by the enemy, of whom he killed several, driving the remainder back until they surrendered. This brave soldier was afterwards unfortunately killed, but for his most conspicuous gallantry he was posthumously awarded the Victoria Cross.

Jemadar Pancham Sing Mahar won the Military Cross by his dashing leading of a party which advanced across the open in face of a severe fire, capturing a machine gun and a number of prisoners.

The Garhwalis, having accomplished all they were asked to do, now consolidated the position, and parties proceeded to search the houses for snipers. Here the Berkshires were seen on the left working through the village, and shortly afterwards touch was established with the 2nd Rifle Brigade on the east. There they halted, and by evening the position had been made defensible, and the battalion remained in support of the 2/3rd Gurkhas facing the Bois du Biez.

In consolidating the line we were greatly assisted by a lucky find of a large quantity of sandbags, hurdles and entrenching tools in a house which had evidently been used by the Germans as a depôt.

On the whole, there was little hostile fire during the progress of the work, beyond a few shells and an occasional burst of machine-gun fire, Jemadar Ghantu Sing being killed at this time. In this first phase, the 2/39th Garhwalis lost 1 Garhwali officer and

26 other ranks killed, 2 Garhwali officers and 71 others wounded, and 31 missing.

The battalion carried out its task with the greatest dash and bravery. The comparatively small casualty list was greatly due to the foresight of Lt-Colonel Drake-Brockman, who made use of slight cover in front of his parapet to get his men out during the preliminary bombardment, thus obtaining to the full the advantage of surprise.

The 2/3rd Gurkhas, under Lt-Colonel V. A. Ormsby, on the signal being given, crossed to the first German trench with very slight losses, as the enemy appeared to be utterly overcome by the violence and accuracy of our bombardment.

A company of the 3rd Londons and one of the 2/39th Garhwalis took up the work of consolidating the position, the Gurkhas sweeping on over the second trench with little opposition and crossing the road with the second line close up in support. Here they were met by rifle and machine-gun fire from parties of the enemy still occupying houses in the south end of the village near the Brewery, which also caused considerable trouble to the Leicesters, who were making a frontal attack.

Seeing that there was great danger of the enemy rallying at this point, Major Tillard, D.S.O., at once determined to take the responsibility of exceeding his orders, and pushed straight on for the Brewery, driving the Germans, after a sharp struggle, out of the houses and capturing a large number. His determined action undoubtedly had a great effect at a critical moment, and gained for him a mention in despatches.

Havildar Bahadur Thapa distinguished himself

at this juncture by heading a bombing party, which entered a house held by the enemy and stormed a barricade, killing 16 Germans and capturing 2 machine guns. For his conspicuous bravery the havildar was awarded the 2nd Class, Indian Order of Merit.

A dramatic incident occurred at this time. Rifleman Gane Gurung, observing that heavy fire was being kept up from a particular house, most gallantly entered it by himself, cowed into surrendering and brought out single-handed eight Germans at the point of his bayonet. At this moment the 2nd Rifle Brigade came on the scene, and on seeing the little Gurkha driving eight burly Germans out of the house, gave him three ringing cheers. This rifleman had previously shown great bravery, and for his daring on this occasion was awarded the 2nd Class of the Indian Order of Merit. In the course of a speech eulogizing the services of the battalion, Sir James Willcocks subsequently remarked that there was probably no other instance in English history of an individual Indian soldier being cheered for his bravery by a British battalion in the midst of a battle.

The question as to which unit, British or Indian, was the first to enter Neuve Chapelle on this occasion has been much argued. The honour would appear to belong to the 2/3rd Gurkhas, who attacked half an hour before the 8th Division; moreover, it was only after the Gurkhas had reached the Brewery and were fighting among the houses that the Rifle Brigade came up and witnessed the incident just described. During their advance, the Gurkhas captured a large number of Germans, but the total cannot be stated, as the prisoners were handed over to other regiments to send back.

Lt-Colonel Ormsby, who had throughout the campaign, and especially in this battle, shown great qualities of leadership, was appointed a Companion of the Bath.

Subadar-Major Gambhir Sing Gurung displayed great gallantry during the assault, and did excellent work in the battle. For his services he received the 2nd Class of the Indian Order of Merit, and later, that of the Order of British India.

Captain H. H. Grigg, though wounded early in the action, continued to command his double company, and gave an inspiring example to his men, for which he was mentioned in despatches.

Subadar Bhim Sing Thapa performed repeated acts of pluck, especially distinguishing himself by his coolness in leading his men, thus gaining the 2nd Class, Indian Order of Merit.

Lance-Naik Harak Sing Gharti, a signaller, showed great devotion in continuously carrying messages under heavy fire. He subsequently commanded his section when his senior was shot, and here again showed conspicuous gallantry. He was awarded the 2nd Class, Indian Order of Merit.

Jemadar Puran Sing Thapa received the Indian Distinguished Service Medal for having, after being wounded at the start, continued to command his section till the following evening, when, after getting his wounds dressed, he returned to the firing line, and was again wounded.

Rifleman Kharakbir Pun, who behaved with great bravery on several occasions, was wounded at the commencement of the battle, remained throughout the day's fighting, and was finally ordered to hospital in a state of collapse. He received the Russian Medal of St George, 3rd Class.

During the attack a very gallant act was performed by Naik Khan Zaman, of the 32nd Lahore Divisional Signal Company. The cable from the front to Divisional Head Quarters was continually being cut. Naik Khan Zaman went back along the line, repairing it in many places. He was out for 3½ hours under very heavy shell fire, and had twice to cross a zone of 400 yards which was swept by rifle fire as well. By a miracle he escaped unwounded, and was awarded the Indian Distinguished Service Medal.

So far all had gone well with the attack, but the 1/39th Garhwalis under Colonel Swiney, whose advance we shall now follow, were fated to meet with misfortune, against which they fought heroically and eventually won through, but with terrible losses, especially in British officers.

On our bombardment lifting, Nos. 2 and 4 Companies, the former under Captains Clarke and Owen, the latter under Captain Kenny and Lieutenant Welchman, went over the parapet. Captain Clarke, who was on the left, was ordered to keep touch with the Leicesters, but from the start No. 2 Company bore too much to the right, thus forcing No. 4 Company out of its direction. Pushing on, with the bravery which has always marked the work of this battalion, they got up close to the German trench in the face of a murderous machine-gun and rifle fire. But here a check was caused, as it was found that the German wire had hardly been touched by our guns, and the trench was practically intact.

This was, of course, only to be expected, as, owing to the loss of direction, the assault was being delivered on a section of trench outside the radius of the bombardment.

The casualties during this pause were very heavy, both amongst the British officers and the rank-and-file. Seeing what had occurred, Colonel Swiney ordered Captains Murray and Sparrow to reinforce the leading companies, and the whole line together carried the enemy's trench after a sanguinary struggle, in spite of the terrific fire and the losses already sustained; but Captain Kenny and Lieutenant Welchman were the only British officers to reach the trench alive, and were then themselves killed almost immediately.

Captains Clarke, Murray, Sparrow, and Owen were killed during the check and subsequent rush. Captain Kenny, before being killed in the enemy's trench, had already been twice wounded, but held on with superb courage.

During the advance of the second line, Lieutenant G. A. Cammell, R.F.A., who was observing in the Garhwalis' trench for his battery, saw that the British officers had been shot down, and that the men were inclined to hesitate. As his telephone wire had been cut, and his occupation was gone, he rushed out of the trench, and putting himself at the head of the line, led them on, four men keeping abreast of him. He had hardly gone twenty yards under the appalling fire, when he and three of the four men by his side were wounded.

Seeing the officer fall, Lance-Corporal V. Thompson, of the 2nd Black Watch, at once ran out and brought Lieutenant Cammell in, being himself wounded in doing so. For their bravery Lieutenant Cammell received the D.S.O., and Lance-Corporal Thompson the Distinguished Conduct Medal.

The net result of this attack was that some 200 yards of trench were carried, but a gap of about the same extent existed between the left of the Garhwalis and the right of the Leicesters. This space was packed with Germans, practically untouched by our bombardment, and still full of fight. The survivors of the assaulting party of the Garhwalis were thus completely isolated, and, what was worse, were without a single British officer. Repeated attempts were made by small parties to reach them, but the result was invariably the same. All who tried to cross were killed or put out of action.

It speaks volumes for the courage and training of the men that under the command of their Garhwali officers, headed by Subadar Kedar Sing Rawat, who received the Indian Distinguished Service Medal for his gallantry, they held on with the greatest determination throughout the day, in spite of frequent attacks by the enemy, and the fact that they had run short of bombs and ammunition.

At about 9.30 a.m. Colonel Swiney telephoned for reinforcements, and at about 10 a.m. he was severely wounded in the thigh by a shell splinter, but, plucky as ever, he had a field dressing put on, and held out till after midnight, when he was so reduced by pain and loss of blood that he had to be removed to hospital. At about the time that Colonel Swiney was wounded, Lieutenant Lemon, who was with him in Port Arthur, was hit in the throat. Shortly after this, two companies of the 1/3rd Londons were sent to Colonel Swiney's aid.

To bring the attack into line, it is now necessary to follow the 2nd Leicesters. At the appointed moment B Company under Captain Morgan, M.C., and C Company under Captain Weir, went over the parapet, and advancing at a steady double, jumped the remains of the enemy's trench, forced their way through the many obstacles and debris, and gained their first objective in about twenty minutes. Captain Morgan was wounded by shrapnel in no less than six places just as the assault was launched. In spite of the terrible injuries, from which he has even now not recovered, he staggered on in front of his company, but collapsed before he had gone many yards.

The second line, consisting of A Company under Lieutenant Buxton, followed at a distance of about thirty yards, succeeded by Captain Romilly with D Company as reserve, and dealt with small parties of the enemy in outlying trenches and houses which had not been touched by the first line. The whole front of the battalion was thus cleared, and the men began to dig themselves in. It was then found, as previously related, that a gap, full of the enemy, existed between the Leicester right and the left of the 1/39th Garhwalis.

The problem of dealing with the situation was a difficult one, as the wire in front of the Germans was practically undamaged, and a frontal attack, whether successful or not, was certain to entail very heavy losses.

Captain Romilly of the Leicesters at once led a platoon of the reserve company at the enemy, and with great skill and courage bombed them back about 100 yards along their trench, shooting five of them with his revolver. For this conspicuous bravery Captain Romilly was awarded the D.S.O. He then sent back for Sappers, who arrived under Captain Hobart, R.E., and found a lively bombing match going on between the Leicesters and the Germans.

The Sappers went up to the furthest point occupied by the Leicesters, and thence Sapper Shaikh Abdul Rahman and two others went back and brought up more bombs, under fire, with which Captain Hobart, Colour-Havildar Chagatta and some Sappers, with the Leicesters, advanced another 20 yards along the trench, and there succeeded in building a sandbag barricade to a height of 4½ feet, when their work was interrupted by our own mortar bombs falling on a house occupied by the enemy a short distance away.

Captain Hobart was then ordered to retire, which he did without a single casualty. For the great gallantry displayed during this work, Captain Hobart received the Military Cross, while Colour-Havildar Chagatta, who already possessed the Indian Order of Merit and the Indian Distinguished Service Medal, was later awarded the Russian Cross of the Order of St George, 4th Class.

Sapper Shaikh Abdul Rahman received the 2nd Class, Indian Order of Merit.

Captain Weir, 2nd Leicesters, received the Military Cross for the gallantry displayed by him during the battle.

During this attack, and again on the 12th March, Private William Buckingham, 2nd Leicesters, on several occasions displayed the greatest bravery and devotion in rescuing and aiding wounded men.

[*Central Press*.

PRIVATE WILLIAM BUCKINGHAM, V.C., 2ND BN LEICESTERSHIRE REGIMENT.

239.]

Time after time he went out under the heaviest fire and brought in those who would otherwise almost certainly have perished. In the performance of this noble work, Private Buckingham was severely wounded in the chest and arm. For his conspicuous valour he was awarded the Victoria Cross. This very valiant soldier was killed during the fighting on the Somme in September, 1916.

The story of the 2nd Leicesters throughout the campaign is full of instances of bravery and self-devotion, of which it is unfortunately impossible, within the scope of this history, to mention more than a few. Amongst others of the battalion who received the Distinguished Conduct Medal for services in the battle was Private G. Hill, who, during the attack of the 10th March, showed a supreme contempt for danger by continually carrying messages across the open under very heavy fire, the enemy being only 100 yards away. Later in the day he was wounded by a bomb while engaged in clearing the Germans out of a trench.

Corporal R. Keitley and Private C. Oakes were granted the same decoration for displaying great courage and the utmost devotion to duty in removing the wounded from the firing line to the aid post during three whole days, without rest and with hardly any food. Throughout they were under very heavy fire.

Sergeant H. E. Ruckledge dressed the wounds of several men after being himself wounded in the leg. He then collected sandbags and took them to the firing line, receiving another wound in the wrist. Next, he went to the aid of a seriously wounded officer. All these gallant actions were performed under heavy fire. Private J. Steeples voluntarily went out into the open with another man under severe close-range fire and carried a wounded officer under cover. In both cases the Distinguished Conduct Medal was awarded.

These are a few instances of the spirit which inspired this splendid battalion.

To resume the story. After the barricade had been built, it was held by two platoons of the Leicesters until, at about 5 p.m., the preparations to deal with the situation were complete. It was arranged that two companies of the 1st Seaforths should assault the trench from the left in co-operation with a frontal attack. Accordingly, the Seaforths took up their position among some ruined houses on the left flank, while two companies of the 1/3rd Londons (Territorials) with a party of the 1/39th Garhwalis were to make a frontal attack, issuing from the same point in the trenches from which Captain Clarke had led the assault in the morning.

As soon as Colonel Swiney saw that the Seaforths had advanced, and that their bombing party was making progress, he launched the attack of the 3rd Londons and Garhwalis. C Company of the Seaforths under Captain Baillie-Hamilton and D Company under Captain Wicks had to move under rifle and machine-gun fire over difficult and intersected ground, and were for a time held up by our heavy artillery, which began to shell the neighbourhood.

The enemy then brought up a trench mortar, by which, amongst others, Captain Wicks was wounded. This officer had shown marked courage and ability on many occasions in face of the enemy, and on this day he again led his company with equal dash and judgment.

A Company under Lieutenant the Hon. D. Bruce and B Company under Captain Murray, were then ordered to co-operate in the attack, as it was getting late (4 p.m.), and the advance of the Dehra Dun Brigade on the Bois du Biez was being retarded by this unfortunate situation. B Company at once set to work to bomb the Germans along the trench from the left, and at this point Captain R. Murray was wounded, dying the next day. A number of men distinguished themselves during the attack.

Corporal A. Hunter outdistanced the rest of his company, and got in ahead of them in the charge.

Lance-Corporal J. Muir showed great bravery in leading the bombing party and driving the enemy out of traverse after traverse.

Sergeant J. Porter performed a valuable service by taking a portion of his platoon under fire to a position well in rear of the German trench, whence he brought a very effective fire to bear on the enemy.

The services of these non-commissioned officers and men were recognized by the award of the Distinguished Conduct Medal.

While the trench was being cleared of the enemy, 2nd Lieutenant Kirkaldy was killed.

The Seaforths pushed on still further, but by now the enemy was thoroughly cowed, and about 120 of them surrendered. The casualties of the Seaforths during this brief but sharp action amounted to 2 officers and 17 men killed, 7 officers and 49 men wounded.

The Londons, on receiving the order to assault,

swarmed over the parapet of Port Arthur, and rushed across the open ground under very heavy fire. Losing heavily as they went, and splendidly led by their officers, they never hesitated for a moment, and got into the trench side by side with the party of the 1/39th Garhwalis.

The Distinguished Conduct Medal was awarded to the following for marked bravery during the charge:—Lance-Corporal Brewster, Company Sergeant-Major Murray, and Sergeant Newman.

When the trench was reached the Germans put up a half-hearted fight, which ended in a number being killed and about 20 surrendering.

The assaulting companies were commanded by Captains Moore and Livingstone. The former was awarded the Military Cross for his conspicuous ability and gallantry in handling the two companies during the attack and the remaining days of the battle. This fine battalion, whose first real baptism of fire it was, showed on this occasion what good work might be expected from our Territorial troops. Their casualties in the battle amounted to 8 officers and 160 other ranks.

Up to now Colonel Swiney had continued to direct operations from Port Arthur, in spite of the intense suffering and weakness caused by his wound, but towards 10 p.m. Major MacTier of the 2/39th was sent up to relieve him, and at about midnight Colonel Swiney was carried to hospital. He testified to the great gallantry and devotion to duty shown by Captain J. Taylor, I.M.S., the medical officer of the 1/39th, who continued without ceasing to attend to the wounded throughout the day and most of the night, although himself wounded, working under shell fire for the greater part of the time. Captain Taylor was awarded the D.S.O. for his services during this trying period.

Colonel Swiney survived his wound and eventually returned to France, but lost his life on his way to India, when the P. & O. s.s. *Persia* was torpedoed in the Mediterranean on the 30th December, 1915. By his death the 1/39th were deprived of a most gallant, competent, and much beloved Commanding Officer.

The 1/39th were now fully installed in the section of trench which it had been intended that they should take in the morning, but their casualties had been very serious, and by the night of the 12th March they had lost 7 British officers killed, Major MacTier, Captains Sparrow, Clarke, Kenny, Owen, Murray, and Lieutenant Welchman, as well as 3 Garhwali officers and 98 rank-and-file; while 5 British officers, Colonel Swiney, Captain Mainwaring, Lieutenants Mankelow and Lemon, and Captain Taylor, I.M.S., with 2 Garhwali officers and 190 men, were wounded. In addition to this, 22 men were missing, of whom the majority were probably killed.

The position on the night of the 10th March, from left to right, was as follows, the line being divided into three sections :—

Section 1: 2/3rd Gurkhas, under Lt-Colonel V. Ormsby.

Section 2: 2nd Leicesters, under Lt-Colonel Gordon.

Section 3: 1st Seaforths, 1/3rd Londons, and 1/39th Garhwalis, all under Lt-Colonel Ritchie of the Seaforths.

On the left of the 2/3rd Gurkhas touch was

established with the 2nd Rifle Brigade, 25th Brigade, 8th Division.

During the whole of the 11th and night of the 11th–12th March the process of consolidating the position was continued without much interference on the part of the enemy.

CHAPTER XVII

BATTLE OF NEUVE CHAPELLE—*Continued*

Neuve Chapelle cleared of the enemy—Condition of the village—Work of the Sappers and Miners—Activity of hostile snipers—Camaraderie between British and Indian soldiers—Attack of 23rd Brigade held up—Gallantry of Middlesex Regiment and Scottish Rifles—Delay in bringing up reserves of 4th Corps—Attack by the Dehra Dun Brigade held up—8th Division fails to advance—General Jacob in consequence has to retire—1/4th Seaforth Highlanders—Further attack delayed by inability of 8th Division to advance—Dehra Dun Brigade relieved by Sirhind—General Jacob's appreciation of 2/2nd and 1/9th Gurkhas—Attack by Sirhind and Jullundur Brigades—Anticipated by heavy German attacks—Completely repulsed—Enemy's heavy losses—Gallantry of Captain Lodwick and Lieutenant Mankelow—Work of Signallers—Captain Collins, 1/4th Gurkhas, wins the D.S.O.—Our attack held up owing to failure of 25th Brigade to advance—Heavy losses of 1st Highland Light Infantry—Failure of our second attack—Third attack countermanded by Sir James Willcocks—Further active operations suspended by Sir Douglas Haig—Losses of British forces in the battle—Losses of Indian Corps—Material and moral results of the battle—Appreciation of Indian Corps by Sir John French—Sir Douglas Haig's special order—Telegram from Sir John French to the Viceroy of India—Curtailment of ammunition for our artillery—Improvements in enemy's defences after Neuve Chapelle.

THE Indian Corps was now firmly established in a line of trenches running down the eastern side of Neuve Chapelle and facing the Bois du Biez, the assault on which was to form the second phase of the operations.

The task of clearing the village of such of the enemy as had survived the bombardment was necessarily a grim proceeding. The houses had for the most part been blown to bits, but isolated parties of the bolder spirits amongst the Germans still lurked in the cellars, or held the upper floors of disroofed buildings, while machine guns did their deadly work from the shelter of piles of ruins. Our men went systematically through the village, house by house, bombing or bayoneting such as resisted, and taking a large number of prisoners, so that by 11 a.m. the village was completely cleared.

The effect of our bombardment resembled that of a very violent earthquake. The church had been completely shattered, and the churchyard was pitted from end to end with yawning shell holes, the graves in many cases being burst open, exposing in a very terrible fashion long-buried bodies to view. Many trees had been blown up by the roots, and over all was the stain and pungent reek of lyddite.

The rôle of the Sappers and Miners in an action is to follow up the infantry as closely as possible, and to wire and consolidate captured positions. This, as can be imagined, is no light task, entailing as it does heavy labour under constant fire. The party of Sappers who were entrusted with the work on the new line in front of Neuve Chapelle, made their head quarters in the cellars of the Brewery, on the walls of which the late occupants had written many times the benevolent phrase, "Gott strafe England." By day the company rested, spending the whole night in consolidating the line.

The Brewery, formerly a substantial three-storied erection, was a favourite target of the German gunners, who pounded it persistently with every kind of shell. Gradually the remaining walls and floors were demolished, but the gallant Sappers still held on in their underground fastness. The climax came on the third day, when the cellar roof was split, and a "crump" bursting outside extinguished the solitary candle at the far end, and other arrangements had to be made.

The Sappers and the 107th Pioneers laboured with such a will that our new line was consolidated before that of the enemy, and we were thus enabled to bring fire to bear on the German working parties, and to break them up. To have done so before would have been to draw the enemy's fire on our men, a proceeding always to be avoided.

The German snipers were particularly active and bold at this period. On the 14th March two men of the 4th King's (Liverpools) were shot through the head soon after daylight, evidently by a sniper. There appeared to be no very suitable positions for these gentry in the neighbourhood, but a close scrutiny of the ground in front revealed a slight movement among some dead Germans lying just beyond our wire, and a further examination disclosed the presence among the corpses of a sniper, who was greeted with a volley which put a stop to his further operations.

As an instance of the different ways in which our men meet misfortune when it comes, the case of Havildar Ismail Khan of the 21st Company, 3rd Sappers and Miners, may be quoted. This havildar, while working in front of the line, was shot through both legs, one being smashed. His first expression of opinion was one of admiration for the German sniper, who, he considered, had carefully waited until his legs were in line, so as to damage both with one shot! The havildar, who expressed his view with grave and measured approval, evidently looked upon this feat as a fine example of war economy.

The camaraderie existing between the British and Indian soldiers was very marked during the battle. Cigarettes were freely exchanged as well as friendly greetings, the latter evidently unintelligible, but apparently eminently satisfactory to both parties. Often when a detachment of Sappers was returning from work, the British would give them cigarettes and insist on their warming themselves at their fire buckets, generally heralding their arrival by the cry of "Gangway for the Suffering Miners."

The attack of the 23rd Brigade on the left had not met with the same success as that of the Indian Corps, but through no fault of their own. The 2nd Scottish Rifles and the 2nd Middlesex advanced with splendid determination against a hail of bullets from rifles and machine guns, only to find that the enemy's wire had been but little damaged by our guns.

Both battalions fought magnificently, tearing at the wire with their hands and breaking it with the butts of their rifles, but nothing could live against such fire as was brought to bear on them at a range of a few yards, and they were compelled to fall back and to lie in the open, scraping up such cover as they could. Further to their right the 25th Brigade had met with little difficulty, as the wire in their front had been completely destroyed, and they were enabled to turn the southern flank of the enemy's defence in front of the 23rd Brigade, which then succeeded in getting through to the north-east corner of the village, where they linked up with the 25th Brigade on their right and the 24th Brigade on their left.

The losses of the Middlesex and Scottish Rifles were fearful; the latter regiment came out about 150 strong, under the command of a second lieutenant, having lost 15 officers, including the colonel.

This would have been the opportunity to push on with the utmost possible speed, while the element of surprise still existed and the enemy was demoralized by the bombardment, but the check sustained by the 23rd Brigade had thrown the machinery out of gear, and our front had to be reorganized.

An unexplained delay also occurred in bringing up the reserves of the 4th Corps. Sir John French, in his despatch dated the 5th April, 1915, remarked, "I am of opinion that this delay would not have occurred had the clearly expressed orders of the General Officer Commanding First Army been more carefully observed. The difficulties above enumerated might have been overcome at an earlier period of the day if the General Officer Commanding 4th Corps had been able to bring his reserve Brigade more speedily into action. As it was, the further advance did not commence before 3.30 p.m."

It is no part of the duty of those who are only concerned with the fortunes of the Indian Corps to examine the reasons which prevented the prompt employment of the reserve Brigade of the 4th Corps. The results, however, of this failure did much to neutralize the splendid efforts of the Indian Corps in this great battle.

It will be seen later that the successive assaults were held up by the enfilade fire of the enemy, the left flank of the Indian attack being in each case in the air, owing to the inability of the 8th Division to advance.

At about 4 p.m. on the 10th March, the Dehra Dun Brigade, under the command of Brigadier-General C. W. Jacob, which had hitherto been in support of the Garhwal Brigade, moved up and deployed along the road running south-west of Neuve Chapelle towards Port Arthur, facing the Bois du Biez. The Brigade had, however, been weakened by the detachment of the 1st Seaforths to assist the Garhwal Brigade.

At 5.30 p.m., by which time it was almost dark, the assaulting troops advanced towards their objective, the Bois du Biez, the 2/2nd Gurkhas on the right, the 1/9th Gurkhas on the left, with the 1/4th Seaforths in close support. The front line of the 2nd Gurkhas was composed of No. 3 Double Company under Major Nicolay and 2nd Lieutenant Clifford on the left, and No. 4 Double Company under Major Watt, with Captain Dallas Smith on the right. No. 1 Double Company under Major Sweet and Captain McCleverty was in support on the right, and No. 2 under Captain Mullaly on the left. Leading the 1/9th Gurkhas were Nos. 1 and 2 Companies, with 3 and 4 in support.

The attack at once came under fire from both flanks, a machine gun on the left being particularly active, and as each line deployed into the open, casualties occurred. Captain McCleverty was here shot through the arm and put out of action.

Luckily, the River Des Layes, an obstacle which it was feared would cause much trouble, was to a great extent in dead ground, *i.e.* not exposed to the direct fire of the enemy, and did not seriously impede the advance, as eight portable bridges had been brought up, over which the troops crossed rapidly.

Major Watt and Captain Dallas Smith led the assault with great dash, and reached the edge of the wood with few casualties. No. 3 Double Company, in attempting to keep touch with the 9th Gurkhas on the left, lost connection with No. 4 Company, and some confusion arose, which ended in a portion of No. 3 being held up by machine-gun fire. Nos. 1 and 2 Double Companies then closed up in rear, and the whole battalion began to dig itself in at the edge of the wood, sending out scouts to search the adjoining houses, from which snipers were giving much trouble.

Major Watt subsequently received the D.S.O. for the conspicuous bravery and ability shown by him in leading his company during this attack. On the following day he was wounded, but continued to command his double company until he collapsed.

Captain Dallas Smith and Lieutenant and Adjutant Corse-Scott were awarded the Military Cross for their services in the battle.

Here four Germans were captured by No. 4 Company, and another, who had lost his way, walked into the middle of No. 2 Company and was made prisoner. At about this time Major Nicolay was missing, and it was believed that he had been captured by the Germans, but subsequently it was ascertained that he had been killed in an attempt to establish touch between his position and that of No. 4 Company.

Our scouts could find no enemy or hostile trench in our immediate front, but a prisoner stated that there were 1200 Germans on our left. While exploring the neighbourhood, a searchlight was discovered mounted on a limber, and, as it could not be removed it was rendered unserviceable before the subsequent retirement.

In the darkness touch had been lost with the 1/9th Gurkhas, and the position of No. 4 Double Company being very precarious, it was withdrawn to the support line outside the wood. Several German scouts were there captured, and it was found that a strongly traversed trench lay at a short distance from our front.

The 1/9th Gurkhas on the left had reached the River Layes with very slight casualties, and Nos. 3 and 4 Companies moved up to establish connection with the 2nd Gurkhas. They arrived at the edge of the wood after a brief but sharp tussle, in which five Germans were killed and seven taken prisoner.

Subadar Mehar Sing Khattri was very prominent in this episode. He spotted some Germans in a trench and sent a bomber to attack them, covering his advance with fire. The Subadar then rushed the trench, and by his gallant leading gained the 2nd Class, Indian Order of Merit.

In this position both battalions remained until about 8 p.m., the enemy continually making strenuous efforts to work round the flank of the 1/9th Gurkhas, but every attempt was frustrated by the fire of our machine guns under Lieutenant R. G. H. Murray, who met all onslaughts with such vigour that the enemy was compelled, after considerable losses, to desist. Lieutenant Murray was awarded the Military Cross for marked gallantry and ability on this and the succeeding day.

The advance had now been brought to a standstill, and General Jacob had at once to decide whether it was advisable to hold on where he was, or to retire to a stronger line. In coming to a conclusion, he had to take into consideration several points. He had been led to expect co-operation by the 8th Division on his left, but one Brigade had been stopped by a strongly held bridgehead ; another could make no headway against machine-gun fire from the cross-roads near the village of Piètre. The 7th Division also was held up at the River Layes, and by the strength of the hostile position at the Moulin du Piètre ; the 1st Brigade, which was brought up in support from the 1st Corps, arrived after dark, when it was not considered advisable to put it in. The result was that both flanks of the Dehra Dun Brigade were in the air, the left flank especially being heavily enfiladed by machine guns. In fact, the Brigade was isolated.

Information obtained from prisoners and by our scouts showed that the enemy had rushed up reinforcements, and that the wood was strongly held, two German regiments being known to have assembled there.

The absence of the 1st Seaforths with the Garhwal Brigade had seriously weakened General Jacob's command, but in spite of this, he was confident that, had the 8th Division been able to co-operate, he could have maintained his position on the edge of the wood. As it was, he was forced to the conclusion that a retirement to the line of the River Layes was imperative, in which opinion General Anderson commanding the Meerut Division, as well as Sir James Willcocks, subsequently concurred.

The force then withdrew in good order under continual fire, but without further casualties, thanks to General Jacob's skill, to the western bank of the River Layes, all wounded who could be found being collected and removed. In the absence of any signs of activity on the part of the enemy, the troops spent the night in digging themselves in.

During the retirement Riflemen Manjit Gurung, Partiman Gurung, Ujir Sing Gurung, and Jagtea Pun, 2/2nd Gurkhas, gained the 2nd Class, Indian Order of Merit by attending to wounded men under fire and carrying them back. Rifleman Hastobir Roka earned the same distinction by bringing up machine-gun ammunition across ground swept by fire, although already wounded in the arm.

Meanwhile, operation orders were issued for an attack to be made at 7 a.m. on the 11th March by the Meerut Division, with the Bois du Biez as its first objective, the Jullundur Brigade being lent as a support, while the Divisional Artillery was strengthened by that of the Lahore Division with No. 1 Group of G.H.Q. Artillery.

Early in the morning Lt-Colonel MacFarlane commanding the 4th Seaforths was wounded, and Major Cuthbert took over command. Throughout the day this officer led his battalion with great courage and ability, although he was suffering severely from a wound in the head. For their services during this battle Lt-Colonel MacFarlane and Major Cuthbert were awarded the C.M.G. and the D.S.O. respectively.

General Jacob, in his report on the part taken by his Brigade in the battle, speaks in the following terms of high praise of this splendid unit:—

"The 4th Seaforths, a Territorial battalion, showed itself to be the equal of any Regular regiment. They worked with a will, and with such regularity that it was a pleasure to see this battalion advance to attack with confidence and self-reliance that left little to be desired."

As showing the feeling of comradeship which existed between the British and Indian soldiers, the winning of the Distinguished Conduct Medal by Private A. McLeod, 1/4th Seaforths, may be instanced. This soldier voluntarily left his trench on the 11th March and spent a quarter of an hour under very heavy machine-gun and rifle fire in bandaging a seriously wounded Gurkha.

In addition to the attack on the Bois du Biez, the Meerut Division was ordered to seize any opportunity of advancing southwards from the Rue du Bois to co-operate with the 1st Corps, which was continuing its attack east of Givenchy. The assaulting troops were again supplied by the Dehra Dun Brigade, the 2/39th Garhwalis taking the place of the 1st Seaforths, who had not yet rejoined.

Seven o'clock on the morning of the 11th arrived, but the attack of the 8th Division was held up, and it was consequently unable to get into line with the Dehra Dun Brigade, whose advance, in turn, was prevented by a thick fog and by heavy fire from the Bois du Biez, as well as from the left front and rear from points which could not be located.

At 9 a.m. the Jullundur Brigade was moved up to Neuve Chapelle in readiness to support. This situation continued till 10 a.m., there being still no signs of any advance by the 8th Division.

Meanwhile our guns were shelling the wood heavily, the only response from the enemy being in the shape of machine-gun and rifle fire; but a considerable amount of movement among the Germans was observed, especially opposite the 2/39th, and it was evident that they were collecting in large numbers.

Our men were by this time in a very exhausted condition, many of them having had no food, except what they carried in their haversacks, since they left Richebourg St Vaast on the night before the attack. The appearance of the 2/8th Gurkhas with rations was therefore very welcome. The battalion was employed to a great extent during the action in bringing up stores and ammunition to the firing line. General Anderson records that this duty was steadily carried out under heavy shell fire, with considerable casualties, and that the behaviour of all ranks reflected much credit on the regiment, the work being arduous, dangerous, and not very inspiring.

During the operations of the 11th March, the ration party of the 1/9th Gurkhas lost a number of men from machine-gun fire. Jemadar Shibdhoj Mal saw one of the wounded lying out under fire. Accompanied by Havildar Gambhir Sing Bohra and four of the 1/9th, he went out and brought in several men, the enemy keeping up intense machine-gun fire all the time. The Jemadar received the 2nd Class, Indian Order of Merit and the Havildar and Riflemen the Indian Distinguished Service Medal.

At 11.30 a.m. the Sirhind Brigade was moved up to Richebourg St Vaast in case of emergency.

Meanwhile it was ascertained by General Jacob personally, from the nearest battalion of the 8th Division, that the cause of the delay in their advance was that the left of the 25th Brigade was heavily engaged, and that the right had strict orders not to move forward till the situation was adjusted. Still more delay, until at 12.45 p.m. orders were received for the infantry attack from the line of the River Layes to take place at 2.15 p.m., provided that the 8th Division had come up; the Dehra Dun Brigade to assault the Bois du Biez, supported by the Jullundur Brigade.

From thenceforward until dark the enemy kept up a constant bombardment of the trenches; the slightest movement at once drew heavy enfilade machine-gun fire on our front line, which, hastily dug as it had been, afforded very incomplete cover, and the casualties were numerous.

When 2.15 p.m., the appointed time for the attack, arrived, there were still no signs of any advance on the part of the 8th Division. The two leading battalions of the Dehra Dun Brigade were therefore precluded by operation orders from moving, but some platoons of the 4th Seaforths, out of sheer eagerness, left their support trenches and doubled forward. They came at once under heavy machine-gun fire, and, after losing a number of men, were forced to crowd into the Gurkha trenches.

It was felt that this unsatisfactory situation should not be allowed to continue, and inquiry was again made by General Jacob of the nearest battalion of the 25th Brigade as to the reason of the delay in the advance. *The reply was that nothing was known of any intended attack at* 2.15 *p.m.* This was reported to General Anderson, who at 6 p.m. informed General Jacob that he would be relieved by the Sirhind Brigade.

At 1.20 a.m. on the 12th the Sirhind Brigade

arrived, and Dehra Dun moved off in the pitch darkness, losing a few men on the way from shell fire.

The casualties of the various units of the Brigade during the fighting from the 10th to the 12th March were as follows:—

1st Seaforths: 1 officer and 34 men killed; 9 officers and 117 men wounded; 5 men missing.

4th Seaforths: 2 officers and 34 men killed; 6 officers and 136 men wounded; 3 missing.

1/9th Gurkhas: 1 British, 3 Gurkha officers and 50 other ranks killed; 2 Gurkha officers and 76 others wounded; 1 Gurkha officer and 1 man missing.

2/2nd Gurkhas: 2 Gurkha officers and 17 others killed; 2 British, 1 Gurkha officer and 44 men wounded; 1 British officer and 28 men missing.

General Jacob speaks in these words of the work of the Gurkhas:—

"The Gurkha battalions (2/2nd and 1/9th) had an opportunity of making up for the terrible ordeals they had been through in the earlier days of the war, and they took full advantage of it. Their spirits were high, and nothing could stop their dash."

Brigadier-General Jacob, who has since risen to the command of an Army Corps, was appointed a Companion of the Order of the Bath in recognition of the ability shown by him during the battle, Lt-Colonel G. T. Widdicombe, 1/9th Gurkhas, receiving the same distinction, while Major E. P. R. Boileau, 2/2nd Gurkhas, was promoted to brevet Lt-Colonel.

On the relief of the Dehra Dun Brigade, the Jullundur Brigade moved up to Neuve Chapelle. This Brigade had gone through a very trying experience during the previous day, as it had been lying out in the open, exposed for the greater part of the time to severe shell and rifle fire, by which 286 casualties were caused. During the march to Neuve Chapelle, it was subjected to continued shelling by heavy artillery and field guns, which broke up the formation and forced units to disperse in search of any cover they could find; 300 casualties occurred during this short march, and some units were much disorganized.

The Sirhind Brigade, while marching up to relieve Dehra Dun, also came under shell fire, but luckily with few casualties.

The general plan of operations on the 12th March was as follows :—

Artillery fire was to be concentrated from 10 to 10.30 a.m. on the enemy's positions and on houses in front of the 8th Division, which, as soon as the bombardment ceased, was to assault and then to continue its advance in conjunction with the Indian Corps. The attack of the latter was timed for 11 a.m., to be preceded by concentrated artillery fire on the hostile positions along the road on the north-east edge of the Bois du Biez to the road junction 600 yards south-east of Port Arthur, also on redoubts and houses on the La Bassée road.

The Sirhind and Jullundur Brigades were to carry out the attack under Brigadier-General Walker, on a two-Brigade front.

The second objective was the eastern edge of the Bois du Biez; the third objective being a line through La Hue and Ligny-le-Grand to La Cliqueterie inclusive.

The time of attack was subsequently postponed

for two hours, *i.e.* to 12.30 p.m. for the 8th Division and 1 p.m. for the Indian Corps, as a heavy morning mist made it impossible to carry out adequate registration.

At 5.45 a.m. the Bareilly Brigade, which was still holding our original trenches, reported that the Germans were assaulting from a point slightly south of Port Arthur up to our extreme left in front of Neuve Chapelle. This Brigade, although it did not take part in the attack, had also been going through a very trying time, as the enemy's artillery had kept up an almost continual bombardment of varying intensity. During the action on the 10th March, the Brigade assisted by bursts of machine-gun and rifle fire, with a view to subduing any counter-attack on the right of our assault.

At 11 a.m. the 4th Black Watch was ordered up from Brigade reserve to take over from the Garhwal Brigade two strong points which were to be established in the captured trenches. This operation the battalion carried out with great dash and determination.

Lieutenant S. H. Steven charged at the head of the leading platoon, and gained his objective with fine courage, in spite of the heavy enfilade fire to which the movement was exposed. He was awarded the Military Cross for his conspicuous gallantry. By its behaviour on this its first appearance in the front line, the battalion gave promise of the reputation which it has since acquired.

The enemy's attack on the 12th was heralded by a heavy bombardment of Roome's trench, Port Arthur and the "Crescent," which commenced at 5.20 a.m. At 5.45 a.m. dense masses of Germans appeared, coming on at their usual jog-trot. In the uncertain light they resembled Highlanders, their overcoats giving the appearance of kilts, but when they arrived within 100 yards of our line, the spikes of their helmets could be discerned.

It seemed at first as if no fire could stop them, so impressive was the sight of this great multitude of men. The effect of concentrated machine-gun and rifle fire must, however, be witnessed to be fully appreciated. The surging mass came on much as a heavy swell rolls towards the seashore. At one moment the very earth seemed to be advancing towards our line, and nothing apparently could save us from being overwhelmed. The next instant a furious fusillade broke from our trenches. It ceased just as daylight appeared, and where before were swelling lines of men moving on in their awe-compelling progress, now, as an officer relates, nothing was to be seen but heaps of dead and wounded Germans.

Piles of wriggling, heaving bodies lay on the ground, and the air resounded with shrieks, groans, and curses. The wounded tried to shelter themselves behind parapets formed of the bodies of their dead comrades, while some attempted to dig themselves in. For hours afterwards wounded Germans continued to crawl into our line, where they received medical attention and were sent off in ambulances as soon as possible.

The slaughter was prodigious. In front of the Leicesters, 1st Seaforths, and 2/3rd Gurkhas, some 600 dead were counted, and General Anderson in his report calculated, as a minimum, that the enemy's losses in killed alone on the front captured by the

Meerut Division amounted to 2000, to which must be added heavy casualties caused by our bombardment of the Bois du Biez. One of the writers himself, on a careful estimate, counted 1200 Germans lying dead or wounded in front of a portion of our line.

The repelling of a massed attack such as this gives the machine-gun officer his own peculiar opportunity, and, as usual, he was not slow to seize it. Captain Lodwick, 2/3rd Gurkhas, gained the D.S.O. by his courage and skill in the performance of his duties as machine-gun officer of the Garhwal Brigade during the battle. In order to ascertain the best positions, he reconnoitred at great risk the whole of the captured trenches, and by his masterly disposition of 20 guns he was very largely responsible for the overthrow of this heavy attack. Unfortunately, this brave officer, like Colonel Swiney, lost his life when the *Persia* was torpedoed on the 30th December, 1915.

At 9 a.m. the enemy made a second attempt, which fared no better than the first. Similar scenes were enacted, and in no place did the attack reach our trenches.

On the right of the 1/39th Garhwalis the Germans repeatedly endeavoured to work up the trench against the flank of the battalion, and even came into the open in rear, but each attempt was thwarted, largely through the instrumentality of Lieutenant A. H. Mankelow, in charge of the regimental machine guns, who had throughout the action shown the greatest determination and ability, remaining at duty, although he had been wounded on the 10th March. For his services Lieutenant Mankelow received the

Military Cross. This gallant young officer was killed on the 14th May, 1915.

Jemadar Guman Sing Negi, who was with the guns under Lieutenant Mankelow, showed great devotion to duty. The enemy were using trench mortars with much effect, and only one man of a gun team was still unwounded. The Jemadar continued himself to fire the gun, and although wounded and shaken by a bomb, he remained at his post till relieved on the night of the 13th March, receiving the Indian Distinguished Service Medal for his bravery, as did also Lance-Naik Dangwa Ramola, one of the team of another gun, who was twice shot in the head, but still went on trying to fire.

Rifleman Jawarihu Negi (1/39th) and Sepoy Baliram (30th Punjabis attached) won the same reward by their bravery during the attack in getting out in the open and throwing hand grenades at the enemy. The former also threw an unexploded bomb, which had fallen in his trench, over the parapet. He thus saved a number of casualties. The latter was killed while bombing the enemy.

All this time our artillery kept up a terrific fire on the Bois du Biez, causing, there is every reason to believe, very heavy casualties, as for days afterwards the enemy was observed to be removing bodies from the wood for burial in the fields behind it.

As always, the work of the Signallers at this arduous time was carried on with the utmost coolness and skill. During an action, the ground in rear of attack and defence alike is subjected to a tremendous artillery fire, which ploughs up the earth and destroys the telephone wires connecting the front line with Brigade and Divisional Head Quarters. It is the duty of the Signallers to repair the lines at all costs, and what such work means can easily be imagined. In the midst of a tornado of every description of fire a few men are seen in the open, calmly attending to their task, repairing the wires with as much coolness as if the scene of the breakage were in a London house instead of on a bullet-swept battlefield. A man falls ; another takes his place ; and the work goes on, whatever may be the toll of life involved.

Amongst those who specially distinguished themselves was Captain C. J. Torrie, 30th Punjabis, commanding No. 35 Signal Company, of whom it is recorded that the successful work of the Division at Neuve Chapelle was to a very great extent dependent on the efficiency of the communications established and maintained by him under very heavy fire. The value of Captain Torrie's services was recognized by the award of the D.S.O.

It is only possible to mention a few of the non-commissioned officers and men who gained the Distinguished Conduct Medal by their gallantry on signal duty.

Corporal W. Gurdon, a motor cyclist of the Meerut Signal Company and a member of the 2nd Presidency Volunteer Rifles, showed conspicuous bravery from the 10th to the 13th March in constantly carrying important messages under fire by day and night, always with success.

Private P. E. Sones, 4th Suffolks, attached Lahore Signal Company, received the Medal for great courage on the 12th and 13th March, when he carried messages for 48 successive hours under very heavy rifle and machine-gun fire.

Corporal Chadwick, R.E., attached to the same

Signal Company, carried messages on three occasions for a distance of $1\frac{1}{4}$ miles over ground swept by very heavy and continuous shell fire.

A volume could be filled with the deeds of these men, but the few instances cited above will suffice to show the nature of their work.

On the 12th March the enemy made frequent use of handkerchiefs tied to rifles, as white flags, often even at a distance of 800 to 1000 yards, and officers were seen in the background trying, by the persuasion of their revolvers, to induce their men to advance.

During the whole of the 12th and 13th March the Garhwal Brigade went through the terrible test of holding a line under continual heavy bombardment. An officer describes this experience as a foretaste of hell, an opinion with which others who have suffered in a like manner will agree. The enemy also kept up a heavy fire on Neuve Chapelle and Port Arthur, it being estimated that 3000 shells fell in the latter section during the 12th alone.

The Sirhind and Jullundur Brigades had been brought up during the night of the 11th–12th, Sirhind relieving Dehra Dun in the trenches, with the 1st Highland Light Infantry and 1/4th Gurkhas in rear of the portion of the line held by the 2/3rd Gurkhas, while Jullundur occupied a position in rear of Sirhind.

At about 11.30 a.m. on the 12th, it was reported that the Germans in front of the right of the 1/4th Gurkhas were showing signs of wishing to surrender. In dealing with a foe so given to treachery, it was always necessary to be on one's guard. Captain L. P. Collins, 1/4th Gurkhas, who was in command at that point, considered that the opportunity should at once be seized to attack, as the occupation of that portion of the enemy's trench was in conformity with the general plan, and would facilitate the extension of the 1/4th Gurkhas to the right.

Acting on his own responsibility, Captain Collins at once assaulted and took 150 yards of the trench with very slight loss. He then saw that a number of Germans were holding the trench further to the left. These he attacked, when about 100 surrendered and some 50 were shot as they bolted. Captain Collins's losses were slight, but they included Subadar Durgia Gurung, who could ill be spared, as his work both in and out of action had been of great value to the regiment. For his conspicuous gallantry in this affair, and for the initiative displayed by him, Captain Collins was awarded the D.S.O.

The attack timed for 1 p.m. was organized on a two-Brigade front, the Sirhind Brigade being on the right with two battalions, the 1st Highland Light Infantry and 1/4th Gurkhas, in the front line, the 15th Sikhs and 1/1st Gurkhas in support. The two Brigades were under Brigadier-General Walker, Lt-Colonel Anderson, 1/1st Gurkhas, commanding the Sirhind Brigade in his place.

Originally it was intended that the Jullundur Brigade should attack on a front of three battalions, *i.e.* the 1st Manchesters on the left in touch with the 25th Brigade, 8th Division, the 47th Sikhs in the centre, and the 4th Suffolks on the right, with the 59th Rifles in Brigade reserve. During the morning, however, it was reported that the Suffolks now consisted of about 140 rank-and-file, while the 59th Rifles numbered only some 125 men.

The cause of this very serious diminution of

numbers was that the Brigade had suffered heavy casualties while lying in the open on the previous day, coming also under very severe shelling on the march to Neuve Chapelle. Great confusion arose in the darkness, and in addition to casualties, a large number of men of the Suffolks and 59th were unable to rejoin their units. The result was that in order to occupy the length of front allotted to the Brigade, the 59th Rifles had to be added to the Suffolks in the front line, thus leaving no Brigade reserve.

At noon the bombardment on the 8th Division front began, but their attack had only progressed about a hundred yards by 1 p.m. Shortly before our guns opened on the Indian Corps' front, about 100 Germans came over and gave themselves up. They were a miserable-looking lot of men, and appeared to be more or less starving, as they eagerly devoured the chupatties given to them by the Indians.

At 12.30 p.m. our artillery poured a very heavy shrapnel fire into the Bois du Biez, and at 1 p.m. the infantry attack commenced.

The Manchesters, heroes of Givenchy, advanced with their accustomed determination and steadiness, but the moment the first line of two companies appeared, the enemy opened a staggering fire, and Captain Browne, commanding No. 1 Company, was wounded, while men were falling fast. By 1.30 p.m. the leading companies of the battalion had succeeded in reaching the front line trenches held by the Garhwal Brigade, but here they became mixed up with the 2/3rd Gurkhas, while the first and second ines and the communication trenches were completely blocked by troops.

The remainder of the battalion was held up for some time, owing to the necessity of crossing gaps in the trenches where roads and ditches intersected them. These gaps were marked down by the enemy and swept by machine-gun fire, all attempts to pass them ending only in heavy casualties. The Manchesters, however, are hard to beat, as the enemy has so often found to his cost, and Nos. 3 and 4 Companies eventually made a most gallant rush and reached the front line, but with much-diminished ranks.

The 47th Sikhs, who had so greatly distinguished themselves at Neuve Chapelle in October, 1914, fared little better. Scarcely had their advance commenced, when Captain Combe was wounded, as well as several Indian officers. Captain Hogge then took command, but was hit shortly afterwards, being succeeded by Captain Talbot, who was himself slightly wounded, as were also Captains Abbay and Cormack, but all remained at duty.

Subadar Harnam Singh was killed while leading his half-company. His bravery had been most conspicuous throughout the campaign, and had won for him the Indian Order of Merit at Festubert in December, 1914, in which action his only son was killed. The Subadar, after his death, was granted the Order of British India, 2nd Class.

Shortly after this Captain Brown was killed and Captain Story wounded, the casualties in the ranks being also very heavy, and when the front line trenches were reached, it was found to be impossible to make any further progress in face of the terrific fire.

During the advance, a wounded man was seen to be lying out in a most exposed position.

Havildar Gajjan Singh and Sepoy Rur Singh volunteered to attempt to bring him in, and went over the parapet. The Havildar was at once wounded, but Rur Singh managed to drag him back under cover, and went out again to rescue the wounded man by himself, but was unable to move him. Lieutenant Allardice (14th, attached 47th Sikhs) then went out, and with Rur Singh succeeded in getting the man into our trench. He had, however, been wounded in so many places while lying in the open that he succumbed. This conspicuous act of bravery was performed in a most exposed position, when any movement drew heavy machine-gun fire from both flanks. Havildar Gajjan Singh and Sepoy Rur Singh received the 2nd Class, Indian Order of Merit.

For his services during the campaign, in which he was twice wounded, Lt-Colonel Richardson was promoted to Brevet-Colonel, while Lt-Colonel Gunning (35th Sikhs attached) received the C.M.G.

The 4th Suffolks, who on the 11th had lost Lieutenant Row and 19 men killed, Lieutenant Turner and 100 men being wounded, now again suffered severely, Captain Garrett and 7 men being killed, Captains Cockburn and Mason, Lieutenant Hoyland and 74 men being wounded.

The 59th Rifles were even more unfortunate. On the preceding day they had lost 1 British officer killed and 2 wounded, as well as 2 Indian officers. They went into this attack with only 5 British and the same number of Indian officers.

During the advance to the support trenches, Lt-Colonel P. C. Eliott-Lockhart, of the Guides, a most gallant and able Commanding Officer, was wounded, and died shortly afterwards. A little later Captain

Hore was killed at the head of his company, as well as Captain Reed of the machine guns, and Captain Burn was severely wounded.

For some time after this quick succession of casualties the regiment was left without a British officer, as Captain Inskip, the last left, was badly shell-shocked and could not rejoin till later. The losses of the 59th in British officers, up to date, had been very heavy, amounting to 10 killed and 19 wounded out of an average war strength of 13 officers.

Sepoy Zarif Khan, throughout the 11th and 12th March, behaved with the greatest gallantry in continually carrying messages under very heavy fire. He was killed on the 12th March, while performing this duty, but was posthumously granted the 1st Class of the Indian Order of Merit. This brave soldier had already won the 2nd Class of the Order during the early days of the war.

The failure of the Jullundur and Sirhind Brigades to reach their objectives, in spite of the great dash and bravery with which their advance was carried out, was due to the fact that the 25th Brigade on their left was unable to advance, the Brigades on its left again having been held up. This enabled the enemy to bring heavy enfilade fire to bear on the Indian attack from the left, while at the same time pouring in oblique fire from a redoubt at the north-west extremity of the Bois du Biez.

The Sirhind Brigade met with more success in its attack. In the front line were the 1st Highland Light Infantry under Lt-Colonel E. R. Hill on the left, and the 1/4th Gurkhas under Major D. C. Young on the right, the 15th Sikhs being in rear of the 1/4th Gurkhas, the 1/1st Gurkhas in reserve, and the 4th King's (Liverpools) further back, for it was only intended to use this battalion, which had recently arrived from England, in case of emergency.

Before the attack on the first main objective, the Bois du Biez, could be developed, two advanced positions had to be captured: (*a*) a line of trench parallel to and just north-west of the River Layes; (*b*) a trench parallel to and 200 yards south-east of the river.

As soon as the bombardment ceased, the Highland Light Infantry advanced with A Company on the right in the firing line, under Captain Halswelle, and B Company on the left under Captain Knight, with C and D Companies in reserve.

The Sirhind Brigade, having relieved Dehra Dun during the early morning, was already some distance in advance, and the Jullundur Brigade having been held up, the left flank of the Highland Light Infantry was exposed to a very heavy oblique as well as frontal fire at a range of about 500 yards. This caught the battalion the moment it began to advance, and a number fell at the start, as well as at each successive rush.

Captains Knight and Halswelle led their men with great dash, nobly seconded by their subalterns, 2nd Lieutenants Gibbs, Maclean (killed), Knox and Wornham.

The advance lay over absolutely bare ground without a vestige of cover, but the men swept on in spite of the heavy losses caused by the enemy's accurate fire. With the last rush the line of trench (*a*) was carried, after a hand-to-hand fight, in which a large number of Germans were killed and about

200 captured. A few men of A Company under Captain Halswelle succeeded in crossing the river, and held on there until dark.

Colonel Hill then ordered his advanced companies not to attempt to proceed further until the Jullundur Brigade could come up on the left, as that flank was in the air.

An attack by the 25th Brigade on the left, which was timed for 5 p.m., did not develope, and as darkness was rapidly coming on, the ground won was consolidated.

During the action, Private Brooks, seeing Corporal Hawke lying badly wounded in the open at a distance of about 30 yards from our trench, went over the parapet and carried him in under extremely heavy fire, for which act of bravery he received the Distinguished Conduct Medal.

Lance-Corporal Stewart and Private Clifford won the same decoration by their gallantry in going out under very severe fire and relaying a telephone wire which had been cut by shells, after two men had been killed in the attempt.

Sergeant-Major House also received the Distinguished Conduct Medal for his gallant and valuable services in keeping up the supply of ammunition by day and organizing stretcher parties at night.

Brave deeds were numerous on this trying day. Amongst others may be mentioned that of Private Duffy, Highland Light Infantry, who voluntarily went out from his trench and brought in eight wounded men under heavy fire, for which he was rewarded with the Distinguished Conduct Medal.

Of the officers, whose gallantry and leading had been of the highest order throughout, Lt-Colonel

Hill, Captains Halswelle, Knight, Tarrant, Stewart, and Lieutenant Cowan were mentioned in despatches.

The losses of the battalion during the action were very heavy, 8 officers having been killed and 5 wounded, while there were nearly 250 casualties amongst other ranks.

The right half-battalion of the 1/4th Gurkhas, which had captured a section of the enemy's trench under Captain Collins earlier in the day, had reformed with their right in touch with the Leicesters, the left half-battalion coming up shortly afterwards.

At about 2 p.m. a number of casualties occurred among the British officers of this battalion in their endeavour to rescue a wounded private of the Leicesters, who was lying about 20 yards in front of the Gurkha parapet. Major Young, Jemadar Gangabir Gurung and Rifleman Wazir Sing Burathoki went out together to try to bring the man in. In doing so, Major Young was mortally, and the rifleman severely, wounded. Captains Hogg and McGann, without a moment's hesitation, rushed out to help, but both were at once hit. Captain McGann managed to crawl back unaided, and Jemadar Gangabir with the help of some Gurkhas eventually succeeded in bringing Captain Hogg back. For their gallantry and devotion, the Jemadar and Rifleman Wazir Sing Burathoki received the 2nd Class of the Indian Order of Merit; the latter was also subsequently awarded the Russian Medal of St George, 3rd Class.

It is typical of the spirit of the Corps, and indeed of the whole Army, that three British officers and a number of Indian soldiers should have risked their lives to rescue a single private soldier of the Leicesters.

The battalion remained in readiness to attack, but as the left of the line was still held up, the assault was not delivered.

The 15th Sikhs in support got up close behind the Garhwal trenches, where they lay down under cover. Captain Waterfield was wounded in getting out of the trench at the very commencement of the advance; Subadar Gajjan Singh was killed and one Gurkha officer was wounded, there being 60 casualties amongst other ranks.

The 1/1st Gurkhas moved up in close support. As they advanced Major C. E. B. Champain, who was in temporary command in the absence of Lt-Colonel Anderson, was shot through the lungs. He was pulled under cover by men of the Highland Light Infantry, and survived to command his battalion in Mesopotamia. Captain and Adjutant G. S. Kennedy, one Gurkha officer and 15 other ranks were killed, and 51 wounded.

Insistent orders were now received from the 1st Army to press the attack on the Bois du Biez. In consequence, the Dehra Dun Brigade, which had just got back to well-earned billets, was recalled to Richebourg St Vaast, and the whole Lahore Division, now placed under its own Commander, General Keary, was ordered to push on to the wood at all costs.

At 5.50 p.m. our guns bombarded for 15 minutes, when a second attack was attempted; this, however, could not debouch from the trenches, being smothered by the enemy's frontal and enfilade fire.

In view, however, of the urgency of the orders

from Sir Douglas Haig, General Keary arranged for an attack by the whole of the Lahore Division to take place at 10.45 p.m., preceded again by 15 minutes' bombardment. This operation was vetoed by Sir James Willcocks, as not being feasible in pitch darkness, over unknown ground, and with such a large body of troops. No competent critic who has studied the facts will question the wisdom of this decision.

At 10.5 p.m. on the 12th, orders were received from Sir Douglas Haig, to suspend further active operations and to consolidate all positions gained. The Sirhind Brigade was then placed at the disposal of the Meerut Division, the Jullundur and Ferozepore Brigades being withdrawn.

So ended the battle of Neuve Chapelle, the first action on a large scale during the war in which the British had a predominance in artillery as well as in men.

The losses of the British forces engaged were: 190 officers and 2337 other ranks killed; 359 officers and 8174 other ranks wounded; 23 officers and 1728 other ranks missing; making a total of 12,811 casualties.

Included in these losses were the following casualties of the Indian Corps :—

	British officers.	Indian officers.	Other ranks (British).	Other ranks (Indian).
Killed	41	22	364	408
Wounded	91	36	1461	1495
Missing	1	2	87	225
Total	133	60	1912	2128

The question as to whether the success achieved was worth the losses involved has been much argued.

The material gain consisted of an advance of our

line on a front of two miles to a depth of 1000 yards. By this advance the dangerous salient known as Port Arthur was straightened out, thus, in Sir James Willcocks' words, removing a considerable source of anxiety to the various Corps which had been responsible for its safe custody.

To this gain in ground must be added the losses of the enemy in men and in moral. On the front captured by the Indian Corps alone the German dead numbered at least 2000, while many were buried by the enemy behind the Bois du Biez. In addition to these, Sir John French mentions, in his despatch before quoted, that he was in possession of positive information that upwards of 12,000 German wounded were removed to the north-east and east by train. It is possible that this estimate was exaggerated, but it is certain that 30 officers and 1657 other ranks of the enemy were captured, the share of the Indian Corps being 12 officers and 617 men. It is not improbable that the German losses approached the number of 18,000, leaving a balance in our favour.

As regards the question of loss of moral by the enemy, there can be no doubt that this sudden turning of the tables by the employment of overwhelming masses of artillery had a most demoralizing effect on the Germans, who, accustomed to view with exultation the effects of their superior concentrations of guns, were loud in their denunciations of similar practices by us.

The effect was felt far behind the hostile line, for it is known that at Lille the state of affairs was much akin to a panic. The principal hospital was removed to Tournai, to which place went many officers and the paraphernalia of the German Head Quarters, while the inhabitants of Lille openly expressed their joy at the prospect of the arrival of the British.

On the other hand, the change from the unutterable weariness of the winter months in trenches to the activity of a vigorous offensive put new life into our men. They were cheered too by the thought that the old, bad time had come to an end, and that in future the adequate support of our guns would enable them to give as much as they got. How far this belief was justified will be seen, but at least it was beneficial.

On the whole, then, the battle of Neuve Chapelle, on a strict balancing of accounts, was not entirely a failure. We attained our first objective at a cost which might well have gained us a further goal.

The mistakes which occurred were, perhaps, to be looked for in a first attempt at the adoption of the French methods of attack. The artillery preparation, almost perfect on the Indian front, was not everywhere so efficacious, as witness the effect of the bombardment on the 23rd Brigade front. In some cases, mostly due to the cloudy and foggy weather, artillery observation could not be adequately carried out, with the result that our guns sometimes shelled our own troops, leaving the enemy's line untouched.

Still, the reference to the behaviour of the Corps made by Sir John French, in his despatch dated the 5th April, 1915, shows that, whatever mistakes may have occurred in other parts of the field, the Indian Corps had every reason to be satisfied with its share in this battle. He remarks :—

"While the success attained was due to the magnificent bearing and indomitable courage displayed by the troops of the 4th and Indian Corps, I consider that the able and skilful dispositions which were made by the General Officer Commanding First Army contributed largely to the defeat of the enemy and to the capture of his position."

In the same despatch Sir John French continues:—

"I can best express my estimate of this battle by quoting an extract from a Special Order of the Day which I addressed to Sir Douglas Haig and the First Army at its conclusion: 'I am anxious to express to you personally my warmest appreciation of the skilful manner in which you have carried out your orders, and my fervent and most heartfelt appreciation of the magnificent gallantry and devoted, tenacious courage displayed by all ranks whom you have ably led to success and victory. My warmest thanks to you all.'"

In publishing this order of the day, Sir Douglas Haig added the following appreciatory remarks:—

"I desire to express to all ranks of the 1st Army my great appreciation of the task accomplished by them in the past four days of severe fighting. The 1st Army has captured the German trenches on a front of two miles, including the whole village of Neuve Chapelle, and some strongly defended works. Very serious loss has been inflicted on the enemy, nearly 2000 prisoners are in our hands, and his casualties in killed and wounded are estimated at about 16,000. I wish also to thank all concerned for the careful preparation made for the assault. Much depended on this thoroughness and secrecy. The attack was such a complete surprise to the enemy that he had neither a Corps nor an Army Reserve at hand, and had to draw on the adjoining army for help.

"The absolute success of the operation of breaking through the German lines on the first day is not only a tribute to the careful forethought and attention to detail on the part of the leaders, but it has proved beyond question that our forces can defeat the Germans where and when they choose, no matter what mechanical contrivances or elaborate defences are opposed to their advance.

"The results of the successful action just fought are not, however, confined to the material losses sustained by the enemy. The organization of the German forces from Ypres to far south of the La Bassée Canal has been thrown into a state of confusion. Reinforcements available to oppose the French in the battle which is taking place at Notre Dame de Lorette or destined for other parts of the line have been drawn into the fight opposite the 1st Army, and, in many cases, very severely handled.

"The losses sustained by the 1st Army, though heavy, are fully compensated for by the results achieved, which have brought us one step forward in our efforts to end the war; and the British soldier has once more given the Germans a proof of his superiority in a fight, as well as of his pluck and determination to conquer. The spirit and energy shown by all ranks augur well for the future, and I feel confident that the success achieved by the 1st Army at Neuve Chapelle is the forerunner of still greater victories which must be gained in order to bring the war to a successful conclusion."

In an order of the day dated the 14th March, 1915, the following telegram, received from Field-Marshal Sir John French, was published by Sir James Willcocks:—

"I have cabled following to Viceroy, India. Begins: I am glad to be able to inform your Excellency that the Indian troops under Sir James Willcocks fought with great gallantry and marked success in the capture of Neuve Chapelle and subsequent fighting which took place on the 10th, 11th, 12th, and 13th of this month. The fighting was very severe and the losses heavy, but nothing daunted them; their tenacity, courage, and endurance were admirable, and worthy of the best traditions of the soldiers of India. Message ends. Please make this known to the Corps under your command. Accept yourself and repeat to all Troops my warm and hearty appreciation of their services, and my gratitude for the help they have rendered, which has so much conduced to the success of the operations."

In common, then, with the other troops engaged in this memorable battle, the Indian Corps had every reason to be proud of itself. The general recognition of their valiant efforts encouraged officers and men to further deeds of courage and endurance. Moreover, fresh heart was put into the troops, so long accustomed to possess their souls in such patience as they might under the constant torment of an overpowering hostile artillery, by the exhibition of the power of our own guns so strikingly given at Neuve Chapelle. They felt that at last they had come into their own, and that the nightmare of the past months could not be repeated.

Their hopes were doomed to disappointment,

for within a few days of the end of the battle, the state of affairs was as bad as ever. The German guns again kept up their never-ceasing hideous din; again were our parapets battered down; once more our guns were almost silent; and this was to continue for months, save for our partially successful but costly attacks of May, 1915.

At the cause of this disheartening state of things the ordinary officers and men could only guess; presumably the supply of ammunition was insufficient. How far this was the case can be gathered from an order dated the 16th March, 1915. By this order the only guns for which the expenditure of ammunition was unrestricted were the 2·75, 60-pounder, and 6-inch; but even in regard to these the greatest economy was enjoined. The 3-pounders were put on a miserable ration of 2 rounds per day; 15-pounders were absolutely to hold their peace; 18-pounders, the ordinary field guns, were allowed to speak three times in the 24 hours; but no high explosive was available; and so on up to "Mother" and "Grandmother," the 9·2 and 15-inch howitzers, whose venerable mouths were on no account to be filled.

It is not strange that the troops began to doubt whether the nation was aware that it was at war with Germany, and not with some small tribe on the Indian Frontier.

A further result of our lavish expenditure of big-gun ammunition at Neuve Chapelle was the enormous improvement and strengthening of the enemy's defences. The trenches captured by us from the Germans in March, 1915, were on the whole hardly as good as our own. The enemy, however, never slow to learn, at once set about rendering his defences, as far as possible, safe against artillery fire.

In May and September, 1915, the positions taken at the battles of Festubert and Loos were very different from those of Neuve Chapelle. Every art of the military engineer had now been called into play. Heavily armoured machine-gun emplacements had been made; the dug-outs were no longer the old simple affairs, but elaborate underground systems, strengthened in every conceivable way with concrete and steel girders. It has therefore sometimes been doubted whether the battle of Neuve Chapelle was an unmixed blessing, or whether it would not have been wiser to have left the Germans in their innocence until we were prepared in every way for a violent and sustained effort. Further, had we succeeded in our aim of occupying the high ground commanding the approaches to Lille, Turcoing, and Roubaix, the enemy would have been compelled to run grave risks in order to readjust the situation.

Could we, in face of the serious shortage of artillery ammunition, have held the captured positions?

To reply to this question it is necessary to await the fuller information which may be available at the close of the war; but it is permissible to doubt whether we could have clung to our success.

Casualties up to the 1st April, 1915:—

	Killed.	Wounded.	Missing.
British officers . .	147	265	42
Indian officers . .	66	144	35
Other ranks, British .	726	2876	662
Other ranks, Indian .	1364	6253	1936
Total .	2303	9538	2675

CHAPTER XVIII

THE SECOND BATTLE OF YPRES

New front taken over by the Indian Corps—Establishment of bombing schools—Arrival of 40th Pathans—Lahore Division leaves for Ypres—Attack by Jullundur and Ferozepore Brigades under disadvantageous conditions—Corporal Issy Smith, 1st Manchesters, wins the V.C.—Severe casualties of the Manchesters—Death of Colonel Rennick, 40th Pathans—Heavy losses of the Pathans and 47th Sikhs—Gallantry of officers and men of the 57th Rifles and Connaught Rangers—French Colonial troops driven back by gas, carrying with them a great part of the Lahore Division—Parties of Connaughts, Manchesters, and Indians hold on under Major Deacon—Captain Ingham's D.S.O.—Major Deacon's D.S.O. and Legion of Honour—Jemadar Mir Dast's V.C.—Bravery of officers and men of the Lahore Signal Company and Army Service Corps—Jullundur and Ferozepore Brigades withdrawn on relief by Sirhind—C.R.E.'s experiences in Poperinghe.

The battle of Neuve Chapelle may be considered to have ended at 10 p.m. on the 12th March, when orders were received from General Sir Douglas Haig to suspend further operations and consolidate the positions gained.

The Meerut Division continued to hold the line, Bareilly being on the right, Garhwal on the left, with Sirhind supporting Garhwal from Neuve Chapelle.

The night of the 12th–13th passed quietly, and the Jullundur and Ferozepore Brigades were withdrawn. During the 13th the enemy several times threatened to attack in front of the left of the Indian Corps from north-west of the Bois du Biez, but the attacks could not develope in face of the heavy shrapnel fire which we brought to bear on likely points of debouchement.

The remainder of March passed without special incident beyond frequent heavy shelling by the enemy of Neuve Chapelle, Port Arthur, and Richebourg St Vaast. The weather continued to improve, and, the ground drying up, life became more bearable in the trenches. On the 19th March, however, a fall of snow served to remind the troops that winter had not yet struck its last blow.

On the 21st March orders were received for the Indian Corps to take over a new line of trenches from the cross-roads just north-north-east of Neuve Chapelle to a point near Chapigny, relieving the 4th Corps and handing over its former front to the 1st Corps. The Bareilly and Dehra Dun Brigades accordingly relieved the Brigades of the 8th Division during the night of the 23rd–24th March, and on the 31st March the Lahore Division relieved Meerut in the front line.

On the 28th March a reorganization of Brigades was effected, of which a complete detail is here given.

Lahore Division.

Commander: Major-General H. D'U. Keary, C.B., D.S.O.

Jullundur Brigade.

Commander: Brigadier-General E. P. Strickland, C.M.G., D.S.O.

1st Manchesters.
4th Suffolks (Territorials).
40th Pathans (arrived 8th April).
47th Sikhs.
59th Rifles.

Sirhind Brigade.

Commander: Brigadier-General W. G. Walker, V.C., C.B.

1st Highland Light Infantry.
4th King's (Liverpools) (Special Reserve).
15th Sikhs.
1/1st Gurkhas.
1/4th Gurkhas.

Ferozepore Brigade.

Commander: Brigadier-General R. M. Egerton, C.B.

Connaught Rangers.
4th London Regiment (Territorials).
9th Bhopals.
57th Rifles.
129th Baluchis.

Divisional Cavalry.

15th Lancers.

Divisional Battalion.

34th Sikh Pioneers.

C.R.A.: Brigadier-General F. E. Johnson, C.M.G., D.S.O., R.A.

C.R.E.: Lt-Colonel C. Coffin, R.E.

MEERUT DIVISION.

Commander: Lt-General C. A. Anderson, C.B.

Dehra Dun Brigade.

Commander: Brigadier-General C. W. Jacob.

1st Seaforths.
4th Seaforths (Territorials).
6th Jats.
2/2nd Gurkhas.
1/9th Gurkhas.

Garhwal Brigade.

Commander: Brigadier-General C. G. Blackader, D.S.O.

2nd Leicesters.
3rd London Regiment (Territorials).
The Garhwal Rifles.
2/3rd Gurkhas.
2/8th Gurkhas.

Bareilly Brigade.

Commander: Brigadier-General W. M. Southey.

2nd Black Watch.
4th Black Watch (Territorials).
41st Dogras.
58th Rifles.
125th Rifles.

Divisional Cavalry.

4th Cavalry.

Divisional Battalion.

107th Pioneers.

C.R.A.: Brigadier-General R. St C. Lecky, R.A.
C.R.E.: Lt-Colonel G. A. J. Leslie, R.E.
C.R.A. with Corps Head quarters: Brigadier-General A. B. Scott, C.B., D.S.O., R.A.
C.R.E.: Brigadier-General H. C. Nanton, C.B., R.E.

By this time the importance of the part played by bombs in the war had been fully recognized. Divisional schools for instruction in bombing were established, each class lasting three days, and consisting of one officer per regiment, one sergeant or havildar per company, and two men per platoon. These schools did extremely good work, and our bombing, which had hitherto not been organized on a scientific basis, soon showed marked signs of improvement.

On the 8th April the 40th Pathans, under Lt-Colonel F. Rennick, joined the Corps on arrival from China, and were posted to the Jullundur Brigade. On the 12th April the Meerut Division relieved Lahore in the front line.

During the first three weeks of April, no events of special importance took place on the Indian front, but the lull was not destined to continue much longer. On the 23rd orders were received from the 1st Army for the Lahore Division to hold itself in readiness to move at short notice to an unknown destination, and on the 24th the Division marched in two columns, viâ Merville and La Gorgue, under the command of Major-General Keary, with orders to establish its head quarters at Godewaersvelde on the main road from Hazebrouck to Poperinghe.

After a very trying march, the Division arrived at its halting-place, Boeschepe, during the evening and night. The Transport had an especially harassing time, as it became involved in the hilly country round the Mont des Cats, and only arrived at dawn at Boeschepe, whence it had again to push on after a very short rest. The head of the Division arrived at the hutments near Ouderdom, about four miles north-west of Ypres, at 10 a.m. on the 25th, the men footsore and tired after a weary tramp of about thirty miles over the unyielding surface of cobble-paved roads, slippery with the rain which fell during the march.

It was evident to all that the Division was about

to take part in a great battle, for the booming of guns was continuous, and heavy shells could be seen bursting in and around Ypres.

To enable some estimate to be formed of the importance of the part taken by the Lahore Division in the second battle of Ypres, it is necessary to review very briefly the chain of circumstances which had rendered it necessary to summon the Division so hastily to the scene of conflict, leaving the front of the Indian Corps, already sparsely held, to the care of only one Division. This, it will be remembered, was the third occasion on which the Corps had been called upon, under circumstances of urgent necessity, to step into the breach, the earliest occasion being during the first battle of Ypres in October, 1914, and the second in the same month, when the Corps, newly arrived and not yet complete, was rushed to the front just in time to relieve the hard-pressed 2nd Corps opposite La Bassée.

The second battle of Ypres, reviewed dispassionately in the light of subsequent events, may be considered as the result of our operations at Hill 60, in themselves merely an heroic episode in such a war, but destined to be fraught with tremendous consequences.

Sir John French has informed one of the writers (and permits him to mention the circumstance) that in his judgment the Second Battle of Ypres was not less grave and critical than the First Battle.

On the night of the 17th April we exploded seven mines under a point known as Hill 60, our troops then rushing the position and occupying it. The importance of this so-called hill—in reality merely a mound formed chiefly by the earth excavated in making a cutting through an undulation for the Ypres—Lille railway—lay in the fact that it afforded the Germans an excellent position for artillery observation towards the west and north-west.

From the 17th April to the 5th May the struggle for possession of the hill continued. On the latter date, as the result of a furious effort by the enemy, supported by volumes of gas, the position passed out of our hands, but the hill, for so many terrible days and nights the scene of astounding deeds of heroism, no longer presented the same advantages to the possessor, almost demolished as it was by the furious cannonades which had been directed against it.

The question as to whether the battle which followed our capture of Hill 60 formed part of the German plan to force a way to Calais has been much argued, and for the most part without any definite conclusion having been reached. The more probable view is that a local offensive met with unexpected success, and that the enemy thereupon developed his activities into an important battle which might easily have produced strategic results of the first consequence.

The main difference between the first and second battles of Ypres lies in the fact that on the former occasion the enemy had concentrated at least half a million men against a force which never exceeded 150,000 ; on the latter occasion there seems to have been at the outset no formidable massing of troops, which would at once have been detected by the weakening of the German line elsewhere. At the second battle, such reinforcements as were brought up appear to have been taken from the ordinary local reserves.

In the absence, then, of strong evidence to the contrary, it is permissible to believe that the original object of the enemy was the capture of Ypres, with attendant loss of prestige for us and corresponding gain by the Germans.

The actual commencement of the second battle of Ypres would appear to date from the evening of the 22nd April, when, at about 5 p.m., after a terrific bombardment, the enemy attacked the French Colonial Division holding the line from Steenstraate to the east of Langemarck. Previous to the assault, it was reported that thick yellow smoke was issuing from the German trenches. The meaning of this phenomenon was not at once grasped, but the smoke was rapidly borne down upon the French line by the north-easterly breeze, and in a short time hundreds of men were writhing in agony from the effects of the poisonous fumes of asphyxiating gas, now employed for the first time. Within an hour the strain had become too much for human nature to bear, and the whole position was abandoned by the French Colonials, who were totally unprovided with any means of protection against such an attack.

Sir John French, in his despatch of the 15th June, 1915, lays emphasis on the fact that no blame could attach to the French, and expresses his conviction that if any troops in the world had been able to hold their trenches in the face of such a treacherous and altogether unexpected onslaught, the French Division would have stood firm.

By the retirement of the French, the left flank of the Canadian Division on their right was exposed, and there appeared to be serious danger of the

Canadians being overwhelmed, and of the British troops in the east of the salient being cut off. To protect their flank, the Canadians retired on St Julien, with their left thrown back, fighting hard as they went, with the wonderful gallantry which did so much to save the situation.[1]

The Germans followed up the gas, and swept on their way over the French trenches, bayoneting numbers of men whom they found dying in horrible torture.

Heavy fighting went on all night with alternating success. Early on the 23rd we counter-attacked northwards in co-operation with the French, but after meeting with some initial success, we were forced to retire, struggling hard for every inch of ground, and counter-attacking at every opportunity. By nightfall on the 24th our line was re-established at a distance of about 700 yards in rear of St Julien, slightly to the north of Fortuin.

Sir John French remarks:—

"In the course of these two or three days many circumstances combined to render the situation east of the Ypres Canal very critical and most difficult to deal with.

"The confusion caused by the sudden retirement of the French Division, and the necessity for closing up the gap and checking the enemy's advance at all costs, led to a mixing up of units and a sudden shifting of the areas of command which was quite unavoidable.

"Fresh units as they came up from the south had to be pushed into the firing line in an area swept

[1] For a full account of this stage of the battle, see Lord Beaverbrook's "Canada in Flanders," vol. i.

by artillery fire, which, owing to the capture of the French guns, we were unable to keep down."

It is thus clear that Sir John French considered it to be vitally necessary to check the enemy's advance at all costs, and it was because of this necessity that the Lahore Division was so suddenly flung into the battle. How nobly the Division played its part will be seen, not only from the record of its deeds, but from the heavy price in blood which it was once again compelled to pay.

On Sunday, the 25th April, a strong counter-attack was organized by Brigadier-General Hull, under the orders of Lt-General Alderson, with a view to retaking St Julien. Although not successful in its object, the move effectually checked the enemy's advance in this direction. As an example of the unavoidable confusion mentioned by Sir John French, it may be remarked that Brigadier-General Hull, at one moment of the attack, was called upon to control, with the assistance only of his own Brigade Staff, parts of battalions from six separate Divisions, all of which were quite new to the ground.

In the early morning of the 26th, operation orders were issued by General Sir Horace Smith-Dorrien, commanding the 2nd Army, under whose orders the Lahore Division came, for an attack which was to take place in the afternoon.

The general plan was as follows:—

The French, strongly reinforced, were to attack the enemy in their front, with their right resting on the Ypres—Langemarck road.

That portion of the 2nd Army which was facing north was to assault in co-operation with the

Second Battle of Ypres

Situation of Lahore Division

From 1·20 p.m. 26th April 1915 to the morning of 1st May 1915.

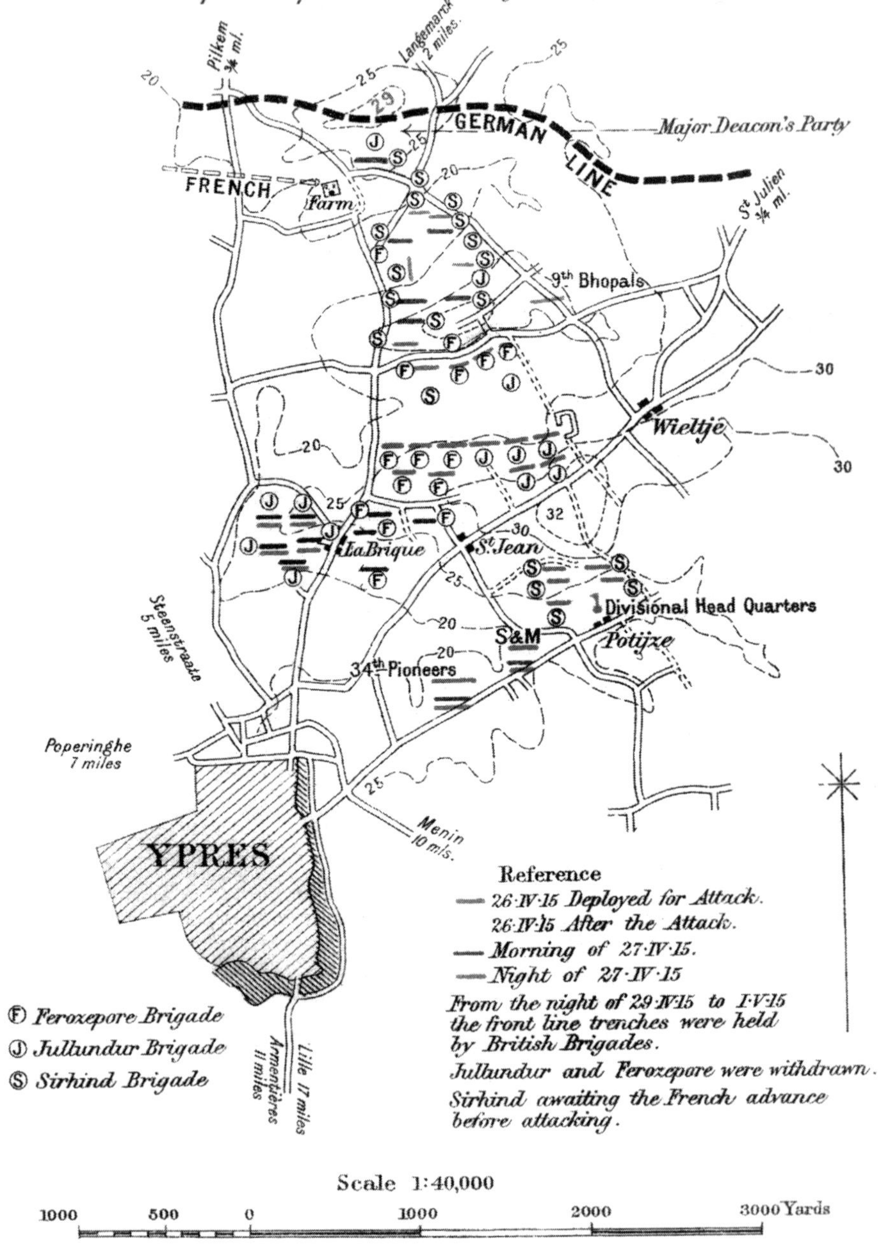

French, with a view to driving the enemy out of his positions.

The left of the Lahore Division was to rest on the Ypres—Langemarck road, where it would be in touch with the French right.

The 5th Corps was ordered to co-operate, mainly on the right of the Lahore Division.

The Division moved to its positions of assembly as follows :—

The Jullundur Brigade marched on Wieltje, starting at 7 a.m., by the road passing by the moat round Ypres on the south.

Ferozepore, starting at 5.30 a.m., proceeded to St Jean viâ Vlamertinghe.

Sirhind, which was detailed for Divisional reserve, followed the route of Ferozepore to a position more or less under cover, south-east of St Jean.

The Jullundur Brigade, under Brigadier-General Strickland, while passing close to the moat round Ypres, came under heavy shell fire. Many of the shells fell into the moat or struck the ancient walls of the town without at first doing any serious damage, and the men often cheered when a projectile fell into the water. But suddenly a big shell dropped right in the Yusufzai (the centre) company of the recently arrived 40th Pathans, wounding a Jemadar and causing 22 casualties among the men.

This was the first experience of the Pathans of shell fire, and it would have been excusable had the incident caused some confusion ; but there was none. The ranks closed up and the regiment marched on without a pause. The Jemadar pluckily kept going, and was present at the attack, only reporting his wound the next day.

Captain Hodge, the medical officer of the regiment, remained to attend to the wounded, the stretcher-bearers as usual behaving splendidly, and although the spot was heavily shelled for some time, the dead were buried and the wounded were successfully removed.

As soon as the Brigade formed up in the fields near Wieltje, the enemy began bombarding the village, and put three shells amongst the 1st Manchesters, causing 12 casualties. These shells were filled with a form of gas which, at a distance of 50 yards, caused the men's eyes to water to such an extent as to render them unable to use a rifle for some minutes.

The Ferozepore Brigade, under Brigadier-General Egerton, also came under heavy fire while marching to St Jean, and casualties commenced early in the day. Captain D. H. Acworth, 55th Rifles, who was officiating as Staff Captain, was wounded by a shell while conducting the Connaught Rangers through the northern outskirts of Ypres, the same shell killing two men and wounding Lt-Colonel Murray, Captain Foster, and five men of the Connaughts.

The Sirhind Brigade got into its supporting position south-east of St Jean with few casualties although the road was heavily shelled.

The chief sufferers were the 4th King's (Liverpools), their losses being 2nd Lieutenant Lydden (who died next day from his wounds), 2nd Lieutenant Soden wounded, with 10 casualties amongst other ranks.

The Division was lucky to escape so lightly, for the enemy, well aware that all reinforcements, supplies, etc., must come through or round Ypres, had for days past been pouring shells into the town and on the approaches.

When General Keary moved up to his advanced head quarters near St Jean, he found the road strewn with corpses and dead animals. He himself had a narrow escape, for a shell, bursting in close proximity to his car, blew his kit off the roof, but luckily did no more serious damage.

The three Brigades were in their assembly position by 11 a.m., and the enemy's aeroplanes at once became very busy in observation. For some unknown reason they were able to carry on their operations almost with impunity. The difference between the attitude of the German airmen at and before the battle of Neuve Chapelle, and at the second battle of Ypres, was so marked as to give rise to much comment. Whereas at Neuve Chapelle the German planes were practically unable to show themselves, at Ypres they flew as they liked over the British positions, with the result that our artillery was located, and the enemy's fire was accurately directed both on our guns and on our infantry.

The attacking force laboured under heavy disadvantages. The Lahore Division, with the laurels of Neuve Chapelle still fresh upon it, had carried out an exhausting march of 30 miles, and was pushed up almost on arrival. The exact position of the enemy's line was unknown, air reconnaissance, if made, having apparently failed to reveal it, and it was therefore impossible for our guns to register, whereas the German artillery, ably assisted by their airmen, had ample opportunity to register on our successive positions.

Registration is considered to be a luxury, not a necessity, and in theory guns should be able to pick up a target sufficiently rapidly without its aid. In practice, however, the side which has been able to register possesses a very great advantage, especially where, as in this case, the position of their target is unknown to the opposing artillery.

It was subsequently found by reconnaissance that the German line ran along a crest at a distance of about 1500 yards from our position of deployment. From this point of vantage the flash of our guns, hastily concealed as they perforce were, was spotted, and by this means some of our batteries were at once roughly located by the enemy.

Artillery fire, again, cannot be efficiently directed without good observing stations. With the short time at our disposal, we were at first greatly dependent on local information as to the position of suitable points of observation. On examination, these were generally found to be of little use, as they afforded no continuous view of the ground on which the enemy's position was believed to lie. It was not until late on the following day that satisfactory observation posts could be established.

Throughout the battle it was remarked that our artillery fire, both in preparation and support, was insufficient. For this, however, no blame can be attached to the officers and men of the artillery. As observed by the commanding officer of a distinguished regiment, they worked like heroes, but were unable to compete with the weight of metal opposed to them and the other solid advantages possessed by the enemy.

At 12.30 p.m. the Brigades moved out to their positions of deployment, the Jullundur Brigade, with its right resting on a farm slightly west of Wieltje, occupying a front of 500 yards, while the

Ferozepore Brigade continued the line to the left as far as the Ypres—Langemarck road, where touch was obtained with the French.

From right to left the units of the front line of the Jullundur Brigade were disposed as follows:— 1st Manchesters, 40th Pathans, 47th Sikhs.

The second line, at an interval of 400 yards, was composed of the 59th Rifles in rear of the Manchesters, and the 4th Suffolks (Territorials) supporting the 47th Sikhs.

In the Ferozepore Brigade the 129th Baluchis were on the right, the 57th Rifles in the centre, the Connaught Rangers on the left.

Supporting the Connaughts were the 4th Londons, while the 9th Bhopal Infantry were in reserve.

As the result of a conference with the C.R.A. 5th Corps, it was decided that he should support the advance and assault with all batteries west of the Canal. The exact position of the German line being unknown, two Canadian 18-pounder batteries and one howitzer battery, together with one 18-pounder and one howitzer battery of the Lahore Division, were placed under the orders of the Brigadiers of the two attacking Brigades, so as to afford them close support.

The French assault being timed for 2.5 p.m., that of the Lahore Division, which was echeloned slightly in rear of the French, was ordered to commence at 2 p.m. to enable the Division to get up in line.

The country to be crossed before the actual assault could be delivered was extremely unfavourable to the attacking troops, being absolutely open and devoid of cover. For the first 500 yards the ground rose slightly to a crest, thence gently declining for another 500 yards, after which it ascended in a smooth glacis-like slope to the German front line trenches.

At 1.20 p.m. the bombardment commenced, and continued for 40 minutes, gradually increasing in intensity. Immediately the guns opened, the attacking troops advanced, with a view to reaching assaulting distance before the fire ceased. The general direction of the attack was due north, but from the commencement, the Jullundur Brigade on the right inclined slightly north-north-west, and thus crowded in on the right of the Ferozepore Brigade, forcing it to overlap the road which formed the dividing line between the French and the Lahore Division. This at once led to such a confusion of units that men of the centre battalion of Jullundur actually got mixed up with the Connaught Rangers on the extreme left of the Ferozepore Brigade.

The enemy's guns were very active from the beginning of the attack, and when the troops reached the crest, they came under a perfect inferno of fire of all kinds, machine-gun, rifle, and every variety of shell, many of which were filled with gas. On crossing the ridge, the Manchesters at once began to feel the effect of the fire, officers and men falling everywhere.

At about this time Lieutenants Huskinson, Crawhall, and Robinson were wounded. This left only one officer, 2nd Lieutenant Williamson-Jones, with No. 1 Company. Shortly afterwards he too was hit, and Captain Buchan, commanding the firing line, was gassed by a shell, but saved himself to a great extent by covering his mouth and nose with a

[*Central News.*

CORPORAL ISSY SMITH, V.C., 1ST BN MANCHESTER REGIMENT.

wet handkerchief. Going up the final slope, Captain Paulson and Lieutenant Roberts were wounded, the latter in five places. He died shortly afterwards.

Corporal Issy Smith won the Victoria Cross by his devotion in leaving his company and going far forward towards the enemy's position to assist a severely wounded man, whom he carried for a distance of 250 yards, although he was all the time exposed to heavy machine-gun and rifle fire. Subsequently Corporal Smith voluntarily helped to bring in many more wounded men, and attended to them, regardless of danger.

Sergeant J. Bates received the Distinguished Conduct Medal for his coolness and bravery at a critical time in the advance. When troops on the left of the Brigade were checking under the torrent of fire, he rallied men of several units and led them forward.

The Manchesters, as stubborn and superb here as at Givenchy, still pushed on, the casualties increasing with every yard gained, until they reached a road at a distance of only some 60 yards from the German trench.

During this last stage, Corporal Dervin gained the Distinguished Conduct Medal by his gallantry and determination in advancing, after his officers had been killed or wounded, and maintaining his position close to the enemy. Previous to this he had rescued a wounded man who had fallen into a brook and was in danger of drowning, and under heavy fire got him back to cover.

Private F. Richardson also received the Distinguished Conduct Medal for his bravery in leading on the men when his officers were put out of action, and establishing himself close to the German trench. He then went back, moved his wounded Company Commander to a safer place, and rejoined his company.

After a short pause, Lieutenant Brunskill, 47th Sikhs, who, as before related, had received the Military Cross for an audacious reconnaissance, observing that a number of the enemy were bolting from a section of their trench, rushed forward with one man of the Manchesters and one of the Connaughts, followed by a small mixed party.

Between our firing line and the Germans was a ditch which he managed to reach in one rush. In his second rush he got to within a very short distance of the enemy, who had now been reinforced by a new regiment wearing *pickelhaubes* instead of the round caps which the men who bolted were wearing. Here practically the whole of the party were knocked over. Lieutenant Brunskill was wounded in three places, his left leg being shattered. He lay for several hours under shelter of a refuse heap, and was finally rescued with the greatest devotion and bravery by Lance-Corporal R. Reilly, Connaught Rangers, who came up under a terrible fire and succeeded in reaching the wounded officer. He then took off his putties, tied Lieutenant Brunskill's legs together, and, himself walking erect, dragged him back through a hail of bullets, both arriving without further damage after a wonderful escape.

For his great gallantry Lance-Corporal Reilly was selected to receive the Russian Medal of St George, 4th Class.

The Adjutant of the Manchesters, Captain Heelis,

was wounded during the afternoon while taking a message to Brigade Head Quarters under heavy fire, and at about 9.30 p.m. Lt-Colonel Hitchins, Commanding the Battalion, was killed by a stray bullet while crossing the ground between the French and British trenches.

During this battle the Manchesters sustained and, if possible, increased their splendid reputation, but at a great cost, their casualties amounting to 1 officer and 15 men killed, 11 officers and 206 men wounded, and 56 men missing.

Here for the moment we must leave them and follow the other units in their progress.

The 40th Pathans, next on the left to the Manchesters, were led by A Company under Major Perkins, who made the pace very fast, and thus enabled the greater part of the regiment to cross the first zone with comparatively few casualties, but the last company and the machine guns, under Lieutenant Munn, met the full blast, the machine-gun detachment having 9 casualties out of 18 men.

Only some 300 yards from the start, the Commanding Officer, Lt-Colonel Rennick, fell mortally wounded, and the Adjutant, Lieutenant Campbell, got him into a ditch, where he lay till dusk. This gallant officer's last thoughts, before being taken away on a stretcher, were for his regiment. He asked that two of his faithful Pathans might accompany him, as he wished them to be with him in case he died on the way. Colonel Rennick expired in a motor ambulance *en route* to Hazebrouck.

On crossing the first ridge, the regiment came under a terrible fire. Men fell in heaps, and the effect of this tornado of bullets is aptly compared by an officer who went through it to that of a scythe being drawn across the legs of the troops as they advanced. At one moment they were moving forward as if nothing could stop them; the next second they had simply collapsed.

The machine guns under Lieutenant Munn followed the regiment, but at first could find no target. The officer went ahead with a few men, all carrying ammunition, to discover a better position. At the bottom of the downward slope was a small brook, which they reached in safety; the remainder, including those carrying the guns, were mown down.

Sepoy Muktiara, undeterred by the fate of his comrades, at once volunteered to bring up one of the guns, and succeeded in crossing the 250 yards of open ground swept by enfilade machine-gun fire. With the help of Sepoy Haidar Ali, who also showed wonderful coolness, a gun was eventually set up, when to their dismay it was found to be useless, for it persisted in jamming, as the result of a fall into a stream when the carriers were hit. Eventually the guns were brought back.

For his gallantry Lieutenant Munn was awarded the Military Cross; Sepoy Muktiara received the Russian Medal of St George, 4th Class; while Sepoy Haidar Ali was awarded the Indian Distinguished Service Medal.

The Pathans got on by short rushes, but by the time they arrived within assaulting distance, their losses were very serious. The heroic Captain Dalmahoy, already four times wounded, got to within fifty yards of the enemy, when he was again hit in the head and spine. Brave and unselfish to the last, he begged Lieutenant Adams, who crawled over to help him, to leave him and get under cover. At that moment Adams was very severely wounded, and had only just strength to roll over and over till he reached a trench where his men attended to him.

Almost at Captain Dalmahoy's side, Captain Christopher, his company officer, was killed, and on the bank of the little stream at the bottom of the slope lay Captain Waters, shot through the brain.

Hairbreadth escapes were numerous. Lt-Colonel Hill, on whom devolved the command when Colonel Rennick was mortally wounded, had his revolver case cut off by a bullet; another went through his breast pocket from left to right, piercing a note-book, but leaving him unhurt.

Major Perkins, who led the attack with splendid dash, got up close to the German trench, but was then killed.

Lieutenant Thornton, the bomb officer, got to within 40 yards of the enemy, when he was wounded, and, unable to move, lay for six hours under cover of a manure heap.

During the latter part of the attack, Jemadar Lehna Singh displayed great coolness and courage in bringing his support up through the front line. He then occupied and held a position with wonderful tenacity under heavy fire at close range. For his conspicuous bravery he received the 2nd Class, Indian Order of Merit.

Subadar Jahandad Khan also did splendid service in reorganizing and leading the men of a support which had lost very heavily from shell fire. This gallant officer was unfortunately killed, but his services were subsequently recognized by the grant of the 2nd Class, Indian Order of Merit.

The losses of the 40th Pathans during the battle amounted to 3 British, 2 Indian officers and 23 other ranks killed; 5 British, 10 Indian officers and 258 others wounded, to which must be added 19 missing.

The 47th Sikhs fared even worse. Although the road was heavily shelled, they got up to their place of assembly with only three casualties; but their trouble was to come. In common with the rest of the Brigade, the loss of direction led to great confusion in the ranks. Casualties occurred as soon as the regiment advanced, and on crossing the ridge, Major Talbot and Captains Cook and Scott were killed, as well as Lieutenant Allardice, to whose gallantry at Neuve Chapelle reference has been made. In addition to these, by the time the regiment began its upward course towards the German trenches, all the other British officers, except Lieutenant Drysdale, had been put out of action, while the men were falling in swathes.

Lieutenant Drysdale, a subaltern of only five years' service, was thus left in command of the remnant of the regiment. He rose most nobly to his task, cheered the men forward and led them under an infernal fire to a point within seventy yards of the enemy, where he held on, and by his most determined courage gained the Military Cross.

The losses of the 47th reduced the regiment to a mere shadow of its former self. Its strength on going into action was 11 British, 10 Indian officers and 423 other ranks. On the morning of the 27th April, when a muster was taken, the regiment numbered 2 British, 2 Indian officers and 92 others, its losses being 9 British, 8 Indian officers and 331 other ranks or 78 per cent.

No regiment could wish, and none in the Army possesses, a prouder record than that of the 47th Sikhs at the attack on Neuve Chapelle in October, 1914, the battle of Neuve Chapelle in March, 1915, and the second battle of Ypres.

The attack of the Ferozepore Brigade on the left progressed under much the same conditions as that of the Jullundur Brigade.

The right battalion, the 129th Baluchis under Major Hannyngton, C.M.G., advanced steadily, but its movements were much cramped by the pressure caused by the Jullundur Brigade bearing too much to the left.

The critical stage was reached when the first crest was crossed. Here officers and men began to fall, and, as was the case with the other units, there was a natural disposition to bunch under cover of farm buildings on the left.

The front line, however, continued to push on, and eventually reached a point near a farm at a distance of about 300 yards from the German trenches. Communications had, as usual, been cut by the enemy's fire, and great difficulty was experienced in sending back reports.

Sepoy Raji Khan earned the 2nd Class, Indian Order of Merit, by his bravery in carrying an urgent message under heavy shell and rifle fire. A shell burst only about three yards from him during his progress, wounding and almost putting him out of action, but he managed to struggle on and delivered the message.

Later in the day, at a critical moment, when the troops were labouring under the tortures of gas, Major Holbrooke was wounded and lying in the open. Sepoy Ghulam Hussein, attached from the 124th Baluchis, dashed out and carried him under heavy fire into a safer position. He then collected a number of men and set them to work at a trench to form a rallying point. For his splendid example of bravery and coolness, Sepoy Ghulam Hussein received the Indian Distinguished Service Medal.

The losses of the 129th during the attack were as follows:—1 Indian officer and 11 other ranks killed; 7 British, 6 Indian officers and 171 other ranks wounded; 35 others missing.

For his gallant leadership Major Hannyngton received the D.S.O., and Lieutenant Griffith-Griffin was awarded the Military Cross for his conspicuous bravery during the action.

Next on the left were the 57th Rifles commanded by Major Willans. This regiment which, with the Connaught Rangers and 129th Baluchis, had distinguished itself at the first battle of Ypres in October, 1914, arrived at its position of deployment without casualties, although frequently shelled. During the first part of the advance, only a few men were hit, but in crossing the fateful ridge, the regiment came into an absolute inferno, and from here onwards officers and men fell fast.

By the time the bottom of the slope was reached, Lieutenant Bainbridge had been overcome by a gas shell, and Major Willans had been wounded, as well as Captain Radford. Captain Mahon, who had been hit in the knee early in the advance, managed to hold out till the end of the day.

The 57th swept on, in spite of their losses, and the remnant succeeded in reaching a point about 80 yards from the German line. Here Major Duhan, Captain Banks (attached from the Guides) and Captain Mackie were killed, as were also Subadar Badawa Singh and Jemadar Kirpa Singh, four other Indian officers being wounded.

Captain Banks's orderly, a Sikh named Bhan Singh, also attached from the Guides, was following his officer, although himself severely wounded in the face early in the action. On seeing Captain Banks fall, Bhan Singh's one thought was to bring him back, alive or dead. Weak as he was from his wound, he staggered along under an appalling fire, carrying the body, until he fell from exhaustion and was forced to give up the attempt, contriving, however, to bring in the dead officer's accoutrements. There have been few more striking instances of the deep attachment which exists between the British officer and the Indian soldier. For his signal act of devotion and bravery Sepoy Bhan Singh was awarded the Indian Distinguished Service Medal, and eventually received the Russian Medal of St George, 3rd Class.

This quick succession of casualties left the 57th with only two British officers, Captain Mahon already wounded, and Lieutenant Deedes of the 31st Punjabis. The latter, although suffering severely from the effects of a gas shell, was at work on the left flank trying to bring his machine guns into action from the farm.

Havildar Sar Mast was in charge of one of the guns, which he brought up several times, but was forced out of his position by the retirement of our line. In spite of this, he persevered until the attack was abandoned. He was rewarded for his gallantry with the Indian Distinguished Service Medal.

Another member of the machine-gun detachment, Naik Atma Singh, helped to bring a gun up to near the firing line, and got it into position under a hot fire. Here he held on until the front line was driven out by gas, but he himself declined to budge until Lieutenant Deedes ordered him to retire. For his conspicuous gallantry Naik Atma Singh received the 2nd Class, Indian Order of Merit.

Major Willans, who had led his regiment with the greatest courage and dash, was awarded the D.S.O., and Lieutenant Deedes received the Military Cross for bravery in this as well as in other actions.

During the day's fighting, the 57th lost 3 British, 3 Indian officers and 36 other ranks killed; 4 British, 7 Indian officers and 215 others wounded; 7 men being returned as missing. Among these casualties were many men of the Guides and of other regiments who were attached to the 57th Rifles.

The Connaught Rangers, on the extreme left of the Ferozepore Brigade, had, as before related, experienced bad luck during their march up through Ypres. All through the morning they lay out under heavy shelling, and were lucky to escape with only two men killed and three wounded.

On advancing from the place of deployment, the battalion was much impeded by thick hedges, through which the only means of passage was a few gaps. This kept the regiment back, and it had not reached the farm when our bombardment ceased, with the result that it met the full blast of the enemy's unchecked fire.

One of the first to be hit was Lieutenant Badham, who was wounded by a shell splinter and lost an eye. This young officer had previously distinguished himself at the first battle of Ypres and in subsequent actions, for which he was awarded the Military Cross.

As was the case with all the regiments, the Connaughts suffered severely on crossing the ridge, but, true to their reputation, never faltered, and, still losing heavily, eventually reached a point about 120 yards from the German trenches.

During the advance Sergeant Coldwell, whose never-failing courage has before been mentioned, again distinguished himself by taking command of his company after all the officers had been hit, and leading them with the finest determination. This splendid non-commissioned officer had already received the Distinguished Conduct Medal, and was subsequently awarded the 4th Class of the Russian Cross of St George.

Amid the storm of fire, the stretcher-bearers, with the spirit of self-sacrifice which has marked their work throughout the campaign, were moving about on their errand of mercy. Amongst them was especially distinguished Bandsman Gillan, who showed the utmost contempt for danger, and saved many lives by his fearless devotion to duty, for which he received the Medal of St George, 3rd Class.

Sergeants Finegan and Murphy received the Medal of St George, 2nd Class, and Lance-Corporal

Reilly that of the 4th Class, for gallant conduct, while Corporal Flynn was awarded the Médaille Militaire.

Private Duffy, transport driver, displayed great courage in bringing up ammunition through the enemy's barrage between Vlamertinghe and La Brique at a time when supplies were running short, for which valuable services he received the Medal of St George, 4th Class.

Captain Callaghan gained the Military Cross by his conspicuous gallantry throughout the day, in the course of which he was wounded.

The bravery of our Irish regiments is well known; the following figures of the casualties of the Connaughts during this attack will show with what intrepidity they were led, and with what determination they fought:—

Of 20 officers actually in action, 3 were killed and 12 wounded, including the Commanding Officer, Lt-Colonel Murray.

Of an approximate strength of 900 other ranks, 361 were killed or wounded.

The front line battalions of both Brigades were now in the most advanced positions to which the attack as a whole was destined to attain, although, as will be seen later, detachments of various units succeeded in reaching a point in close touch with the enemy, and maintained themselves there until relieved.

The position was critical. The only cover available was that which the men were able to throw up, all the time exposed to a terrible fire at close range. Units had been so reduced during the advance as now to be mere shadows of their former selves.

To make matters worse, the loss of direction at the commencement, coupled with the natural inclination to make use of cover wherever, as was seldom the case, it existed, had conspired to cause an inextricable confusion, British, Indians, and French being hopelessly mixed up. In spite of all, it is the opinion of officers who took part in this terrible day's fighting that we could at least have held on to the position, had not the enemy again resorted to the use of gas.

The British supports had followed the attack at a distance of about 400 yards, and although they had not undergone such a severe test as those in the front line, they had by no means escaped scathless.

The losses of the 59th Rifles amounted to 62, including 4 British officers wounded.

The 4th Suffolks lost 6 officers and 20 men wounded, 3 men being killed.

The 4th Londons escaped much more lightly, with 2 men killed, 1 officer and 10 men wounded.

Terrible as had already been our experiences, the worst was yet to come.

At about 2.20 p.m. the ominous signs of gas were seen proceeding from the German trenches, and in a few minutes dense volumes of yellowish vapour were borne by the wind across the front of the line from right to left. The effect of the gas in such volume and at such a short distance was more than even the oft-tried resisting power of the Indian Corps could support.

The troops were quite unprovided with any means of warding off the effect of the fumes. The most they could do was to cover their noses and mouths with wet handkerchiefs or pagris, and, in default of this poor resource, to keep their faces pressed against the scanty parapet. It was of little avail, for in a few minutes the ground was strewn with the bodies of men writhing in unspeakable torture, while the enemy seized the opportunity to pour in a redoubled fire.

The direction of the wind caused the French and the Ferozepore Brigade, especially the former, to suffer more than the right of the attack, although the whole line was more or less affected. The French were forced to give way, leaving the ground covered with their dead and dying. In their retirement they carried with them the greater part of our line. Mixed in hopeless confusion, French, British, and Indians streamed back, and many of the men reached La Brique before it was possible to rally them.

Only a small band, heroes every one of them, men whom no amount of devilry could deter, persisted in carrying on under these torturing conditions. Amongst this party were about 60 of the Connaughts under Major Deacon, who was joined by Lieutenant Henderson with some 50 men of the Manchesters. Added to these were a few of the 40th Pathans, 47th Sikhs, 129th Baluchis, and 57th Rifles.

For a short space they held on where they stood, but the enemy then counter-attacked, and the valiant little detachment was forced back about 80 yards, when it again pulled up and established itself, remaining in that position, in spite of all the efforts of the enemy to dislodge it, until relieved by the Highland Light Infantry under Captain Tarrant at 2.30 a.m. on the next day. For an exhibition of

[*Central News.*

FIELD-MARSHAL EARL KITCHENER AND SUBADAR MIR DAST, V.C., 55TH COKE'S RIFLES.

sheer valour, of indomitable tenacity, this exploit could scarcely be surpassed.

With the party of Connaughts was Captain Ingham, who had led his men until he was finally brought up short by the enemy's fire at a range of about 60 yards, when he set about organizing the position, exposing himself meanwhile with an absolute disregard of danger. Coming through the ordeal unscathed, he subsequently brought in a number of wounded. For his conspicuous gallantry he was awarded the D.S.O.

Lieutenant Henderson of the Manchesters, who was prominent during this episode, had taken command of his company after his seniors had been killed or wounded, and throughout the day set a splendid example of courage, for which he received the Military Cross.

Major Deacon, the commander and guiding spirit of the defence, was awarded the D.S.O., and later received the Cross of Officer of the Legion of Honour.

When the French and British were thrown back in confusion, Jemadar (now Subadar) Mir Dast, 55th Coke's Rifles, attached 57th, remained behind in a trench after his officers had been killed or wounded. He rallied all the men he could find, amongst them many who had been only slightly gassed and were beginning to recover, and with them he held on until he was ordered to retire after dusk. During his retirement he collected a number of men from various trenches and brought them in. Subsequently he assisted in bringing in eight wounded British and Indian officers, being himself wounded in doing so. This splendid Indian officer already possessed the 2nd Class, Indian Order of Merit, for his gallantry in the Mohmand Expedition, and now for his most conspicuous valour was awarded the Victoria Cross, being the fourth Indian soldier to receive that honour.

Amongst those who had been rendered unconscious by the gas and subsequently rescued by Jemadar Mir Dast, was Havildar (now Jemadar) Mangal Singh. On recovering consciousness, in spite of intense suffering, he went out time after time and helped to bring in the wounded under fire. For his bravery and devotion he received the 2nd Class, Indian Order of Merit.

Lieutenant Mein, also of the 55th, displayed the greatest skill and coolness in bringing up rations and ammunition for the regiment under heavy shell fire, often passing through Ypres when the town was being subjected to a terrific bombardment. He divided his time between this duty and helping in the front line when only two officers were left with the regiment, and he took part in the second attack on the 27th. For his gallant conduct Lieutenant Mein was awarded the Military Cross.

The 55th have every reason to be proud of their representatives at this great battle.

The retirement of the French and the majority of the British troops exposed the left of our meagre line, and the Sirhind Brigade was therefore brought up to La Brique in readiness for any eventuality on that flank.

General Keary, on becoming aware of the precarious position of the small body of men under Major Deacon, who was now completely isolated, ordered the Highland Light Infantry and 1/1st Gurkhas up to carry the Jullundur Brigade forward to Major Deacon's assistance. The Ferozepore Brigade was directed to hold on wherever it could, to support the movement, and, if possible, to advance. Later, however, it was reported that to push up the two battalions in face of the heavy fire would only entail a fruitless loss of life, and the plan had to be abandoned.

At 7 p.m. the 15th Sikhs and 1/4th Gurkhas were detached from the Sirhind Brigade to Ferozepore with a view to a fresh attack. The advance was made with the Gurkhas on the right and the Sikhs on the left. Streams of wounded and gassed men were encountered on the way, the blackened and swollen faces and protruding eyes of the latter giving evidence of the torture to which they had been subjected.

Overhead the monster shells of the German 42-centimetre guns could be heard hurtling through the air on their way to spread further devastation in Ypres, now a city of the dead, deserted by all else. The sound of these enormous projectiles resembled nothing so much as that of an express train tearing through the air, a resemblance which was, in fact, embodied in the name by which they were known, that of "the Wipers Express." To illustrate the destructive power of these shells, it is sufficient to mention that a hole made by one of them in the ground near Ypres measured 72 feet across by 48 feet deep.

The night was fine and clear, but by this time it was quite dark, and the air was sickly with the smell of chlorine from the German gas, the effects of which were felt as far as Poperinghe, seven miles west of Ypres. Communication with the front line had been so scanty, owing to the telephone wires being continually cut by shells, that even at this late period of the day the position of the enemy was not known to the regiments not actually engaged in the attack.

After much wandering in the dark, the Sikhs and Gurkhas, under Lt-Colonel J. Hill, D.S.O., arrived at a point on the right of the French, who had by this time been reinforced. Inquiry was then made from the officer commanding the French, but even he was unable to give any information as to the whereabouts of the British trench.

The attack was halted, and officers went forward to attempt to ascertain the situation. At last a man of the Manchesters was met, who led Colonel Hill to a trench where he found the battered remnants of the gallant little body of men under Major Deacon, still holding on amidst their dead and wounded.

Here the sinister information was received that the German trenches were about 100 yards in advance, at the summit of a glacis-like slope devoid of all cover, and protected by uncut wire. Further, it appeared that our trench ended on both flanks in the air.

At the moment there was little firing, so Colonel Hill returned and reported the situation to Brigadier-General Egerton, who, after consulting Brigadier-General Strickland, decided to abandon the attack (as there was no sign of any advance by the French) and to occupy the gap on the right of Major Deacon and slightly in rear, the farm held by the French being on the left front. At 1 a.m., then, Colonel Hill's men dug themselves in, and, assisted by a company of the 34th Sikh Pioneers, made every preparation to cling to their precarious position.

This episode has been described in greater detail than its importance would appear to warrant, were it not that it gives a good idea of the character of the operations of this most harassing day. It shows clearly the danger of an attack on a strongly sited and held position which had been reconnoitred neither from the air nor the ground, and whose defences had defied an insufficient and undirected artillery preparation.

During this and later phases of the operations round Ypres many gallant deeds were performed by others than those actually engaged in the attacks. The devoted work of the Signalling Companies has before been described, and in this battle they added to their already high reputation for bravery and skill.

Major W. F. Maxwell, R.E., Commanding the Lahore Divisional Signal Company, worked unceasingly to keep up the communications. Regardless of danger, he continually exposed himself to fire while directing the repair of lines which had been cut by shells. His valuable services gained for him the D.S.O.

Lance-Corporal E. Humphries (Royal Scots, attached to the Signal Company), on the night of the 26th, when it was vital that communication should be restored between the front and Divisional Head Quarters, volunteered to go out alone under heavy shell fire, and repaired the line, remaining out all night at his work. His gallant conduct earned him the Distinguished Conduct Medal.

Sergeant F. Birley (Madras Volunteer Rifles, attached) received the Distinguished Conduct Medal for bravery from the 26th April to the 3rd May in carrying, as a motor cyclist, despatches under heavy fire. On one occasion he was blown off his bicycle by a shell, but finished the journey, although severely shell-shocked.

Private J. Holman (1st Highland Light Infantry, attached) showed a splendid example of indifference to danger and pain in the performance of his duty. He repeatedly carried messages under heavy fire, and his right hand was eventually shattered by a shell. He still tried to go out with messages, and was only stopped on being three times ordered to desist. He also received the Distinguished Conduct Medal.

Sappers Jai Singh and Gujar Singh earned the Indian Distinguished Service Medal by their great courage in constantly repairing the lines under fire.

The work of the drivers of motor cars during this war, although it does not come much into the limelight, is fraught with considerable danger, and has been performed with great skill and coolness.

Sergeant G. W. Staunton and Private J. D. Collins, Army Service Corps, won the Distinguished Conduct Medal by their bravery in continually bringing officers and supplies up through Ypres and from Poperinghe to Potijye under the heaviest shell fire. The greater the danger the more cheerfully they performed their duties.

In another branch of non-combatant service, the Reverend F. Peal, Roman Catholic chaplain attached to the Connaught Rangers, was indefatiable in ministering to the wounded, although the aid post at La Brique was continually under heavy shell fire. His Commanding Officer records that the work of this brave priest amidst these scenes of horror was beyond all praise. The devotion of the chaplains of all creeds has been a marked feature of this war, and many have been decorated for bravery.

To resume the main story. At about 3 a.m. on the 27th April, the Jullundur Brigade was relieved in the front line by Sirhind. Ferozepore and Jullundur then withdrew to La Brique, while the Sirhind Brigade, assisted by the 3rd Sappers and Miners and 34th Pioneers, proceeded to consolidate the front line.

The Sappers and Miners, as usual during an action, had been going through a strenuous time. Lt-Colonel Coffin, Commanding the Royal Engineers, who subsequently was awarded the C.M.G., had established his head quarters in Poperinghe on the 26th. During the afternoon a terrific explosion took place, which shook the town to its foundations. On investigation it was found that several houses at a distance of only about 100 yards had been destroyed by a shell, believed to have been fired from a 42-centimetre gun at a range of about 15 miles. More of the same kind arrived at intervals of five minutes, and as the War Diary tersely puts it, "It was deemed advisable to visit other parts of the town till the shelling was over." The entry in the Diary characteristically concludes with the remark, "Weather fine. Temperature 52°."

Such is the cool spirit which has won for the Scientific Corps the admiration of the whole Army, and has enabled its officers and men to carry out the most dangerous duties with unflinching courage and never-failing skill.

CHAPTER XIX

THE SECOND BATTLE OF YPRES—*Continued*

Reconnaissances by Captains Kisch and Nosworthy, R.E.—Attack by Sirhind and Jullundur Brigades—Gallantry of 4th King's Regiment—Heavy losses—Major Beall's D.S.O.—Abandoned French guns recovered by 1/1st Gurkhas—2nd Lieutenant Pyper, 4th London Regiment, wins the Military Cross—Composite Brigade under Colonel Tuson joins Lahore—2nd attack—Death of Lt-Colonel Vivian, 15th Sikhs—French driven back by gas—Our attack held up in consequence—Gallant defence of Captain Tarrant's company, Highland Light Infantry—Death of Captain Tarrant—German aeroplane brought down—Jullundur and Ferozepore Brigades withdrawn—Attack by Sirhind on 1st May—Valuable services of the medical officers and their subordinates—Captain Wood, I.M.S., gains the Military Cross—Attack stopped and Lahore Division withdrawn—Casualties during the battle—General Keary's remarks—Appreciatory letters from Generals Smith-Dorrien and Plumer.

DURING the night of the 26th–27th April, 1915, very daring and valuable reconnaissances of the enemy's position were made by Captains Kisch and Nosworthy, R.E., both of whom had distinguished themselves on previous occasions in the campaign, the latter especially having taken a leading part in our attack on Neuve Chapelle in October of the previous year. The work was done under conditions of great danger, as the Germans continually sent up flares which revealed the slightest movement on the open ground between the lines, while rifles and machine guns searched every yard of No Man's Land.

In the course of his reconnaissance Captain Kisch

was wounded, but, determined at all costs to obtain the information which meant so much to his comrades, he went on with his work, approaching within a few yards of the German trenches, and succeeded in making a plan of the whole of the enemy's position in front of the Jullundur Brigade. In spite of his wound, Captain Kisch remained at duty till the evening of the 27th.

Captain Nosworthy, although he had previously been badly shaken and gassed by a shell, also succeeded in making a sketch of the enemy's position and escaped untouched, only to be dangerously wounded for the second time during a further reconnaissance on the 28th April.

For his conspicuous gallantry during the campaign in France, as well as in Mesopotamia, where he was again wounded, Captain Kisch received the D.S.O., Captain Nosworthy being awarded the Military Cross for his services, especially at Neuve Chapelle.

As a result of these reconnaissances, the nature and position of the enemy's line were ascertained, and more definite plans could be made for the infantry attack and artillery support than had been possible on the previous unhappy day.

It was decided that the French Moroccans, on the left of the Lahore Division, should attack at 1.30 p.m. on the 27th, the Sirhind Brigade being in touch with the French right, the dividing line as before being the Ypres—Langemarck road, and the Ferozepore Brigade prolonging the line to the right. The latter Brigade, on the morning of the 27th, was lying in hastily prepared trenches between La Brique and St Jean, with the exception of the

4th Londons, who were further north in support of the Sirhind Brigade, which was holding the front line. The artillery of the 5th Corps and Lahore Division were to co-operate with the Canadian Artillery in the preparation and support of the infantry attack.

The commencement of our bombardment was timed for 12.30 p.m., when Ferozepore would at once move forward so as to arrive in line with Sirhind by 1.15 p.m., at which time the guns would lift on to the enemy's second line and works in rear.

On the bombardment commencing, the Ferozepore Brigade moved off and deployed for attack as follows :—

The 9th Bhopal Infantry on the right of the front line, the 4th Londons on the left keeping touch with the Sirhind Brigade. In support were the Connaught Rangers following the Bhopals at a distance of 400 yards. The 57th Rifles and 129th Baluchis were in Brigade reserve, both battalions being mere skeletons, as a result of their share in the operations of the previous day.

The Brigade came under heavy shell fire while advancing across the open ground, but casualties were minimized by making the best use of the slight cover afforded by hedges and folds of the ground. The Sirhind Brigade did not wait for Ferozepore to come up in line, but advanced as soon as the bombardment started. It seemed indeed to General Walker that it was better to face the risks of outdistancing the troops on his flanks than to lose artillery support by waiting for the Ferozepore Brigade.

Of the Sirhind Brigade, one company of the

Highland Light Infantry, under Captain Tarrant, was holding a trench parallel to the German line and about 100 yards from it, in which it had relieved Major Deacon and his brave little detachment of Connaughts and Manchesters during the night. Three companies of the Highland Light Infantry were in support of Captain Tarrant, and on their left were the 15th Sikhs under Lt-Colonel J. Hill.

About 300 yards behind the supports were the remaining units of the Brigade, the 4th Liverpools, 1/1st and 1/4th Gurkhas in shelters. The Jullundur Brigade was in Divisional reserve at La Brique, where it remained throughout the day.

The Sirhind Brigade advanced on a two-battalion front, the 1/4th Gurkhas under Major Brodhurst on the right, and the 1/1st Gurkhas commanded by Lt-Colonel W. C. Anderson on the left, with the 4th Liverpools and the remainder of the 1st Highland Light Infantry and the 15th Sikhs in support.

In passing the ridge, the attack came under severe frontal cross fire from rifles and machine guns, as well as from several other directions. The enemy had registered the range of every likely spot with great accuracy; hedges and ditches which would give any sort of cover had all been marked down, and casualties were heaviest in their vicinity.

Major Brodhurst, commanding the 1/4th Gurkhas, was killed early in the attack, the Adjutant, Captain Hartwell, being wounded by his side at the same moment.

Three British officers and about thirty men succeeded in reaching a large farm at the bottom of the slope, which had apparently been used as a

Canadian R.E. depôt. Here they held on under a desperate fire, but no help could reach them until about 4 p.m., when Lt-Colonel Allen, commanding the 4th King's, seeing that the 1/4th Gurkhas were held up, determined to reinforce.

The King's, splendidly led by their officers, advanced by short rushes, with the enemy pumping lead into them and men falling in heaps. A number, under Major Beall, succeeded in getting to within 200 yards of the hostile line, but it was evident that the wire in front of the German trench was untouched, and it was impossible to push on further. This spirited dash, however, enabled a number of the 1/4th Gurkhas to join the small party which was holding on to the farm.

The 4th King's had not been long in showing their quality, for the battalion had only landed in France during the preceding month, and had already been present at Neuve Chapelle. Its losses in this attack were very heavy, 2nd Lieutenant R. A. Lloyd being killed and 8 officers wounded, while there were 374 casualties amongst other ranks.

Lt-Colonel Allen received the C.M.G., and for his conspicuous courage and able leadership Major Beall, who not only led his men in the attack, but also returned across the bullet-swept open to bring up reinforcements, was awarded the D.S.O.

Lance-Sergeant M. Vincent won the D.C.M. by his gallantry on this date and on the 1st May, when he carried a wounded signaller into safety under heavy fire.

Private W. Elmer gained the same distinction by his conspicuous bravery in attending to a wounded officer under fire, and for volunteering on the 1st

May to carry messages under circumstances of particular danger.

By this time three more officers of the 1/4th Gurkhas had been wounded, Captain Collins, Lieutenant Moore and Captain Lentaigne, but the last-named continued to command his company in spite of his wound.

The 1/1st Gurkhas, like the 1/4th, suffered severely from heavy enfilade fire on their way to some enclosed ground on the downward slope, being compelled to swing round towards the left to face it. One company under 2nd Lieutenant Fry, I.A.R.O., succeeded in advancing to a ruined farm distant only about 250 yards from the Germans. Here it held on under heavy fire until withdrawn after dusk. The remainder of the battalion was brought to a standstill at a distance of about 400 yards from the enemy's trenches.

Just then, Lieutenant and Adjutant G. St George was shot through the chest by the side of Colonel Anderson, and died the next day in hospital. At this juncture, too, Captain Evans was wounded. Rifleman Phalman Gurung, seeing his Company Commander fall, ran over to him, dug a hole, threw up rough cover round it, and, always under heavy fire, placed Captain Evans in it, thus undoubtedly saving his life, for which act of gallantry he received the Indian Distinguished Service Medal.

Rifleman Ramkishan Thapa was awarded the 2nd Class, Indian Order of Merit, for his bravery in continuing to lay a telephone line behind the battalion as it advanced. Twice he was forced to return to the base to renew his detachment, all of his men having been killed or wounded. Eventually he brought the line up by himself and returned on two occasions to repair it under very heavy fire. Of the 13 signallers then with him, 2 were killed and 9 wounded.

Rifleman Khamba Sing Gurung earned the Indian Distinguished Service Medal by his bravery in carrying a wounded officer of the 4th King's back to cover under heavy fire.

The battalion came out of action with only Colonel Anderson and 2nd Lieutenant Fry unhurt, the remaining five British officers having been wounded; 15 other ranks were killed; 2 Gurkha officers and 71 others were wounded during the attack, and 9 others were missing.

Although the objective was not reached, the 1/1st Gurkhas were able to establish their position in advance of some French guns which had been abandoned, and during the night these were safely removed.

In the meantime, the Ferozepore Brigade, led by the 4th Londons and the 9th Bhopals, had been moving on towards their goal, a farm on the right of the line of attack, but they fell into a devastating fire from artillery, rifles, and machine guns, which caused such heavy losses as to a great extent to break up the formation.

Among the Bhopals, Major Jamieson, a gallant officer who was to the fore in the action at Neuve Chapelle in October, 1914, and has since been killed in Mesopotamia, was wounded early in the day, and Captain Etlinger, acting Adjutant, was killed at about 3 p.m.

The losses of the Bhopals were 1 British officer and 15 men killed, 2 British, 2 Indian officers and 97 other ranks wounded, and 5 missing.

The 4th Londons, who had not so far to go, suffered very heavily, but pushed on until the attack was smothered by an overwhelming fire, when only 30 men remained of one of the leading companies. During this period, Lieutenant Coates, who had carried out a useful reconnaissance on the previous day, was killed at the head of his platoon.

The two companies in support moved up to reinforce, and, in spite of heavy losses, reached their goal. Captain Saunders, commanding D Company, fell mortally wounded during this advance, still cheering on his men.

The machine-gun detachment suffered very severely in crossing the open to take up position. Here the men were shot down in rapid succession as they advanced. When one of the guns had been rendered useless, the whole detachment being either killed or put out of action, 2nd Lieutenant J. R. Pyper, although already wounded, pushed forward with the remaining gun and continued in action with it until he was ordered back after dark. For his conspicuous gallantry he received the Military Cross.

Lance-Corporal Colomb and Lance-Corporal Ehren won the Distinguished Conduct Medal, the former for bravery in rescuing, under heavy shell and rifle fire, a man who was lying about 50 yards away. He rendered first aid, and got him back to cover, in doing which he was himself wounded. Lance-Corporal Ehren continually carried reports, and on one occasion left his trench and brought in a wounded man, being exposed to heavy fire the whole time.

The attack was eventually held up after it had come into line on the right of the Sirhind Brigade.

During this period the French had been steadily attacking, and, although losing very heavily, they still continued to form a firing line.

At 2.40 p.m. the Commander of the 2nd Army ordered the assault to be pressed on vigorously, at the same time placing a composite Brigade under Colonel Tuson at the disposal of the General Officer Commanding Lahore Division. This Brigade consisted of the West Riding Regiment, the Duke of Cornwall's Light Infantry, the York and Lancaster Regiment, and the 5th King's Own. All these battalions had already suffered heavy losses, and the entire Brigade hardly numbered 1300 men.

Colonel Tuson started forward at once with orders to get into touch with the Sirhind Brigade, and to report whether there was a sufficient interval between our front line and that of the enemy to allow of a further bombardment without danger to our troops. At 4.25 p.m. a report arrived from the Sirhind Brigade, announcing that the bombardment was practicable, and at 5.30 p.m. it commenced, all available batteries joining in. Under cover of our guns, the 1st Highland Light Infantry and 15th Sikhs pushed forward. The Sikhs managed to assemble behind a strong earthwork which had served to screen a French battery before its withdrawal on the night of the 26th.

The moment the battalion emerged from this cover and began to cross the open ground, a terrible crossfire was poured into it from the German trenches, while the shrapnel, if possible, increased in violence.

Just then Lt-Colonel Vivian, while rushing with his company over the fire-swept zone, was shot through the heart and died immediately. The loss of this splendid officer was very keenly felt, as throughout the campaign, in which he had already been wounded, he had shown most marked ability and courage.

Among the many stories of his daring is the following. In December, 1914, it was necessary on one occasion to ascertain whether a German trench in front of the 15th Sikhs was occupied. Knowing the risk, Colonel Vivian preferred to take it himself. Accordingly he crawled out 120 yards along a ditch which ran towards the hostile position, but, on arrival unobserved at the end of his perilous journey, he found himself unable to see into the trench. Determined not to be baffled, he proceeded to climb a tree at a distance of only a few yards from the enemy. The Germans spotted him and began firing. Colonel Vivian felt a shock, and thought that a bullet had gone through his body. He dropped out of the tree, and, fired at all the way, managed to crawl back to our trench, when he was found to be unhurt, the bullet having gone through the numerous winter garments which he was wearing, causing no more damage than a graze.

On Colonel Vivian's death Major Carden took command of the front line. Shortly afterwards, Captain Muir was hit. Major Carden went over to help him, and was wounded in the side. He lay in a ditch until the regiment retired. While he was being taken away on a stretcher, both bearers were wounded, and Major Carden, being again hit, succumbed. This incident will give some idea of the violence of the fire to which our troops were subjected.

During this attack, communications had, as usual, been cut by shells and, when it was urgently necessary to get a message through, it had to be carried by hand. Sepoy Bakshi Singh twice volunteered to take messages over a space of some 1500 yards, which was literally swept by fire. On both occasions he was successful, and returned with the replies. On the 1st May he again distinguished himself by going out several times to repair the telephone wires which had been cut by shells. For his gallant conduct he was rewarded with the 2nd Class, Indian Order of Merit.

The men were now falling fast, and any fresh advance could only be possible with the assistance, on the left, of the French, who had launched a further attack under cover of a very heavy bombardment, at 7 p.m.

At 7.10 p.m. Colonel Hill, on looking round to ascertain the extent of the French advance, saw that they had been driven back by the fire of the enemy and by dense clouds of gas.

The position was very critical. Had the Germans then seized the opportunity to attack, our resistance could not have been prolonged, for the trenches which the Sirhind Brigade had vacated when they advanced had not been manned by other troops, and there was consequently no support.

The left half battalion, which was then leading, was at once ordered to retire to the trenches occupied by the right half battalion. This movement was carried out without further casualties. The din of battle gradually died away as the French Colonials retreated, and parties were sent out to bring in the wounded and bury the dead.

At the close of the day, the strength of the 15th Sikhs amounted to 4 British, 11 Indian officers and 369 other ranks, the casualties having been 2 British officers and 9 others killed, and 1 British officer and 86 other ranks wounded.

The Highland Light Infantry had no better fortune than the 15th Sikhs, and when the French Moroccan Brigade was driven back on the left, the battalion dug itself in and held on where it was.

Great anxiety was felt as to the fate of B Company under the gallant Captain Tarrant, who were left utterly isolated in their position only 100 yards from the German line. It was feared that they had been overwhelmed, or at the least had been forced back, but when matters had quieted down, it was found that this heroic little detachment had held on without flinching against all the attempts of the enemy, culminating in the final discharge of gas which drove back the Moroccans. This splendid effort, however, cost the life of Captain Tarrant, who was killed during the afternoon.

Captain Tarrant is described as an exceptionally able and gallant officer, a description which is borne out by the skill and determination shown by him in the defence of his precarious position in face of a terrible fire and volumes of gas; by his stubborn refusal to retire when isolated and liable at any moment to be overwhelmed; and by his heroic death, which, as his Commanding Officer testified, was a heavy blow to the regiment.

When Captain Tarrant took over the hastily dug trench from the Manchesters and Connaughts, it was necessary to get ammunition up to him as quickly as possible, but daylight arrived before the party carrying the supplies could reach the trench, and on the way 9 of the 10 men were hit. Captain Tarrant called for volunteers to go out and bring the ammunition in. Company Sergeant-Major R. Bell headed the party, and under a very heavy fire succeeded in bringing up the sorely needed supplies. For his bravery on this and other occasions he received the Distinguished Conduct Medal.

The casualties of the Highland Light Infantry on this day amounted to 1 officer killed, 1 wounded, and 108 other ranks killed, wounded, or missing.

The night of the 28th April passed fairly quietly as far as the troops were concerned, but a number of 42-centimetre shells hurtled overhead on their way to complete the ruin of Ypres.

On the morning of the 28th, the Lahore Division was placed under the orders of the 5th Corps, and later in the day was incorporated with Plumer's Force, which had just been formed.

From the French operation orders, it was gathered that their main attack would be from their left, the right co-operating if it saw an opportunity. The Sirhind Brigade was ordered to assist with fire, and to be ready to take advantage of any decided success on the part of the French by attacking. The Divisional Artillery was also ordered to help the French, whose attack, however, which was timed for 2 p.m., was finally postponed till 7 p.m.

At 1 p.m., nevertheless, an artillery bombardment began, but, as before, the superior weight of metal of the enemy told at once, and from that hour till

4 p.m. the whole area was ploughed up by the German shells.

The French attack did not develope, and the fight was confined to an artillery duel.

At about 5 p.m. the German aeroplanes again became active, but as usual flew very high. One daring pilot, however, descended rather lower than the others, and paid for his temerity by being brought down by our rifle fire, falling in our lines in the direction of St Julien.

The night again passed quietly, and the opportunity was seized to strengthen our position. It was very noticeable that, whereas at the commencement of the campaign the Indian troops did not appreciate the importance of digging really strong trenches, by this time they so fully understood the necessity that, as an officer remarks, the only difficulty was to get them to stop digging.

An attack by the French was timed for noon on the 29th April, and the Sirhind and Ferozepore Brigades were ordered to assist as before, but after the operation had been postponed till further orders, it was eventually cancelled.

During the night of the 29th–30th, the Jullundur and Ferozepore Brigades were withdrawn to the huts at Ouderdom by General Plumer's orders, and their share in this great battle came to an end.

The story of the 30th April is very much the same as that of the previous twenty-four hours.

A French attack was timed for 11.15 a.m., the bombardment commencing at 10 a.m. The Sirhind Brigade stood ready for action during the whole day, and bombardments took place one after another, as the attack was postponed from hour to hour.

The co-operation of the Canadian Artillery, which had throughout rendered most valuable assistance, was very marked during this period, when the guns were served under the heaviest shell fire.

Finally, at 6 p.m., Colonel Savy, Commanding the Moroccan Brigade, informed General Keary that his losses had been so heavy as to preclude any further advance without reinforcements. The attack was therefore indefinitely postponed.

It was then explained by General Plumer to the Commander of the French Army in Belgium, that the Sirhind Brigade, the only one available, could be utilized to support the French right in an attack on Hill 29. (See Map.) Arrangements were accordingly made for the enemy's wire on Hill 29 to be cut by our artillery, and a certain section of his line to be subjected to a heavy bombardment to keep down machine-gun and rifle fire, as this section swung round in a semicircle towards the right of the Sirhind Brigade and flanked our attack.

The position from which Sirhind was to attack was left to General Walker's discretion, provided only that he advanced at the same time as the French. It was then learnt from General Plumer that the French thoroughly understood that our move depended on theirs, and that the two attacks would not converge. It was finally decided that the French should attack at 3.10 p.m. on the 1st May, their advance being preceded by a prolonged and heavy bombardment. To bring it level, the Sirhind Brigade would advance at 2.50 p.m., the movement being supported by artillery fire.

Using the discretion allowed him, General Walker

decided to move up through the farm on the left of the line near the trench formerly held by Captain Tarrant, a morning reconnaissance having shown this to be the most favourable course. It would have been preferable to have moved the front lines of the Brigade up to the forward trenches now held by the 12th British Brigade during the night, but this could not be done, as the orders for attack were not received till 4 a.m., when day was dawning; moreover, the forward trenches were already fairly full of men.

The Brigade was disposed as follows:—

Right attack: 1/4th Gurkhas, supported by the 1st Highland Light Infantry.

Left attack: 1/1st Gurkhas, supported by 1/4th King's (Liverpools), the 15th Sikhs holding the front line of trenches.

The leading line advanced from the point where the road running east and west crosses the Langemarck—Ypres road. In order to reach assaulting distance, it was necessary to pass down a long steep slope exposed to the enemy's machine-gun and artillery fire, and the Commanding Officers of the two leading Gurkha battalions decided to cross this danger zone at the greatest possible speed.

The sensation of being amongst even the low hills round Ypres had caused the Gurkhas to feel more at home than amidst the dreary plains and mud in which they had fought for so many months, and the two battalions covered the ground at a tremendous pace, passing through our front line trenches, the occupants of which stood up and cheered them as they tore through. The result of this rapid advance was that the perilous passage was accomplished before the enemy's artillery fire had time to develope, and the attack reached a point on the final upward slope at a distance of only some 250 yards from the Germans with comparatively few casualties.

The losses of the 1/1st Gurkhas during this operation amounted only to 1 British officer, Captain Johnson, and 1 Gurkha officer wounded, while 6 men were killed, 62 wounded, and 3 missing—a small casualty list for an attack in the face of such odds.

Lt-Colonel W. C. Anderson, Commanding the 1/1st Gurkhas, received the C.M.G. in recognition of the marked qualities of command displayed by him during this battle and on other occasions.

Our bombardment had now ceased. The ground between our line and that of the enemy was a smooth slope devoid of cover, and it was apparent that the wire in front of the German position was still intact. At a distance of about 150 yards in front of the spot where the attack halted was a trench, the ownership of which was doubtful.

It was necessary to ascertain at once whether the trench was occupied by friends or enemies, but, exposed as the ground was, the task of obtaining the information was highly dangerous. Havildar Bhakat Sing Rana, of the 2/4th Gurkhas, undertook the duty, and leading a small party across the open, succeeded in getting through the enemy's fire. Having ascertained that the position was held by the French, he returned and reported. For his gallantry the havildar received the 2nd Class, Indian Order of Merit.

The 4th King's, in support of the 1/1st Gurkhas,

lost Captain Lumsden killed, Major Beall and 2nd Lieutenant Mason wounded, with 43 casualties amongst other ranks.

During this period of the attack, the bodies of two Indians were seen suspended by the neck from a tree near the hostile lines, another outrage being thus added to the long list of German crimes.

By 4.30 p.m. the 1/4th Gurkhas had succeeded in reaching some new trenches to the east of the farm. The Highland Light Infantry then reinforced, which led to the trenches becoming overcrowded, as they were also occupied by men of the Essex Regiment and by some of the French.

The losses of the 1/4th Gurkhas during this attack were light, amounting only to 7 men killed, 2 Gurkha officers and 49 men wounded.

The casualties of the 1st Highland Light Infantry were: 2nd Lieutenant J. L. McIntosh (Indian Army attached) killed, 2nd Lieutenant C. P. Johnstone wounded, and 80 casualties amongst other ranks.

All through the battle, the work of the medical officers and their subordinates had been beyond praise. Captain C. A. Wood, I.M.S., 1/4th Gurkhas, gained the Military Cross by his bravery and unceasing energy in collecting the wounded, even after he had himself been hit, and in arranging for their safety after his first-aid post had become a target for the enemy's artillery. Throughout the campaign this officer had shown himself to be utterly regardless of danger in the performance of his duty.

Riflemen Patiram Kunwar and Deotinarain Newar, of the 1/4th Gurkhas, were in charge of stretcher parties. On two occasions especially they had particularly hard work in collecting the wounded on the battle-field under very heavy fire; they showed great courage in doing so, and brought in all the wounded, amounting to nearly 200 on each occasion. For their bravery and devotion to duty they were awarded the Indian Distinguished Service Medal.

Luckily, during this attack the wind was from the west, and there was no danger of gas, but shortly after our front line reached its most advanced position, the enemy set up an impenetrable barrage of fire, which cut off half of the 4th King's (Liverpools) and prevented them from reinforcing. Any further forward move was now out of the question, unless it could be made in conjunction with the French and under cover of heavy fire.

Our Allies, however, had suffered under an extremely heavy bombardment during the previous night and the greater part of the day. At 10 a.m., especially, the Germans opened a terrific fire on the whole area occupied by the Moroccan Brigade, which had already sustained very serious losses in the battle. At 6.30 p.m., then, General Walker, who, as usual, was well up in front in the trenches of the 15th Sikhs, having ascertained that there was no prospect of any advance on the part of the French, reported the situation to General Keary, and orders were issued for the Brigade to collect the wounded, bury the dead, and withdraw after dark.

This movement was successfully carried out, and the troops returned to the hutments at Ouderdom, arriving there at 5.20 a.m. on the 2nd May. On the 3rd, General Walker remarks that, although the Brigade had been under shell fire from the

27th April to the 1st May inclusive, the behaviour of the troops had been excellent throughout, and, in spite of heavy casualties, the moral of the Brigade was unaffected, all ranks after two days' rest being quite fit for further work.

On the 3rd May the Lahore Division proceeded to rejoin the Indian Corps, having within a period of less than two months taken a prominent part in two of the greatest battles in the world's history.

The casualty list was very heavy, as will be seen from the following table.

The strength of the Division on the 23rd April, the day preceding its departure for Ypres, was as under:—

British officers.	Indian officers.	Sabres.	Rifles (British).	Rifles (Indian).	Artillery (British).	Artillery (Indian).	Total.
421	166	475	5439	6808	2390	281	15,980

The casualties were as follows, showing killed, wounded, and missing:—

British officers.			Indian officers.			Sabres.			Rifles (British).			Rifles (Indian).			Artillery (British).			Artillery (Indian).		
K.	W.	M.	K.	W.	M.	K.	W.	M.	K.	W.	M.	K.	W.	M.	K.	W.	M.	K.	W.	M.
28	105	—	6	57	1	2	4	—	180	1096	345	177	1684	209	6	47	—	—	1	—

The total casualties of all ranks amounted to 3889.

In order, however, to arrive at a fairly correct estimate of the proportion of casualties to troops actually engaged in the various attacks, it is necessary to deduct the strength and the casualties of the Artillery and Cavalry.

The combined strength of these two arms amounted to 3146, excluding officers, their casualties being 60, also excluding officers, amongst whom there were 9 casualties, all in the Artillery.

The strength actually engaged at one time or another in the attacks therefore comes to 12,834 of all ranks, with a total of 3829 casualties, giving a percentage of very nearly 30.

General Keary's remarks, in the summing up of his report on the operations, show very clearly the adverse conditions under which the troops had to fight; the figures above quoted demonstrate the spirit with which those conditions were met.

General Keary reports:—"In conclusion, I consider that the troops did all that it was humanly possible to do under most trying circumstances. They had to pass along some miles of road and narrow streets under a hail of shell fire, advance to a position of assembly over open ground, and from thence to a position of deployment under the same conditions.

"The Germans had prepared a position which required the most accurate and intense gun fire to reduce it. Owing to the hurried nature of the attack, it was impossible to reconnoitre sufficiently to ensure such a fire. Nor were the guns registered. During the first two days the Infantry advanced against a position on an open glacis which was virtually unshaken.

"After the first two days only one Brigade was in action, and its action depended on that of the French, whose right never advanced to the attack.

"In spite of all these disabilities the carrying of the position by the French and British was only prevented by the use of asphyxiating gases."

Where all had done splendid service, General Keary considered that the following units deserved special mention:—

1st Manchesters.	Connaught Rangers.
1st Highland Light Infantry.	4th King's (Liverpool) Regiment.
47th Sikhs.	57th Rifles.
40th Pathans.	

From the time of its arrival till the morning of the 28th April the Division was under the orders of General Sir Horace Smith-Dorrien, Commanding the 2nd Army. On the 7th May the following letter was received from General Smith-Dorrien:—

"Having read the very complete and excellent report on the work of the Lahore Division in the heavy fighting near Ypres on the 26th and 27th April, 1915, the Commander of the 2nd Army is confirmed in the views he formed at the time that the Division had been handled with great skill and determination by Major-General Keary.

"Sir Horace Smith-Dorrien fully realizes the disadvantages under which the attack was made: insufficient artillery preparation on our side, and an open glacis-like slope to advance over in the face of overwhelming shell, rifle, and machine-gun fire; and the employment of poisonous gases on the enemy's side; and that in spite of these disadvantages the troops, although only partially successful in wrenching ground from the enemy, prevented his further advance, and thus ensured the safety of the town of Ypres.

[*Swain, London*

GENERAL SIR HORACE SMITH-DORRIEN, G.C.B., G.C.M.G., D.S.O.

"Sir Horace, whilst deploring the heavy casualties, wishes to thank the Divisional General, Brigadiers and Commanding Officers and all ranks of the several arms employed for the great service they performed for the 2nd Army on those eventful two days. In this respect he would especially mention the following regiments: 1st Manchester Regiment, Connaught Rangers, 1st Highland Light Infantry, 4th King's (Liverpool) Regiment, 47th Sikhs, 57th Rifles, 40th Pathans."

From the 28th April till its departure on the 3rd May the Division was under the orders of Lt-General Sir Herbert Plumer, Commanding Plumer's Force. On the 2nd May, Sir Herbert Plumer wrote as under to General Keary:—

"Will you please convey to the Brigadiers, Commanding Officers, and all Officers, Non-Commissioned Officers and men of your Division my thanks for the assistance they have rendered in the recent severe fighting, and my appreciation of the way in which they have carried out the very arduous duties entrusted to them while under my command?

"I deeply regret the very heavy casualties they have suffered."

These letters of appreciation, proceeding from such quarters, speak for themselves, and it will be agreed that General Sir James Willcocks had every ground for sending the following message to General Keary:—

"Please convey to all ranks of the Division my own and all their other comrades' best congratulations on having taken part in the battle near Ypres. We are proud of you all. Well done."

It is only necessary to add that two days after

rejoining the Indian Corps, the Lahore Division relieved the Meerut Division in the trenches: such was the spirit and stamina of these men; and such were the necessities of the times.

Casualties up to 1st May, 1915:—

	Killed.	Wounded.	Missing.	Other deaths.
British officers .	177	376	45	2
Indian officers .	74	194	35	4
Other ranks, British	1000	3945	1253	?
Other ranks, Indian	1837	8036	2189	406
Total	3088	12551	2522	412

Grand total, 18,573.

CHAPTER XX

THE BATTLE OF FESTUBERT

Events on the Eastern Front—French offensive in Woevre—Combined operations in May, 1915, by French and British to relieve pressure on Russia—Distinct objective of British offensive—General instructions —51st Highland Division joins the Indian Corps—Weather extremely unfavourable—Dispositions for attack—Inadequate bombardment—Two attacks of the Dehra Dun Brigade fail with heavy losses—Temporary success of 8th Division—Terrible condition of communication trenches—Two attacks by 1st Division fail—Second attack of 4th Corps breaks down—Bareilly attack fails with serious losses —Enemy's defences strengthened as result of Neuve Chapelle—Progress by the French—Further operation orders—Garhwal attack fails with very heavy casualties—Second attack also breaks down —Sirhind takes over trenches captured by 2nd Division—Situation on 18th May—Lieutenant J. G. Smyth, 15th Sikhs, gains the Victoria Cross—Attack by Sirhind on 18th May—Further attack on 21st May—Attack withdrawn—Captain Douie, R.E., gains the D.S.O.—General Walker's reasons for failure of Sirhind attack—Magnificent courage of the troops throughout the operations—Sir John French's remarks.

THE month of May, 1915, was destined to leave its mark deep cut in the Indian Corps. For the greater part of this period fighting was continuous, and although our object was not gained in its entirety, there can be few pages in the history of the war which testify to greater gallantry than that displayed by the Corps in its prolonged heroic struggle against the impossible.

During April the eyes of the world had been fixed on the operations on the Eastern front, where great events were in preparation, the result of which, it was then hoped, would place Russia in a commanding position for her great summer offensive.

Within the limits of this history it is impossible to go into detail. It will be remembered that the Russian plans aimed at the possession of the crest of the Carpathians, the domination of which was necessary, whether the ultimate objective was the Oder by way of Cracow, or the plains of Hungary, from which the Germans drew vast quantities of grain. By the 25th April it seemed that the Russian blow would be successful, and that the Carpathian line would shortly be in General Ivanov's hands,

During this and the preceding month, however, there had been ominous signs of a revival of German activity, which at first took the form of operations by the Baltic Fleet, in the course of which Libau was bombarded, while a little later the enemy advanced towards the Dubissa. These moves were generally construed as efforts to take the Russian pressure off the Carpathian region, where the position of the Central Powers had reached a critical stage.

The Germans kept their secret well, for the true meaning of their preliminary operations appears not to have been understood until Mackensen's thunderbolt fell at the close of April, and the contemplated Russian offensive was turned, as it were in an instant, into a desperate defence.

For some time past the French had been engaged in sanguinary, but successful, fighting in Woevre, their ultimate aim, apparently, being a crushing advance into Alsace and Lorraine, with a view to breaking down the German left.

The course of events on the Russian front brought a rapid awakening from these dreams. Any advance into Alsace-Lorraine must perforce be slow, directed as it would be against a portion of the enemy's line which was covered by fortresses such as Metz ; moreover, no main arteries of communication could be severed by such a move.

Whatever was to be done had to be done quickly, and the section which appeared to offer the most speedy means of diverting the enemy's attention from the Eastern front seemed to be that containing the important railway junctions of Valenciennes and Douai, through which passed a network of lines supplying three German armies. If these communications could be cut, the enemy's position from Lille to Soissons would become untenable, and there would be no alternative to a retreat.

In May, therefore, the French commenced an offensive towards Lens, the British at the same time undertaking active operations further north. To quote the words of Sir John French in his despatch dated the 15th June, 1915 :—

"In pursuance of a promise which I made to the French Commander-in-Chief to support an attack which his troops were making on the 9th May between the right of my line and Arras, I directed Sir Douglas Haig to carry out on that date an attack on the German trenches in the neighbourhood of Rouges Bancs (north-west of Fromelles) by the 4th Corps, and between Neuve Chapelle and Givenchy by the 1st and Indian Corps."

Although the British offensive was undertaken chiefly in support of the French, it had also a distinct and important objective, that of wresting from the enemy the famous Aubers Ridge, our principal aim at Neuve Chapelle, the possession of which would menace Lille, Tourcoing, Roubaix, and La Bassée.

On the 13th April secret instructions for the forthcoming operations were issued. Therein Sir Douglas Haig laid emphasis on the fact that the projected offensive was intended to be much more sustained, and that it was hoped that more far-reaching results would be obtained than from the operations at Neuve Chapelle.

The object was to co-operate with a vigorous offensive on a large scale by the French, with a view to breaking the enemy's front for a considerable width, and then to follow it up by such action as would cause a general retirement of a great part of the enemy's line.

Our aim, then, was not a local success and the capture of a few trenches, nor even of a portion of the hostile position on a more or less extended front, but to employ the entire force at our disposal, and to fight a decisive battle. At the same time general instructions were issued, the details of which were to be worked out by the Corps and Divisions concerned on the same lines as those for the attack on Neuve Chapelle.

The general instructions were briefly as follows :—

The 1st Army was to operate with a view to breaking through the enemy's line and gaining the La Bassée—Lille road between La Bassée and Fournes, after which an advance on Don would take place.

The 1st Corps, with its right on Givenchy, would attack from the vicinity of Richebourg L'Avoué, on as broad a front as possible, and advance on the line Rue du Marais—Illies.

The Indian Corps was to cover the left of the 1st Corps and to capture the Ferme du Biez, its subsequent advance being directed on Ligny-le-Grand—La Cliqueterie Farm.

The 4th Corps would operate so as to break through the enemy's line near Rouges Bancs with the double object of organizing a defensive flank from the vicinity of La Cordonnerie Farm to Fromelles, and of turning the Aubers defences from the north-east.

After gaining these objects the Corps would advance on La Cliqueterie Farm in the hope of effecting a junction with the Indian Corps.

The 2nd Cavalry Division was to remain in readiness near Estaires to act as the situation might develope.

The lesson of Neuve Chapelle had been learned, and the most minute instructions were now issued to prevent the delay caused by the late arrival of reserves, which on that occasion proved fatal to our plans. The importance of preserving communications between commanders and the front line of attack was especially impressed on all concerned, detailed instructions as to the method of attaining this end being given.

On the 18th April secret orders were issued by Sir James Willcocks for the operations of the Indian Corps. The Meerut Division was to attack on a front of 600 yards, reinforced by the artillery of the Lahore Division, and by any other guns which might be placed at the disposal of the Corps, the line being held by the Lahore Division, of which one Brigade would be in Corps reserve.

The various stages up to the first objective were defined as—

(*a*) Assault on the enemy's first line trenches.

(*b*) Capture of the village of La Tourelle on the La Bassée—Estaires road.

(*c*) Capture of the Ferme du Biez near the southern extremity of the Bois du Biez.

The subsequent objectives of the Indian Corps were to be the occupation of Ligny-le-Petit, Ligny-le-Grand, the Bois du Biez and La Cliqueterie, where junction would be effected with the 4th Corps.

All was in readiness for an attack at an early date, when orders were received for the Lahore Division to march to Ypres, where, as already related, it took part in the second battle, rejoining the Indian Corps on the 3rd–4th May. The operations intended for April had therefore to be postponed pending the return of the Lahore Division. At the commencement of May our front line was held by the Meerut Division.

The Germans were evidently suspicious of an attack on the 1st May, for at 4.45 a.m. on that date they opened a very heavy bombardment with howitzers on Port Arthur and the eastern end of the Rue du Bois, but our front line trenches were left severely alone. There was no sign of any infantry attack, and it was evident that, fearing an assault on our part, the enemy was searching for supports and reserves, and was seeking to destroy the communication trenches.

The chief sufferers were the 2nd Leicesters, 2/8th Gurkhas, and 39th Garhwalis, but the total of only 44 casualties was light considering the severity of the bombardment. By 6.30 a.m. all was calm again, and the cuckoo was heard calling amongst the ruins of Neuve Chapelle, as serenely as if the voice of a heavy howitzer had never been heard in the land.

On the 2nd May the Corps received a valuable addition in the shape of the 1st (afterwards known as the 51st) Highland Division (Territorials), under the command of Major-General Bannatine-Allason, C.B.

The Territorial battalions already with the Corps had established such a reputation that the advent of a whole Division of similar units was warmly welcomed, but their stay was unfortunately brief. On the 6th May the Jullundur Brigade relieved the Garhwal Brigade in the northern section of the Corps front, which now fell under the Lahore Division.

The Highland Division was not long in getting to work, for on the night of the 6th May the 1st Highland Brigade R.F.A. was ordered into action, while the remainder of the Division was moved into billets as far forward as possible, in readiness for any eventualities.

The advance of the 1st Army, originally fixed for the 8th May, was put off for 24 hours, partly on account of the thick mist, and partly because of the postponement of the French operations further south. The weather during the few preceding days had been of a very uncertain nature, alternating between steamy heat and heavy rain. In the evening of the 4th May a violent thunderstorm burst, and during the night more rain fell, as had also been the case during the preceding night. The trenches were, in consequence, once more converted into quagmires, and the prospect of an attack over heavy holding mud did not seem very bright.

The 6th was a day of brilliant sunshine, but on the 7th there was again rain.

The dispositions of the Meerut Division for the attack were as follows :-

The assault on the first objective, the enemy's trenches opposite to them, was to be delivered by the Dehra Dun Brigade on a three-battalion front, the Bareilly Brigade being in support, and the Garhwal Brigade, less two battalions which were detailed for another purpose, was to be in Divisional reserve. A separate force under the command of Lt-Colonel Drake-Brockman, was to be organized as a complete unit with its own Staff, signalling arrangements, and ammunition supply.

Colonel Drake-Brockman's Command was composed of the Garhwal Rifles, the 2/8th Gurkhas and two bomb guns. His orders were to move up into the front line trenches as soon as they were vacated by the Dehra Dun Brigade, and eventually to secure the eastern edge of the Bois du Biez and to capture La Russe.

The morning of the 9th May broke fine and clear. By 5 a.m. our guns had completed their registration, which had been carried on for several days previously in order not to rouse the suspicions of the enemy. At that hour the bombardment commenced and lasted for 40 minutes. It was noticed in our trenches that the fire was not so terrific as was expected, and, although by 5.20 a.m. the enemy's wire appeared to have been satisfactorily cut, the German parapet was seen to have suffered very slightly. Many of our shells burst short or over, some of them falling in our own trenches amongst the 1st Seaforths and 2/2nd Gurkhas, Captain Mullaly and several men of the latter battalion being wounded in this way.

The units of the Dehra Dun Brigade, which were to deliver the assault were, from right to left, the 2/2nd Gurkhas, 1/4th Seaforths, and 1st Seaforths, the 6th Jats and 1/9th Gurkhas being in support. One company of the 6th Jats was sent forward to close a small gap which would otherwise have existed between the left of the 1st Division and the right of the 2/2nd Gurkhas.

At 5.25 a.m. the assaulting troops went over the parapet and lined out, preparatory to an advance as the guns lengthened their range. The intention was that the front line should creep up as close to the enemy's position as our bombardment would allow, but in consequence of so many shells falling short, the men were not able to make any appreciable advance before the time fixed for the assault.

At 5.40 a.m., at the first signs of a move on our part, the enemy's parapet was manned, many Germans were seen to look over, and an appalling machine-gun and rifle fire was opened on us, the machine guns firing apparently from ground level.

On the right, two platoons of the 6th Jats attempted to advance with the 2nd Gurkhas, but were mown down at once, Captain Dudley and Subadar Lekh Ram being killed, and all the men either killed or wounded. The second line fared no better, Lieutenant Hebbert being severely wounded, and most of the men put out of action. In the 2/2nd Gurkhas also, all the British officers who went over the parapet were at once shot, Captain Mullaly, who was leading in spite of his wound, and Lieutenant Collins being killed.

The men fell in heaps, but the survivors dashed forward and gained the cover of the ditch in front of the parapet, where they lay down, thousands of bullets sweeping through the air just over their heads.

In the centre, the leading platoon of No. 3 Double Company, led by Captain Park, moved out in support of No. 4, but could get no further than the ditch. Captain Park, who, though very ill at the time, had insisted on taking part in the attack, was mortally wounded.

The 1/4th Seaforths in the centre were held up in the same manner, numbers of men being put out of action the moment they began to advance. The remainder pushed forward in the face of a sleet of bullets, and as many as could reach it took cover in the ditch, where they were forced to remain. Others were lying in the open or in shell holes, unable either to advance or retire.

This situation continued until orders were issued for any men who could crawl back to do so ; but few succeeded, as the slightest movement drew a terrific fire. More men managed to regain our trenches during the subsequent attack of the Bareilly Brigade, but the majority were compelled to lie out under fire until darkness set in.

The battalion suffered severely during the action.

Lieutenants Railton and Tennant, 2nd Lieutenant Bastian and 62 other ranks were killed, 5 officers and 127 men were wounded, while 19 men were missing.

The experiences of the 1st Seaforths on the left were of an equally harrowing nature. The moment they attempted to advance, officers and men were cut down as if by an invisible reaping machine, the sound of the fire from a distance resembling the purring of a multitude of gigantic cats.

By 6 a.m. it was evident that the attack had failed, although it was believed that some men of the 2nd Gurkhas had reached the German trenches, only, however, to be shot down or captured. In the meantime the remainder were lying out in the open between our trenches and the enemy, unable to move.

The German guns, which till then had not been much in evidence, now poured a heavy and continuous fire on our trenches and the ground in rear, as well as on the Rue du Bois. This bombardment caused a large number of casualties amongst the Bareilly Brigade in its assembly position north of the Rue du Bois, the 41st Dogras suffering severely, while the 1/4th Black Watch sustained 14 casualties from premature bursts of our own shells.

On the right of the Indian Corps the attack of the 1st Division had also broken down with very heavy losses under machine-gun fire, and preparations were being made for a second bombardment. Heavy howitzers were now turned on to the enemy's parapet, after which the 1st Seaforths made a second gallant attempt to advance, but this, as well as a subsequent attack, was held up as before by fire through which there was no passing.

At 9 a.m., seeing that the task was absolutely impossible, that most of the officers had been shot, and that the men were lying out under a terrible fire of all kinds, the Commanding Officer of the 1st Seaforths ordered all who were able to move to get back to the trench whenever they could. A number succeeded in doing so, but many had to remain for hours, some returning at 3.40 p.m., when the Bareilly Brigade attacked, the remainder crawling back after dark. The losses of the 1st Seaforths during this terrible day were 7 officers and 131 other ranks killed, 10 officers and 346 others wounded.

The 8th Division of the 4th Corps on the left had at first met with considerable success, capturing the front line of German trenches near Rouges Bancs, while detachments even penetrated to a considerable distance behind the enemy's front; but eventually enfilade fire rendered the captured positions untenable, and by the morning of the 10th the Division was compelled to retire to its original line.

It was now observed that the enemy was being strongly reinforced in front of the Dehra Dun Brigade, and there appeared to be danger of a counter-attack. The 1/9th Gurkhas were accordingly ordered to support the 1st and 4th Seaforths, but by this time the communication trenches were so congested that only 200 of the battalion could get up to the front.

These trenches, difficult to pass through even when occupied only by the ordinary traffic, were now in a state which beggars description. The German guns had been pouring high explosive and shrapnel into them all the morning; in numerous places the parapet had been blown in and blocked the way, while numbers of dead and wounded were lying at the bottom of the trenches. The direction boards had in many cases been destroyed, and men were wandering about, vainly attempting to find the nearest way to their units or to the aid posts. The nearer one got to the front, the more of a shambles the trenches became; wounded men were creeping and crawling along amidst the mud and debris of the parapet, numbers of them, unable to extricate themselves, died alone and unattended, while amidst this infernal scene the German shells were continually bursting.

At 7.45 a.m. on the 9th May, a special bombardment by howitzers of the enemy's trenches commenced and lasted till 8.45 a.m., under cover of which the Dehra Dun Brigade was to make a further assault. In the meantime news was received that the second attack of the 1st Division had failed owing to the enemy's wire not having been cut, the 2nd and 3rd Brigades having lost very heavily. The attack of the Dehra Dun Brigade was therefore postponed, and arrangements were made to organize another assault to synchronize with that of the 1st Division, which could not be got ready under two hours.

Eventually, operations were fixed for 2 p.m., to be undertaken by the Bareilly Brigade in relief of Dehra Dun. In consequence, however, of the crowded and battered state of the communication trenches, it was found to be impossible for the Bareilly Brigade to assault at that hour. The bombardment was therefore ordered to commence at 3.20 p.m., the assault, both of the 1st and Meerut Divisions, to take place at 4 p.m.

In the interval the Germans had been strongly reinforcing their second line, and at noon General Southey, Commanding the Bareilly Brigade, reported that the enemy's position had been in no way weakened by our bombardment, and that the machine-gun fire which had checked Dehra Dun was not lessened, while three of his battalions had already suffered severely from shell fire.

In spite of this report, Sir James Willcocks, in

order to conform with the general plan of operations, directed the attack to take place as directed, and to proceed at all costs.

The relief of Dehra Dun by Bareilly had been in process since 10.30 a.m., but the movement was observed by the enemy, who kept up a constant heavy shell fire, which, coupled with the congested state of the trenches, greatly delayed the completion of the arrangements for the assault.

By this time the 2nd Black Watch had relieved the 2/2nd Gurkhas on the right, and the 58th Rifles succeeded the 1/4th Seaforths in the centre, while the 41st Dogras replaced the 1st Seaforths on the left. It was a most pathetic sight to watch the poor remnant of this magnificent battalion, before the action over 1100 strong with 26 officers, returning to billets a mere skeleton, with a solitary piper marching at its head.

The 1/4th Black Watch were in reserve in the Crescent and Blackader trenches with the machine guns of the 125th Rifles. The Sirhind Brigade was placed in reserve to the Meerut Division, sending two battalions, the 1/4th King's (Liverpools) and 1/1st Gurkhas, into Corps reserve with the Dehra Dun Brigade.

It had now been ascertained that the machine-gun fire, from which the 1st Seaforths had suffered such terrible losses, was proceeding from the south-west corner of the Bois du Biez. General Anderson arranged for artillery fire to cope with this during the next bombardment, and directed General Southey not to make any attack east of the Estaires—La Bassée road, the left of the 41st Dogras being directed on the west of that road which, being on a low

[*Central Press.*

LANCE-CORPORAL DAVID FINLAY, V.C., 2ND BN BLACK WATCH.

embankment, afforded partial protection from the east and north-east.

Some idea of the severity of the fire to which the Bareilly Brigade had been subjected during its move up to relieve Dehra Dun may be gathered from the fact that No. 3 Company of the 58th Rifles lost Lieutenant Mackmillan mortally wounded, two Indian officers killed, and 45 casualties amongst other ranks; in consequence, one company of the 1/4th Black Watch had to be lent to the 58th.

Meanwhile a report had been received that the second attack of the 4th Corps had also failed and that a further effort was being organized.

The artillery bombardment commenced at 3.20 p.m. on the 9th, and at 3.40 p.m. the assaulting troops began to cross our parapet and form up ready to advance. The right battalion, the 2nd Black Watch, and the right company of the 58th Rifles in the centre were met with an accurate and heavy machine-gun and rifle fire the moment they appeared over the parapet, with the result that only very few succeeded in crossing the ditch in front, the majority being killed or wounded before they reached it. This ditch, which was full of water and mud, ran almost parallel to our position at a distance varying from 10 to 30 yards, and had proved a very serious obstacle to each successive attack. Seeing that any further advance under such circumstances was out of the question, the Commanding Officer ordered the rest of the attack to remain in our trench.

During the advance Lance-Corporal David Finlay, 2nd Black Watch, performed a number of heroic deeds. Shortly after crossing the parapet he was knocked over by the explosion of a shell, but on finding his feet again, he led forward a bombing party of twelve men, rushing from one shell hole to another until ten of his men had been put out of action. Seeing that further progress was impossible, he ordered the two survivors to make the best of their way back, but himself crawled over to a wounded man and carried him in safety to our trench, crossing, in doing so, for a distance of about 100 yards, a zone which was being swept by a terrific fire of every kind.

Lance-Corporal Finlay was awarded the Victoria Cross for his valour and devotion, but later met his death, like so many brave men of the Indian Corps, in Mesopotamia.

In this brief period the losses of the 2nd Black Watch were:—Killed: 3 officers, Lieutenants the Hon. K. A. Stewart, W. L. Brownlow, and R. Sinclair; other ranks, 69. Wounded: 5 officers and 157 others. Missing: other ranks, 36. Total: 270 out of approximately 450 actually engaged.

The majority of these casualties were from bullet wounds, as the battalion had not suffered to any great extent from shells.

The wounded lay out in the open exposed to a fiendish fire till darkness enabled them to be brought in; then too those who had reached the cover of the ditch managed to creep back to our trench.

The left of the 58th Rifles succeeded with great gallantry in advancing about 100 yards, but here all further progress was barred by our own guns, which continued till 4.10 p.m. to plaster the ground about 130 yards in front of the enemy's trenches with lyddite, and thus pinned our men down. The enemy's guns were knocking the parapet about badly, and succeeded in landing a shell on top of one of the machine guns of the 58th, killing 2 men and wounding 4; but the other gun continued in action in spite of the heavy fire.

After 5 p.m. those of the men who were still lying out under any slight cover they could find began to crawl back, some returning through holes dug under the parapet, and others climbing over the top. Many were hit during the process. The stretcher-bearers went out after dark, and with their usual devotion brought in all the 58th wounded, and many of the Seaforths and Black Watch.

The casualties of the 58th were 3 British officers wounded, of whom Lieutenant Mackmillan died that night; 2 Indian officers and 38 other ranks killed, 5 Indian officers and 197 others wounded; 7 others missing; total, 252.

The 41st Dogras had been exposed to an extremely accurate high-explosive fire, as well as shrapnel, while moving up through the Pioneer trench, one company being reduced to 28 men. The remnant of two and a half companies crossed the parapet and pushed forward, but Captain Nixon, 91st Punjabis, who was leading No. 2 Company, was at once severely wounded, and the majority of the men were put out of action.

Lt-Colonel Hutchinson and Lieutenant Vaughan, I.A.R.O., led on No. 1 Double Company, and with the remains of No. 2 succeeded in getting a little further forward, but here Colonel Hutchinson was severely wounded in both legs and one hand, while Lieutenant Vaughan had his right arm shattered. At the same time, Lt-Colonel Tribe, the Commanding Officer, who had been watching the advance over the parapet, was wounded in the chest by a shell splinter.

The men lay down under whatever cover they could find to wait for 4 p.m., at which time the assault was to be pressed home, but the whole advance had now been held up. Subadar Jai Singh, 37th Dogras, who was the sole unwounded officer, British or Indian, sent back word that he was ready to assault and was only awaiting the signal.

The casualties, however, both amongst the attacking companies and those still in our trench, had been so serious as to preclude all idea of any further move forward, and the Subadar, who had meanwhile been wounded in two places, was ordered to abandon the attack, and await darkness before attempting to get back to the trench.

About this time Major Milne, 82nd Punjabis, was severely wounded while bringing his men up to the front line.

From 5 p.m. the artillery and rifle fire on both sides died down, and the opportunity was seized to reorganize companies and repair the trenches, as well as to remove the dead and evacuate the wounded.

The losses of the 41st Dogras during this attack were: 5 British officers wounded; 1 Indian officer killed and 6 wounded, as well as 354 other ranks; while 35 others were killed or believed to have been so. Total: 401 out of 645 engaged.

This was the first assault in which the battalion had taken part during its seven months of trench warfare, but under the magnificent leadership of its British officers it held its own and made a lasting reputation for itself, no small achievement on a day when all units engaged showed such heroism. For his services on this occasion Lt-Colonel W. Tribe, who has since been killed in action, was granted the C.M.G., Lt-Colonel Hutchinson the D.S.O., and Captain Brind, 37th Dogras, machine-gun officer, the Military Cross; while Subadar Jai Singh received the Russian Cross of the Order of St George, 3rd Class, a number of decorations being also awarded to the other ranks.

By this time the Commanding Officers of all the battalions engaged had come to the conclusion that to attempt any further advance would only mean useless loss of life. They were led to this opinion by the fact that our artillery preparation had been ineffectual, and that neither the enemy's parapet, personnel, nor machine guns had been seriously weakened. It was stated by the officers commanding the 2nd Black Watch and 58th Rifles that they saw the German marksmen deliberately standing up behind their breastworks during our bombardment and shooting our men while assembling, and it was only by the use of the regimental machine guns and the Brigade trench guns that the enemy could be kept down during the advance.

General Southey was of opinion that, although at Neuve Chapelle a forty minutes' bombardment was entirely successful, the enemy's parapet and lines generally had been much strengthened since that battle, necessitating a far longer and more sustained battering of the hostile trenches before an infantry attack could be made with any prospect of success.

At 6.15 p.m. orders were received for the relief

of the Bareilly Brigade by Garhwal as soon as possible. The relief was completed by 1 a.m. on the 10th, Bareilly remaining in close support of the Garhwal Brigade. As a tribute to the gallantry of the Bareilly Brigade in the face of tremendous odds, the words of General Southey's report are worthy of quotation.

"I wish to bring to the notice of the Lieutenant-General Commanding the gallant behaviour of all the regiments engaged. They saw in front of them the hundreds of men of the Dehra Dun Brigade lying out on our front wounded and dead. They knew the enemy were unshaken, seeing them with their heads over the parapet firing, and thoroughly realizing that what had happened to the Dehra Dun Brigade would in all probability happen to them: but not a man faltered, and as they boldly advanced over the parapet, only to be shot down, British and Indian ranks alike did their level best to reach the enemy's line. Even when the attack had failed, the moral of the Brigade remained unshaken, and, had another attack been ordered, they would have undertaken it in the same spirit."

During the day news was received of good progress by the French in their operations between Lens and Arras. By nightfall our Allies had captured three lines of trench on a five-mile front, taking 3000 prisoners and a number of guns. Their infantry assault had been most thoroughly prepared, and the bombardment was the heaviest yet witnessed on the Western front, lasting for hours, and absolutely obliterating the German front line trenches, while cutting off all reinforcements.

As regards the British front, the position on the

morning of the 10th May was unaltered, such ground as had been gained having been evacuated by us as untenable in face of the terrific enfilade fire maintained by the enemy. Early in the morning of the 10th orders were issued for the day's operations, but were cancelled later. During the night of the 10th–11th the Indian Corps took over a small portion of the line on the left of the 1st Corps.

The approximate casualties of the Corps up to midnight 10th–11th May were as follows:—

Meerut Division:—British officers, 69; Indian officers, 24; others, British, 1055; others, Indian, 823.

To these must be added 122 of all ranks of the Lahore Division, making a total of 2093.

Nothing of special note occurred during the 11th and 12th.

On the morning of the 13th May instructions were received from the 1st Army for operations on the 14th.

The general plan of the main attack was as follows:—

(1) To continue pressing forward towards Violaines and Beau Puits, establishing a defensive flank along the La Bassée road on the left and maintaining the right at Givenchy.

(2) The line to be established in the first instance, if possible, on the general line of the road Festubert—La Quinque Rue—La Tourelle cross-roads—Port Arthur. This position to be consolidated, the troops reformed, and communication established.

(3) During this process a bombardment on the whole front would continue, with fire specially directed on the next objectives, the Rue d'Ouvert—

Rue du Marais, after which a fresh advance on this line would take place.

The assault was to be carried out simultaneously by the Indian Corps and the 1st Division, commencing at 11.30 p.m. on the 14th May. The attacking troops of the Indian Corps were to be the Meerut Division, less the Dehra Dun Brigade, whose place was taken by Sirhind. The Lahore Division was to continue to hold its front and to assist with rifle and gun fire.

During the 13th and 14th considerable rain fell. Observation was in consequence extremely difficult, and many of our shells failed to burst on account of the softness of the ground. The operations ordered for 11.30 p.m. on the 14th were consequently postponed for 24 hours, as it was found that the bombardment had not been very successful. It was accordingly continued throughout the 15th, drawing a strong reply from the enemy's guns on the trenches held by the Meerut Division.

At 11.30 p.m. the guns lifted and our assault was launched. The 2nd Leicesters were on the right with 6 machine guns, the Garhwal Rifles with a similar number of machine guns on the left, the 3rd Londons and two companies of the 2/3rd Gurkhas were in support, the remainder of the 2/3rd being in Brigade reserve.

A number of portable bridges had been provided to enable the troops to cross the ditch which had proved such a serious obstacle to previous assaults. The placing of these bridges in position was no easy task. The enemy continually sent up flares which illuminated every inch of the ground, and followed them with bursts of rifle and machine-gun fire. Moreover, the ditch had in many places been much widened by shell holes on the banks, and trunks of trees felled by shell fire blocked many places where the bridges might otherwise have been placed. The work was, however, quickly and skilfully carried out with few casualties.

As soon as the bridges were in position the assaulting troops filed out, a portion of each battalion lying on the enemy's side of the ditch, another portion on our side, while the remainder were in or behind the front-line trench ready to support. These movements were also completed with small losses.

The moment the men advanced, the enemy opened a murderous fire from rifles and machine guns, at the same time sending up flares and throwing in front of their parapet a species of fire ball, which burst into flame on striking the ground, the result being that the night was literally as light as day. At the same time they covered the ground round the ditch with trench-mortar bombs and shrapnel, while a searchlight exposed every movement of our men.

As each successive line came under fire, the bridges got blocked, and the obstruction caused by shell holes and fallen trees so impeded movement that no effective support could be given. Repeated attempts were made to press forward, but they all ended in the same way. No living thing could penetrate the storm of bullets which screened the German trenches.

There seems reason to believe that the enemy was aware, not only of the hour of the intended attack, but also of the exact front on which it was to be delivered. During the evening preceding the assault the Germans were heard to call out, "Come on, we are ready for you." Moreover, when they opened fire as our troops began to advance, only the actual front occupied by the assaulting companies was swept, and not the ground to the east of it, as might have been expected.

At about midnight it became evident that there was not the slightest prospect of success, however gallantly the assault might be pressed. The Leicesters and Garhwalis were therefore withdrawn, their place being taken by the 2/3rd Gurkhas and 3rd Londons.

The casualties of the 2nd Leicesters in this attack were:—Killed: 2nd Lieutenants Gandy, Tayler, Brown, and 22 other ranks. Wounded: 6 officers, of whom one, Lieutenant Crosse, died, and 192 others. Missing: 5.

The 39th Garhwalis lost:—Killed: 4 men. Wounded: Lieutenant G. S. Rogers, 2 Garhwali officers and 136 men. Missing: 11.

At 2.45 a.m. on the 16th May we commenced afresh the intense bombardment, and at 3.15 a.m. the 3rd Londons and 2/3rd Gurkhas attacked. Owing to the early dawn, it was not possible to get the men out before our bombardment ceased. Even before the assault started, the enemy was keeping up a very heavy fire on our parapet, and numbers of men were shot as they crossed the top.

In the 2/3rd Gurkhas, Lieutenant Robertson and 2nd Lieutenant Nott-Bower led two platoons each. Lieutenant Robertson led the remnant of his men over the ditch by the few remaining bridges, and was advancing by short rushes from shell hole to shell hole when he was stunned by a shrapnel bullet in the head. The attack was shortly afterwards held up all along the line, the Londons on the left and the Worcesters of the British Division on the right being unable to advance.

The situation was reported, and orders were issued for the line to be held, but no further attempt at advance to be made. In retiring from the position reached during the assault, 2nd Lieutenant Nott-Bower was killed in a gallant attempt to bring in a badly wounded private of the Leicesters. Captain Grigg was also killed during the morning by shell fire.

During the attack Captain F. F. Hodgson, 84th Punjabis, machine-gun officer of the Bareilly Brigade, was mortally wounded. He had distinguished himself, while attached to the 58th Rifles, during the fighting of the 20th–22nd December, 1914, and his loss was keenly felt, for he was an officer of great promise and much esteemed by all ranks.

At 6 a.m. the front line was vacated to allow of our artillery bombarding the German parapet, the troops again occupying the trenches at 2 p.m.

The losses of the 2/3rd Gurkhas were 2 British officers and 9 other ranks killed, 64 others wounded, 1 missing.

The 3rd Londons lost 10 men killed, 3 officers and 86 men wounded, 5 missing.

In view of the extraordinary strength of the defence, it was decided that no further attempts should be made to advance on this front, but that troops should be pushed through the opening on the right of the Indian Corps. The Sirhind Brigade was now put under the orders of the General Officer Commanding 2nd Division, as also were the 107th Pioneers and No. 4 Company Sappers and Miners.

On the night of the 16th, Bareilly relieved the Garhwal Brigade in the front line. Throughout the darkness our guns continued to hammer at the Germans in order to give them no rest, and to keep them from sending out working parties. Our scouts made repeated attempts to get close to the hostile line, but were always prevented by the constant rifle and machine-gun fire, and the never-ceasing flares.

On the 17th May the Sirhind Brigade took over from the 5th Brigade a portion of the trenches captured by the 2nd Division. This relief was carried out with the greatest difficulty, owing to the communication trenches being blocked with wounded and also knee-deep in mud and water, through which the men, heavily laden with 300 rounds of ammunition, bombs, sandbags, etc., had to plod their way. The result was that the relief was only partially completed when dawn broke on the 18th, and there was considerable confusion.

The whole area of the support and fire trenches bore witness to the terrible fighting which had taken place there on the previous day. The parapets were in many places levelled and the trenches filled up; the ground was everywhere pitted with huge shell holes, and might almost be described as carpeted with dead bodies.

At 4 a.m. the enemy made a half-hearted attack on the left of the 15th Sikhs, but was easily beaten off by rifle fire.

The 1st Highland Light Infantry, who relieved their own second battalion, suffered a number of casualties from the incessant shell fire during the relief and on the previous day, 2nd Lieutenant Davidson being killed, Lieutenants Henderson,

Cowan, McNeill, and Murray wounded, while there were 70 casualties amongst the rank-and-file.

The battalion found the trenches in a shocking condition, as many corpses and wounded were still lying there; 104 dead of different units were interred by the company in the front line during the night of the 18th May. The Germans had buried many bodies in the parapet from which our shelling had unearthed them; mangled remains were trodden into the deep mud at the bottom of the trenches, and it was not till some days later that they could be extricated. The conditions in the meantime cannot with decency be described.

At noon on the 18th May the position of the Meerut Division and Sirhind Brigade was as follows:—

The Bareilly Brigade and 2/8th Gurkhas were holding the line from the La Bassée road to a point near the cinder track on the Rue du Bois, where a communication trench had been cut to the newly taken position.

Of the Sirhind Brigade, the 15th Sikhs and one company Highland Light Infantry were in the captured trenches, with the 4th King's (Liverpools) in our old trench to the west. The 1/1st and 1/4th Gurkhas were in support.

Of the Garhwal Brigade, one battalion was at Lansdowne Post, the remainder in billets and in second-line trenches at Croix Barbée. The Dehra Dun Brigade was in reserve.

On the night of the 17th May a company of the 15th Sikhs under Captain K. Hyde-Cates relieved the 2nd Highland Light Infantry in a section of the captured trench known as the "Glory Hole" on account of its dangerous position and the number of casualties which had occurred there, the enemy being only separated from us by barricades.

In the early morning of the 18th Captain Hyde-Cates observed that attempts were being made to reinforce the enemy, swarms of Germans being seen rushing towards the further extremity of the trench. Rapid fire was opened on them, but in the dim light the effect could not be ascertained. When day broke, it was found that the hostile trench was packed with men, and an attack seemed certain.

Shortly afterwards the Germans commenced heavy bombing, to which the 15th replied vigorously, and succeeded in holding their own till noon when all our dry bombs had been expended, the remainder having been rendered useless by the incessant rain and the mud. The situation at once became very critical, as without bombs the position could hardly be held.

At 3.30 p.m. Lieutenant J. G. Smyth, 15th Sikhs, was ordered to attempt to take bombs and a bombing party from the support trench (our former front line) to Captain Hyde-Cates. The distance to be covered was about 250 yards over open ground. The only means of communication was a shallow trench half full of mud and water, and in many places exposed to the fire of the enemy's snipers and machine guns. The trench was crammed with the dead bodies of British and Indian soldiers, as well as Germans. Lieutenant Smyth took with him ten bombers from No. 4 Company, selected from the crowd of volunteers who at once responded to the call.

The names of these heroes deserve to be put on record. They were Lance-Naik Mangal Singh,

[Gilman Oxford.

LIEUT J. G. SMYTH, V.C., 15TH SIKHS.

Sepoys Lal Singh, Sucha Singh, Sapuram Singh, Sarain Singh, Sundur Singh, Ganda Singh, Harnam Singh (the last four being all of the 19th Punjabis), Fateh Singh and Ujagar Singh, both of the 45th Sikhs.

The party took with them two boxes of bombs containing 48 each. For the first 50 yards the trench gave cover from the enemy's view, but on emerging from this portion the men came under enfilade shrapnel fire from the German field guns, which was so severe as to force them to crawl off to the right and take refuge in a small stream where the water reached chest-high. Here the first man was hit.

They waited until the shelling slackened, and then, returning to the trench, continued their laborious progress. But now man after man was killed or wounded, for it was necessary to crawl over the top of the dead bodies, and the sides of the trench had been in many places broken down, exposing the party to the full view of the enemy, who, well aware of the object of the enterprise, pumped torrents of bullets into the trench. By the time Lieutenant Smyth had arrived within 30 yards of Captain Hyde-Cates' position, he had only three men left, and the slightest attempt to rise from a lying-down position brought a shower of bullets.

Up to this point the boxes had been pushed or pulled along by means of pagris attached to them, but with the few men left, this was no longer possible. Lieutenant Smyth now gave orders for the boxes to be opened, and for each man to carry two bombs in his hands. While opening a box, another man was shot through the head and killed. There was nothing for it but to leave the bombs in the communication trench to be brought in after dark.

The officer, Lance-Naik Mangal Singh, and one sepoy managed by crawling through the mud and water to reach Captain Hyde-Cates' trench, being the sole survivors of the little band of eleven.

So ended one of the most gallant episodes of the war. For his most conspicuous valour Lieutenant Smyth was awarded the Victoria Cross and later the 4th Class of the Order of St George. Lance-Naik Mangal Singh received the 2nd Class, Indian Order of Merit, while the Indian Distinguished Service Medal was conferred on all the sepoys of the party.

An attack by the Sirhind Brigade on the Ferme du Bois was timed for 4.30 p.m. on the 18th May, in conjunction with an assault by the Guards Brigade on the Cour d'Avoué. As a first move, Sirhind was intended to bomb along the German trenches in their front and thus establish a *pied à terre* from which to launch an attack on the Ferme du Bois. After the capture of the farm, the Brigade was to conform to the progress of the Guards' attack.

Our artillery bombardment commenced at 2 p.m., from which time till 4 p.m. it was slow and deliberate in order to ensure proper observation of the effect. At 4 p.m. the guns quickened up till 4.20 p.m., ending with intense fire till 4.30 p.m., when the attack was to be launched.

At 4.20 p.m., however, the bombing parties of the Sirhind Brigade were still held up in their own trenches by the heavy artillery fire which deluged our line and the ground in rear with shells of all calibres, from the "pipsqueak" of the field guns to the "coal boxes" or "black Marias" of the heavy howitzers. The Highland Light Infantry attempted to dribble men up the communication trench to the firing line with their bombing parties, but they were at once spotted, and their losses prevented them from making any further progress. The attack of the 4th King's could not develope in face of the terrible fire, and by 6.30 p.m. the attempt died away, although the artillery on both sides continued an intermittent bombardment.

Already the company of the 15th Sikhs in the front line under Captain Hyde-Cates had lost approximately half its strength, but still held on bravely until relieved by No. 2 Company under Captain Beattie-Crozier at 8.30 p.m. With them the machine guns under Captain Daniell moved up to the front line, and a section of the 1/4th Gurkhas relieved a party of the 2nd Highland Light Infantry. The Germans were thoroughly on the alert, and at once opened a heavy fire, wounding two Indian officers and a number of men.

In the meantime the Guards Brigade had made some progress by short rushes, and a night attack by Sirhind was now ordered to take place as soon as the reliefs of the 2nd Division on the right were completed. At 10 p.m. Brigadier General Walker, V.C., Commanding the Sirhind Brigade, reported that the strength of the German position round the Ferme du Bois was such as to render the chance of success of an attack very doubtful; that any advance would entail useless loss unless our present front could be properly consolidated and a base for the attack assured.

Sir James Willcocks, while again impressing on

General Walker the desirability of making the attack, left it to his judgment on the spot to decide whether to assault or not. At 11.10 p.m. it was definitely decided by General Walker that the attack should not take place, and with his decision Sir James Willcocks, for the reasons given, agreed.

The weather during this period continued to be atrocious, rain frequently fell, and the trenches were half full of mud and water.

The 19th May began badly for the 15th Sikhs, for news was received early in the morning that Captain Beattie-Crozier and Lieutenant Thomson had been mortally wounded, and further, that the Germans on the left were bombing slowly along the trench, while of No. 2 Company in the front line and the machine-gun section only 48 men remained unhurt, and that assistance was badly required. This was at once reported, and a company of the 1st Highland Light Infantry was sent up to reinforce the 15th with a bombing party. At the same time artillery, rifle, machine-gun and bomb-gun fire was directed on the Germans, with the result that by 6.25 a.m. the situation had been adjusted. It was found later that the 15th had not yielded an inch of ground.

Artillery fire continued on both sides throughout the day, the Germans shelling our supports with shrapnel, while their heavy artillery attended to the reserve trenches and any likely positions for head quarters in rear of the line. A number of heavy shells burst in an open field at a distance of only about 100 yards from the 15th Sikhs' head quarters, without, however, doing the slightest damage.

During this period Captain Waterfield, of the

15th, was mortally wounded in the head by a shell while talking to Captain Finnis and Lieutenant Smyth of his plans for his next leave. He died during the night without regaining consciousness, the Regimental Diary testifying that the loss of this gallant officer was most keenly felt by the officers and men of the regiment.

During the 19th May the 4th King's were relieved by the 1/4th Gurkhas, and the 15th Sikhs by the 1st Highland Light Infantry. The 4th King's had suffered severely during the shelling of the 18th May, losing 7 men killed, Captain Jenkins and 82 men wounded.

On the 20th May Sir James Willcocks impressed on General Anderson that the Ferme du Bois must be captured before the morning of the 22nd. The general idea of the operations was that the Canadian and Highland Divisions should work southwards, and capture a group of houses south of the Cour d'Avoué, while the Indian Corps was to carry on continuous active hostilities with a view to harassing the enemy and wearing down his resistance.

The Sirhind Brigade, as a first objective, was ordered to secure the Ferme du Bois, preparation for the assault on this position being made by occupying certain important tactical points in advance of the general attack which was to be carried out by the Brigade.

During the night of the 20th–21st a thorough reconnaissance of the position was made and a picquet established slightly to the west of the Ferme du Bois. Our artillery bombardment was timed to commence at 1 p.m. on the 21st May, and to continue till 5 a.m. on the 22nd, being directed on the enemy's trenches and the area round the Ferme du Bois, at the same time forming barrages to prevent the arrival of reinforcements.

The Sirhind Brigade was disposed for attack as follows:—

Right attack: the 1/4th Gurkhas.

Centre attack: the 1/1st Gurkhas.

Left attack: the 1st Highland Light Infantry.

The 4th King's were in support, with the 15th Sikhs in Brigade reserve.

The troops got into position correctly, and the attacks were launched punctually at 1 a.m. The ground over which the assault had to advance was broken up by old trenches, ditches and hedges, and, a satisfactory daylight reconnaissance not having been possible, direction was to some extent lost and units in places became mixed up. At first there was very little firing on the part of the enemy.

On the right the 1/4th Gurkhas were led by Major H. E. Moule, and for a time all went well, but suddenly they found themselves up against a ditch full of water on the further side of which was barbed wire little damaged by our bombardment. Part of the company was held up by the ditch, but Major Moule, a brother officer relates, with his usual dash and courage, accompanied by Captain Robinson and a few men, overcame all the obstacles and reached the enemy's trench. He was seen to climb the parapet, and there is no doubt that he was killed in a hand-to-hand fight, together with Captain Robinson and the men, for of this gallant party not one returned.

As a distinguished General remarks, "Major Moule led his men most gallantly, and did his duty as well as it could be done, and no man can do more."

In spite of repeated attempts to advance, the remainder of the right attack was held up. The only unwounded British officer with the Gurkhas returned at 1.50 a.m. to fetch up reinforcements. Unfortunately, two machine guns of the 4th King's, which were attached to the right attack, were lost. The officer in charge, 2nd Lieutenant F. A. Ballinger, had been ordered to follow up in rear of the last company of the Gurkhas, which was carrying entrenching tools and ammunition, but in his keenness to get forward he did not wait, but pushed right up to the wire in front of the enemy's trench, where he and most of the gun teams were killed. An exhaustive search was made for the guns on the following night, but without success, for doubtless they had been carried off by the enemy.

The losses of the 1/4th Gurkhas were: Major Moule and Captain Robinson missing, believed killed; 2 riflemen killed; 1 Gurkha officer and 76 men wounded; 18 missing.

The 1/1st Gurkhas in the centre met with more success, which unfortunately was not known until it was too late to take advantage of it.

Lieutenant Heyland led the first company, and Captain Mellis the second, but owing to the darkness touch was soon lost with the troops on both flanks. The two companies were together when the outskirts of the farm were reached, and up to that point had not been met with any serious fire. Unfortunately the men started cheering, on which very heavy machine-gun and rifle fire was opened on them, especially from the right rear.

Our shells were still falling in front of the Gurkhas, and as Captain Mellis was anxious, before advancing further, to get into touch with the Highland Light Infantry on his left, he ordered Lieutenant Heyland to turn the ditch which the men were then lining into a defensible trench.

The Gurkhas were now falling fast, and at this moment both officers were hit; Heyland died at once, and the trench was soon full of dead and wounded men.

Captain Mellis sent back for reinforcements with entrenching tools, but after waiting for some time, as there were no signs of help, he dragged himself out of the ditch, collected as many of the wounded as could move, and managed to get back to our line.

Lieutenant Sutcliffe had been wounded early in the attack, and 2nd Lieutenants Herbert, Fry, and Gamble were killed in the ditch while waiting for reinforcements.

When all the British officers were out of action, Subadar Jit Sing Gurung took command and asked for reinforcements. By this time, however, the troops on both flanks had been withdrawn, and Colonel Anderson was compelled to order the Subadar to retire, which he did, capturing on the way a man of a German patrol. He received the 2nd class, India Order of Merit for his gallantry.

The casualties of the 1/1st Gurkhas, who behaved throughout with great bravery, were: 4 British officers killed; 2 wounded; 115 other ranks killed or wounded.

Lt-Colonel Anderson particularly brought to notice the very adequate support which his battalion received from the artillery during the advance.

For his gallant leading in this attack Captain Mellis was awarded the Military Cross.

The 1st Highland Light Infantry on the left met with much the same fate as the 1/4th Gurkhas on the right. They reached the ditch with comparatively slight losses, but were here stopped by machine-gun fire, which caused heavy casualties amongst both officers and men. At 1.50 a.m. it was reported that the attack had been completely held up. The three Commanding Officers of the attacking units, after consultation, decided to order a withdrawal at once in order to complete the movement before daylight.

The losses of the Highland Light Infantry were:—Killed: 2nd Lieutenant Agnew. Wounded and missing: 2nd Lieutenant B. Ivy. Wounded: Lieutenant Murray-Lyon, 2nd Lieutenants Mummery, Westwater, and Wright. The casualties in the ranks amounted to 120.

At the close of this attack, after day had fully dawned, a wounded man was observed to be lying within 80 yards of the German parapet, from which the enemy were firing at him. Captain F. M. Douie, R.E., M.C., regardless of the apparent hopelessness of the attempt, at once went over the parapet, accompanied by his orderly, Sapper Jiwa Khan, No. 3 Company 1st Sappers and Miners, and, in spite of the enemy's close-range fire and the fact that the German trench was being shelled by our guns, they succeeded in rescuing the man. Captain Douie also helped to bring in another wounded soldier on a stretcher under very heavy fire. He had previously won the Military Cross by his gallantry in action during November, 1914, and was now awarded the D.S.O., while Sapper Jiwa Khan received the 2nd Class, Indian Order of Merit.

In General Walker's opinion the failure of the attack was due to the following reasons :—

(i) The excessive casualties among the British officers with the assaulting companies. When the attack was finally held up there remained with the Highland Light Infantry only one subaltern, with the 1/1st Gurkhas no British officer, with the 1/4th Gurkhas one subaltern.

(ii) The deep ditch in front of the objective. Though not an insuperable obstacle, it was a very serious one at night, and effectually stopped the impetus of the attack.

(iii) The hour fixed for the attack, 1 a.m., was too late. The organization of a second assault before daylight was impossible, nor would the troops have had time to dig themselves in.

(iv) The want of aeroplane photographs showing the German trenches.

General Walker further considered that the Commanding Officers were right in withdrawing their men in view of the approach of daylight.

The total losses of the 9 companies actually engaged were very heavy, amounting to 16 British, 2 Indian officers, 137 other ranks British, and 173 Indian. This attack marked the conclusion of our active operations during May, 1915.

The Sirhind Brigade was relieved by Dehra Dun on the 23rd May, and went into billets for a well-earned rest, the first which it had enjoyed since it left to take part in the second battle of Ypres on the 23rd April. All ranks were feeling the strain of the past month ; regiments were mere skeletons, and required thorough reorganization before they could become fit for any further offensive operations.

The Indian Corps failed to attain its objective through no fault of its own, but owing entirely to the misfortune of being faced by an extraordinarily strong position, an experience shared by the British 4th Corps operating on its left. Had success been possible under the circumstances, it would have been achieved by the troops, British and Indian, who had so recently covered themselves with glory at the battles of Neuve Chapelle and Ypres.

Sir John French, in his despatch dated the 15th June, 1915, sums up the results of the battle in the following words:—

"In the battle of Festubert above described the enemy was driven from a position which was strongly entrenched and fortified, and ground was won on a front of four miles to an average depth of 600 yards. The enemy is known to have suffered very heavy losses, and in the course of the battle 785 prisoners and 10 machine guns were captured. A number of machine guns were also destroyed by our fire."

Casualties to date:—

	Killed.	Wounded.	Missing.	Other deaths.
British officers . .	213	501	58	2
Indian officers . .	88	260	35	4
Other ranks, British .	1376	6,073	1724	?
Other ranks, Indian .	1943	10,650	2504	447
Total . .	3620	17,484	4321	453

CHAPTER XXI

CHANGES IN COMPOSITION OF THE CORPS

The 8th and 49th West Riding Divisions attached to the Corps—The Highland Division transferred to the 4th Corps—Strength of the Indian Corps on the 5th June—Arrival of the 69th and 89th Punjabis, relieving the 9th Bhopals and 125th Rifles—Success of sanitary measures under Colonel Pike, D.S.O., R.A.M.C.—Temporary success of the 4th Corps—49th Division transferred to the 2nd Army—The Highland Division rejoins, the 8th Division going to the 3rd Corps—Adventures of Naik Ayub Khan, 129th Baluchis—Indian units taken out of the line for reorganization—Opportunity thus given for Musalmans to observe the Ramazan—The 19th Division joins the Corps—Gallant work by Captain Roe, 1/4th Gurkhas—Bravery of Subadar-Major Senbir Gurung—Fall of Warsaw—The 6th Jats, the 15th Sikhs, and 41st Dogras leave for another theatre of war.

On the 31st May, 1915, the 51st Highland Division was transferred to the 4th Corps, while the 8th Division of that Corps and the newly arrived 49th West Riding Division of the New Army were attached to the Indian Corps. The month of June opened with the line held by portions of the Meerut, Lahore, 8th, and 49th Divisions.

This month was destined to see many changes in the composition of the Corps, and the departure for fresh battlefields of several regiments which had carved their names deep on the roll of honour of the Indian Army.

The strength of the Corps on the 5th June was as follows:—

Formation.	British officers.	Indian officers.	Sabres or lances.	British rifles.	Indian rifles.	Artillery personnel, British.	Artillery personnel, Indian.	Guns.	Machine guns.
Lahore Division	346	129	440	5077	4916	2438	283	64	42
Meerut Division	390	158	482	4734	6216	2460	280	68	48
8th Division	539	—	132	14,345	—	2818	—	58	60
49th Division	483	—	127	12,007	—	2793	—	52	48
Corps Troops	12	1	—	257	98	—	—	5	9
Totals	1770	288	1181	36,420	11,230	10,509	563	247	207

The total strength of the Corps, including artillery, therefore amounted to 59,903, a striking contrast to the 15,700, all told, with which it held the front taken over from the 2nd Corps in 1914.

On the 4th June the 89th Punjabis, and on the 5th June the 69th Punjabis, arrived to take the place respectively of the 9th Bhopals and the 125th Rifles, the two latter battalions leaving for Egypt. The 89th were posted to the Ferozepore Brigade, and the 69th to Bareilly.

The weather, as a whole, throughout the month, was an agreeable contrast to that experienced during May, being generally fine and warm. It was feared that the advent of sultry weather might cause an epidemic of typhus, to which the inhabitants of the surrounding country are, even in normal years, particularly liable. This fear, however, happily proved to be unfounded, but the immunity of the troops must be ascribed to the perfection of the sanitary measures carried out by the medical officers under Colonel W. W. Pike, D.S.O., the Deputy Director of Medical Services, to which more detailed reference will be made hereafter.

On the 15th June the 4th Corps on the left of the Indian Corps resumed the offensive in the direction of the Rue d'Ouvert, on the northern end of which the 51st Highland Division was directed, while the 7th Division attacked the southern end and Chapelle St Roch, the Canadian Division forming a defensive flank. In conjunction with this the Lahore Division carried out a minor operation for which the Sirhind Brigade and other troops were detailed. The enemy, however, was too wide-awake, and the attempt to capture one of his advanced posts, with a view to bombing down his trench, had to be abandoned.

The 4th Corps twice captured the entire front line of the enemy, but on each occasion was driven back by concentrated gun and bomb fire.

On the 26th June the 51st Highland Division again joined the Corps, the 8th Division going to the 3rd Corps. The Indian Corps now consisted of the Lahore, Meerut, and 51st Highland Divisions, as the 49th (West Riding) Division was transferred to the 2nd Army.

On the night of the 21st June Naik Ayub Khan, 129th Baluchis, was ordered to go out with a patrol between the lines. When the patrol returned, Ayub Khan was missing. He had last been seen close to the German wire, and it was feared that he had either been killed or taken prisoner. Failing either of these contingencies, the only remaining supposition was that he had deserted to the enemy. This, however, the officers of the regiment stoutly refused to admit as possible, for the naik in question was well known as a good and courageous soldier.

On the 22nd June Sir James Willcocks visited the trenches south-east of Neuve Chapelle which were held by the 129th Baluchis. Lieutenant Lewis, M.C., to whose company Ayub Khan belonged, at once begged Sir James to allow him to go out at night and search for the naik, who, he was sure, was lying dead or wounded near the German line. General Willcocks, while fully appreciating the spirit which inspired the request, felt unable to give permission for an officer to undertake such risk with so little prospect of success.

The 22nd passed and the night of the 23rd arrived, and at 11.30 p.m. in stalked Naik Ayub Khan, none the worse for his experiences, bringing with him his rifle and ammunition.

The story of his adventures is unique in the history of the war, and illustrates the peculiar histrionic capabilities which are possessed by so many Orientals, coupled with a sangfroid under circumstances of concentrated danger which could hardly be surpassed. It appeared that, on nearing the German wire, Naik Ayub Khan made up his mind to visit the enemy in his trench and to pick up whatever useful information he could obtain. He concealed his rifle and ammunition, and then, taking his life in both hands, boldly walked up to the wire, where he stood calling out "Musalman." German heads appeared over the parapet, and for a moment his life hung in the balance. An officer came up, however, and called to him to come in, which he did. At first the occupants of the trench, fearing a ruse, were all for shooting Ayub Khan offhand, but milder counsels prevailed, and he was conducted along the trench to the Bois du Biez, through which he was taken behind the lines, and eventually found himself at the head quarters, presumably of the 13th Division, VIIth Corps, at Marquillies. All this time he was keeping his eyes and ears very wide open, and making mental notes of everything of value.

At Marquillies he was taken before the General, and was closely interrogated by the Staff through the medium of an officer who spoke extremely bad Hindustani, learned doubtless during a tour in India with a view to the future discomfiture of his hosts. This interrogation was a very trying ordeal, for on the nature of his answers the naik's life hung. He was anxious, of course, not to give any information of value to the enemy, but had at the same time to avoid arousing suspicion. He was asked, amongst other matters, many questions about our troops in this portion of the line and particularly about the 69th and 89th Punjabis which had recently arrived. To unimportant questions he sometimes replied correctly; in other cases, while giving a general appearance of truth to his answers, he nullified their value by supplying incorrect details.

The Germans talked about the supposed disaffection in India, and impressed on Ayub Khan that it was very wrong of Musalmans to fight against the friends of Turkey, dexterously ignoring the fact that the policy of these friends of Islam has been to undermine the Mahomedan religion in their colonies by every possible means, as has been proved by secret documents captured in Africa. Ayub Khan was asked whether there was not considerable disaffection in his regiment, and whether a large number of men were willing to desert as he had done. To these questions he returned a vigorous affirmative, and offered to bring back with him at least 20 men. This offer was greedily accepted, and he was promised 400 marks (Rs. 300) if he brought over 20 men, *i.e.* at the rate of 20 marks per man.

He remained at the head quarters throughout the 22nd, and was well fed and looked after, evidently with a view to impressing on him the kindly nature of the Germans. Many men came to see him, and he kept a careful note in his mind of the numbers on shoulder-straps, the various kinds of uniform, etc., details which were subsequently fully confirmed by the statements of prisoners and deserters, and were of considerable value to our Intelligence Branch.

On the night of the 23rd he was taken by a Staff officer and the interpreter in a motor car to the Bois du Biez, and thence through the trenches to the spot at which he had entered them. There he bade an affectionate farewell, and with one eye over his shoulder in case the Germans might at the last moment change their minds and put a bullet through the departing guest, he returned to our trench, retrieving on the way his rifle and ammunition.

Naik Ayub Khan was able to describe the paths through the Bois du Biez, and to give a good idea of the strength and the units by which the enemy's line was held. Further, he was able to report that there was no installation of asphyxiating gas in the trenches through which he had passed, a detail of no small importance to us at the time.

His story was an extraordinary one, but as before stated, any lingering doubt of its veracity was removed by corroborative evidence obtained from other sources. In order to make the enemy believe that we had discovered Ayub Khan's intention of deserting with 20 of his comrades, a notice was put up outside our trench to the effect that the traitor had been shot by us. Whether the Germans credited the statement or not was never discovered.

For his great daring and skill Naik Ayub Khan was promoted to Jemadar and was awarded the 2nd Class of the Indian Order of Merit.

There were no further events of special interest during June. The weather underwent a change for the worse towards the end of the month, and heavy rain fell at intervals, which rendered life in the trenches once more uncomfortable.

July found the Corps holding a line from La Quinque Rue to a point slightly south-east of Picantin, opposite Laventie. Each of the three Divisions had 2 Brigades in the front line and a Brigade in reserve, the front of each Division being roughly 3400 yards.

The casualties up to the 1st July, 1915, were as under :—

	Killed.	Wounded.	Missing.	Other deaths.
British officers . .	223	531	58	2
Indian officers . .	88	274	35	4
Other ranks, British .	1465	6,517	1747	?
Other ranks, Indian .	2002	11,285	2508	483
Total . .	3778	18,607	4348	489

On the 9th July instructions were received from

the 1st Army for the 1st Corps to take over, as a temporary measure, a portion of the Indian Corps front. This change was made with a view to the reorganization of the Indian units of the Corps, a measure of which they stood sadly in need. The heavy fighting in which they had been engaged at Neuve Chapelle in March, at Ypres in April and during May, had necessitated the repletion of the ranks, for which purpose drafts of other units or recruits from India had arrived. The immediate result was that a large proportion of the men were quite unknown to their officers, and required, moreover, thorough training in the methods of warfare obtaining in France.

Sir James Willcocks, with his usual solicitude for the welfare, moral as well as physical, of his troops, suggested to Sir John French that the period of reorganization might be so arranged as to coincide as far as possible with the Musalman Fast of Ramazan. The suggestion was approved, and the Musalmans of the Corps were thus enabled to observe their religious rites during at least a portion of the prescribed period, a boon for which they were sincerely grateful.

All the British units were now grouped together in the Lahore Division, which was to continue to hold the line, the Indian battalions being assembled in the Meerut Division, which was withdrawn into reserve.

Units were exchanged by Brigades as follows: Dehra Dun with Jullundur, Garhwal with Sirhind, and Bareilly with Ferozepore.

This reorganization was completed on the night of the 15th–16th July, the Lahore Division thus being composed entirely of British, and the Meerut of Indian units.

The original intention was that the Indian regiments should remain in reserve for a full month, but war necessities made shipwreck of this expectation. On the 19th July instructions were received for the Lahore Division to relieve the Highland Division south of the Fauquissart—Aubers road by 6 a.m. on the 23rd.

To carry out these orders it was necessary to strengthen each Brigade of Lahore by about 1000 rifles of Indian units taken from the affiliated Brigade in the Meerut Division. This relief took place on the night of the 23rd, and the rest of a large proportion of the Indian troops came to an abrupt conclusion.

On the 24th July the 19th Division, under the command of Major-General Fasken, joined the Corps, its strength being as follows: 552 officers, 133 sabres, 13,379 British rifles, 2783 artillery personnel, 64 guns, 39 machine guns.

At the commencement of July a very skilful and daring reconnaissance was carried out by Captain C. D. Roe, 1/4th Gurkhas. The battalion was then in trenches near Neuve Chapelle. In front of the position, "No Man's Land" was covered with thick long grass, which lent itself to daylight reconnaissance by either side, and tussles between patrols were frequent.

On the night of the 1st July, Captain Roe, accompanied by Lieutenant Manson and acting Subadar-Major Senbir Gurung, made a reconnaissance, and the following morning the same party, strengthened by two riflemen, went out at 3 a.m., with a view to ascertaining which of the network of trenches in front was actually held by the enemy, whether some ruined houses were occupied, the exact position of two snipers' posts (the occupants of which had been giving considerable trouble), the amount of wire in front of the German trenches, and finally, what use the enemy was making of a re-entrant in their line.

The party crawled out through the long grass, and meeting with no opposition, managed to get right up to the front line of trench, which they investigated, and ascertained exactly which position was occupied by day. Creeping along, Captain Roe explored the buildings in the hope of finding a sniper asleep, but failed in his quest, although he made a systematic search through each house. He was able, however, to locate the haunt of the snipers by finding about 100 empty cartridge cases which had evidently been recently fired, while five yards to the left was a dummy machine gun.

Still crawling along, the party found that the whole of that part of the line was wired in the most formidable manner, and that unless cut by artillery fire, passage through it would be impossible. Further, a most important point was now cleared up. It was evident from the arrangement of the wire that the enemy intended to use the re-entrant as a trap for us in any future attack, hoping that we would make for it and thus be taken from every angle by machine-gun fire. At another point Captain Roe found a barricade which was occupied and doubtless concealed a machine gun.

The adventure was destined to end with some excitement, for as the party was creeping on, they saw a German officer at a distance of about 250 yards in the act of getting over the parapet. Captain Roe and the Subadar-Major fired together and hit the officer in the hip, knocking him backwards. Immediately another man showed his head and shoulders, evidently trying to discover where the bullets came from. Captain Roe fired again, and the man fell. The result of a third attempt at another man who looked over could not be observed. The only reply was one wild shot fired at an angle of about 45 degrees away to the left. The party eventually returned in safety, having completely carried out their programme.

On the 3rd July two men of the battalion were hit while on listening patrol. Captain Roe decided to go out next morning and try to discover their fate, and further, to ascertain whether the enemy had occupied the ruins near which his men had fallen.

In view of the probability that some opposition would be met, the preparations were now more elaborate. Covering fire was to be supplied from the trench of the 1/1st Gurkhas, and a small party under Lieutenant Manson was posted in a suitable position to assist in case of emergency. Another party under Subadar-Major Senbir Gurung was put out on the right of Captain Roe's line of advance, and six men accompanied the officer to search the ruins. At the same time the 84th Battery R.F.A. was to assist with the fire of one gun towards the left, and on a new communication trench made by the enemy. Captain Roe carried five bombs himself, while the Subadar-Major also had five, and 24 were kept handy in reserve.

At 8.10 a.m. the expedition started, and after

posting Lieutenant Manson's party, Captain Roe pushed along up a communication trench, and had just arrived at his pre-arranged position when the 84th Battery fired its first shell. At this moment three bombs were thrown at the party from a distance of about 20 yards, followed almost at once by two more. All five exploded round Captain Roe and his orderly, partially burying them. The six men behind them, thinking they were killed, retired towards the British line. Subadar-Major Senbir, however, at once rallied and brought them up to where Captain Roe was busily engaged in bombing the Germans. Lance-Naik Lachman Gurung, a bomber, rushed up and took the enemy from the front, and with this assistance they were driven back with the loss of five of their number. They retreated until they were seen to be joined by an officer and about 25 men.

Captain Roe had now used all his bombs, and had to retire to the spot where he had left his reserve supply. Armed with these, he again advanced and bombed the officer's party steadily back. Then it was found that the enemy had got round on both flanks, and they soon made their presence felt by bombing and firing.

Subadar-Major Senbir was now hit by a bomb which shattered his left leg, but in spite of his suffering he held on in the most gallant way, and continued to direct his men. At this juncture Lieutenant Manson caught sight of the Germans and at once opened rapid fire. The enemy were seized with panic, and were bolting through the ruins, when two shrapnel shells fired by the 84th Battery burst right over them and added wings to their flight.

By good luck our bombs had outlasted those of the enemy, and it was due to this fact and the assistance of the 84th Battery that Captain Roe was able to return with only one casualty, Subadar-Major Senbir Gurung. This Gurkha officer had throughout the campaign behaved with the greatest gallantry, having especially distinguished himself at Ypres, and whenever he got near the enemy, to use the words of his Commanding Officer, Lt-Colonel H. B. Champain, "he showed amazing coolness and resource."

Thus ended a most dashing little episode, the skilful and daring execution of which obtained for us information of considerable value and proved the worth of our men, when led by British officers, in hand-to-hand fighting against superior numbers. For his conspicuous gallantry and leadership Captain Roe was awarded the D.S.O., while Lieutenant Manson received the Military Cross, and Subadar-Major Senbir Gurung the 2nd Class, Indian Order of Merit.

Lance-Naiks Lachman Gurung and Asbir Rana with Rifleman Garbha Sing Gurung, who had stuck to the two officers and had behaved throughout with great bravery, were awarded the Indian Distinguished Service Medal.

On the 1st August a melancholy illustration of the chances of war occurred.

Lieutenant E. G. Bullard, of the Indian Postal Service, was proceeding on duty in a car near Croix Barbée, when a German shell exploded practically in the motor, killing him and the chauffeur instantaneously.

This young officer had, by his kindly disposition

and zeal in the performance of his important duties, endeared himself to his comrades in the Corps, and his loss was keenly felt.

The occurrence was particularly unfortunate, as he was to have proceeded on leave the next day, while the chauffeur was only taking the duty of another man.

By the 2nd August the Corps had once more been reorganized into its normal formation, and the front was held by the Lahore and Meerut Divisions, while the 19th Division, in reserve billets, was receiving instruction in trench warfare.

On the 5th August loud cheering was heard in the German lines, after which a notice board was placed just outside their wire with the following inscription: "Warchaou * conquered." To this we replied by a similar board bearing the legend, "Another Zeppelin brought down."

The German notice remained in position, although riddled with bullets by us, and several unsuccessful attempts were made to bring it in under cover of darkness. On the night of the 16th August, however, Lance-Naiks Kale Singh and But Singh, of the 47th Sikhs, succeeded in crawling up to the board and cutting the wire which attached it to the German parapet. While doing this, four bombs were thrown at them, but they escaped uninjured, and bore the notice back in triumph to the 47th, by whom it is treasured as a souvenir of an audacious feat.

The remainder of the month passed without any event of special importance. A deserter gave himself up on the night of the 28th August, and, apparently by way of justifying his existence, in-

* Warsaw.

formed us that the enemy had installed gas in his trenches with a view to an attack on the 30th August. To ascertain the truth or otherwise of his story, a bombardment of the enemy's front line took place on the 29th and again on the 30th, but although the parapet was badly damaged and heavy timber, sandbags and earth were thrown up into the air, there were no signs of any preparation for a gas attack.

On the 17th August the 6th Jats under the command of Captain Ross, who subsequently received the D.S.O., the 15th Sikhs under Colonel Hill, D.S.O., and the 41st Dogras under Lt-Colonel Tribe, C.M.G., left for another theatre of war, where they have since fully maintained the great reputation which they had won in France. It is pleasing to note, as testifying to the spirit which existed between our Allies and ourselves, that the War Diary of the 6th Jats records the great reluctance with which the regiment parted with their interpreter, Monsieur Henri Le Gros, who, it is remarked, had served with them since their arrival in France, in October, 1914, without a day's absence, had rendered invaluable service and become almost one of the regiment.

CHAPTER XXII

THE BATTLE OF LOOS

Front held by Indian Corps at the commencement of September—General Sir James Willcocks succeeded by Lt-General Sir Charles Anderson—Preparations for offensive on a large scale—Reasons for choice of Champagne as scene of main operations—Minor "holding" actions to be undertaken—Operations orders—Gas and smoke to be used—Doubt as to advisability of gas—Prolonged bombardment of enemy's positions—Rainy weather unfavourable to attack—Enemy's bomb bursts gas cylinders in our trench—Wind unfavourable to gas attack—Our mine exploded—Field guns and Hotchkiss employed in front trenches—Presence of mind of gas detachments prevents a disaster—Assault of the Garhwal Brigade—Right attack held up—Lieutenant Bagot-Chester—Rifleman Kulbir Thapa, 2/3rd Gurkhas, wins the Victoria Cross—Great gallantry of 2/8th Gurkhas—Colonel Morris mortally wounded—Captain Buckland, D.S.O.—Subadar Sarbjit Gurung—Splendid stand by Subadar Ransur Rana—Terrible losses of the 2/8th Gurkhas—Congested state of the trenches delays attack by Dehra Dun Brigade—Unsuccessful assault by 39th Garhwalis and 2/2nd Gurkhas—Causes of failure of attack—Remarks by Brigadier-General Blackader.

At the commencement of September, 1915, the line of the Indian Corps was held as follows:—

On the right lay the 19th Division, with two Brigades in the front trenches, and one in reserve.

Southwards the line was continued by the 1st Corps.

The right of one Brigade of the 19th Division rested on a point almost opposite Le Plantin, the left being slightly north-west of the Cour d'Avoué Farm.

Thence the Lahore Division continued with

Ferozepore, the remaining two Brigades in reserve, the front of the Division extending to the southern edge of the La Bassée—Estaires road, whence the line was held by the Garhwal and Bareilly Brigades of the Meerut Division with Dehra Dun in reserve, a Brigade of the 3rd Corps carrying on to the left from Winchester Road, the total front of the Indian Corps being about 9500 yards.

The casualties of the Corps up to the 31st August, 1915, amounted to :—

	Killed.	Wounded.	Missing.	Other deaths.
British officers . .	234	559	59	2
Indian officers . .	90	290	35	6
Other ranks, British .	1562	7,069	1748	?
Other ranks, Indian .	2084	12,058	2518	578
Total . .	3970	19,976	4360	586

During the first few days of the month the weather was inclined to be changeable, and on the 3rd September heavy rain fell, once more converting the trenches into morasses, although much had now been done to improve them by drainage, by boarding the footways, and by strengthening the sides.

On the 6th September the Corps sustained an irreparable loss by the sudden departure of Sir James Willcocks. This is neither the time nor the place in which to enter into the causes which led to so untoward an event. With the simple loyalty to duty which has marked General Willcocks' entire career, he has preserved a silence which the present historians have no right, while the war continues, to break.

The blow was keenly felt by both officers and men of the Corps. General Willcocks' knowledge of the Indian Army is unique, and throughout the campaign he had never spared himself in his zeal for the welfare and efficiency of the troops under his command. It is not too much to say, and those who know the extreme difficulties of the position will agree, that it was largely owing to his personal influence, his never-failing sense of justice, his infinite patience, and his constant cheerfulness, that the Corps was able to hold its own against the superb troops which, during these critical months, did their utmost to destroy its spirit and undermine its moral.

Never in the history of the Indian Army has a command fraught with such mixed and onerous responsibilities been placed upon the shoulders of a British officer. Composed as the Corps was, at various stages of its career, of English, Irish, and Scotch regiments, battalions of Gurkhas, subjects of a foreign state, of units largely formed of Trans-Frontier men, Imperial Service Troops, and even Indian police—a medley of religions and customs, in a foreign country and amid strange and depressing surroundings—to command such a body of troops with success called for the firmness of Kitchener, the patience of Job, and the tact of Talleyrand.

To what extent Sir James Willcocks succeeded can be judged by the fact that the Corps, in spite of its losses, in spite of the substitution of reinforcements mostly far inferior to its original Indian personnel, in face of the cruel and always growing losses of British officers, continued to the end of his command to preserve its special character and to hold its place amongst that vast concourse of the best fighting material of the British Empire.

The future historian, writing when the dark places have been made light, and tongues, now sealed, are free, will be able to give Sir James Willcocks his due niche in the Temple of Fame, till which time he will rest content with his place in the hearts of those whom he commanded in a dark and bloody season. He will not, we predict, be counted in the passionless scales of history the least of the heroes who stood for England in the autumn of 1914.

General Willcocks, who for his services during the war had been created a Knight Grand Cross of St Michael and St George and a Grand Officer of the Legion of Honour, was succeeded by Lieutenant-General Sir Charles Anderson, K.C.B., who had commanded the Meerut Division since the commencement of the war, and on whom had fallen the brunt of several important battles, notably that of Neuve Chapelle. He took over the command under the best auspices, as a personal friend of his late chief whose last recommendation was that he should succeed him.

To his brilliant career as a soldier, General Anderson united the indispensable qualifications, although himself an artillery officer, of long residence in and intimate knowledge of India. The Corps profoundly regretted the loss of Sir James Willcocks, but it was agreed that his mantle could have fallen on no more competent shoulders than those of Sir Charles Anderson, whose sympathetic, dare-devil, Irish nature appealed strongly to the Indians, creatures always of impulse and temperament, more easily to be led than driven.

By September, 1915, the preparations of both sides had advanced long stages towards such completion as is possible in a war where nothing can be complete until the opposing army has been finally crushed.

LIEUT-GENERAL SIR CHARLES ANDERSON, K.C.B.

402.]

The Germans had learnt many lessons from Neuve Chapelle, and their defences were now of a totally different class from those which we had met and overcome on that occasion.

We, in our turn, slow as we are to learn, had at last grasped the fact that the success of infantry attacks depended on adequate artillery preparation and support. Throughout the summer every nerve had been strained to bring us abreast of our opponents in this respect, and with such success that it was now deemed possible to make a serious offensive move on a large scale, although it was felt that we could not hope to arrive at a thoroughly satisfactory position in the matter of munitions until, at the earliest, the spring of 1916.

Our French Allies had been even more successful than ourselves, and between us we possessed at least an equality of gun power with the Germans, while the preponderance of man power on the Western front was, at the moment, certainly in our favour.

The position at the commencement of September was briefly as follows :—

The 2nd Army, commanded by Sir Herbert Plumer, held the line from Boesinghe, north of Ypres, to a point slightly south-west of Armentières. Next came the 1st Army, under Sir Douglas Haig, which reached as far south as Grenay, north-west of Lens. Here the line was taken up by the French 10th Army, which, continuing to a point south of Arras, separated our new 3rd Army under Sir Charles Monro from the remainder of the British forces. The front of the 3rd Army extended to the south as far as the Somme.

In the September operations Champagne was

chosen as the area for the main attack. It is not possible to discuss in detail the reasons which governed this decision, but one obvious object was to cut, if possible, the communications which brought up supplies from the Rhine, and thus to limit the enemy to the use of his northern network of railways. Added to this was the remote possibility of isolating the Crown Prince's Army opposite Verdun.

In conjunction with the main operations, a number of subsidiary actions was necessary to prevent the enemy from reinforcing his line in Champagne from other sectors of his front. The scene of the chief of these operations was the area between La Bassée and Arras, the object now being the same as in May, *i.e.* to cut the German communications between Lille and Soissons by an advance on Douai and Valenciennes, always with the idea of Lille in the background.

From north to south the holding engagements were as follows:—

(*a*) By the 5th Corps under General Allenby, plus the 14th Division lent by the 6th Corps, the objective being Bellewaarde Farm, situated to the east of Ypres.

(*b*) By General Pulteney's 3rd Corps near Bois Grenier.

(*c*) By the Indian Corps in the vicinity of Neuve Chapelle.

(*d*) By the 2nd Division of the 1st Army near Givenchy.

The purpose of this history being to present an intelligible account of the operations of the Indian Corps, reference will only be made in this complicated phase of the war to such occurrences in other areas of the fighting as may be necessary to that end.

Verbal instructions were given on the 30th August, followed, on the 20th September, by detailed orders.

The general idea was for the Indian Corps to carry out an attack, in conjunction with the main operations, with a view to holding the enemy and preventing him from sending reinforcements southwards; also with the object of inducing doubt in his mind as to the real point of the main attack.

Three objectives were laid down for the Corps.

(*a*) To attack the enemy's line between Sunken Road and Winchester Road, and to establish our line along the road running from Mauquissart to the "Duck's Bill."

(*b*) To press on, with the left in front, until the high ground between Haut Pommereau and La Cliqueterie Farm was gained.

(*c*) To continue the advance from that point in a south-easterly direction, in order to assist our main offensive in the south by turning the La Bassée defences from the north.

For the first time gas was to be used by the British troops, a step which was taken with the greatest reluctance, and not until it was forced upon us by the enemy's continual use of this barbarous method of warfare. Gas, however, as the enemy has more than once found to his cost, is an untrustworthy servant. At a conference held at the commencement of September, grave doubts were expressed as to the utility of the device, unless, in the event of the gas being a failure on the Indian Corps front, adequate artillery support was to be forthcoming. Later events were to prove that these doubts were well founded.

It was felt that gas should not be used unless the wind were in a pronouncedly favourable direction, and in amply sufficient strength to carry it away from our line on to the German trenches. In consequence, two programmes were drawn up, the second for adoption if it appeared unwise to employ gas and smoke.

As will be seen later, the gas was a failure upon the Indian Corps front, for it caused no inconvenience to the enemy and very seriously interfered with the movements of our troops.

The attack was to be delivered by the Meerut Division, now commanded by Brigadier-General C. W. Jacob (who was succeeded in the Dehra Dun Brigade by Lt-Colonel W. J. Harvey, of the 2nd Black Watch), the 19th and Lahore Divisions holding the whole of the front except that section from which Meerut was to advance. The 20th Division of the 3rd Corps on the left was to co-operate with Lahore in covering the flanks of the Meerut Division with its fire.

The assault was to be preceded by (1) four days' deliberate bombardment by artillery and trench mortars, the enemy at the same time being prevented by rifle, rifle-grenade and machine-gun fire from repairing the damage done to his obstacles and defences; (2) the explosion of a mine under the enemy's parapet, opposite the left of our attack, two minutes before the gas and smoke commenced; (3) a gas and smoke attack immediately before the assault; (4) the formation of thick smoke barrages on each flank of the assaulting troops.

Profiting by the lesson learned in the May fighting, field guns were now placed in the front parapet, with a view, by point-blank fire, to destroying machine guns and their emplacements, while a Hotchkiss gun was also to be used for the same object.

The Garhwal Brigade was detailed for the right assault, Bareilly for the left, with the Dehra Dun Brigade in Divisional reserve, each assaulting Brigade having three battalions in the front line and two in reserve.

It was calculated that, in order to ensure the success of the gas attack, it would be necessary to employ 1100 cylinders, and the requisite shelters were prepared in the trenches by the 6th September. It was subsequently found that only 160 cylinders would be available, and the whole plan had to be recast, distributing the gas in such a way that it could be used from the salients if the wind proved to come from the south-east, south, or south-west. By the night of the 23rd–24th September the cylinders had been placed in position by Lieutenant Kent of the 189th Company Royal Engineers

In addition to the arrangements for gas, dispositions were made to cover the advance of our troops by a screen of smoke along the entire front, supported by barrages of smoke on either flank. To this end a number of appliances were used, such as smoke candles and phosphorus smoke bombs, which were hurled out by catapults and proved most effective, attaining a range of 350 yards. Bombs were also thrown out of 95-millimetre and 2-inch trench mortars with very satisfactory results.

On the 21st September the deliberate bombardment commenced and lasted throughout four days and nights, a weary time for the gunners, but their strength and spirits were sustained by the hope that for the first time there would be sufficient ammunition to enable them to strike at the enemy effectively and continuously.

Observation was very difficult, owing to the haze and dense clouds of smoke which hung over the German trenches during the first three days, and it was rendered still more difficult by rain and mist on the 24th. By the evening it was reported that the enemy's wire had been satisfactorily cut, except in one section in front of the Garhwal Brigade. This failure was destined to cost us dear, as it held up our men under terrible fire, while they were seeking a way through the web of death.

Throughout the bombardment we kept up a constant fusillade from the front line with rifles, grenades, machine guns and trench mortars, as well as indirect machine-gun fire from points in rear, thus practically limiting repairs to the placing of rolls of wire in some of the gaps caused by our artillery. In spite of the fact that his parapets were being gradually destroyed, the enemy's guns showed very little more than their usual activity, and our casualties were slight.

On the 22nd September the Lahore Division made a feint of attack. The artillery fired for five minutes on the enemy's front line and then for five minutes on his support trenches, after which bayonets were shown over the top of the parapet, while a number of dummy heads, which had been previously prepared, were raised with an accompaniment of shouting.

This probably led to the enemy crowding his trenches with men to receive the attack which, however, did not come. In its place our guns rained shrapnel with great accuracy over the opposite trenches, causing, it was hoped, considerable loss. In spite of this, the enemy could not be drawn into retaliation. A similar feint was carried out by the 19th Division on the following day, but the Germans utterly declined to take any interest in it. On this date the 93rd Burma Infantry, under the command of Lt-Colonel Stevens, joined the Corps, and was posted to the Dehra Dun Brigade.

A party of seven civilians paid an ill-timed visit to the enemy's trenches at the commencement of the bombardment. Of these, with the German sense of the fitness of things, three wore top hats, two bowlers, and one a soft grey hat, while the seventh carried a top hat in his hand. Unfortunately for them, their arrival was noticed by one of our snipers perched in a tree, and he at once gave the whole of his attention to them. Yells were heard; top hats were seen falling in every direction; and the party, or such of it as survived, returned home with a real experience of trench warfare.

The weather, which for the greater part of the month had been extremely good, now showed signs of change, and from the evening of the 23rd September it became rainy and unfavourable generally. By the evening of the 25th there was a foot of water in the trenches and movement was very difficult.

During the 24th all thoughts were concentrated on the question as to whether the wind would be favourable to a gas attack. At this time a gentle breeze was blowing from the west, but during the night it changed, veering round from west to south and from south to south-west, till at 3.15 a.m. on the 25th it was again blowing from the west with a velocity of three miles an hour.

At 4.40 a.m. a German bomb burst in the "Duck's Bill," a projecting portion of trench on the right which was held by the 1/3rd Londons. The explosion blew off the heads of several cylinders of gas, which escaped in large volumes. Although masks were ready, the vapour filled the front and support trench in such density and with such rapidity that one officer and 18 men of the Londons were put out of action, as was also a bombing party of the Manchester Regiment which had been sent to the "Duck's Bill" preparatory to the attack. The officer in charge of the gas detachment was himself "gassed," and the senior non-commissioned officer at once gave orders that no gas was to be liberated in view of the change in the wind.

The Londons behaved with great coolness under this unexpected contretemps; the cylinders were promptly covered with earth, and by this swift action more serious losses were prevented.

The wind, slight as it was, had changed, and was now blowing rather towards than from our trenches. General Jacob, in his report on the action, suggests that in future the responsibility for using gas should rest with the officers commanding on the spot, who would alone be in a position to decide as to the advisability of its use in the event of the wind suddenly veering round as it did on this occasion. Had officers commanding been allowed to exercise their discretion, there can be little doubt that gas would not have been used. As it was, it was solely due to the initiative of the detachments, who took the responsibility of turning off the gas as soon as it was found to be blown back into our trenches, that a serious disaster was prevented.

At 5.48 a.m., with a deafening roar, which was heard and felt at a distance of many miles from the scene of the explosion, the mine on the left of our attack went up. Charged as it was with one ton of guncotton, the effects were awe-inspiring. The point of the German salient disappeared; enormous masses of earth flew high into the air, and over all hung a dense cloud of dust and smoke. The crater was afterwards found to measure 92 feet in breadth, and for a considerable distance around piles of debris were lying.

At 5.50 a.m. the intense bombardment commenced and lasted till 6 a.m., when the guns lifted. The two field guns and the Hotchkiss in the front line took an active part in this phase of the preparation. One gun, owing to the "striker" breaking, fired only 47 rounds of high explosive, but the other, in the "Duck's Bill," fired 76 rounds in 4½ minutes. The first five rounds of the latter gun were observed to be direct hits, which did enormous damage to the enemy's parapet. The smoke barrage rendered further observation impossible, but from the reports subsequently received from the infantry, there was no doubt of the complete success of this novel departure in trench warfare.

At the moment of the commencement of the intense bombardment, the gas should have been turned on, but the direction of the wind rendered its liberation unsafe in some sections of the line, and in others a sudden change brought the poisonous fumes back into our trenches. Seeing this, the gas detachments, on their own initiative, at once closed the valves. An officer records that, in spite of wearing two masks, he suffered from soreness of the throat, while one of the gas detachment was lying at his feet, quite overcome, and groaning horribly. In fact, as he remarks, every one was glad when the order came to go over the parapet.

At 6 a.m., amidst dense clouds of smoke, the infantry assault commenced, and from the moment the troops advanced they were lost to sight, as the wind bore the right barrage down in a north-easterly direction and utterly obscured all view in front of our line.

From right to left the assaulting troops were disposed as follows:—

Garhwal Brigade. 2/3rd Gurkhas, 2nd Leicesters, and 2/8th Gurkhas. On the extreme right the 1/3rd Londons continued to hold the "Duck's Bill," while the 39th Garhwal Rifles held the Home Counties trench in rear of the centre of the Brigade.

Bareilly Brigade. 1/4th Black Watch, 69th Punjabis and 2nd Black Watch in the front line, the 33rd Punjabis being next to the Garhwalis in the Home Counties trench, and the 58th Rifles in the trenches along the Rue Tilleloy in rear of the Brigade.

The Dehra Dun Brigade, which was in Divisional reserve, had orders to concentrate, as soon as the assaulting troops advanced, in the Home Counties and Tilleloy trenches, posting picquets only in the front line. The object of this disposition was to ensure that the Brigade would be concentrated and ready to move at once in any required direction.

The 2/3rd Gurkhas had been warned that the German wire in their front had probably not been destroyed, and the advance was therefore made on a narrow front. No. 4 Double Company, under Lieutenants Bagot-Chester and Wood, led the assault, closely followed by No. 3, under Lt-Colonel Brakspear and Lieutenant Tyson. They got into good line, but found themselves faced by a wall of smoke and gas of such density that it was only possible to see a few yards ahead. At first not a shot was fired from the German trenches, and it was hoped that perhaps, after all, the gas had inflicted more damage on the enemy than on ourselves, and that they might be lying in their trenches out of action.

The distance to be covered was about 200 yards, and for the first 80 yards the smoke hid our troops, who advanced at a quick walk, from the Germans, but the moment the Gurkhas came into view, they were met by a blizzard of bullets. They put on the pace at once, but Lieutenant Bagot-Chester saw his men dropping all round him until, when he reached the German wire, which was quite uncut, he and the very few left were forced to run along the front of the position, seeking in vain for a passage by which to get to grips with the enemy. A number, partly overcome by our own gas and blinded by the smoke, charged headlong to the right, until they were brought up by the projecting "Duck's Bill" held by the 1/3rd Londons.

A moment later Lieutenant Bagot-Chester was knocked over by a terrific blow on his right shoulder. Luckily for him, he fell close to a "pipsqueak" hole, into which he at once rolled. The hole unfortunately was very small and shallow, and was already tenanted by a wounded Gurkha, Budhiman Gurung by name.

As an example of the experiences through which wounded too often pass, it is instructive to follow the pair in their perilous adventures. Looking cautiously over the edge of the hole, the officer could see several dead Gurkhas, and one or two others mortally wounded and writhing in agony; a couple more were lying flat, apparently unwounded, but even as he looked they were hit several times. In front of him lay the German wire and trench.

It was evident the attack had failed, and the only chance of life was to lie absolutely still for the rest of the day, within 15 yards of the enemy, with shells bursting all round and the alternatives of being blown to bits or shot by the Germans. In the hole there was only room to shelter their heads and bodies; their legs had to remain outside.

Soon Lieutenant Bagot-Chester heard a squeal from Budhiman on being hit a second time by the enemy, who were following their usual practice of shooting at the wounded. Next the officer received a piece of iron in his groin. Then Budhiman was hit again. Still there they had to lie, unable even to move sufficiently to get out the morphia which was in Lieutenant Bagot-Chester's pocket. The Germans kept up their fire, and the officer was again wounded by a piece of bomb in the left foot, followed almost at once by another which entered his left leg below the knee.

Shortly afterwards (according to the Regimental Diary, at about 3 p.m.), it began to rain, which was a blessing in disguise, as it appeared to reduce the firing. It fell in sheets, and the hole rapidly filled with icy water and mud. After a time the rain stopped and dusk crept slowly on. The gallant Budhiman, sorely wounded as he was, was all for starting back the moment it grew dusk, but Bagot-Chester, combining prudence with valour, thought it better to wait for complete darkness before beginning the horrible pilgrimage.

At about 8 p.m. the crippled pair started, but were soon separated. The officer was so much damaged and had lost such a quantity of blood that he was unable to stand. The rain, however, had made the ground slippery, and he was able to slide along on his back, every minute of progress a year of torture. Frequently he came upon a dead body, and it taxed the poor remnant of his strength to work his way round it. By the time he had accomplished half his journey, he found that he could just stand on one foot and the heel of the other, and thus he completed his way, collapsing every few yards, and being eventually found at about 10 p.m. by Captain Burton, D.S.O., who has since himself been killed.

Lieutenant Bagot-Chester had throughout the campaign been conspicuous in the regiment for his bravery and skill, especially in reconnaissance and patrol work, and a detailed account of his experiences on this occasion has been deemed worthy of insertion, as showing what the human body can suffer, and yet survive, when animated by such a spirit as that of this young officer. After months of suffering he rejoined his regiment, was wounded at the tomb of Samuel in Palestine on the 23rd

November, 1917, again recovered, and finally succumbed to further wounds on the 28th March, 1918. A more gallant and admirable British officer can hardly be imagined. He was mentioned in despatches.* Of his Double Company, Lieutenant Wood was killed, and of a total of 120 men who went into action, 86 were killed, wounded, or missing, a percentage of nearly 72.

Lieutenant Wood proved himself worthy of his leader, for he is reported to have fought his way with only four men through the wire into the trench, where all were killed in a hand-to-hand fight.

The wire was, in places, piled four and five deep with dead and wounded Gurkhas.

Lt-Colonel Brakspear and Lieutenant Tyson, with No. 3 Double Company, had followed closely behind Lieutenant Bagot-Chester, but, bearing away a little to the right, came up against high wire entanglement absolutely untouched, as at this point in the line there were a number of trees which prevented the full force of our wire-cutting bombardment being felt. Colonel Brakspear, who had given many proofs of his bravery during the war, tried, with Lieutenant Tyson, to force his way through the entanglement, but it was impossible, and both officers, with many of their men, were mown down. Lieutenant Fisher, with No. 2 Company, found the attack held up, and likewise failed to get through the wire, being wounded in the attempt.

For some unknown reason it had been reported to Colonel Ormsby, commanding the 2/3rd Gurkhas, that our distinguishing flags had been seen waving

* Lieutenant Bagot-Chester was awarded the Military Cross in February, 1918, for gallantry in Palestine.

in the German trenches, but that a gap existed between the left of the Gurkhas and the right of the Leicesters. To fill this gap, Subadar Bhim Sing with A Company was sent forward, and he too disappeared into the haze. On reaching the vicinity of the German line, he found that the attack had failed, and that the parapet, wherever any of it remained, was strongly manned, while enfilade machine-gun fire was being poured into our men from both flanks.

He reported that the remnant of the Leicesters and 2/3rd Gurkhas were taking cover in ditches as best they could, and orders were soon received to try to dribble the men back as opportunity offered. The Gurkhas were finally relieved by the Dehra Dun Brigade at 1 p.m., the relief being much delayed by the numbers of wounded who were still crawling in over the parapet.

The 2/3rd Gurkhas suffered heavy losses in this action, in which they fought with the utmost gallantry, but no gallantry can prevail against uncut wire and enfilade machine-gun fire. Thirty-five dead Gurkhas were seen lying on the front of the German parapet, and it was believed that a small party of men fought their way into the trench, where, as far as is known, they were, with one exception, killed, *as the total number of prisoners of war belonging to this battalion does not exceed ten for the whole campaign.*

The casualties were as follows:—Killed: Lt-Colonel W. R. Brakspear, Lieutenant T. P. Wood, 2nd Lieutenant Tyson, 2 Gurkha officers, and 31 other ranks. Wounded: Lieutenants W. G. Bagot-Chester and G. T. Fisher, 3 Gurkha officers and 126 others. Missing: 64 other ranks; a total of 231.

During this attack deeds which could hardly be surpassed for sheer bravery and self-sacrifice were performed by Rifleman Kulbir Thapa. He is the exception noted above, as having entered the German trench and escaped alive. Kulbir succeeded, after being wounded, in penetrating the wire in some extraordinary way and charged straight through the German trench. In rear of it he found a badly injured man of the 2nd Leicesters. The wounded man begged Kulbir Thapa to leave him and save himself, but the Gurkha refused to do so, and remained by his side throughout the day and the following night.

Luckily, there was a heavy mist on the morning of the 26th September, of which Kulbir took advantage to bring the man out through the German wire. He succeeded, after hairbreadth escapes, in doing this unobserved, and put the wounded man in a shell-hole. Not content with this, he returned and rescued, one after the other, two Gurkhas. He then went back again and brought in the British soldier in broad daylight, carrying him most of the way under fire.

For these successive acts of valour Rifleman Kulbir Thapa received the Victoria Cross, and it will be agreed that seldom, if ever, has this supreme reward been more splendidly won. The deaths of officers and men who won the V.C. have so often been recorded in this history, that it is a relief to mention that Kulbir Thapa survived his wound, proceeded to Egypt with his regiment, and eventually returned to India.

The barbarity of the Germans has seldom been more vividly illustrated than during this action. In addition to the incident already related of their

RIFLEMAN KULBIR THAPA, V.C., 2ND BN 3RD GURKHA RIFLES.

firing on Lieutenant Bagot-Chester while lying wounded, at a distance of 15 yards, it is on record that on the morning of the 26th September, during the dense fog which enabled Kulbir Thapa to perform his deeds of heroism, numbers of Germans left their trenches for the express purpose of shooting and bayoneting our wounded. This information was supplied by wounded men who escaped by feigning death, and the evidence is sufficient to establish the charge.

The 2nd Leicesters, on the left of the 2/3rd Gurkhas, sent their first line over the parapet at 6 a.m., closely followed by the second, the third and fourth lines at once filling their places in the trench. They moved forward rapidly, but a number were affected by the gas, and great difficulty was experienced in keeping the right direction owing to the smoke.

Casualties began as soon as our men were in the open, and the third line was sent out to fill up gaps, followed by the fourth line. The attack dashed on, but A Company, on the extreme left, ran into heavy rifle and machine-gun fire, which caused a large number of casualties, including all the officers and most of the non-commissioned officers of the company.

Major Lewis showed conspicuous gallantry and ability during this action, in which he was second in command. Shortly after the attack was launched, he was wounded in the neck by shrapnel, but remained at his post for three hours, and returned as soon as his wound had been dressed. When Colonel Gordon was wounded at about 3.30 p.m., Major Lewis took command of the battalion. He had previously been brought to notice for gallant conduct, and was later awarded the D.S.O.

Still undaunted, the left of the Leicesters went forward, and, scrambling through the wire, were in the German front line by 6.10 a.m., when their distinguishing flag was seen flying over the enemy's position. Carrying on their rush still further, a portion of the left of the battalion was reported to have reached the road from Mauquissart to the "Duck's Bill."

Captain Wilson, whose name had several times been brought to notice for gallantry and determination, was severely wounded while issuing final instructions to his men before the advance, but he refused to give in, and went forward with the attack until he could see that the men were over the German parapet. He was then taken back in a state of collapse. For his conspicuous gallantry he received the D.S.O.

The general position was now extremely obscure. Conflicting reports came in one after the other, and at first it was believed that the enemy's front line had been captured. This was later found to be incorrect, and at 7 a.m. there was no doubt that the right of the Garhwal Brigade had been held up by the German wire, in which such gaps as existed had been filled by the enemy with rolls of French wire. On the left, however, the 2/8th Gurkhas and a portion of the 2nd Leicesters had got through the front trenches, but only with very heavy losses, especially in officers.

The progress of this action cannot be recorded with accuracy, owing to the impossibility of observation from our front-line trenches, due to the impenetrable wall of smoke and gas, which was rendered even more opaque by the dampness of the air. Secondly, as reported by General Jacob, the heavy losses of officers, especially of those who would have been able to throw light on obscure points, prevents certainty as to the details. The main story, however, can be reconstructed without grave inaccuracy.

As regards the Leicesters, the position remained unchanged throughout the day until, at 4.30 p.m., orders were received for the survivors to get back to our trenches as opportunity offered. The battalion had fought with all the bravery for which it was famous, and, had the wire in front of the right of the Garhwal Brigade been cut, there is little doubt that the whole of the enemy's first-line trenches would have been captured. As it was, the holding up of the right and right centre attacks exposed the right of the left attack and rendered its temporary success of no avail.

The losses of the Leicesters were very heavy. Killed: Captain Romilly who had won the D.S.O. at Neuve Chapelle, Captain Deane, M.C., R.A.M.C., Lieutenant Browne, and 72 men. Wounded: 10 officers and 217 others, amongst whom was Lt-Colonel Gordon, D.S.O., the Commanding Officer. Missing and believed killed: 2 officers. Missing and known to have been wounded: 1 officer. Missing and no trace found: 3 officers. Of the rank-and-file 96 were missing. In addition to these casualties, 1 officer and 42 men were gassed, making a total of 20 officers and 427 men.

Captain Deane won his Military Cross on the 22nd August, 1915, near Fauquissart, when one of our patrols was bombed at night. Without stopping to consider the possible strength of the enemy, he at once got over the parapet and ran by himself to the spot under rifle and machine-gun fire.

On finding that four men of the patrol had been wounded, he returned for stretchers and got them safely back.

The notification of the reward mentioned that this was not the first time that Captain Deane's gallantry under fire had been brought to notice.

Inseparably bound up with the record of the 2nd Leicesters in the war is the name of the Reverend Ronald Irwin, the regimental chaplain. Coming from India with the Corps, he was present at all the actions in which the battalion was engaged, and, non-combatant though he was, showed on many occasions as high a degree of heroism as any soldier could attain. He accompanied the Indian troops to Mesopotamia, where he again displayed the greatest bravery and devotion to his duties, attending the wounded and dying under the heaviest fire, and he was eventually very severely wounded in carrying a man out of action. Subsequently he returned to France, where he was again wounded. For his conspicuous gallantry he has received the D.S.O. and the Military Cross with a bar.

At 6.30 p.m. the remnant of the battalion was relieved by the Garhwal Rifles, and moved into support and local reserve close in rear.

The 2/8th Gurkhas, under Lt-Colonel G. M. Morris, were also destined to play a very gallant part during this day's fighting. The battalion, it will be remembered, had undergone a terrible experience within a few hours of its first arrival in the trenches on the 30th October, 1914. On that date it lost a large number of officers and men. The deeds of the regiment on the 25th September, 1915 will never be forgotten, and the memory of their fallen comrades was fully avenged, although at a terrible cost to the battalion.

When, as before stated, the gas was turned on at 5.50 a.m., the wind at once brought it back into our trenches, and the valves were therefore closed.

At 5.59 a.m. No. 3 Double Company, under Captain Buckland, D.S.O., crossed the parapet, lined up outside, and advanced. Owing to the dense smoke and mist, it was impossible to form an accurate idea of the exact direction, but as straight a line as possible was taken towards the German position, which was reached without much difficulty. The right of the company entered the trench unopposed, but on the left the enemy put up a fight. Lieutenant Inglis led his men straight at them, and was shot in a hand-to-hand struggle, which ended in the death or capture of all the defenders of the trench, numbering about 50 men.

The Company then pushed on to the next German line with its right resting on the road near a clump of trees on the right of the objective. A position was taken up on some rising ground and the men began to dig themselves in. Patrols were sent out to both flanks to endeavour to establish touch, but could find no trace of the battalions on the right or left. At this point eight Germans were captured in a dug-out, and two men of the Leicesters came up by themselves, but could give no news of the whereabouts of the remainder of the battalion.

No. 2 Company, under 2nd Lieutenant Meldrum, which formed the second line, advanced immediately behind Captain Buckland, but in the fog must have swung to the left and become mixed with the 4th Black Watch. Pressing on, they rushed the German trench, where a fight ensued, in which Major Kemball, who had come up with two platoons in support, was put out of action, and a number of other casualties occurred. The trench was taken, and Lieutenant Meldrum, advancing still further, began digging himself in astride of a communication trench, a party of the 4th Black Watch being on his right and some of the 33rd Punjabis eventually arriving on the left.

The 3rd line, which now formed the new support, followed closely on Major Kemball's heels, and came under heavy rifle and shell fire on its way up, Lieutenant Taylor being wounded and taken back, while a number of the men fell. With this company was Subadar Ransur Rana, who was slightly wounded in the chest, while two men alongside him were killed. The Subadar, however, seized one of their rifles and shot a German in front of him.

A few of the enemy were found in the trench, but they at once put up their hands and were taken prisoners.

Moving down the trench to the right sixteen more Germans were captured and sent back under escort of one rifleman and a wounded man. Apparently the prisoners overcame the escort and escaped, for Subadar Ransur Rana next met the rifleman in captivity in Germany.

No Germans were found in the second line, which was occupied with very few casualties, as was also the third line.

The objectives had now been reached, so No. 1

Company began to dig in at a distance of about 300 yards from the fourth line, but with its right flank in the air, as the enemy was still in possession of his second and third lines on that flank.

In the meantime the bombing parties had come under heavy fire, and Lieutenant Bampton was wounded, as well as Captain Browning of No. 4 Company.

Subadar Pahalsing Gurung then brought up his company, and with it a fresh supply of ammunition, losing heavily during the advance.

Colonel Morris and Lieutenant Harington, the Adjutant, came on with the last of No. 4 Company, but at a point about 50 yards from the British parapet the former was mortally wounded, and subsequently died in hospital at Merville. Lieutenant Harington at once tried to get his Commanding Officer back into our trench, but was wounded in the attempt, and Colonel Morris was eventually rescued under heavy fire by Lance-Corporal S. W. Evans, 2nd Leicesters. Dying as he was, but ever forgetful of himself in his care for others, he specially re quested that this brave soldier might be rewarded for his gallantry.

At the same time two machine guns came up, but the officer, Lieutenant Ryall, was mortally wounded.

The position at this juncture was as follows :—

Captain Buckland, with the survivors of a party of 150 men and two machine guns, was holding his ground near the Moulin. In front was a strong party of Germans, who were keeping up an incessant fire. These Captain Buckland engaged and finally dispersed.

Lieutenant Meldrum with 60 men was astride a

communication trench in front of the Moulin du Piètre, which was very strongly held by the enemy, who poured a hail of bullets on to the devoted little party.

By 7.30 a.m. about 300 men of the battalion had reached the foremost position, but between 9.30 and 10 a.m. the enemy made a strong counter-attack on the Gurkhas and on the 1/4th Black Watch on their left, at the same time keeping up heavy artillery fire on our original front line trenches, and thus preventing the arrival of reinforcements.

The unequal fight went on until about 11.30 a.m., by which time our numbers had been much reduced, and the 4th Black Watch were compelled to fall back, losing the while very heavily from machine-gun fire.

Captain Buckland saw that, unless at once reinforced, the situation would rapidly become very critical. He made up his mind to risk crossing the fire-swept zone between his position and our original front line, and taking two men with him to ensure the arrival of the message in the event of his being killed on the way, he succeeded in reaching our trench.

He then took two of his own signallers to attempt to lay a telephone line up to the advanced position. With them went the artillery observing officer, but before they had gone far, the artillery officer was killed, and presumably the signallers also, as Captain Buckland was the only one to complete the journey. On his arrival he found that the Germans had begun to come in from the right, bombing along the trench. They had been most gallantly counter-attacked by a party led by Subadar Sarabjit Gurung, which fought with superb bravery against overwhelming odds, but was killed to the last man, one of our machine guns being also put out of action by a bomb.

Subadar Sarabjit Gurung was posthumously awarded the 2nd Class, Indian Order of Merit in recognition of his bravery and self-devotion.

The fact was that the Germans, finding that our right attack had been finally held up, had occupied some houses on that flank, where they had posted a machine gun, and the footing which they thus obtained in the front trench enabled them to bomb the Gurkhas from behind.

Captain Buckland was now in a most dangerous position, as his small party was isolated, and, with the exception of himself, all the British officers were out of action, Lieutenant Meldrum having just then been killed. On his death, Jemadar Rimani Thapa took command, and held on until one of our own shells burst in the middle of his party, reducing its number to about 30 men. On his way he made stands in the German trenches before finally retiring to the British line.

Captain Buckland swung back his right and attempted to hold off the attacks on that flank. On his left were some small parties of the 4th Black Watch, with whom he established communication. Our bombs had run out, but a number of German bombs were collected and used with good effect on the enemy, who were still pressing on.

It was, however, evident that disaster was imminent unless reinforcements were immediately forthcoming. Once more Captain Buckland accepted the risk of going back. He left Subadar Ransur Rana in charge, with orders to hold out until assistance should arrive. He then returned with a havildar and two men, one named Bahadur Pun carrying our damaged machine gun, and the other, Ratbaran Gurung, a captured German gun.

Together they crawled along under very heavy fire, still clinging to the guns for which they had risked so much. Bahadur Pun arrived with his gun at our parapet, and Ratbaran Gurung was eventually found wounded in a field ambulance, having, after all, succeeded in bringing in his trophy.

Captain Buckland and the havildar got safely back, in spite of the heavy fire through which they passed, and the former, as the senior officer left with the battalion, was ordered to take command in our trench and to issue instructions for the 2/8th to hold on to their position, bombing up both flanks to gain touch with the Leicesters on the right and the 4th Black Watch on the left.

The orders were easy to issue, but impossible to carry out. The advanced party of the 2/8th, under Subadar Ransur Rana, had been in touch with a few men of the 4th Black Watch, but the latter had been forced back, while the Leicesters had not reached the enemy's second line, and touch could therefore not be established with them.

The havildar who had accompanied Captain Buckland was sent back with a signaller, but was heavily fired on and had to return with the report that it was impossible to get through. It was now obvious that the Germans were again holding their front line, and had cut off Subadar Ransur Rana and his party. The subsequent fate of this very gallant detachment has at last been ascertained.

At about 11.30 a.m. the enemy, finding both

flanks of the Gurkhas exposed, quickly pushed his attack in, first on the right and then on the left, and, moving through his second line trenches, completely enveloped Subadar Ransur Rana and his men.

Luckily a party of the 39th Garhwalis under a Naik had managed to bring up a small quantity of ammunition, and a number of German bombs were found and used, but the enemy crept closer and closer, and gradually the Gurkhas were split up into small groups, which were rushed successively, and by 1.30 p.m. all was over. Of the 300 men only 170 survived to be captured, and of these about 60 were wounded. Among the survivors were Subadar Ransur Rana and Jemadar Mahatbir Thapa.

The losses of the 2/8th Gurkhas were as follows, and the mixed condition to which many Indian regiments had now been reduced can be gathered from the list of the officers :—

Killed : Lieutenant C. N. D. Inglis, and 2nd Lieutenant A. E. Meldrum, Indian Army Reserve of Officers.

Died of wounds: Lt-Colonel G. M. Morris (2/8th Gurkhas), Lieutenant A. M. Taylor (1st Brahmans), and Lieutenant R. W. Ryall (2/8th Gurkhas.

Wounded: Major G. Kemball (31st Punjabis), Captain E. R. L. Browning (1st Brahmans), Lieutenant H. R. Harington (1/8th Gurkhas), 2nd Lieutenant J. A. H. Bampton (I.A.R.O.).

It is thus seen that of the 9 officer casualties out of a total strength of 12 combatant officers, only 2 belonged to the battalion.

Of the Gurkha officers, 2 were killed, 1 was

wounded, and 5 were missing. In the ranks there were 18 killed, 151 wounded, and 295 missing, making a total of 481 casualties.*

Captain Buckland, Lieutenant Harington, and Subadar Sarabjit Gurung were mentioned in despatches.

Of the two battalions in reserve, the 1/3rd Londons continued to hold the "Duck's Bill" throughout the day, and escaped with a casualty list of only 52. Amongst these were 2nd Lieutenant Gedge killed, and Major Beresford gassed.

The 39th Garhwalis, under Lt-Colonel Drake-Brockman, had orders to move up as soon as the mine was exploded, and to hold the front of the Brigade. Accordingly they at once began to file up the three communication trenches, but were soon totally blocked by the numbers of wounded and gassed men of the Leicesters and 2/3rd Gurkhas who were crowding back; only the left company of the Garhwalis was able to get into its place in the front trench.

At about 8.30 a.m. the Garhwalis were ordered to send half the battalion and two bombing parties to reinforce the left of the Leicesters, and then to clear the German trenches so as to assist the Leicesters' right frontal attack. By 9 a.m., however, it was very doubtful whether the Leicesters had succeeded in breaking through any portion of the enemy's front, so the Garhwalis were directed to put in half the battalion and two bombing parties behind the 2/8th Gurkhas to work towards the right, the remaining half-battalion and bombers meantime working towards the left.

* The total casualties (excluding sick) of the 2/8th Gurkha Rifles in France amounted to 40 British, 27 Gurkha officers, and 1356 other ranks.

The idea of this move was to work inwards, and, by attacking the enemy's line in front of the 2/3rd Gurkhas and Leicesters, to assist their advance.

The message was received at the Leicesters' head quarters at 10.15 a.m., but took an hour longer to reach Colonel Drake-Brockman. This was due to the fact that the Garhwalis were occupying a front of about 600 yards, while the congested state of the trenches, which were also deep in mud and water, rendered movement almost impossible, even a single man taking a long time to advance fifty yards. To add to the trouble, the Dehra Dun Brigade now began to arrive, and the trenches were completely blocked, rendering it impossible to organize the Garhwalis' attack, and it was not until 2.30 p.m. that the companies could be got into position. By this time the propitious moment had passed.

The original orders, received at about 10.30 a.m., were for the Dehra Dun Brigade to advance through the German trenches and establish itself on the line Haut Pommereau—La Cliqueterie, and by 2.15 p.m. the Brigade was concentrated in position to advance in the following order from right to left: 4th Seaforths, 2/2nd Gurkhas, 1st Seaforths, 9th Gurkhas.

It became necessary, however, to cancel these orders when it was certain that the attack of the Bareilly Brigade, at first highly successful, had been driven back, and that the Germans had reoccupied their front line. Orders were then issued for the Brigade to attempt to establish touch with any British troops still remaining in the German trenches.

Accordingly a company of the 1st Seaforths was ordered to advance on the left and a company of the 2/2nd Gurkhas on the right. Before the move commenced, it was reported that no British troops, other than killed or wounded, were now in the enemy's trenches on the left. The advance of the Seaforth company was therefore countermanded. As there was still some doubt as to the situation on the right, one company of the 2/2nd Gurkhas and two of the 39th Garhwalis were launched.

A small German flag was now seen floating over the enemy's front line, and the second that our men crossed the parapet they came under a hot fire from all directions, chiefly from machine guns, and were held up at the first rush, when they had at once to take what cover they could find in the long grass and the folds of the ground. It was obviously impossible to make any further progress without a fresh artillery preparation, so the attacking troops were ordered to get back as opportunity offered.

The company of the 39th Garhwalis was led by 2nd Lieutenant Rana Jodha Jang with great courage, which, coupled with his gallantry on a subsequent occasion, gained him the Military Cross.

The casualties of the 2/2nd Gurkhas were: 3 killed, 18 wounded, and 2 missing; while the 39th during the day lost 4 men killed, 1 British officer, 2 Garhwali officers and 40 men wounded, 26 men being missing.

Our inability to attain the whole objective was attributed to the following chief causes:—

(1) The fact that the wire was uncut in front of the Leicesters and 2/3rd Gurkhas.

(2) The unfavourable wind and weather conditions. These induced a thick fog between our line and that of the enemy, which lasted over an hour, and prevented all observation of the progress of the

attack. It hampered our men instead of the Germans, and caused several of the lines of assault to lose their direction owing to its density. The gas also recoiled and added to the congestion in the trenches by forcing our men back. This led to a delay in getting up reserves, as messengers could not circulate freely.

In conclusion, the words of Brigadier-General Blackader, Commanding the Garhwal Brigade, may be quoted :—

"I would bring to notice the gallant conduct and fine spirit that animated all ranks of the assaulting battalions. They did all that was possible, and a sufficient testimony is the number of dead and wounded that lay in front of the German wire which barred their further advance."

CHAPTER XXIII

THE BATTLE OF LOOS—*Continued*

Attack by the Bareilly Brigade—Effects of our gas on the 2nd Black Watch—Enemy's lines penetrated up to the Moulin du Piètre—Gallantry of all units engaged—Captains Park and Buchan, 2nd Black Watch, win the D.S.O.—Enemy reoccupies front-line trenches—Our troops, outflanked on both sides, compelled to retire—Heavy losses of troops engaged—Remarks by Generals Jacob and Norie—Causes of failure of attack—Remarks by Sir John French and Sir Douglas Haig.

WE must now turn to the operations of the Bareilly Brigade under the command of Brigadier-General C. Norie.

As before mentioned, the order of battalions from right to left was as follows: 1/4th Black Watch, 69th Punjabis and 2nd Black Watch in the front line, with the 33rd Punjabis and 58th Rifles in reserve.

At 6 a.m. two minutes after the explosion of our mine, which was situated at a distance of about 130 yards from the trench occupied by the 2nd Black Watch, the assaulting infantry advanced with a rush.

The 2nd Black Watch, under Major Wauchope, D.S.O., who were to leeward of the Brigade front, received the full effects of our gas, which was at once blown back across the parapet. A number of men were disabled by this unlucky occurrence, but the remainder raced out of sight into the pall of smoke which hid them alike from our view and that of the enemy.

No. 1 Company, under Captain W. Wilson, got across with few casualties and occupied the enemy's trench. Meeting with little opposition, they pressed on, the wire having been thoroughly disposed of by our guns. No. 2 Company under Captain Park and No. 3 under Captain Denison followed close on their heels, leaving No. 4 under Captain Buchan to bring up ammunition and tools. With No. 3 Company went Major Wauchope.

By 7 a.m. Captains Park and Denison had secured the left flank of their advance up to this point, and double-blocked the German trenches. No. 4 Company, although the last to start, had caught up and pushed on for the Moulin du Piètre and the enemy's second line of trenches, pressing back the Germans as they advanced.

Major Wauchope now established his Head Quarters in the German first line, and along the whole front of his battalion the enemy was being steadily driven back on to his second position. This was reported, and arrangements were made for the left to be held by a battalion of the 60th Brigade of the 3rd Corps, as that flank was dangerously exposed for a distance of some 600 yards. The 69th Punjabis were meantime doing good work on the right, and some of the 58th Rifles also came up, and together all fought their way towards the Moulin du Piètre.

A number of officers and men of the 2nd Black Watch had been overcome by the gas before they reached the German front line, and by 7 a.m. 12 officers out of 20, as well as a large number of men, had been put out of action.

In order immediately to close as much as possible of the gap of 600 yards, Subadar Tika Khan of the 58th Rifles, by Major Wauchope's orders, took his Double Company out of the second line, which was overcrowded, and lining a ditch which ran back in the required direction, filled up about 180 yards.

Moving to the right, Major Wauchope found Colonels Ridgway (33rd Punjabis) and Walker (1/4th Black Watch), and with them came to the conclusion that unless the Garhwal Brigade as a whole succeeded in getting forward, the 4th Black Watch, whose right flank was exposed, would be unable to hold on. At this moment, however, some of the 2/8th Gurkhas were seen on the right, and it was hoped that that flank was fairly secure. To make doubly sure, Colonel Walker kept the 1/4th Black Watch in a trench in rear of the 2/8th, while Colonel Ridgway remained where he was, the 33rd thus forming a central reserve against a possible attack from either flank.

The enemy was now keeping up a very severe shell and rifle fire and casualties were numerous.

At 11 a.m. the situation was very mixed. Captain Buchan, with about 80 men, was holding the enemy's second line opposite the Moulin. To his left rear, 200 men of the 58th Rifles occupied about 180 yards on the flank, while in his right rear were parties of the 58th, 69th, and 33rd. Lieutenant Meldrum, with about 80 of the 2/8th Gurkhas, was holding the ground immediately on Captain Buchan's right, while a short distance behind him were most of the 4th Black Watch.

At about this time the first touch was established with the 60th Brigade, when a detachment of the 12th Rifle Brigade took over the blocks established by Captain Park on the left of the German first line. They further extended from the enemy's front-line trench towards the Moulin, one company being placed in a natural ditch by Major Wauchope.

Captain Park reorganized his men and moved towards the right of the Moulin du Piètre, but before he had got half-way, saw our troops retiring.

The cause of this retirement was threefold.

(1) The left of the line was blocked by Captain Buchan's party, but there was no natural feature in his rear to give protection, and the Germans broke through the gap on his left.

(2) The right of the Brigade was unguarded except by a detachment of the 2/8th Gurkhas, who had gallantly fought their way through to a point on the right of the Moulin and to the right front of the 69th. This party held on while the enemy was trying to get round them.

(3) The heavy losses of officers made reorganization very difficult, while the crushing rifle fire and bombing which were kept up by the enemy rendered it almost impossible to take up a new position immediately in rear.

About 11.30 a.m. the Germans made a powerful counter-attack, bombing and pouring in on our right flank which gave way after a brave but vain attempt to stem the flood. The troops in front of the Moulin were now attacked from their right rear, and shortly afterwards those on the left found themselves almost cut off, with the result that each section had to give ground in order to preserve a possible line of retreat.

The gap on the left of the line appears to have been caused by the non-appearance of the remaining companies of the 12th Rifle Brigade, which were intended to fill the opening between the company which Major Wauchope had placed in a ditch running towards the Moulin and the 58th Rifles. Had this gap been filled, it was believed that the left flank would have been secure, but before noon, when the retirement commenced, Major Wauchope saw no signs of the advance of the rest of the 12th Rifle Brigade, and the bombs of the one company which was in the line had run out at a very early stage. Those also of the Bareilly Brigade were soon expended, and the intense fire kept up by the enemy prevented further supplies from being brought up.

The result was that from the moment the German counter-attack commenced, we were outbombed. One officer reported: "We held the flanks until all our bombs were finished, using in the process 35 German bombs." Another states: "The men were most ready to make a series of stands during the retirement, but whenever a stand was prolonged, the Germans came bombing up from trenches on either flank." Again: "The two companies of the Rifle Brigade apparently relied on their Brigade bombers both for bombers and supplies of bombs, and when pressed by German bombing parties, were unable to resist them, having few, if any, trained bombers or bombs. They were driven from the 'blocks' they had taken over."

The German re-action was pressed with the utmost vigour and method from the front and both flanks. A number of the enemy still lurked in the trenches which we had captured, but had not sufficiently searched. These men now fired into our troops from behind, and appear to have singled out officers, for our loss in this respect was very heavy.

At about noon the situation was as follows.

On the right of the Moulin du Piètre no British troops remained, all having been forced back, with the exception of Subadar Ransur Rana's detachment of the 2/8th Gurkhas, which was rapidly being enveloped by the enemy. Those in the centre were slowly retiring with their right rear threatened. The troops on the left, opposite the Moulin, consisting chiefly of 2nd Black Watch and 58th Rifles, were still holding on, but the Germans, in consequence of the retirement of the 12th Rifle Brigade, were able to pour fire into them from trenches in their left rear. By 12.30 p.m. they were pushed out towards their right rear, both flanks were in the air and the direct line of retreat was almost cut. Immediate withdrawal was the only course open.

This delicate operation was most successfully and steadily performed, the men halting and firing at intervals, until finally most of them got back into our front line on both sides of Winchester Road, the light casualties during this movement, in spite of the heavy and accurate fire of the enemy, being due to the steadiness of the men and the skill with which the operation was conducted.

Major Wauchope, who had been half stunned by a bomb, but was, as always, resolute to remain in action, was the last to retire. With him were eight of the 2nd Black Watch, and the party, closely followed by bombs and rifle fire, reached our front trench by about 1.30 p.m.

The losses of the 2nd Black Watch in officers were very heavy, a large number occurring during the first 15 minutes of the attack. These were:—

Killed: Captain A. C. Denison, Lieutenants

Balfour-Melville, Henderson, Sotheby, and Macleod. To these must be added 10 officers wounded, making a total of 15 out of 20 actually in action.

In the ranks: killed, 38; wounded, 261; missing, 49. Total of all ranks, 363.

Captains Park and Buchan were very prominent during the fighting, and received the D.S.O. for their conspicuous gallantry. The former led his company throughout with the greatest dash, personally directing the bombing parties in continuous hand-to-hand fighting for four hours, during which he drove the enemy back about 400 yards along two lines of trench and established three blocks, which he held until he was relieved.

This officer again distinguished himself on the 8th October. On the previous day the enemy was discovered to be mining close under our parapet. The tunnelling company, with the bravery which has so often been displayed by them, managed to explode one of the mines at the very last moment, in fact, the sound of tamping was heard at the time, indicating that the mine would very shortly have been blown up by the enemy. A few hours later the Germans blew up another mine, and at about 5 a.m. two more within 20 yards of our parapet, much of which in front of No. 2 Company of the 2nd Black Watch was destroyed.

Captain Park and about 50 men were half buried in the debris, three men being killed, but the remainder were got out, and with the supports, rushed to the broken-down parapet, which they held in spite of heavy rifle and shrapnel fire. A German bombing party, advancing out of one of the mine craters, was driven back and, owing to the steady fire kept up by Captain Park's company, the enemy made no further attack.

Captain Buchan showed conspicuous gallantry throughout the action on the 25th September. At the commencement, when he and his men were suffering from the effects of gas, he rallied and led them on over three lines of trenches, his company being the first to enter the enemy's position near the Moulin du Piètre. He only retired when the troops on both flanks had been forced back by a counter-attack and he himself had been wounded.

The foregoing account has been principally concerned with the doings of the 2nd Black Watch, mention only being made of other units where necessary to make a connected story.

The 69th Punjabis were on the right of the Highlanders. This regiment, after seeing service in Egypt and Gallipoli, arrived in France on the 29th May, 1915, joining the Indian Corps on the 5th June. Their losses commenced at once, for on the next day two of a party of officers, Major Copeland, Second in Command, and Lieutenant Dill, the Adjutant, who went to see the trenches of the Meerut Division, were caught by shell fire on their way back and killed.

On the 25th September, when a bouquet of day signals was sent up at 5.50 a.m., marking the commencement of our gas attack, No. 1 Double Company under Major Bingham and 2nd Lieutenant Geary, and No. 4 under Lieutenants Moberley and Gray, were standing ready, and at 6 a.m. the assault was launched.

The second line, consisting of No. 2 Double Company, under Captain Nelson, on the right, and

No. 3, under Lieutenant Brooke, on the left, followed close in rear, and with them went the Commanding Officer, Major Stansfeld, and the Adjutant, Lieutenant Lumby.

The right of No. 1 Company came under machine-gun fire, but the line advanced with great élan, and bursting through the enemy's front system, took a machine gun and joined hands with the 2nd Black Watch, 2nd Lieutenant Geary (I.A.R.O.) being very conspicuous by the dash with which he led his men.

No. 4 Company was temporarily held up by a party of Germans, who were, however, quickly disposed of with the bayonet, and the men swept on.

Lieutenant Brooke was wounded shortly after the advance commenced, but his company, though left without a British officer, went straight on in support of No. 4. Lieutenant Lumby, on reaching the enemy's front line, saw some Germans working along towards the centre, hotly pursued by Captain Nelson's bombers. While helping to round them up, he was very severely wounded in the leg, which had eventually to be amputated.

Shortly afterwards Major Stansfeld was mortally wounded by a bomb, while leading Nos 2 and 3 Companies, and by his death the regiment lost, in the language of Brigadier-General Norie, "an exceptional Commanding Officer."

In quick succession, Captain Nelson and Lieutenants Moberley and Fraser (I.A.R.O.) were then killed. These casualties left the battalion with only four officers still in action, namely, Major Bingham, Lieutenants Gulland and Gray, and 2nd

Lieutenant Miller-Sterling (I.A.R.O.). Amongst the Indian officers, as well as in the ranks, the casualties had been very heavy.

Still the battalion held on to its position near the Moulin du Piètre until forced to retire by the causes which have already been described.

The retirement was greatly facilitated by the pluck of Subadar Muhammad Khan and Jemadar Sardar Khan, who took up a position in the centre communication trench where they made a block, from the cover of which they held back the enemy and prevented him from pressing too closely on the heels of their comrades.

Lieutenant Gulland, the regimental machine-gun officer, who had fought his guns with great gallantry throughout the action, was wounded at this juncture, and was taken prisoner with his orderly, Sepoy Kirpa, who stuck to him to the last, thus affording another example of the attachment of the Indian soldier to his British officer.

The retirement was conducted by Major Bingham with Lieutenants Gray and Miller-Sterling. Major Bingham, who had led the attack throughout with great gallantry, was mentioned in despatches, as was also Major Stansfeld the Commanding Officer, who was attached from the 74th Punjabis.

The losses of the 69th were :—

Killed : Major Stansfeld, Captain Nelson, Lieutenant Moberly, 2nd Lieutenant Fraser, 3 Indian officers and 36 men.

Wounded : 3 British, 6 Indian officers and 261 other ranks.

Wounded and a prisoner : Lieutenant Gulland.

Missing : 34 other ranks.

Total: 348 out of a strength of 663 of all ranks actually engaged.

The 1/4th Black Watch (Territorials) had 3 and 4 Double Companies in the front line under Captains O. S. Moodie and Couper respectively. In the old support line, about 30 yards in rear, was No. 2 Double Company commanded by Captain Campbell, and behind them again was No. 1 Double Company under Captain N. C. Walker.

At 6 a.m. the front line went over the parapet, and at the same moment Major Tarleton, the Adjutant, was wounded as he was cheering on the men.

Nos 1 and 2 Companies then crossed and followed closely in rear of the leaders. With them went the Commanding Officer, Lt-Colonel H. Walker, C.M.G., and the Second in Command, Major Tosh. In crossing over to the German front line, the latter was hit by a bullet and fell. Sergeant Petrie immediately ran to his help and was carrying him towards our trench on his back when Major Tosh was again wounded, and this time mortally, by a fragment of shell.

As No. 2 Company went over the parapet, Captain Duncan was hit, both his legs being broken. A few minutes before this, 2nd Lieutenant Bruce of the same company had been wounded.

Nos 3 and 4 Companies got on well, the enemy making very slight resistance, and the front line was taken with little difficulty.

The enemy's snipers were extremely active throughout this day's fighting, and it was obvious that officers were being singled out by them.

Our losses in the ranks in capturing the front trench were light, but Captain Walker and Lieutenants

Steven and S. L. Watson were all wounded at this point, and were subsequently returned as missing, believed killed. About the same time Captain Campbell was wounded and missing, while, to add to the misfortunes of the battalion, 2nd Lieutenant Anderson, who was second in command of the Brigade bombers in reserve, was killed by a shell in our own trench.

The front line quickly settled with the bayonet such of the enemy as had not been disposed of by our bombardment, and who still resisted, but these were few. For the most part the Germans surrendered, and palefaced batches of them, still with their hands up, were marched back to our lines.

Generally speaking, the prisoners were young, strongly built men, but they begged abjectly for mercy. There were also a few older men among them who scowled at their captors, but otherwise did not seem very much upset by their position. The prisoners were taken charge of in some cases by Highlanders and in others by Gurkhas, grinning broadly with pleasure and pride.

The bombers went rapidly along the line, searching the dug-outs for concealed Germans, and then Nos. 3 and 4 Companies, joined by 2nd Lieutenant Cunningham with some of No. 2 Company, pressed on towards the enemy's next line, headed by Captains Moodie and Air. The mist was still thick and it was very difficult to keep the right direction. Frequently dim forms loomed up out of the fog and were, just in time, recognized as some of the Indian troops.

The German reply to our guns, which at first

had been very slight, was now seriously to be reckoned with. The ground between their line and the British was being accurately searched by their artillery, while a barrage of shrapnel prevented the arrival of any further reinforcements on our side. Our artillery unfortunately appeared to be inadequate to deal with this fire.

A small number of men lost direction in the mist, and moving too much to the left, found themselves mixed with Indians and held up opposite the Moulin du Piètre. The main body of the battalion reached a trench at a distance of about 50 yards from the mill, and advantage was taken of the cover to reorganize and rest the men, many of whom at once produced their pipes and began to smoke.

No. 1 was still pushing on in support of No. 2, and in crossing the enemy's second line, Lieutenant L. Wilson and 2nd Lieutenant Watson were wounded, which left only Captain McIntyre with the company. At that moment he, too, was wounded, but with great pluck, he managed to carry on for two hours more. No. 1 then lined a hedge and dug a trench in support of the advanced companies.

Nos 3 and 4 Companies, after taking the German first system, which comprised about five lines of trench, advanced over the open towards the second position, at a short distance from which they began to dig themselves in. With them were Captains Couper, Moodie, Air, Lieutenant Sturrock and 2nd Lieutenant Williamson.

In spite of the search made by the bombers as each successive line was taken, it was now evident that some of the enemy still lurked in the captured trenches. One after the other the officers were wounded by shots fired from the rear, until Captain Air was the only one still uninjured. It was discovered that these losses were due to the presence of a party of six snipers, who were at once rounded up, and the harassment ceased.

Captain Air sent back repeated requests for reinforcements and ammunition, but with the exception of one subaltern of the 2nd Black Watch, who came up with about 30 men, no supports arrived. A number of the rifles had now jammed, owing to being clogged with mud, and our bombs gave out.

Simultaneously the enemy surged forward in masses and our advanced trench was hidden in the smoke of their exploding bombs. In the absence of substantial reinforcements the position was untenable, and Captain Air ordered his few remaining men to retire. Almost as he gave the command, he was wounded. Earlier in the day an attempt had been made to establish communication between our own and the German front line, but as fast as the wire was laid, it was cut by shell fire.

Something had to be done, and that at once, so Colonel Walker, whose entire Staff was now out of action, started to cross to our front trench to bring up reinforcements. In this gallant attempt he fell mortally wounded.

Shortly afterwards a retirement took place along the whole line of the Brigade, and by 1 p.m. the remnant of the battalion had got back into our front trenches.

The 1/4th Black Watch lost heavily on this occasion, but nobly sustained the high reputation which this fine Territorial battalion had made for itself.

Killed: Lt-Colonel Walker, C.M.G., Major Tosh and 2nd Lieutenant Anderson.

Wounded: 8 officers.

Missing, believed killed: 4 officers, amongst whom was the gallant Captain Air.

Missing: 5 officers, including Captain Moodie.

In the ranks, 7 were killed, 141 wounded, 8 missing, making a total casualty list of 20 officers and 235 men out of a strength on going into action of 21 officers and 423 other ranks. This gives a percentage of 57, a terrible price to pay, but as the Regimental War Diary, in the true soldierly spirit, remarks, "It had been a grand advance, but at a great cost. We had forced the enemy to turn on many of his heaviest pieces against us and compelled him to bring up very large reserves. Attacks were made at other parts of the line that day, and the enemy's reserves had to be drawn off."

As soon as the 2nd Black Watch advanced to the attack, the 58th Rifles, under Lt-Colonel C. Davidson-Houston, D.S.O., moved up and occupied the trenches which they had evacuated, as directed in operation orders. In the front line were No. 4 Double Company under Captain McKenzie and No. 2 under Lieutenant Nicolls, the former on the right.

In support were No. 3 Double Company under Captains Harcourt and Flagg, and No. 1 under Captain Wardell and 2nd Lieutenant Deane-Spread.

In Brigade operation orders it was distinctly laid down that the battalion was not to move beyond our own front line without definite instructions, unless the 2nd Black Watch were in urgent need of assistance and communication with Brigade Head

Quarters had been broken. Brigadier-General Norie remarks, "Although the 2nd Battalion Royal Highlanders were in no urgent need of assistance and although communication with Brigade Head Quarters was intact, the Officer Commanding took his regiment across in support of the 2nd Battalion Royal Highlanders. This action added to the subsequent confusion which resulted in front of the Moulin."

The orders were clear and left no loophole for doubt. It is, however, impossible to believe that Colonel Davidson-Houston, a commander of oft-tried competence, a man known for coolness of judgment under the most trying conditions, could have been guilty at such a critical moment of deliberate disobedience of orders.

To appreciate the situation several points have to be considered.

General Norie states that communication with Brigade Head Quarters was intact at the moment when the 58th advanced.

It is, however, a matter of common experience that, under the conditions of a modern battle, many telephone messages fail to get through even when the line is intact.

Unfortunately the soldier who acted as Houston's telephonist, and who was with him till he was killed, is, if still alive, a prisoner in German hands, and his evidence, which would be conclusive, is not obtainable.

We must, then, in common justice to the memory and reputation of a gallant soldier, believe that Colonel Houston attempted to obtain telephonic orders, but failed to get through; and having failed, that he considered the urgency of the situation to be such as to compel him to accept the grave responsibility of an immediate advance on his own initiative.

If this view be accepted, it only remains to consider, from such facts as are on record, whether sufficient grounds existed for so serious a step.

It must be remembered that at the commencement of the advance, the gas was blown back into our line; it penetrated even into the communication trenches where the 58th, while filing up to the front, were ordered to put on masks and, as an officer relates, "even then the smell was suffocating."

The conditions in the front line were still worse. Numbers of men were staggering about, suffering from the effects of our gas; to add to the congestion many men of an unit not belonging to the Indian Corps had found their way into the trench, and it was only with the utmost difficulty that the 58th could take up their position in support, while it was at once evident that it would be highly dangerous to remain long in such a poison-laden atmosphere.

Lastly, but most important of all, Colonel Houston was aware that Major Wauchope depended entirely for the protection of his left flank, without which protection the attack was foredoomed to failure, on the immediate assistance of an entire battalion of the 60th Brigade, which assistance was not forthcoming.

He foresaw also that any advance from our front-line trenches would shortly be rendered impossible by the ever-growing violence of the enemy's fire.

Having considered these points, and having failed to get a message through to Head Quarters, he accepted the responsibility, and, as noted in the Regimental Diary, the battalion crossed the parapet at 6.15 a.m. " in support of the Black Watch."

The correctness of Colonel Houston's action must be judged greatly by the results, of which Major (now Brigadier-General) Wauchope, commanding the 2nd Black Watch, was in the best position to form an opinion.

The following extracts from a recent letter give his considered views on the subject :—

" I say without hesitation that had Colonel Davidson-Houston's soldierly instinct not directed him to strengthen and partly fill the gap on the left of the Bareilly Brigade at an early hour, it would then have been open to the enemy to force our left flank.

" After an attack such as was made on the 25th September, telephone lines, if not cut by artillery fire, are apt to be temporarily blocked.

" Knowing Colonel Houston as not only one of the bravest of officers, but also as free from any inconsiderate rashness, I have no doubt that he first tried and failed to communicate with Brigade Head Quarters, and then acted on his own initiative and, as he thought, in accordance with the wishes of his superior.

" If this be partly surmise, there is no doubt that this prescience was justified by events ; he sent his battalion where and at the time it was needed. Had he awaited orders, his battalion would have been sent to the same flank, but an opportunity would have been given the enemy to break in on our left before his battalion had arrived."

It is believed that the foregoing statement presents a just and temperate consideration of a much-discussed incident.

In the front line were Nos. 2 and 4 Double Companies. The former pushed on through the enemy's position to the bend of Winchester Road, where Lieutenant Nicolls was killed. No. 4 Company also lost its commander soon after crossing the German trench, as Captain McKenzie was mortally wounded; 2nd Lieutenant Durnford took the company forward for a further distance of 200 yards, where he consolidated his position.

No. 2 Company met with very heavy fire, and the men, left without a British officer, fell back on No. 4.

The support companies, accompanied by Colonel Davidson-Houston, now came up and pushed through until, on reaching the bend of the road in front of Lieutenant Durnford, Captain Harcourt was ordered to dig himself in. At about this time Captain Flagg was mortally wounded, probably by a sniper who was doing a great deal of execution from a clump of trees on the right.

Captain Harcourt then went a short way back to get orders, and met his commanding officer sitting with Major Wauchope by the side of a ditch. Colonel Houston remarked that the battalion would have to hold on where it was until reinforcements arrived.

On returning to his company, Captain Harcourt found that it was much mixed with men of other units and, to add to the difficulties, our own guns began to shell the trench and caused some casualties, but luckily there was no direct hit.

Shortly after this our bombs ran short, and the

Germans, coming to close quarters, showered bombs on our men, who were unable to reply and were forced to retire.

On the way back Colonel Davidson-Houston was seen with Captain Milligan and 2nd Lieutenant Deane-Spread lining a shallow ditch with a few men. It was then reported that the enemy had got round the left flank and were behind the party. The only course was to get away as quickly as possible along the ditch, which was half full of mud. At this moment a heavy shell burst near, killing two of the men, and wounding and almost stunning Captain Harcourt who, on recovering a little, crawled towards a ruined cottage where he was suddenly seized by Germans and dragged down a communication trench.

Colonel Houston, Captain Milligan, and 2nd Lieutenant Deane-Spread appear to have arrived at almost the same spot, where Houston was instantaneously killed by a bullet in the head, and the other two were mortally wounded.

Such was the end of three very gallant men.

Of Colonel Davidson-Houston General Norie records, "He was a commanding officer of unusual value," and another officer, himself of most distinguished courage and ability, writes, "On many occasions I have been in action with Colonel Davidson-Houston; I have known no finer commanding officer, I have met no leader of greater resource. I have served with no soldier more brave, no man more straightforward, no officer of more just judgment. These qualities he showed in every battle."

Could any soldier desire a better epitaph?

The losses of the 58th Rifles, as reported after the battle, were :—

Killed: Captain Flagg and Lieutenant Nicolls.

Wounded: Captain Wardell.

Wounded and Missing: Lt-Colonel Davidson-Houston and Captain McKenzie.

Wounded and a prisoner: Captain Harcourt.

Missing: Lieutenants Milligan and Deane-Spread.

Of the Indian officers, one was wounded, one wounded and missing, and three missing, of whom one, Subadar Bhag Singh, was afterwards ascertained to be a prisoner.

Of other ranks, 40 were killed, 106 wounded and 100 were missing.

Lt-Colonel Davidson-Houston and Lieutenant Nicolls were mentioned in despatches.

To describe in detail the part played by the 33rd Punjabis would involve, to a great extent, repetition of the foregoing accounts.

The battalion had joined the Corps from Egypt in two detachments, half arriving on the 6th, and the remainder on the 22nd September. In this, its first experience of a modern battle, it showed a degree of valour equal in every way to that of the more experienced units. As soon as the 1/4th Black Watch advanced, the 33rd took their place in our front trench.

At 6.37 a.m. No. 2 Company under Major Graham crossed over and set to work to consolidate the trench captured by the Highlanders. Here they found a company of the 58th Rifles under Captain Harcourt already engaged in the same task, and were shortly afterwards joined by the Commanding Officer, Lt-Colonel Ridgway with two more companies.

As happened elsewhere the battalion became divided and mixed with other units, but No. 2 Company and part of No. 4 reached the German line near the Moulin du Piètre, where they held on until their bombs were exhausted and their line of retreat was threatened, when they retired with the remainder of the Brigade.

Their losses were :—

Killed : Captains MacCall and Price, Lieutenant Grasett.

Wounded : Lt-Colonel Ridgway and Captain Vincent.

Missing : Major Kelly.

Of the Indian officers, Subadar-Major Bahadur Khan and Jemadar Akbar Ali were killed, 3 were wounded and a similar number were missing.

In the ranks the casualties amounted to 18 killed, 161 wounded and 69 missing.

Lt-Colonel Ridgway and Major Graham were mentioned in despatches.

General Norie records that he lost an admirable Staff officer in Captain Hewett, who was killed while going forward to ascertain how the situation was developing.

The casualties of the Brigade amounted to 1413, while those of the Lahore and Meerut Divisions together reached the large total of 3973, made up as follows :—

British officers 156 ; Indian officers 44 ; other ranks, British 1891 ; other ranks, Indian 1882.

It is always difficult to form any reliable estimate of the enemy's losses when, as in the case of this action, the ground captured has to be evacuated, but there can be no doubt that our bombardment and the subsequent hand-to-hand fighting caused heavy casualties in the German ranks. In addition to these, 2 officers and over 200 men were captured, as also were several machine guns. The balance of gain and loss must be determined in cool perspective by that historian, whoever he may be, who ultimately describes the Western Campaign as a whole.

Major-General Jacob, Commanding the Meerut Division, made the following remarks on the behaviour of the troops on this most trying day.

"The outstanding feature in the operations is the extraordinary keenness, spirit, élan and dash shown by all units. It was very marked in the period preceding the day fixed for the attack, and the way all ranks worked to make the operations a success was most gratifying. The vigour with which the different battalions made the assault left no doubt as to their determination to get through the German lines at all costs. The charge made by the 2/8th Gurkhas and 2nd Leicesters in the Garhwal Brigade and by the 2nd Black Watch, 69th Punjabis and 1/4th Black Watch in the Bareilly Brigade could not have been finer. It was this keenness and spirit which caused some units to overlook their first objective and to go too far, with the result that some of them were cut off and wiped out."

With regard to the work of the technical troops from the Commanding Royal Engineer (Brigadier-General H. C. Nanton, C.B.) downwards, General Jacob reported that the manner in which the whole programme of work during the preliminary operations was carried out proved the high state of efficiency reached by the Sappers and Miners and the Pioneers: "No praise can be too high for the work they have done throughout the war."

In these words he voiced the opinion of all their comrades-in-arms, for, alike in actual fighting such as at Neuve Chapelle in 1914, and in its more legitimate sphere of organization of work in the field, the accomplishments of this branch of the Service won the admiration of the whole corps.

General Jacob concludes by remarking that the evacuation of the wounded and the preparations for this work were carried out perfectly, reflecting great credit on Colonel J. J. Russell, A.D.M.S., and the officers of the R.A.M.C. and I.M.S. He also mentions the skill and energy shown by Captain Frost, Supply and Transport Corps, in organizing and working the tramways system, which enabled the wounded to be removed so quickly and safely.

The reader will now have gathered that the attack was carried out with the greatest gallantry, but a doubt may have arisen in his mind as to whether the effect of this gallantry was not dissipated by lack of prudence in pushing on too far without first consolidating the captured positions.

The key to the question lies in the remarks of Brigadier-General Norie, Commanding the Bareilly Brigade, in which he mentions, as one of the causes of the failure to hold the salient won, the too rapid advance of the Brigade to the enemy's second line. This he describes as unfortunate, but adds, "So strongly had a continued offensive been insisted upon that it is not surprising that troops who already were so full of offensive spirit should have been misled into going forward too fast and too far. In doing so they omitted thoroughly to examine the enemy's trenches for lurking Germans, they did not sufficiently deal with possible approaches for counter-attacks, and they outstripped the Brigades on their right and left."

Since the battle of Neuve Chapelle no opportunity had been lost of impressing on the troops the necessity of pushing forward when opposition was found to be slight. In the Meerut Division operation order issued on the 20th September, the following instructions were given.

"The immediate objective of the assault is the general line of the road from M. 36. a. 3. 4. to M. 30. c. 7. 9. and thence to the enemy's front parapet at M. 30. a. 7. 6., and is to include the capture of all the enemy's front and supporting lines on that front. Assaulting troops are not to delay in the enemy's front line trenches, but will push on and capture the supporting lines. Bodies of infantry are not to halt if portions of the line are held up but will press on towards their objective. If the opposition of the enemy is unshaken the assaulting troops will consolidate the captured position and will extend their flanks by vigorous bomb attacks along all flank trenches. . . . If the opposition is slight full advantage of the situation is to be taken with a view to (*a*) breaking completely the enemy's line opposite our own front and capturing his supporting batteries in rear of his position; (*b*) taking immediate advantage of the weakening of the enemy's opposition which will follow the success of our main offensive in the South, and assisting this offensive by turning the La Bassée defences from the North."

Such were the instructions transmitted from the 1st Army to the assaulting troops through the medium of Divisional, Brigade, and Regimental orders.

Viewed dispassionately in the light of subsequent events, it appears to be impossible to fix any blame for the non-success of the operations on the troops. They did their part most gallantly and paid the cost themselves. Perhaps, had the front line of the attack allowed prudence to get the better of courage, they might have stayed longer to consolidate the front and support lines when captured, but it must be remembered that they had every right to believe that their advance would be adequately supported. That this was not the case is undeniable, but the failure to support was the result, not of want of forethought or skill on the part of those responsible, but of the congestion in the front line and communication trenches, largely due to the effect of our own gas, which prevented the advance of the Dehra Dun Brigade until too late to be of any avail.

Whether, in view of the strength of the position held by the enemy, this moderate addition to our forces would have sufficed to enable the assault to capture and hold the German second line is one on which competent opinions differ. It must be noted that the operation orders laid down that the Lahore Division, which was holding a part of our front, and the 20th Division on our left, were only to advance when the Meerut Division had reached a point beyond the enemy's second line of trenches. To attempt to solve this question is to invade the realms of speculation and could, in the absence of more complete information as to the enemy's strength and dispositions, lead to no fruitful conclusion.

The final judgment of the success or otherwise of the operations must be left to those in a position hereafter to review the situation as a whole.

Sir Douglas Haig concluded his report, dated the 26th September, 1915, with these words:—

"The General Officer Commanding 1st Army wishes to express his appreciation of the good work done by all ranks and his gratification at the good progress made by the 1st and 4th Corps. Also, though the opposition North of the canal prevented great progress of subsidiary attacks, the G.O.C. is very pleased with the manner in which the 1st, 3rd, and Indian Corps carried out the rôle assigned to them of retaining the enemy on their front."

Sir John French, in his despatch dated the 15th October, 1915, describes the operations of the Indian Corps as a subsidiary attack, designed with the object of distracting the enemy's attention and holding his troops to their ground. Further: "Portions of the 1st Corps assaulted the enemy's trenches at Givenchy. The Indian Corps attacked the Moulin du Piètre, while the 3rd Corps was directed against the trenches at Le Bridoux. These attacks started at daybreak and were at first successful all along the line. Later in the day the enemy brought up strong reserves, and after hard fighting and variable fortunes, the troops engaged in this part of the line reoccupied their original trenches at nightfall. They succeeded admirably, however, in fulfilling the rôle allotted to them, and in holding large numbers of the enemy away from the main attack."

The casualties of the Corps up to the 1st October, 1915, were as under:—

	Killed.	Wounded.	Missing.	Other deaths
British officers . .	267	628	86	3
Indian officers . .	100	322	50	6
Other ranks, British .	1734	8,103	2088	?
Other ranks, Indian .	2289	13,715	3131	594
Total . .	4390	22,768	5355	603

CHAPTER XXIV

THE CORPS LEAVES FRANCE FOR OTHER THEATRES OF WAR

Indian Corps front in October—Enemy's mining operations near Givenchy—Indian Army reserves—Failure of system admitted—Inferior quality of reinforcements—Remarks of Sir John French—Regiments in France reinforced by drafts from battalions in India—Danger of this system—Deficiency of suitable officer reinforcements—Consequent gradual deterioration of the Corps—Orders received for the Corps to move to other theatres of war—Corps relieved by the 10th November—Message from Indian Cavalry Corps—Special order by Sir John French—Last units of the Corps leave Marseilles on the 26th December, 1915—Message from His Majesty the King-Emperor.

At the commencement of October, 1915, the Indian Corps front extended for a distance of 10,825 yards; the 19th Division ran on the right from the La Bassée Canal to Farm Corner, and the line was continued northwards by the Lahore Division as far as Sunken Road. The Meerut Division had been withdrawn to refit after the heavy fighting of the 25th September, but on the 1st October the Bareilly Brigade was brought up to relieve Sirhind in the front line, the latter moving back into Army reserve. The weather for the greater part of the month was fine and cold, varied by short spells of mist and light rain.

On the 4th October a redistribution of the Corps on the same front was completed. By this disposition the Meerut Division held the southern portion of the line with the right of the Bareilly Brigade resting on the La Bassée Canal; the centre of the front was occupied by the 19th Division, and the northern section by Lahore, with the left of the Jullundur Brigade on Sunken Road.

The month passed without any events of special importance. The usual mining and counter-mining operations continued on Givenchy Ridge, which was pockmarked in every direction by the craters formed by previous explosions.

At 8.20 p.m. on the 7th October the first German mine was blown up, followed by others at 4.50 a.m., 4.55 a.m. and 4.57 a.m. on the 8th. Each of these explosions was preceded by heavy artillery and Minenwerfer fire on our support line, and was followed by intense rifle grenade and rifle fire. Our parapet was breached in several places, but the casualties were slight, amounting only to some 25 in all, of whom the majority were wounded. The gallant behaviour of Captain Park and No. 2 Company of the 2nd Black Watch on this occasion has already been described.

The question of reinforcements for the Indian Corps had from the commencement been a source of constant anxiety to Sir James Willcocks, and by this time matters had come to a head. The Indian Reserve organization has now been subjected to a thorough and practical test, and is admitted by the highest authorities to have failed completely. There is, then, no reason to enter into argument on the subject, and it is only necessary to explain the very grave consequences produced by the retention, against the oft-repeated advice of those in a position to judge, of an obsolete and dangerous system.

The Corps landed in France with a reserve of 10 per cent. available to fill gaps in the ranks. Before it reached the front, this reserve, owing to sickness, and the weeding out of unfit men, had practically been exhausted, leaving no immediately available reinforcements in France. The casualty lists at once commenced to swell, and battalions were reduced to a dangerous degree.

Owing to the fighting strength of British regiments in India being fixed at the low figure of 844, they were also affected, as for them too, at first, reinforcements were wholly inadequate.

As a result of the experience gained in this war, two indisputable facts stand out.

(*a*) None but the very best class of Indian troops is fit for European warfare, and then only when led by a sufficient number of trained British officers and stiffened by British units.

(*b*) As a general rule, an Indian soldier of over 40 years of age is unfit for service in the field, and many who can speak with authority put the limit at 35 years. Under the present system men may serve until they attain an aggregate of 25 years' service with the Colours and in the Reserve, when they become entitled to a pension of Rs. 3 per mensem. The natural result is that men are too often allowed to serve on, when quite unfit, for the sole purpose of qualifying for pension.

The Indian units were, generally speaking, of the very best class, and had it been possible to maintain them at their original level with a satisfactory supply of British officers, they could have continued indefinitely to play their part in Europe. The extension of the war had, however, by its innumerable calls on the Indian Army, rendered this impossible.

The first appearance of the Corps in the front line was on the 22nd October, 1914. In twelve days, *i.e.* on the 3rd November, the casualty list of the Indian units alone amounted to 44 British, 33 Indian officers and 1808 of other ranks. By the 1st December the total had increased to 133 British, 95 Indian officers and 4735 other ranks.

The importance of immediate reinforcements of a suitable type will be readily understood when it is remembered that the fighting strength of the Indian units of the two Divisions at this period amounted only to 9500 rifles, with 1700 sabres of the Secunderabad Cavalry Brigade.

How did the Indian system cope with this grave crisis ?

At the commencement of December, 1914, the Officer Commanding the Indian Base Depôt at Marseilles reported that a large number of men who had arrived as reinforcements had, on inspection, been found unfit for service. The total of such men on this occasion came to 331. These were divided into four classes :—

A. 68 pronounced unfit for service in Europe on medical grounds by a Board of Medical Officers.

B. 32 pronounced temporarily unfit.

C. 181 pronounced unfit by Depôt Commanders on military grounds as distinct from medical, *i.e.* old age, weakness, miserable physique, etc.

D. 50 unfit for lack of training. These were recruits of under 6 months' service *who had not fired a musketry course.*

The men of Class C. were mostly reservists who had been absent from the Colours for varying periods, and were nearly all old men with 20 or more years' service, entirely incapable of undergoing the rigours of a winter campaign in Europe. A story was current at the time that, at the inspection of this class, an aged man was asked whether he felt fit and keen. He replied that when he left Bombay, by the mercy of God, he had one upper tooth left. Putting his fingers in his mouth, he removed the one tooth and presented it for examination.

Class A. were at once returned to India, and Class B. went later. Class C., as far as possible, were employed on lines of communication. The training of Class D. was undertaken at the Base Depôt.

In addition to these, 94 men who actually reached the Corps were found unfit for service on account of *age, physical disability, and an absence of military spirit.*

So grave was the situation that Sir John French felt compelled to suggest that, unless men of the best quality were available to reinforce the Indian units in the field, it would be preferable to withhold reinforcements altogether, as inferior drafts not only served no useful purpose, but were an actual encumbrance to the army.

At the commencement of January, 1915, Sir John French further placed on record the fact that 876 men in all had been found unfit, amounting approximately to one-sixth of the reinforcements received up to that time. He noted further that, in addition to these, a considerable number of the reinforcements sent were unsatisfactory, as being far below the standard of military training and knowledge demanded by the present war. Apart from the useless expense involved in transporting, equipping and supplying inferior drafts, they were not only a source of actual danger in the field themselves, but tended to lower the efficiency of those with whom they were placed in contact.

Towards the end of January, 1915, Sir James Willcocks was able to report that the reinforcements then arriving from India were mostly of a very good quality. By this time a new system was being tried, and the drafts consisted partly of detachments from other regiments in India, while no reservist of over 15 years' service was then being sent to France. To continue this method indefinitely was obviously out of the question, as it would have entailed the depletion by degrees of the regiments on which depended the defence of India and the maintenance of internal order. The improved quality of these drafts, therefore, so far from proving the elasticity of the military organization, clearly indicated the probability that India would soon cease to send satisfactory reinforcements, while at the same time many of the best regiments still remaining in India would have suffered by furnishing those reinforcements.

Various other expedients were tried later. Men of Military Police Corps and of the local troops of Indian Chiefs were included in the drafts, but the result merely proved that the whole system had failed to stand the stress of war, the sole purpose for which it had been created.

A further and a very grave question was the supply of officers. The establishment of British officers in an Indian regiment is 13, including the medical officer. The losses of British officers from the commencement were very heavy, to illustrate which the case of one regiment may be quoted. This regiment during its service in France was officered by no less than 70 individuals. Many of these officers came from other regiments in India which could ill afford to lose them: others were from the Indian Army Reserve of Officers, who, gallant though they were, lacked experience and training, and frequently knowledge of the language spoken in the regiment. All battalions were thus heavily handicapped, as the officers and men for the most part were utterly unknown to each other. This bore especially heavily on the Gurkha battalions, the men of which speak no language but their own, and are therefore particularly dependent on their British officers, who are required to pass an examination in that language before they can be permanently appointed to a regiment.

Sufficient has perhaps been said, for in the face of the admission of the authorities that the system has completely broken down, the point requires no labouring.

The result was soon seen. Little by little the Corps deteriorated until, after the fighting on the 25th September, following so closely on Neuve Chapelle, Ypres, and the heavy losses in May, it was felt that the breaking point had been reached. Battalions had now become mere frameworks, skeletons of their former selves, held together only by the few officers and men of tried experience who still remained. How many these numbered can be gathered from the fact that on the 2nd October the casualties to date of Indian units were as follows:—

British officers, 483; Indian officers, 478; other ranks, 19,748; total, 20,709.

Again, to take the instance of two battalions. The 59th Rifles landed in France in 1914 with a strength of 13 British, 18 Indian officers, and 810 other ranks. By the commencement of November, 1915, no British, and only 4 Indian officers and 75 men were serving with the battalion who had not been absent through wounds or sickness for over ten days.

The 47th Sikhs, to apply the same test, had no British or Indian officers and only 28 men left.

For some time past rumours had been current of the impending transfer of the Corps to other theatres of war less remote from its natural base. It was therefore without surprise that information was received on the 31st October that the Indian Corps would be required to embark at Marseilles in the near future, leaving behind it in France the 19th Division which was to join the 11th Corps, the five Territorial battalions and the 4th King's (Liverpools), which belonged to the Special Reserve, as well as the headquarters Divisional Artillery and 3 Brigades R.F.A. (18-pounder) of the Lahore Division. The 11th Corps was to take over the front held by the Lahore and Meerut Divisions.

On the 4th November the relief of the two Indian Divisions by the 11th Corps commenced, and on the 6th the Meerut Division left the trenches for the last time, concentrating in the new billeting area north east of Aire, round Thiennes, Boeseghem, and Morbecque.

On the 7th November the following entrained for

Marseilles:—The Garhwal Brigade, 2/2nd Gurkhas, 107th Pioneers and the working battalion, followed on the 8th by the 4th Cavalry. On the 9th the Corps head quarters moved to Norrent Fontes from Merville.

By nightfall on the 10th the Indian Corps had been completely relieved from the line, which it had held so long and so valiantly.

Abstract of Casualties up to the 19th November, 1915.

	Killed.	Wounded.	Missing.	Other deaths.	Total.
British units—					
Officers . .	124	363	37	?	524
Other ranks .	1806	8388	2089	?	12,283
Total	1930	8751	2126	–	12,807
Indian units—					
British officers .	150	294	49	3	496
„ other ranks	4	34	–	9	47
Indian officers .	103	336	50	6	495
„ other ranks	2345	14,221	3148	661	20,375
Total	2602	14,885	3247	679	21,413
Staff—					
British officers .	2	8	–	–	10
„ other ranks	1	15	–	–	16
Indian officers .	–	–	–	–	—
„ other ranks	4	2	–	–	6
Grand Total	4539	23,661	5373	679	34,252

These figures represent the casualties of the Indian Corps proper, and do not include those of units temporarily attached, such as the 8th, 19th, 49th and 51st Divisions. Figures showing deaths from disease or wounds of British units are not immediately available.

In comparing the casualties it must be remembered

that the fighting strengths of British and Indian units were not the same. British units had 28 officers and 816 other ranks. Indian units had only 13 British officers, including the medical officer, 17 Indian officers and 723 other ranks. On the other hand, in number the Indian battalions largely exceeded the British units. From the date of its completion at the front to the commencement of January, 1915, on an average, the Corps consisted of 6 British and 20 Indian Infantry units. From January to the departure of the Corps it comprised 12 British and 20 Indian battalions.

Owing, however, to the fluctuations of casualties and the vagaries of the Indian Reserve system, the Indian battalions were seldom, if ever, as a whole up to their full fighting strength. For these reasons it has been found impossible at present to calculate with any sufficient degree of accuracy the percentages of losses of the British and Indian units. This will only be feasible at the conclusion of the war, when full data will be available.

On the 19th November the following telegram was received from the Indian Cavalry Corps :—

" All ranks of the Indian Cavalry Corps desire to convey their best wishes to their comrades of the Indian Corps, to wish them the best of luck in the future and to express their admiration of their gallantry and staunchness on many memorable occasions, and throughout long months of strenuous fighting under trying conditions, in which the honour and reputation of the Indian Army have been so splendidly maintained, and which will acquire added lustre in whatever circumstances the gallant Indian Corps may find itself."

To this message from soldiers to soldiers, the following reply was sent :—

"We, officers, N.C.O.s and men of the Indian Corps send our best thanks to our comrades of the Indian Cavalry Corps for their kind words of farewell, and for their appreciation of our endeavour to do our duty during the past year. We wish them the best of luck, and know that when the opportunity comes they will worthily uphold the best traditions of the Indian Army and add to the reputation they have already earned."

On the 22nd November the following special order of the day was issued by Field-Marshal Sir John French :—

"On the departure of the Indian Corps from my command, under which you have fought for more than a year, I wish to send a message of thanks to all officers, non-commissioned officers and men for the work you have done for the Empire. From the time you reached France you were constantly engaged with the enemy until the end of last year. After a few weeks' rest you returned to the trenches, and since then you have continually held some portion of the front line, taking part in the important and successful engagements of Neuve Chapelle and of Richebourg, and in the heavy fighting at the end of September. The Lahore Division was also engaged in the severe actions near Ypres in April and May. That your work has been hard is proved by the number of your casualties. The British troops of the Corps have borne themselves in a manner worthy of the best traditions of the army.

"The Indian Corps have also shown most praiseworthy courage under novel and trying conditions, both of climate and of fighting, and have not only upheld, but added to, the good name of the army which they represent. This is all the more praiseworthy in view of the heavy losses amongst British officers having deprived the Indian ranks of many trusted leaders whom they knew well and of the fact that the drafts necessary to maintain your strength have frequently had to be drawn from regiments quite unconnected with the units they were sent to reinforce. You have done your work here well, and are now being sent to another place where an unscrupulous enemy has stirred up strife against the King-Emperor. I send you all my good wishes for success in the part you will now be called on to play in this great war. I thank you for the services you have rendered while under my command, and trust that the united efforts of the Allies may soon bring the enemy to his knees and restore peace to the world."

By the 30th November the last troops of the Meerut Division had entrained for Marseilles, followed on the 9th December by the first detachments of the Lahore Division. By an order from General Head Quarters issued on the 8th December the Indian Army Corps ceased to exist as such. On the 26th December, 1915, the last transport conveying troops of the Indian Corps left Marseilles.

Owing to the fact that the troops entrained by driblets and that they embarked for the most part at night, there were no demonstrations on such a scale as those which greeted the arrival of the Indians in 1914; but wherever the troop trains stopped *en route*, the stations were crowded with warm-hearted French people who showed in the clearest manner their deep appreciation of the service rendered during the past 13 months.

On the 25th November a parade of representatives of the Indian Corps was held at Château Mazinghem, at which the following message of His Majesty the King-Emperor to the British and Indian troops of the Indian Army Corps in France was read by the Prince of Wales:—

"Officers, Non-Commissioned Officers and men of the Indian Army Corps.

"More than a year ago I summoned you from India to fight for the safety of My Empire and the honour of My pledged word on the battlefields of Belgium and France. The confidence which I then expressed in your sense of duty, your courage and your chivalry you have since then nobly justified.

"I now require your services in another field of action, but before you leave France I send My dear and gallant Son, the Prince of Wales, who has shared with My Armies the dangers and hardships of the campaign, to thank you in My name for your services and to express to you My satisfaction.

"British and Indian comrades-in-arms, yours has been a fellowship in toils and hardships, in courage and endurance often against great odds, in deeds nobly done and days of memorable conflict. In a warfare waged under new conditions and in particularly trying circumstances, you have worthily upheld the honour of the Empire and the great traditions of My Army in India.

"I have followed your fortunes with the deepest interest and watched your gallant actions with pride and satisfaction. I mourn with you the loss of many gallant officers and men. Let it be your consolation, as it was their pride, that they freely gave their lives in a just cause for the honour of their Sovereign and the safety of My Empire. They died as gallant soldiers, and I shall ever hold their sacrifice in grateful remembrance. You leave France with a just pride in honourable deeds already achieved and with my assured confidence that your proved valour and experience will contribute to further victories in the new fields of action to which you go.

"I pray God to bless and guard you, and to bring you back safely, when the final victory is won, each to his own home—there to be welcomed with honour among his own people."

CONCLUSION

On re-reading the chapters in which it has been attempted to tell the story of the Indian Corps in Flanders, the writers are most acutely conscious of their failure to reconstruct as it deserves that long and harrowing tale of anguish and heroism. Indeed, it is not easy to conceive of any literary resources which could faithfully describe the fortunes of any of those Corps belonging to the British Expeditionary Force which supported the terrible winter campaign of nineteen hundred and fourteen. Each Corps deserves and requires a separate historian. The account of the Indian Corps, which has been attempted in the above pages, has no claim to be called popular. The distinguished General who took the Corps to France has, it is understood, in preparation a volume of reminiscences, to be published after the war, of which it may be anticipated that his trenchant pen and vigorous character will find expression in a piquant treatment of many episodes. But the plan proposed to themselves by the authors, and it is hoped conscientiously carried out, has excluded a method of treatment, the interest of which would depend upon the constant presentment of dramatic incidents. They have rather attempted, to the best of their powers, the task of preparing a record, both continuous and complete, of all the Indian Corps did—whether at any given moment it was little or much—during the unforgettable days in which it played so great a part. Nor is it perhaps difficult to defend the method and principle of description which have been adopted.

Each year of the war has produced countless acts of heroism amongst individuals, and battles valiantly sustained by our Armies. The year nineteen hundred and fourteen witnessed, in the summer months, the anguish of the great retreat and the glorious vicissitudes of the Marne. Successive campaigns were rendered alike sombre and immortal by the battles of Neuve Chapelle, Loos, the Aubers Ridge and Festubert. Perhaps the red dawn of victory rose first in the blood-drenched and shell-pitted fields of the Somme. And even as we write, immense British and French Armies, in that greatest struggle of all which is the sequel of the Somme Battle, are making what may prove to be the final attempt to expel the enemy from the soil of France. Each of these struggles deserves—and it may be supposed that in the fullness of time it will receive—its own equipped historian: *Non carebit vate sacro.* But we make bold to think that the master historian of all—to whose task it will one day fall to disentangle and place in perspective the complex and baffling narrative of the British campaigns in France—will assign some special niche of glory to those who sustained the desperate defensive warfare which filled up the interval between the battle of the Marne and the battle of Neuve Chapelle.

It is true that the general public has now realized the decisive and critical nature of the first battle of Ypres; but it is open to grave doubt whether it has ever realized how anxious was every month, and indeed every week and day, during which the long-drawn battle lines deployed from the Aisne to the sea. When this movement on our side first began, it is evident that our higher Command was hopeful that it might be possible to outflank the enemy, and to turn their Aisne positions. But even if this attempt had seemed to them as difficult, and indeed hopeless, as it appears in the light of the comparative resources of the combatants as we know them to-day, it would still have been necessary to make the attempt in order to prevent the enemy doing so. From the moment that the movement began, it was hardly ever certain, and sometimes for considerable periods it seemed highly improbable, that the enemy could be pinned to their ground. Many most gallant offensives have been described in the preceding pages. But in the early stages of the struggle they were always local, and always essentially defensive in their character. He who records them and he who reads them must alike be struck by the complete hopelessness of these valiant attempts so cheerfully and so constantly made. When it is said that they were hopeless, it is not of course intended that each of them did not make an important, if not always a distinguishable, contribution to the ultimately successful defensive; but it is meant that the enterprises must have seemed over and over again tragically hopeless to the individuals who spent their lives upon them. And as we read of them in cold print, years afterwards, nothing is more poignant than to observe that the hero of one struggle, after incredible escapes, is the victim of another; and that if he escapes the second, inevitable death overtakes him in the third. A close study of the diaries of this period leaves on the mind the impression, at once vague and extremely vivid, of constant Homeric fighting, disclosing at every moment deeds of individual valour which were never equalled, nor approached, by the heroes whom Homer has made immortal. And to those who realize how great is the confusion of trench warfare, particularly at night, how the attention of each individual is necessarily given to his own fortunes and not to the deeds of his comrades, it is a tragic reflection that so many heroes worthy of any distinction which could embellish valour, or of any glory which could mitigate death, have perished without a record and without a witness. No research, however careful, among diaries, no inquiries among survivors, be the chronicler never so industrious, can complete or half complete the Roll of Honour. We can only accept and reverently record the fact of death. And where a soldier has died on the field of battle for his country, perhaps no decoration could add to—and no description further ennoble—that which he has done. But the universal experience of all ages has shown that a rare and precious consolation is afforded to father and mother, to wife and child of the dead, by reading and understanding, as far as it may be understood, how and in what adventure the fallen died. Believing this to be true, we have throughout made it our first and principal object, at whatever risk of weariness, to rescue from forgetfulness the names of British or Indian soldiers of every rank, whose ascertained deeds have entitled them to be counted among the immortals.

Much discussion took place when it was first announced that Indian soldiers were to be employed in France as to whether the decision was judicious. Many high authorities felt grave doubts upon this question ; and nothing was more noticeable to those who joined the Staff at Marseilles than that some of its most experienced members believed that they were taking part in a very hazardous experiment. And it was a hazardous experiment. Even in its infancy this war made it clear that the human material engaged in it was to be more hardly tried than the soldiers of any nation, in any war in the world's history, have ever been tried. It was already evident that the war was one certain to make supreme demands even upon European troops fighting in a quarrel which in the main they have understood, and which was so presented as to make a strong moral appeal to their duty and their patriotism. No man could be bold enough to predict the result of flinging Oriental troops into these horrible scenes, in a pitiless climate, to lose life and limb in a quarrel remote from their own experiences, uninspired by fears on behalf of their own people, or even of their own property. It was thought necessary to give six months' training in England to the superb raw material which formed the first Canadian Division ; and many months were allowed to pass before it seemed desirable to send a Territorial Division as a unit to France. And yet those who knew the Indian soldier best were confident, however sudden his immersion into the Great War might be, that his traditions, his loyalty and his sense of duty would carry him through. And they did.

But in fact the discussion is futile as to whether the experiment was risky or not, just as it is tedious to insist upon the admitted risks undertaken by Mr. Asquith's Government when the British Expeditionary Force was sent to France. In each case a hazardous experiment was undertaken by a great nation which was concerned to defend, by the best available methods, however hazardous, its own security and the existence of its Allies. At the moment when the Indian Corps was detailed for service in France the very existence of the Empire required that the experiment should be made. If a quarter only of those who landed in France had stood firm, and the rest had fled, it would still have been worth while to despatch the whole for the sake of that quarter. The cool and high courage of Lord French, the laconic and soldierly quality of his despatches, obscured to some extent the intensity of the crisis which existed at the moment when the Indian Corps began to arrive at Marseilles. He who wishes to form an opinion upon the opportuneness of the Indian contribution should reflect how swiftly the first arrivals were rushed into the firing line; how short was the period of concentration conceded to General Willcocks; and how imperious was the necessity which flung Indian Sappers and Miners into the streets of Neuve Chapelle as assaulting infantry.

It is clear, when once it is realized that decisions in these matters must be conditioned, first upon necessity, and secondly upon the resources available to meet necessity, that it would have been right to make the experiment even if it had wholly failed. But in fact the experiment almost wholly succeeded.

The time has not yet come when any judicious

purpose can be served by explaining the qualification to the claim that in the main the Indian troops engaged arose, with rare and intrepid courage, to the height of the crisis which summoned them to the trenches of Flanders.

It is unnecessary to point out—for every one knows it—how much the Indian troops owed to their British officers, and to the British regiments with which they were brigaded. Indeed nothing is more profoundly touching than the *esprit de corps*, animating all ranks, which forbids them to apportion credit as between British and Indian regiments. They were coadventurers and gallant comrades. They trod together the Valley of the Shadow of Death. It is in this way that they conceived of their own relationship, and so it may be left.

But a singular tribute must be paid to the British officers serving in Indian regiments. The relationship between such an officer and his men is of a very special kind. In no army in the world are the relations between officer and private on a more admirable and soldierly basis than in the British Army. But there are in this matter some features in the Indian Army which are quite unique. Among the private soldiers, and even among the Indian officers, the degree of dependence upon the officer is on the whole greater than is known, or perhaps has ever been known, in any army in the world. And side by side with that dependence, there has grown up on the part of the British officer, however young he may be, the habit and frame of mind of a father, and sometimes, when the occasion requires it, even more the habit and frame of mind of a mother. Each officer looks upon his men as his children. This was the spirit in which a subaltern poet * addressed the fathers of his fallen men :—

> "You were only their fathers;
> I was their officer."

Compared with the officer of a British regiment, the British officer in an Indian regiment must contend against many drawbacks. He misses the common sense of humour, the common outlook upon life, and the common store of inherited associations which a British officer has with men of British blood. He does not inevitably think, as a British officer in a British regiment instinctively and in the very moment of crisis thinks, of the same things at the same moral and psychological angle. And this community of range counts for much in times when human nature is racked and tortured. At such moments the Eton boy and the slum recruit often discover a common point of view derived from obscure affiliations which can neither be explained nor even analyzed. The most intuitive and sympathetic British officer of an Indian battalion can never be quite sure whether his outlook upon events, where those events have transcended their experience and his, retains any contact with that of his men. East is still East; West is still West.

But if a British officer in an Indian regiment is at a disadvantage in these respects, he receives in exchange much which, for the purpose of fashioning an admirable military instrument, must be put in the other scale. If he is the right sort of officer (and they nearly all are), his men bestow upon him, almost from the day he is gazetted, a degree of respect and a depth of loyalty which bring responsibility to the

* Lieutenant Hodgson, M.C.

most volatile and maturity to the most boyish. And there springs from this mutual relationship an atmosphere of all others the most fruitful in gallant enterprises. The British officer knows that his men will obey an order because he gives it, because he sets the example, and because therefore (so the simple reasoning goes) it must be for the best. And the Indian soldier yields the same unquestioning obedience to a trusted officer which a boy who has a profound affection and admiration for his father gives to the admonitions of that father. It is, therefore, no exaggeration to say that when the Corps landed in Marseilles, every battalion was superbly officered, and this circumstance was rightly relied upon by those who believed that the Army would rise to the extreme demands so shortly to be made upon it. And as long as each unit retained a fair proportion of those British officers who had sailed with it from India, and who still seemed to afford some connecting link with home, the battalions retained, even amid the terrible surroundings of Flanders, an astonishing degree of self-confidence, resilience and *esprit de corps.* But a far higher trial came later. A bloody toll was soon taken of the British officers. The Germans were quite acute enough to realize the vital part which they played in the Indian Army. The machine gunners and snipers received urgent orders in this regard.

And so the roll of officers who lost their lives or were hopelessly maimed grew ever and ever longer.

It soon happened that many battalions lost every officer who in far-away India had instructed them in the military art, and who, in the eyes of the Indian troops, were all that remained to remind them, with familiar authority, of their homes and their duty. They felt their bereavement as orphans, old enough to realize their sorrow, feel it. Every ingenuity and every conceivable resource were exhausted by the authorities in the attempt to supply new officers to take the place of the fallen. A constant succession of gallant young gentlemen was drafted from India and from home to fill the gaps in the ranks. But it was not possible to keep pace completely with the losses. And even where the numbers were forthcoming, there was hardly leisure to establish in the necessary degree acquaintance and confidence. This would have mattered comparatively little in a British regiment. Provided his officer is competent, considerate, and brave, the British soldier can support many changes and substitutions in his commands. No such adaptability can be expected, and little is in fact found, among the Indian battalions. Foremost, therefore, among the trials and the difficulties which the Indian troops had to bear, and to which in the main they proved stoically equal, were the cruel losses of officers to whom they had become devoted, and whom they had been in the habit of following through any dangers to any objective.

The question has been much discussed whether India has on the whole made the contribution to the necessities of the Empire which might have been expected from her teeming populations and her great resources. It would be difficult to argue that, if everything had been clearly realized at the beginning of the war, it would have been impossible to train and equip more soldiers in India. And it seems certain that almost an unlimited contribution was, and is, available in India for labour or garrison battalions. But it must not be forgotten that the very decision to employ so many Indian troops immediately on active service removed very many of those who, and who alone, were available for the purposes of instructing recruits; and it is equally important to remember that ever growing numbers of British recruits were at that very time in the most urgent and indeed critical need of officers for training purposes. It was decided, and rightly decided, that the first and paramount duty of the British Government was to provide instruction for the new British Armies. And in the first few months of the struggle everything was properly sacrificed to this view. Thus, on the outbreak of war, there were about 550 officers of the Army in India on leave in this country. All of them were immediately borrowed by the War Office to help in the work of organizing the new Armies. From the beginning of the war until the end of nineteen hundred and sixteen, over 2600 British officers have been drawn from India for Imperial purposes, apart from those who accompanied their units abroad. And the total number of British officers in India when war broke out was less than 5000. On the outbreak of war, the Indian Army Reserve of Officers consisted of forty members. It consists to-day of over 2200, of whom 800 are on active service. Apart from the Indian Army Reserve of Officers, commissions have been given in the Indian Army to 271 cadets from Quetta and Wellington, where military schools modelled upon Sandhurst have been established since the war began. These facts are recalled because, in considering and appraising the effort which India has made, it is very important to bear in mind that she, like the rest of the Empire, was called upon, on the outbreak of war, for an immense effort of improvisation; that improvisation was, from the nature of the case, more difficult for her than for any other part of the Empire; and that in carrying out the task of improvisation, her imperious needs were at every stage subordinated by the compulsion of events to those of others. To these conditions it must be added—familiar as the observation must be to all readers—that the martial races of India do not by any means form an overwhelming proportion of the total population of India. A brief account and analysis of the fighting races living in this great peninsula is contained in an appendix to this History. It is not necessary here to carry the comparison into details, but it is sufficient to point out that before the war many competent observers were of opinion that among two or three of the most illustrious soldier races of India recruiting had been pushed as far as was likely to prove in long perspective expedient or fruitful.

It is not maintained that the fullest possible use has been made of the human reserves of India. The question is too large to be argued here, and it is only distantly relevant to the subject of this work. But the critic, in measuring what India has done, should never forget the extreme difficulty occasioned by the shortage of officers who could speak the necessary languages. Still less should he forget the absolute irrelevance of comparisons and homilies based upon the total population of the country.

It is possible that later writers will answer the criticisms which have been brought by saying that an autocratic conqueror of India, who was preparing for war as Germany was preparing, could and would have made incomparably more of the resources of India than was made by Great Britain. But he may equally decide, in the light of the difficulties referred to above, that the contribution of India on its purely military side has been of surprising importance, and as great as could have been provided, during a period of all-round improvisation, by an Imperial Government which had neglected all preparations for continental warfare. Indian troops have fought with heroic endurance in France, in Egypt, at Aden, on the Suez Canal, in Gallipoli, in East Africa, in West Africa and in Mesopotamia. They were the first of the overseas troops to man with untried qualities the sodden trenches of Flanders. They furnished the first bulwark of British East Africa. They flung back the first Turkish attack on the Suez Canal. The Army in Mesopotamia, alike in its failures and its triumphs, was in the main an Indian Army based upon India. Nearly five hundred thousand men—British and Indian—have left India since the war began to take part in one theatre or another, though before the war the whole Indian Army only amounted to two hundred and thirty-six thousand men. All the units of the Indian forces have been kept supplied with drafts, and on the whole, after the first collapse, with efficient drafts. The establishments of the cavalry regiments in India have been increased by 20 per cent. and the establishments of the infantry regiments by 40 per cent. New units have been created, drawn only partly from the classes or races which were recruited before the war; and nearly thirty thousand Indians of all classes have become associated in one capacity or another with the Medical Services overseas. Nor should the admirable work often done by the Imperial Service Troops be omitted from this survey. The Mysore and Patiala Lancers and the Bikanir Camel Corps are serving in Egypt. The Jodhpur Lancers did good work in France. The Kashmir Rifles, the Jhind Infantry and the Faridkot Sappers were specially praised by General Smuts in East Africa. The Maler Kotla Sappers will not soon be forgotten in companies where brave Engineers meet.

Enough has been said to show that too ready assent must not be given to the more sweeping criticisms directed at those responsible for military policy in India. The topic has been considered in this chapter at some length, for it is by no means irrelevant to the fortunes of the Indian Corps in Flanders. The power of making good the wastage of officers and of sending drafts in substitution for casualties depended greatly upon the demands which were being simultaneously pressed upon India from other quarters. Whatever view is taken of this larger question, the belief is confidently expressed by the authors that every future military historian will do justice to the sufferings and to the stamina of those Indian troops who took part in the Great Flanders Campaign. In an earlier part of this work it was stated that they were destined to a fate as devastating as that which overtook the first British Expeditionary Force. About twenty-four thousand men formed the two divisions which landed at Marseilles. In less than a year more than thirty thousand drafts were sent from India to replace casualties. In other words, *in about eight months six thousand more troops were despatched for the single purpose of replacing the killed, the wounded and the sick than the force contained when it landed.* And the Corps, the original personnel of which had been so completely wiped out, was afterwards sent to Mesopotamia, where it added, if possible, to its glory, and made further and bitter sacrifices in health and life.

Their achievements in this field must be left for others to describe. Our task is completed. We have traced the fortunes, alike in failure and success, of the brave men who fought among the chivalry of France and Britain—equals by the side of equals—against the German legions which swarmed upon Calais in the winter of nineteen hundred and fourteen. May those who survive live long to keep alive by their memories the traditions of martial ardour in India. And upon the heroic dead may the earth rest lightly.

APPENDIX I

DESCRIPTION OF THE INDIAN ARMY

BEFORE this war Indian troops had proved their loyalty and worth in many other parts of the world where smaller issues were involved—in China, Egypt, the Sudan, Ashanti, Somaliland and the Aden Hinterland, as well as in numerous Indian Frontier operations—but never, since the Indian Mutiny, had their loyalty been put to such a test as in the crisis of 1914, which menaced the very existence of the Empire itself.

For the first time Indians were called upon to fight in Europe in a "White Man's War." The manner in which the call to arms from Britain was answered from India, disclosing a brotherhood which seemed not only strange but incomprehensible to the apostles of "Kultur," has been already described.

It will be as well to correct at once a misconception which arose at the commencement of the war as to the status of the Indian Army. It was evident from many remarks which appeared in English newspapers that the Indian Army was believed to consist of volunteers whose services for the war were placed at the disposal of the Empire by the Ruling Chiefs of India.

Certainly the Indian troops were and are volunteers, but in precisely the same way as the British Army, prior to the introduction of compulsory service, was composed of volunteers. They are, however, regular troops, bound by an oath of allegiance to serve their Sovereign under any circumstances and in any part of the world. With the exception of a small force of Imperial Service troops, the

Indian regiments which fought in Europe were as much soldiers of the King as any regiment of Guards, and equally bound to obey his orders. They were ordered to come to Europe, and they came. It is the spirit in which they came, not the fact of their coming, which compels our esteem and admiration.

The purpose of this Appendix is to give a brief and simple account of the various peoples from which the units of the Indian Army Corps were drawn and the different forces which they compose.

It has been well said that the natives of India are "Warriors by tradition and descent." The saying is on the whole, but not entirely, true. Certain classes and tribes appear to be quite without physical courage and unfit for any military service, and among them may be found some of the finest-looking people of India. This would naturally render any system of universal military service unsuitable to the country; but such a system would be as unnecessary as it is unsuitable, the bulk of the people of India being brave and warlike men to whom military service is a source of great honour and prestige, looked upon by them as affording the most fitting career open to a man, whatever his birth or rank.

A clear and accurate description of the various classes of Indian soldiers is a matter of some difficulty. It cannot be dealt with completely by reference to race, locality or regiment. There are other matters necessary to consider, such as caste, religion, custom, temperament, and tradition; and there is so much consequent overlapping of features and characteristics, that scientific or methodical treatment of the subject is scarcely possible. For the present purpose it may suffice to say that the organization of the Indian Army is based mainly on considerations of race, religion, and locality. Thus, we have soldiers of distinct races: the Rajputs, Pathans, Jats, and Gurkhas; of various religions: the Sikhs, Hindus, and Mahomedans; of different localities: the Mahrattas, Dogras, Madrasis, and Punjabis, although it can hardly be said that any of these should be exclusively so classified. The matter may, perhaps, be made fairly clear by the following short account of some of the principal classes and types of fighting men found in the Indian Army.

The Sikhs may with justice be considered the most important class among our Indian soldiers. Not only are they the best known to Englishmen of all the fighting men of India, with the possible exception of the Gurkhas, but they bulk more largely than any other class in the Indian Army. The Sikhs are not, strictly speaking, a distinct race: they are really a community, bound together by a spiritual tie, the Sikh religion. Amongst them there are a variety of sub-divisions of widely divergent origin. Thus the Jats are descended from the Scythians, the Khattris from the Aryans, while the Mazbis, from whom the Pioneer Regiments are largely recruited, are of aboriginal ancestry.

The home of the Sikh is the Punjab. He is generally a fine tall man of strong physique and stately bearing, with the manly virtues inculcated by his religion strongly developed. Tobacco is forbidden to him. His hair is never cut, being worn coiled up on the top of the head, while his beard is drawn back over his ears and tucked under his turban; this is large and often surmounted by a steel quoit with a razor-like edge, which can be thrown with great force and accuracy.

The chief traits of the Sikhs are a love of military adventure and a desire to make money, a combination which has led them to accept military or police service in Burma, China, Africa and other countries beyond the seas.

In the Sikh wars of 1846 and 1849 they fought the British in a manner which compelled admiration for their military genius and prowess, displaying soldierly qualities of the highest order. Since the annexation of the Punjab in the latter year, they have been our loyal adherents, and it speaks volumes for the personality of the British officer that within eight years after the war of 1849 the Sikhs were fighting by our side in the Indian Mutiny.

Three class regiments of Sikhs formed part of the Indian Corps in France, the 15th Ludhiana Sikhs, the 47th Sikhs, and the 34th Sikh Pioneers. The community was, however, largely represented also in the 27th, 33rd, 69th, and 89th Punjabis, and the 57th, 58th, and 59th Rifles, in which the Sikh companies varied from one to four.

The Jats mostly come from the Punjab, Rajputana, Agra, and Oudh. They are a thoroughbred race, generally considered to be of the same stock as, or closely allied to, the Rajputs. In one characteristic, however, they greatly differ from the latter. The Rajput disdains every employment or profession except that of bearing arms; the Jat is generally a landowner engaged chiefly in agriculture, a kind of manual labour especially despised by the haughty Rajput. By religion the Jats are Hindus. In appearance they are tall, large-limbed, and handsome, and they are usually remarkable for their toughness and capacity for enduring the greatest fatigue and privation. They are considered very fine horse-soldiers. In the Mutiny they distinguished themselves greatly against the rebels, and they have since served us well in Afghanistan and other places.

The only class regiment of Jats in the Indian Corps was the 6th Jats.

The inhabitants of the North-West Frontier of India are practically entirely and purely Musalman. From these parts come the Pathans, represented in the Indian Army Corps by a varying number of companies in the 40th Pathans and other units, such as the 27th and 33rd Punjabis, and the 57th, 58th, and 59th Rifles. The Pathans are divided into innumerable clans and are said to be of Semitic descent, even going so far as to call themselves "Beni Israel" (Children of Israel), and their claim is borne out by their features, which are distinctly of a Jewish type.

The Pathan is a tall handsome man, as a rule built in an athletic mould. His easy but swaggering gait speaks of an active life among the mountains, where he engages in constant feud, frequently hereditary, which makes him what he is, an ideal raider or skirmisher, full of dash, but often wanting in cohesion and power of steady resistance, unless led by British officers.

The Afridis come from the Peshawar border, the Khyber Pass, and the surrounding district. They are members of a Pathan tribe, probably of Rajput origin. Intensely democratic and independent in their own home, they make splendid soldiers under good leadership, excelling, like other hillmen, as skirmishers. It has been said that the Afridi has the vices and virtues of all Pathans in an enhanced degree. Casual observers indeed have ascribed to him more vices than virtues, depicting him as ruthless, treacherous and avaricious; but Sir Robert Warburton, who, with his eighteen years' intimate acquaintance with this race, may be accepted as an authority on the subject writes thus :—

"The Afridi lad from his earliest childhood is taught by the circumstances of his existence and life to distrust all mankind, and very often his near relations, heirs to his small plot of land by right of inheritance, are his deadliest enemies. Distrust of all mankind, and readiness to strike the first blow for the safety of his own life, have therefore become the maxims of the Afridi. If you can overcome this mistrust, and be kind in words to him, he will repay you by great devotion, and he will put up with any punishment you like to give him, except abuse." *

The Dogras are Hindus from the district lying between the rivers Chenab and Sutlej on the slopes of the Western Himalayas. Their classification is rather geographical than racial. They are mostly men of high caste and of considerable strength of character. They are noted for their calm courage and obedience to orders, and, as a rule, are thoroughly reliable in moments of peril. In appearance they somewhat resemble the Sikhs, but are rather less in height, more sparely built, and of fairer complexion than most Indians.

* "Eighteen Years in the Khyber," pp. 342-3.

The only Dogra regiment with the Indian Corps was the 41st, but the class was represented by companies in other battalions.

Although the 129th Baluchis took a prominent part in much of the fighting, the name is a misnomer, as the genuine Baluchi is not now enlisted. The 129th consists of 2 companies of Punjabi Musalmans, 3 of Mahsuds, 3 of other Pathans.

The Gurkhas are the sturdy hillmen of Nepal, probably better known, by name at least, to the average Englishman than any other class of Indian soldier. They are a mixture of Mongol and Rajput, the former, as can easily be perceived from their features, predominating. Their appearance is so distinctive and so uniform that it has been said that they look as if they had been issued from the quartermaster's stores. In many ways they resemble the Japanese, being usually little more than five feet in height, but they are of much sturdier build and differ from the Japanese in expression.

There is much about the Gurkha which especially appeals to the British soldier; his friendliness, cheeriness, and adaptability make him easier to get on with than other classes. The present trench warfare is the very antithesis of the Gurkha's idea of fighting. A born shikari, he is in his glory in hill or jungle operations where his sporting instincts can have full play and he has plenty of elbow room. His native weapon is the kukri, a long curved knife with a keen cutting edge and a heavy back. With this he can cut down a tree or a man, or sharpen a pencil with equal skill.

A number of Gurkha battalions served with the Corps in France, namely, the 1st Battalion 1st King George's Own Gurkha Rifles, the 2nd Battalion 2nd King Edward's Own, the 2nd Battalion 3rd Queen Alexandra's Own, the 1st Battalion 4th, the 2nd Battalion 8th, and the 1st Battalion 9th Gurkha Rifles.

The Garhwalis are inhabitants of Garhwal, in the Himalayas, to the west of Nepal. They so closely resemble their neighbours, the Gurkhas, that they have frequently been confused with them. Although they are not generally so thick-set and muscular as the Gurkhas, their resemblance is emphasized by their similar uniforms and weapons, including the kukri. It is said they sometimes complain that their heroic deeds go to swell the credit of the Gurkhas, in consequence of the confusion between the two races and the common ignorance of their separate identity. They are capable of great endurance and can exist for long periods without food or drink.

The Garhwalis were represented in France by the 1st and 2nd Battalions 39th Garhwal Rifles.

The Mahrattas come from the Central Provinces, the Deccan, and the Konkan. They are comparatively small men, without the elegant proportions and strength of the Sikh and Pathan or the sturdiness of the Gurkha, but with very fine constitutions and a tremendous capacity of endurance, which keep them fit for service under conditions which would disable most men. The 3rd Sappers and Miners, the 107th Pioneers, and the 125th Rifles each contained a small element of this class.

The Musalmans, or soldiers of the Mahomedan faith, come from various districts of India, their different classes being distinguished generally by reference to their respective localities. Thus, we have the Punjabi Musalmans, Madrasi Musalmans, Hindustani Musalmans, Deccani Musalmans, and others. Of these the Punjabi Musalmans may be considered the most important, at least as regards numbers. Coming, as the Musalmans do, from various races, their quality is not uniform, but they are good all-round soldiers, with an attachment to their officers which is proverbial. They may, on the whole, be said to be steady and reliable rather than brilliant in any particular respect.

From such men as those described above, and a few other classes of less importance numerically, the Indian Forces have been raised. Passing over the irregular forces of the great Indian Chiefs, with which we need not concern ourselves for the present purpose, we have the Regular

2 K

Indian Army and the Imperial Service Troops, composed of natives of India. The former are directly employed by the Government of India; the latter are specially raised and maintained by Indian rulers themselves and are kept distinct from their ordinary troops, in order that they may be placed at the disposal of the Government when occasion requires.

The French appear to have been the first Europeans to raise Indian regiments during their short period of ascendancy in the middle of the eighteenth century. The English East India Company soon followed their example, and by 1759, two years after the battle of Plassey, had about six regular Indian battalions in Madras, and a few years later, similar units in Bombay and Bengal. These "Presidency Armies" grew and developed during the wars of the later part of the century, and by 1795, when a general reconstruction of the Indian forces took place, we find about 24,000 such troops in Bengal, a similar number in Madras, and 9000 in Bombay, including infantry, cavalry, and artillery. A further reorganization and renumbering took place in 1824. During this period and up to the Mutiny of 1857 these forces again and again rendered us good service, not only in India itself, but in many places overseas, especially during the Napoleonic Wars. As early as 1762, Indian troops from Madras assisted in the capture of Manila; in 1797, forces from Madras and Bengal helped at the capture of Ceylon; and in 1801 Bombay infantry were with us in Egypt. For nearly a century prior to the Mutiny, Indian soldiers had served us so well and had shown such loyalty and attachment to their English officers, that it was difficult to credit the news of their revolt in 1857. On the whole, in fact, the Indian armies remained loyal, the Mutiny being practically confined to the soldiers of Bengal. The armies of Madras and Bombay generally stood by us; so did the Sikhs and Gurkhas; whilst Pathans and Punjabis came freely to our assistance. It may indeed be doubted whether the bulk of the Bengal soldiery were themselves essentially disloyal. They appear rather to have been misled and seduced from their loyalty by a few unprincipled leaders.

The Mutiny, with its consequent transfer of India to the Crown, resulted in a remodelling of the Indian forces, or rather, in the formation of a new Royal Army in place of the Company's Army. The part taken in the Mutiny by the native artillery of Bengal determined the Government to restrict the employment of Indians as artillerymen in the future to a very few light mountain batteries. The cavalry, with some exceptions in Madras, was organized on the "Silladar" system, the main principle of which is that the trooper provides his own horse, uniform, and equipment, with the exception of firearms, and receives considerably higher pay than a soldier of the Non-Silladar Cavalry. This system has been found to appeal to the best classes of horsemen and to produce splendid cavalry.

As regards the Army generally one of the most important questions to be settled was whether there should be "class regiments," or "class companies" and "class squadrons," that is, whether a regiment should consist solely of one race, or members of one religion, or whether the different companies only of a regiment should be so uniformly constituted. In the old army, men of various races or creeds were mixed in a manner which was not, at this later time, considered advisable. Ultimately, most of the regiments became class-company regiments, the Gurkha, Brahman, Rajput, Dogra, Jat, and some of the Sikh regiments remaining entirely homogeneous. So we find, in several of the Punjabi and Sikh regiments, distinct companies of Punjabi Musalmans, Pathans, Sikhs, Dogras, and Afridis; in Mahratta regiments, distinct companies of Mahrattas and Musalmans; in Baluchi regiments, distinct companies of Mahsuds and other Pathans, and Punjabi Musalmans; and other similar combinations.

Since the Mutiny, many changes and reforms in the administration of the Army have been carried out. In 1895 the three Presidency Armies, *i.e.* those of Bengal,

Madras, and Bombay, each with separate administration and Commander-in-Chief, were abolished, being replaced by four Lieutenant-Generals' commands with a Commander-in-Chief of the whole. These reforms were carried on and developed by Lord Kitchener during his term as Commander-in-Chief in India from 1902 to 1909. He abolished the old system of five commands, and at the present day there are two Armies, the Northern and the Southern, each commanded by a Lieutenant-General with his own staff, the supreme command of the whole Indian forces being vested, under the Governor-General in Council, in the Commander-in-Chief, assisted by the Head Quarters Staff.

The Regular Indian Army is now * composed of 39 regiments of Cavalry and 139 battalions of Infantry, besides Mountain Artillery and Sappers and Miners, numbering in all about 160,000 Indian ranks. The system of enlistment is entirely voluntary, recruits being admitted between the ages of 16 and 25, their height and measurements varying for different services. The number of applicants for service is frequently in excess of the vacancies, especially in the Silladar Cavalry.

The superior officers in every Indian regiment are British. The highest rank of the Indian officers in Cavalry regiments is the Risaldar-Major, who is the confidential adviser of the British Commandant in matters relating to the Indian ranks. He may be likened to our rank of Major. Next come the Risaldars and Ressaidars, of whom there are seven in a regiment, answering roughly to our Captains. Each half squadron has its Jemadar, who may be described as the Indian Lieutenant, an officer of this rank also acting as Woordie-Major, or Indian Adjutant. Immediately below these come the Kot Daffadar, or Quartermaster-Sergeant, who is the senior noncommissioned officer, and other Daffadars or Sergeants.

In the Infantry and other branches the corresponding ranks are the Subadar-Major, Subadars, the Jemadars,

* 1917.

of whom one is the Indian Adjutant, the Havildar-Major, the Quartermaster-Havildar, Havildars or Sergeants, and the Naiks or Corporals.

A private in the Cavalry is called a Sowar and in the Infantry a Sepoy.

The other great force of Indian troops upon which we can rely in our hour of need consists of soldiers of the great Feudatory Chiefs of India, specially designed for Imperial purposes, and known as the Imperial Service Troops. They are raised and maintained by the Indian rulers, and are composed entirely of Indian officers and men of the State to which the particular corps belongs, although British officers assist in such matters as training and equipment. They had their origin in 1885, in consequence of the fear of an attack by Russia on the North-West Frontier, at a time when the Indian Army had been reduced after the Afghan War. The danger of the situation impressed the Indian rulers with the necessity of being ready to assist the Government of India in its defence. The Nizam of Hyderabad placed his troops at the disposal of the Government and offered to contribute a large sum of money for the purpose of Imperial defence. Other rulers followed suit, the result of the movement being that almost every State of any size contributed a quota to the Imperial Service Troops. The ready manner in which these forces were placed at the disposal of the Government at the commencement of the present war demonstrates strongly their great importance to the Empire which they had already served so well in China, Somaliland, Chitral, Tirah, and other parts of the world.

Three decorations are especially reserved for the Indian ranks.

1. "The Order of British India," conferred on Indian commissioned officers for long, faithful, and honourable service, has two classes, which carry with them the titles of "Sardar Bahadur" and "Bahadur" respectively.

2. "The Indian Order of Merit," given for personal bravery, irrespective of rank or service. It is divided into

three classes, advancement to a higher class being granted to a man who is already in possession of the next lower class on again distinguishing himself. Each class of both these orders carries with it extra monthly pay.

3. "The Indian Distinguished Service Medal," which is awarded for individual instances of distinguished service in peace or on active service.

APPENDIX II

HEALTH OF THE INDIAN TROOPS IN FRANCE

It was feared that the rapid transition from the dry, warm climate of India to the cold and damp of Flanders would lead to a great increase of sickness among the troops, both British and Indian. These fears happily proved to be unfounded.

In peace time a daily average of 3 per 1000 of admissions to hospital was calculated as a probable standard for war conditions. In practice, it was found to work out at 2 per 1000, and as improvements were made in our method of trench warfare, in the shape of better dug-outs and the draining of trenches, even this average tended to decrease.

This remarkable result must be largely ascribed to the skill and self-sacrificing zeal of the Royal Army Medical Corps and the Indian Medical Service, under the command of Colonel (now Brigadier-General) W. W. Pike, C.M.G., D.S.O., R.A.M.C.

The work of the medical branch of the Service is not one which comes very prominently into the limelight. Its chief reward is found in the admiration and gratitude of the troops over whose health and general well-being the medical officers keep such careful watch.

It was expected that pulmonary affections, such as pneumonia and bronchitis, would be common, but these, as well as malaria and dysentery, were rare, while gastric diseases due to changes of food and water were almost unknown.

Influenza and trench fever occurred among the Indians in much the same proportion as amongst the British. The former, however, were rather more prone to "trench feet" than the latter; on the other hand, they were practically free from that new and insidious disease of the trenches, Albuminuria, although the British in the same area suffered to a considerable degree

Sanitation has been defined as the art of practically applying the laws of hygiene to individual environments. Conservancy is that branch of sanitation which deals with the disposal of waste products. Now, as hygiene is the science of health maintenance, it is obvious that the sanitation of an army in the field is a vital factor in military efficiency.

Those who have lived in India, even for a short period, learn intuitively the elements of sanitation. Deprived of the conveniences of modern civilization, they must adopt the more primitive methods of sanitation and conservancy for their own comfort as well as health.

Indians are being daily educated in these matters, and in regiments, owing to the class of men and the discipline involved, sanitation had reached a high standard before the war. All ranks of the Indian Army Corps therefore entered the field with a sound working knowledge of the important questions of sanitation and conservancy. They not only maintained but improved the standard, as was shown by the health of the troops under very trying and novel conditions of climate and surroundings.

Further adjuncts to health were introduced, such as drying rooms for clothes, laundries, and baths.

In the summer of 1915, when the fly pest was at its worst, a Special Commission was sent to France by the British Museum to investigate the causes and advise as to its prevention. In a subsequent circular the Commission specially commented on the good efforts of the Indian Army Corps to combat this plague, in the following words: "The Commission desires to express its admiration of the able and energetic manner in which potential breeding-places of flies have been dealt with throughout the area occupied by the Indian Corps."

This particular, small perhaps in itself, sufficiently indicates the work done and the importance attached to sanitation by all branches of the Medical Service with the Indian Army Corps.

The method of dealing with the wounded in trench warfare necessitated much consideration, and all existing systems had to be revised and adapted to the new conditions.

It must be remembered that the almost continuous shell fire made the task of the removal of wounded a very difficult and dangerous operation, and the success with which it was carried out speaks for the bravery, devotion, and skill of the Medical Service on which the onus of the work devolved.

During the first few months after the arrival of the Indian Corps, the following were the arrangements in force.

The wounded were attended in the trenches by the regimental medical officers, assisted by two men per company of the battalion, who carried such of the patients as were unable to walk, when a chance offered, to the Regimental Aid Posts which were situated in the safest positions procurable, at a short distance in rear of the trenches.

Next came the posts known as Field Ambulances, each of which was divided into Bearer and Tent sections. The bearers went forward with a small personnel, mostly with horsed ambulances, until they got into touch with the Regimental Aid Posts, when they established positions known as Advanced Dressing Stations, to which the wounded were transferred by stretcher-bearers as rapidly as possible. Thence, after the first field dressings had been inspected and, if necessary, readjusted, the wounded were removed to the Dressing Stations established two or three miles in rear of the trenches by the Tent Divisions of the Field Ambulances. In rear again of the Dressing Stations were the Clearing Hospitals, with their attendant columns of motor ambulances.

At daybreak reports were collected of the number of wounded in the Dressing Stations, after which the motor ambulances conveyed them to the Clearing Hospitals on the line of rail. Here the wounded were carefully attended to, and those fit to travel were got ready for the journey by train to the base and thence by hospital ships to oversea hospitals.

The weak link in this chain was the necessity for transporting the wounded by hand between the Aid Posts and the Advanced Dressing Stations.

A few months after the arrival of the Corps, the Royal Engineers laid a light trolley line from a point about 2000 yards in rear to the firing line, for the purpose of taking supplies up at night. This line was under the charge of Captain Frost, Supply and Transport Corps, to whose good service in this connection during the action of the 25th September, 1915, reference has already been made.

The trucks were then adapted for the carriage of stretchers, and after taking supplies to the front line, they returned with the wounded from the First Aid Posts. This system presented two great advantages.

(1) The more rapid and comfortable removal of the wounded.

(2) Saving of labour, as four to six bearers could manage four wounded men on a truck, instead of at least four bearers to carry each wounded man.

On one occasion 2300 wounded were transported by this method in twenty-four hours.

Since those days light railways have been laid in many places along the line, and experience has improved the method, but it is believed that the Indian Corps can claim to be the pioneers in this direction.

The adoption of a standard system of evacuation of wounded is due to the initiative of Colonel Pike, the Deputy Director of Medical Services with the Indian Corps. After consulting all the medical officers on this important subject, Colonel Pike drafted a pamphlet entitled, "Regimental Medical Aid in Trench Warfare," which was published in the R.A.M.C. Journal and stills holds its place as a guide in any form of stationary warfare.

In this, as in all his strenuous work, Colonel Pike, who has since been awarded the C.M.G. for his invaluable services, was most ably assisted by Captain F. D. Cunningham, R.A.M.C., to whom the Corps in general and the Head Quarters Staff in particular owe a debt of gratitude for his never-failing skill and kindly attention.

Two circumstances have prevented the mention of more than a very few instances of the wonderful gallantry and devotion to duty displayed by the Medical Services of the Indian Corps. Space was limited, and great difficulty was experienced in obtaining particulars of individual acts.

The official list of rewards for services in France granted to all ranks of the Indian Medical Services contains a large number of names, and for each instance of bravery or devotion which has met with recognition, there were numbers of unrecorded cases.

This list includes the humble Kahar or stretcher-bearer of the Field Ambulance. The silent heroism of these men has been remarkable in every war in which Indian troops have been engaged. Unarmed and unwarlike, they have gone about their work on the battlefields, meeting, many of them, the death from which they sought to save others, looking for no reward save the knowledge of duty well performed. However great the danger, the writers have never heard of *a single case in which a Kahar flinched from his duty*. They were all heroes.

To these men and to the gallantry and self-devotion of the regimental stretcher-bearers is due the fact that so few wounded were abandoned upon the battlefields. The Indian Corps will never forget the debt it owes to these courageous men.

As an instance of the spirit which animated these humble servants of the Empire, the following is worthy of record. At the commencement of the battle of Neuve Chapelle an officer of the Royal Engineers relates that he saw two Kahars carrying a wounded man on a stretcher under fire. As they were passing, one of the Kahars was badly wounded by shrapnel. He had just sufficient strength left to sign to his fellow Kahar not to drop the stretcher. They placed it gently on the ground and then this brave man collapsed in a heap. As Captain Bird, the officer who relates the story, remarks, "Perhaps it was only a small episode, but it shows you what the Kahars are."

Finally, as regards the arrangements in the field and in the hospitals, ashore and afloat, for the due observance by Indian soldiers of their religious customs, a short extract from an interview with the heroic Subadar Mir Dast, V.C., reported in the *Times* of India, carries the weight of high authority.

In reply to a question as to whether the feeding arrangements were satisfactory, the Subadar is reported to have made the following remarks :—

"The feeding arrangements were excellent ; they left nothing to be desired. We got all we wanted and our religious susceptibilities were scrupulously respected. The Hindu soldiers had their own cooking arrangements according to their own fashion ; and so had the Mahomedan soldiers. It is this arrangement which has made the lot of the Indian soldier so happy in the battlefield. Even in hospitals our religious feelings are strictly guarded, and we have full liberty and every facility in respect of observing the prayer times, etc. In respect of this, so far as the Pavilion Hospital * is concerned, we are thankful to Colonel Campbell and Colonel Macleod for their great kindness to us."

The magnitude of the task of the medical officers can be grasped from the figures of wounded of the British and Indian units. Up to the 10th November, 1915, these amounted to 23,627. To this total must be added the number of sick who required attention. For these the figures are not readily available, but they can hardly have

* At Brighton.

amounted to less than 18,000 during the same period, at the daily rate of 2 per 1000.

In addition to these cases, the medical officers had to grapple with the heavy work of sanitation and conservancy, as well as the inoculation of the troops against typhoid fever.

APPENDIX III

THE INDIAN SOLDIERS' FUND

No history of the Indian Corps in Flanders would be complete without an account, however brief, of the work of the Indian Soldiers' Fund which owes its inception to the Order of St John of Jerusalem, whose Sovereign Head and Patron is His Majesty the King-Emperor.

The Fund was inaugurated on the 1st October, 1914, when a Committee was formed under the chairmanship of Sir John Hewett, the members being ladies and gentlemen who, from their connection with India in an official or private capacity, were anxious to do everything possible to assist our Indian troops in their severe trials in Europe; with these were associated some distinguished members of different Indian communities.

Lord Curzon of Kedleston very generously provided a Head Quarters by giving the free use of his residence, No. 1, Carlton House Terrace.

The original objects of the Fund were threefold.

(1) To maintain the Lady Hardinge Hospital at Brockenhurst Park.

(2) To supply comforts of all kinds to all hospitals in Great Britain and France in which Indian wounded were treated.

(3) To supplement the clothing and comforts supplied by Government to Indian troops on service.

From the very inauguration of the Fund the late Lord Roberts took the liveliest interest in its welfare, and its Head Quarters was one of the last places visited by him before his final journey to France.

Appeals for subscriptions were made to the general public and to various bodies, with the result that, up to the 20th November, 1915, donations totalling £151,762 had been received.* A leading part in this work was taken by the City Sub-Committee, with Mr C. C. McLeod, formerly a well-known resident of Calcutta, as chairman. With such zeal did this Committee work that, although many of the great commercial houses in London and elsewhere had already been approached, a sum of over £45,000 was obtained, and subscriptions still continued to come in.

In addition to cash, the British public made most generous gifts of clothing, amounting to some 200,000 garments. These were dealt with by the Warehouse Committee under Lady Sydenham, as also were the comforts, of which a large supply was received. A working-party Sub-Committee was further formed under the Hon. Gertrude Kinnaird, with Doctor Carter as Secretary.

The widespread sympathy felt for the Indian troops is well illustrated by the various classes of persons who assisted in this work. Amongst these were invalids, a society of blind girls, old-age pensioners, lonely people in remote cottages, and large, well-equipped working parties in cities under the leadership of the Mayoress. These working parties, in addition to the bales sent direct to hospitals, supplied 44,000 articles, such as shirts, belts, mufflers.

The self-sacrificing spirit in which the Committee and their assistants carried on their work is proved by the fact that the expenditure on Head Quarters establishment amounted, up to the 15th November, 1915, to 0·75 of the receipts and 1·36 of the expenditure, and this standard has since been well maintained.

As regards object (1) mentioned earlier, a hospital named after the late Lady Hardinge of Penshurst was established by the kindness of Mrs Morant in Brockenhurst

* The total donations up to the 30th September, 1918, amounted to over £215,000.

Park near Southampton. The building was erected by the State under the advice of Sir Havelock Charles and Colonel Horrocks. It accommodated 520 patients, want of space alone preventing an extension to 650 beds.

The hospital was staffed by ten retired officers of the Indian Medical Service, under Lt-Colonel Perry, C.I.E. The nursing staff consisted of a matron and assistant-matron with nineteen nurses specially chosen for their knowledge of the languages and requirements of Indian patients. Their work was, strictly speaking, not that of nursing, but of general supervision and control.

The hospital was opened on the 20th January, 1915, and remained open to the 2nd March, 1916, when the main body of the Indian troops had left France. The number of patients treated during this period was 2629.

The mortality was kept down to the surprisingly low figure of 1·4 per cent., a striking evidence of the skill and care exercised in dealing with such large numbers of patients, the majority of whose wounds were septic on admission.

By the kindness of Sir James Clarke, sixty members of the St John Ambulance Brigade were engaged in work at the hospital, all menial service being performed by Indian servants.

The conveyance of sick or wounded Indians with the greatest possible comfort and despatch was facilitated by the gracious gift of a motor-ambulance by Their Majesties and by the generous offer of a motor-ambulance convoy of fifty vehicles by Mr Arthur du Cros, M.P., the Hon. Gideon Murray and others, who also promised to equip and maintain it. To deal with this branch, a Motor Sub-Committee was formed under the chairmanship of Lord Norreys. The convoy commenced work in France on the 1st March, 1915, and performed most valuable service. The total number of patients carried up to November, 1915, was approximately 50,000.

In addition to the Lady Hardinge Hospital, comforts were supplied by the Fund to eight other similar institutions in England, twenty in France, one in Alexandria, and also to nine hospital ships. On the departure of the Corps from France, the Fund continued the supply of comforts to all the Indian units which remained, and to the Indian Hospitals and Casualty Clearing Stations in France, as well as to the Indian Labour Companies. It also continued supplies to the Indian troops in other theatres of war, viz., in Egypt and Palestine.

The extent and variety of the work can be judged by the following figures, taken at random, of articles supplied :—

Socks	78,000	Handkerchiefs	85,000
Balaclava caps	12,000	Sweets	125,000 lbs.
Cigarettes	22,000,000	Envelopes	850,000
Gramophones	40	Periscopes	2000
Religious books	7000	Footballs	130

The well-being of Indian prisoners of war was also not overlooked. Up to November, 1915, the Committee were in possession of the names of 500 prisoners in Germany, and the late General Sir Alfred Gaselee undertook the work of representing the Fund in association with the Prisoners of War Committee.

The first step was to ensure that the prisoners had a proper supply of clothing. Accordingly, a Red Cross kit-bag was sent by name to each prisoner. These bags contained a useful assortment of underwear and comforts. An additional supply of clothing was also despatched and acknowledgments of receipt duly arrived.

Arrangements were made, through Switzerland, for the supply of bread. For Brahman and other prisoners, whose caste restrictions prevented their eating bread prepared by Europeans, material was furnished to enable them to bake their own supply.

Amongst others, as Honorary Secretary of the Regimental Care Committee of the Fund, Lady Melliss rendered invaluable service, as did later Mrs Hannyngton.

The Committee have acknowledged their obligations to numerous subscribers, not only to those who have given money, but also to many, themselves in poor circumstances, who have sent gifts of garments and comforts ; also to the War Office and India Office and to the St John Ambulance Association in India, which latter has been of the greatest assistance in many ways.*

The Fund received most grateful acknowledgments from Sir James Willcocks and Lt-General Rimington and many other officers commanding Indian troops, and its efforts evoked the heartfelt gratitude of the Indian Forces in France and elsewhere.

The writers can testify that it was impossible to visit the trenches, billets, or hospitals without meeting at every turn evidence of the solicitude with which the comfort and well-being of the Indian soldier were considered in every detail.

There can be no doubt that the excellent health enjoyed by the Indian troops, contrary to all expectation, must be greatly ascribed to the devoted work of the Committee of the Indian Soldiers' Fund and their assistants.

* On taking up important work in connection with the National Service Department in January, 1917, Sir John Hewett resigned the chairmanship of the Fund, and was succeeded by Sir Trevredyn Wynne ; Sir John Stanley, who has been Chairman of the Comforts Committee since the inception of the Fund, was appointed Vice-Chairman. Mr Arthur Preston has given his services as Honorary Secretary since December, 1916.

INDEX

A

B

C

D

E

F

I

K

L

N

O

P

Q

R

S

W

THE END